Registration and the Draft

OTHER BOOKS BY MARTIN ANDERSON

Conscription: A Select and Annotated Bibliography

The Federal Bulldozer: A Critical Analysis of Urban Renewal, 1949–1962

Welfare: The Political Economy of Welfare Reform in the United States

The Military Draft: Selected Readings on Conscription

Registration and the Draft

Proceedings of the Hoover-Rochester Conference
on the
All-Volunteer Force

Edited by
MARTIN ANDERSON

**HOOVER
INSTITUTION**

**STANFORD
UNIVERSITY**

Design and Typography

Design and typography by Ted Ligda, Redwood City, California. The typeface for
this book is Baskerville, facsimile of a Roman letter first used in England, about 1760,
by John Baskerville, the greatest type founder of his era. His types, most of which
were based on the letters of Caslon, are of exceptional beauty, the italic forms in
particular being superior to any other created up to that time.

Production

Printed and bound in the United States of America by Braun-Brumfield, Inc.,
Ann Arbor, Michigan.

Hoover Press Publication 242

*The Hoover Institution on War, Revolution and Peace, founded at
Stanford University in 1919 by the late President Herbert Hoover,
is an interdisciplinary research center for advanced study on
domestic and international affairs in the twentieth century. The views
expressed in its publications are entirely those of the authors and
do not necessarily reflect the views of the staff, officers, or
Board of Overseers of the Hoover Institution.*

CONTENTS

PREFACE

The question of how best to raise an armed force is one that has been with us since this country was founded. In recent years this debate on military manpower has centered on the viability of the All-Volunteer Force established by the Nixon Administration in 1971 and on whether or not to return to some form of a peacetime military draft. During the presidential campaign of 1980, the corollary issue of draft registration was introduced into the debate.

The issue of the peacetime draft and registration is one that apparently cuts across traditional ideological and political lines. Although those on either side of the issue feel very strongly about their position, it is difficult, indeed often impossible, to predict someone's views on the basis of his or her political party affiliation or ideological orientation.

Because of the complexity of the issue and the intensity of the convictions that people hold, my colleagues and I felt that a conference of experts — representing a broad spectrum of views — could contribute significantly by casting some intellectual light on the subject and reducing some of the emotional heat. This feeling was intensified by the increasing national political debate that promised to drive the issue to active consideration by the Supreme Court and Congress. After some preliminary discussions between myself and Thomas Moore at the Hoover Institution at Stanford University, a proposal for a draft conference was prepared by Walter Oi of the University of Rochester, with the assistance of William H. Meckling, W. Allen Wallis, and Kenneth E. Clark. The conference was approved and enthusiastically supported by W. Glenn Campbell, Director of the Hoover Institution.

The Hoover-Rochester Conference on the All-Volunteer Force was held at the Hoover Institution on December 13 and 14, 1979. It was the first national conference on the draft to be held since 1966.

The participants in the conference were an especially distinguished group, evenly representing a broad spectrum of views: scholars from the academic world, many of whom had been wrestling with the conceptual problems of conscription for years; officials from government, some of them deeply involved with the demanding task of actually raising military manpower; and others, including elected officials and foundation executives.

Six major papers, prepared in the months preceding the conference, and presented in summary form during the proceedings, constituted the core of the discussion and debate. The complete papers make up Part Six of this volume. Two focus on the question of how well the All-Volunteer Force is working; two deal with the serious constitutional and civil liberty issues of conscription; and two discuss the social and economic equity involved in raising military manpower.

In addition to the basic papers and the spirited and informed discussion they triggered, there was a major address by Richard Danzig, Principal Deputy Assistant Secretary of Defense, and a free-swinging debate between two of the country's most articulate and knowledgeable men in their respective opposition to and support of the draft — Milton Friedman and Congressman Pete McCloskey of California.

The issues identified at the conference, together with the new facts and insights developed in the papers and refined during the discussions, should provide a significant contribution to the nation's understanding of this critical and timely issue.

MARTIN ANDERSON

Washington, D.C.
September 21, 1981

ACKNOWLEDGMENTS

This volume represents the sustained efforts and vision of many who correctly foresaw military manpower as a key issue in the 1980s.

Director W. Glenn Campbell and Senior Fellow Thomas Moore of the Hoover Institution supported the project from its inception. Walter Oi, William Meckling, W. Allen Wallis, and Kenneth E. Clark developed the structure of the conference and drafted the preliminary proposal.

My research assistant, Barbara Honegger, inherited the transcript from the conference and honed and rehoned it into recognizable form. She shepherded the volume through its many stages, including three office moves made necessary by the 1980 presidential campaign.

David Henderson spent hours listening to tapes of the conference to identify speakers. The volume would not have the continuity it does were it not for his timely contribution.

Lise Hofmann meticulously, as always, copy-edited the entire manuscript, checking references and polishing it into its finished form. She also guided the manuscript through the complex typesetting process, only one of her consummate skills.

Ted Ligda singlehandedly set the manuscript in hot type with his inexhaustible patience and professionalism.

Jim Marin and Dianne Erickson designed the distinctive jacket for the book.

Finally, the Hoover Institution Press, under the steady direction of Mickey Hamilton and, later, Phyllis Cairns, oversaw the typesetting, proofreading, and final publication and distribution.

PART 1

How Well Is the All-Volunteer
Force Working?

INTRODUCTION

Thomas Moore

THOMAS MOORE: I'd like to welcome you to the Hoover Institution, and, in particular, to the Hoover-Rochester Conference on the All-Volunteer Force. We are meeting at a very timely point when there is a great deal of interest in how well the All-Volunteer Force is working—whether we should go back to the draft or substitute some other system like universal military service. These are going to be very important issues in the 1980s. I think that we've got an excellent set of papers to illuminate the issues and a particularly distinguished and knowledgeable audience. We should have a very good debate.

The ground rules for the conference will be as follows: Each speaker will be given twenty minutes to summarize his paper. Then discussants will have ten minutes each to comment on the papers. Then, after a short break of about ten minutes, we will reconvene for comments and discussion from the floor.

Now I want to call on our first speaker, William King, who is Professor of Business Administration at the University of Pittsburgh. His paper is entitled "The All-Voluntary Military: Viewpoints, Issues, and Prospects."

I

First Paper:

THE ALL-VOLUNTEER MILITARY: VIEWPOINTS ISSUES, AND PROSPECTS (Summary)

William R. King

WILLIAM KING: Thank you, Tom. I'm delighted to be here this morning.

I'd like to do several things today. First, give you a brief assessment of the past and current performance of the All-Volunteer Force, as I see it; second, try to explain the reasons why many different analysts and advocates have arrived at vastly different conclusions about the merits and failings of the All-Volunteer Force; and, last, to propose a general direction we might follow to resolve the current conflict and debate concerning the All-Volunteer Force.

As I'm sure most of you are aware, there is a great deal of semantic confusion in this debate. People speak about the success or failure of the All-Volunteer Force without clearly defining their terms, and this makes effective communication difficult.

Every time I think about this I recall a series of newspaper ads that seem to me to describe the problem very well. One Monday morning the following ad appeared in the classified section of a small-town newspaper: "FOR SALE: R. D. Jones has one sewing machine. Phone 958 after 7:00 P.M. and ask for Mrs. Kelly who lives with him cheap." The next day the following correction appeared: "We regret having erred in R. D. Jones' ad of yesterday. It should have read: One sewing machine for sale, cheap. Phone 958 and ask for Mrs. Kelly who lives with him after 7:00 P.M." On Wednesday, yet another item appeared: "R. D. Jones has informed us he has received several annoying telephone calls because of the error we made in his classified ad yesterday. It stands corrected as follows: R. D. Jones has one sewing machine for sale, cheap. Phone 958 after 7:00 P.M. and ask for Mrs. Kelly who loves with him." The final correction came on Thursday, and read: "NOTICE: I, R. D. Jones, have no sewing machine for sale. I smashed it. Don't call 958, as the phone has been ripped out. And I have not been carrying on with Mrs. Kelly. Until yesterday she *was* my housekeeper, but she quit."

I think that the problems of communication, made so graphic in this little story, are partially responsible for the apparent contradiction in conclusions coming from professsional studies about the All-Volunteer Force. I hope, somewhat presumptuously, to try to explain the basis of these difficulties this morning.

Almost every day our newspapers are filled with reports about the failure of the All-Volunteer Force. Despite the fact that I have been described in some of these as an opponent of the All-Volunteer Force, a draft advocate, and several other, less polite things, I do *not* believe that the All-Volunteer Force has in any sense failed. Rather, newspaper treatments of the topic tend to present us with the kind of either/or choice—draft versus All-Volunteer Force—that I foresaw some years ago we might be impelled to make. To avoid such either/or thinking we have to recognize that in assessing the merits of any personnel procurement system, whether it be the All-Volunteer Force, the draft, or some other alternative, we need to be aware of its overall impact on society and not simply try to answer questions like "Did we get enough recruits last month, or last year?"

There has been a strong, and I believe dangerous, tendency to focus on such simplistic measures in the debate on the All-Volunteer Force. Perhaps this is because it is simpler to do so; or perhaps because we haven't always had all the information we needed. Until the Gates Commission report, for instance, we may not have fully recognized the burdensome tax that the draft selectively levies on some members of society. And, after the report appeared, it took Morris Janowitz and Charles Moskos, among others, to point out the impact that the All-Volunteer Force is having on our society as a whole. In all these cases, we have taken too narrow a view of what we mean by success and failure; our narrow definition of the problem has constrained our search for solutions. And all along the press has been framing the question in terms of whether we should go back to the draft or stay with the All-Volunteer Force as it is, assuming that it has failed. We've simply allowed ourselves to be steered too long into dealing with the wrong problems and with statements of problems that are too simplistic.

The first thing of substance that I want to do this morning is to state what I see has happened during the All-Volunteer Force era. This will be based on data and analyses reported in a study I did for the Senate Armed Services Committee, though I don't have these in detail with me today.

Though the situation is different today from what it was when I prepared that report, I don't think that what I have to say here will be seriously challenged.

There are seven major points of fact I'd like to make about the All-Volunteer Force:

1. Within a range of error considered acceptable in most fields, our active forces have been maintained at close to desired force levels during the All-Volunteer Force era, just as they were during the era of the draft.
2. On the other hand, our reserve forces have *not* been maintained at target levels and today are seriously undermanned.
3. Through a lowering of standards and the use of monetary and other incentives, the ability of the All-Volunteer Force to meet target manpower levels can probably be maintained for the immediate future.
4. However, as an inevitable consequence of a smaller age-group cohort pool, less attractive financial incentives for the military relative to jobs in the civilian sector, and other factors, it will become increasingly difficult to maintain target force levels through the 1980s.
5. The All-Volunteer Force is, in any case, a peacetime concept and would not be realistically expected to serve as a basis for dealing with our needs in an emergency situation.
6. A number of the supports that were assumed to become a part of the All-Volunteer Force when it was instituted never materialized—like adequate reserves, a registration system, and a back-up draft.
7. And, finally, despite seven years of experience with the All-Volunteer Force, its impact on our society and our ability to meet our defense needs within its context have not been adequately assessed.

These seven points sum up the state of the All-Volunteer Force as I see it today.

But more important than arguing whether the All-Volunteer Force is working in terms of some specific variable, like attrition or recruitment, we must first of all understand why the debate about the All-Volunteer Force goes on and on without people really communicating with one another. In the remaining time I have this morning, I'd like to summarize the reasons I see for this impasse. Along these lines, a number of possibilities come to mind: the role played by analysts, and the impact upon conclusions of differing analytical frameworks, analytical domains, and analytical methodologies. I will address each of these in turn.

First, the role of advocates. As you are all aware, I'm sure, there are advocates on both the pro and the con sides of this issue. They are passionate believers—or disbelievers. I have a desk drawer full of their letters, some of them written in crayon, which represent all points of view on this heated topic. From reading these letters, one suspects that these people base their assessments on philosophical grounds or personal experience, having had a good or bad experience with the draft or the military, or both, and that facts would in no way alter their beliefs. Personally, I don't think this is a great problem, because we can put such viewpoints into perspective. The *real* problem, I think, is that serious analysts *also* appear to substantially disagree with respect to all dimensions of the All-Volunteer Force. This is a far more serious problem, because it confuses the informed and uninformed public alike. I'd now like to address why I think this is so.

Analysts, like less informed advocates to a greater or a lesser degree, come to conclusions that reflect their personalities, backgrounds, values, and analytical frameworks. In his book *The Subjective Side of Science*, my colleague Ian Mitroff reported a study he did of moon scientists in the 1960s. In this book, Mitroff shows very clearly how the personalities, backgrounds, and beliefs of these hard-nosed scientists affected their conclusions in what is supposed to be a strictly objective process. I would assert that manpower analysts who research the All-Volunteer Force are no less subject to these influences.

The analytic framework in which a study is conducted can also affect its outcome. In my paper for this conference I single out economists to make this point because econometric models were emphasized just before and during the period of transition to the All-Volunteer Force. I've therefore suggested that economists' theoretical models, in which everything is given a price and actors are assumed to behave rationally in response to price and quantity variables, are not adequate to assess complex social systems like the All-Volunteer Force. On the other hand, I point out that sociologists' models, which do take into account nonquantifiable or difficult-to-quantify variables, are also limited in the sense that their conclusions are inherently less actionable than those of economists. That is, it is not always clear what policy options one should select based on a sociologist's model, whereas the selection is usually more clear-cut when based on an economist's model. My point is that there is clearly a trade-off, and that it is not a question of one group being right and the other being wrong. Each analytic framework has its costs, and each its benefits. Only when we get two or more groups working within the same agreed-upon framework can we begin to talk about conclusions being right or wrong.

Another factor affecting the results of analyses is what I call their analytic domain. That is a fancy term for the fact that analysts studying different things are very likely to reach different conclusions—the old apple and oranges problem—and that is, in fact, what has happened in the debate over the All-Volunteer Force. Some analysts study the Army because it has the most serious recruiting problem. Others single out a worst-case kind of analysis, like looking only at the reserves because force maintenance and recruiting are at their worst there, or looking only at the problem the Air Force has in recruiting physicians. Sometimes, of course, special-focus studies are necessary and may even be preferable, for some purposes, to relying on the masses of highly aggregated and therefore often misleading statistics we generally have to work with. When we select different analytic domains, then, it is not too surprising that we come up with conflicting conclusions.

Another factor affecting an analyst's conclusions, and closely related to the analytic framework, is the analytic methodology he chooses. Let me give an example. On the basis of their studies, Richard Cooper and Charles Moskos have arrived at conclusions that are almost diametrically opposed.

I don't believe that one is right and the other wrong. Rather, I believe that both are correct within the framework and methodology that they chose to use. It then becomes a question of evaluating conclusions within the context of the analytic domain and methodology of studies, and that is precisely what I propose that we start doing.

How we put our questions, then, reflects our values and determines in great part the answers we will get. Keeping this in mind, I think that we need to state our questions about the All-Volunteer Force broadly enough so that some of the nonquantifiable and difficult-to-quantify issues can be brought to bear on the analyses. The fact is that none of the studies we have been talking about, despite some of them being substantially funded and resulting in some very fine analytical work, has been sufficiently comprehensive to deal with the complex question of what is the best way to maintain a defense establishment to meet our national goals. And that, by the way, is the way I propose we pose the question: How can we use the necessity of maintaining a defense establishment to best meet our national goals?

I state this as the issue only tentatively, however, because whatever group performs these studies has to define its issues and questions in close collaboration with all those who will use the results.

One of the things that I find working in other fields—strategic planning for business people, for example—is that if you don't design a planning system for a firm in close collaboration with the people who are going to use it, it simply doesn't get used. Or, at the very least, it won't get used in the way it was intended to be used. My point is that there really is no way to adequately address a question without incorporating those who will use the results of the analysis into the process. For the All-Volunteer Force, this would minimally mean the Department of Defense and the congressmen who will have to draft and pass legislation implementing any conclusions that may be reached.

It is very important that such studies be conducted by multidisciplinary groups so that the various analytic frameworks, methodologies, and ways of thinking can be incorporated into the analytic process. I have done research for and directed a number of studies based on this kind of multidisciplinary approach, and, though none of these have been of the scale I'm talking about here for the All-Volunteer Force, I know these principles can be applied on a broader scale. The issues to be researched and the data to be gathered need to be developed on the basis of a multidisciplinary consensus, and by that I don't mean farming out the economic aspects of the problem to economists and the social aspects of the problem to sociologists, and so forth. The kind of group I'm talking about reaches working agreements by defining the issues to be researched, setting standards for comparison of data, determining what is going to be compared with what, and incorporating various perspectives on the measures to be used to assess the issues at hand. These are analytical decisions that need to be made within a multidisciplinary working group to avoid the kind of apparent disagreement among experts we are seeing today.

To maximize the impact of such a study, or group of studies, its users must be involved in every stage of the analytic process. That doesn't mean, however, that we need another blue-ribbon, or purple-ribbon, panel. We've all had too many of those. What we need, if I may emphasize it one last time, is a serious multileveled, multidisciplinary approach.

My hope for this meeting is that we might at least be able to better define what we don't agree about and why we don't agree. And I suspect that this will turn out to be a function of the kind of considerations I've been describing this morning—differences in analytic domain, methodology, and so forth. I hope that we can begin the process of agreeing on analytic domains, analytic frameworks, and methodologies, and I look forward to joining you in the next couple of days to try to do that.

Thank you very much.

THOMAS MOORE: Thank you, Bill. Our next paper, "The All-Volunteer Force: Has It Worked, Will It Work?"—was coauthored by Richard Hunter and Gary Nelson. Dick will present the first part of their paper and Gary the second part.

II

Second Paper:

THE ALL-VOLUNTEER FORCE: HAS IT WORKED, WILL IT WORK? (Summary)

Richard W. Hunter and Gary R. Nelson

RICHARD HUNTER.   As Bill has accused us of doing, we're going to try to talk somewhat about data. After all, that is why, I think, we were asked to come—to present some of the data as we see them. One of the things that I do agree with Bill on is that it is very difficult, when you start looking at data, to come to the right kinds of conclusions. The correlations can be perfect, and yet you can come to the wrong answer. It reminds me of an episode in 1964, when the presidential campaign was under way. I was a naval officer, a graduate student, on the Harvard campus; and all of my more liberal colleagues were arguing with me that if I voted for Senator Goldwater we would become involved in a massive land war in Asia. They were correct. I voted for Senator Goldwater and we became involved in a massive land war in Asia.

This whole debate has to be taken with that caution in mind. Just because data correlate, they do not prove cause and effect. I'm going to talk about the first half of our paper, about whether the All-Volunteer Force has worked, and Gary is going to talk about how well it can work. We're going to look at three kinds of measures. We look at the Gates Commission again. The two standards the commission used were, first, the quantity of people needed, and, second, but very important, the measure of quality. Since then, as Bill mentioned, people have reached a third parameter—representativeness.

As for quantity, here are the latest numbers [see Figure 1, page 233]. As you can see, we remain within 1½ percent of active-duty strength. If you're going to use that standard you say, as Bill has indicated, that we're "on strength." The enlisted force looks exactly the same [Figure 2, page 234]. You can see the major changes in the Army: it got bigger for Vietnam and came down most after Vietnam.

This next figure [Figure 3, page 235] is even more important. This is the accession picture. I want to spend a couple of moments here to focus on a few things that I think will be important to you as you observe the 1980s. If you remember, the Army went to three- and four-year enlistments under the encouragement of the Secretary of Defense. In 1976 that gave us a lot of people who had previously been in two-year enlistments. During 1976 we had people come in for three and four years instead of for two. The result: in 1978 we had a very low accession year. Then, in 1979 the three-year people started to get out. And, in fact, instead of being level, as shown in Figure 3, if we had made strength, the Army would have been up in here—near the star in the figure. Now, in 1980, we have the four-year people from 1976 and the three-year people from 1977 and the 15,000 we didn't recruit last year. They all stack up, so 1980 is going to be a tough year. If you make 1980, then 1981 becomes easy and we're back to normal, but General Max Thurman, Commander of the Army Recruiting Command, has his work cut out for him in 1980.

The second thing I'd like to show is the measure of quality. As we have seen from a quantity perspective, we have generally made strength, in spite of the fact that this last year for the first time all four services missed their recruiting objectives. From a quality point of view, however, the answer is not so clear-cut. We now have serious debates focusing on the question: What, in fact, is quality?

One single measure of quality is the use of test scores. The second graph in Figure 5 [page 239] shows five mental groups based on test scores. These are basically the breakdowns from the World War II population: everyone who came in between 1942 and 1945, officer and enlisted, 42 years old and 18 years old. The distribution looked something like the curve on Figure 4, except that it also included mental group V as well as I–IV. We think that's still what it looks like, but it's been a long time; so we're going to make a major effort to renorm these tests and to go back to the population to see how our test scores really are measuring up to the population. Since mental group V is now precluded by law from enlisting, Figure 4 represents our best estimates of the quality distribution of the potential supply of volunteers.

These are raw scores, and the y axis shown is the percentage of the population receiving a particular score. From the perspective of the Department of Defense, this looks about right. So from this, overall chart quality was pretty good. The Navy and the Marine Corps [see fourth and fifth graphs in Figure 5] look about like the average. [The last graph in Figure 5] shows the Air Force. Almost all Air Force recruits were from Groups I, II, and IIIA. [In the third graph] we see the opposite picture, the Army. The Army has had a lot of people right at the III-B–IV line.

This explains what you may have heard about some of the quality problems we have been having. You might ask how such a distribution can occur. If someone gives a kid a couple of questions and answers, he may be able to slide over into a higher group. If he is allowed to retake the test enough times, with luck he will pass once. All of that helps account for the difference between the shape of the Army and the shape of the other services. The first graph in Figure 4 [page 236] shows the trend in number of mental groups I and II, lumped together. I'd like you to focus, though, on the dark black line, which is the DOD total, and you can also look at the Army or whatever other service you prefer. You'll see that the DOD line is surprisingly level. At least I was surprised when I first saw it.

One of the things that's fascinating in this light, I believe, is the impact of the termination of the GI Bill. We found that the peak in high-quality people was the surge as we reached out and got people to come in just before the GI Bill terminated in 1976, and we leveled off at a lower level after that. Perhaps what we are seeing now is a non-GI Bill market for groups I and II as compared to what we had when we had a GI Bill market.

At the other end of the spectrum are group IVs, shown in [the third graph in Figure 4]. The percentage of mental group IV personnel has dropped inordinately under the All-Volunteer Force. We think that this is very important. While there may be some norming problems, the number of recruits from the very low part of the spectrum was a lot higher than it is now. In the 1960s the Air Force took a significant percentage of mental group IV, or below-average Americans. They now recruit almost no mental group IVs. The big increase in recruits under the volunteer force is the result of taking in average Americans, or mental group III, as shown in [the second graph in Figure 4]. Today the Air Force recruits primarily III-As and above. In the Army the increase is mostly in III-Bs, and some of these are very low, as you saw in [the third graph].

The other quality parameter that we use (in addition to test scores) is high school graduation [see Figure 6, page 244]. Its primary importance is as an index of endurance. Those who completed high school have a much better probability of completing their military tour. They get to the end, and that's worth quite a bit, because when people don't get to the end you have to replace them, and not just on a one-to-one basis: not only do you have to replace each one with the soldier that's going to fill in, but you must replace training tail and everything else, so it requires about 1.5 people to replace an attrition loss.

Finally, the third perspective is representativeness. Perhaps the most significant change in representativeness is the increase in the number of blacks, as shown in [Figure 8, page 247]. Now remember, not only is the number of blacks going up, but the overall size of the base—of the whole force—is going down. [Figure 9, page 247] shows the percentage increase in black personnel. The enlisted forces of the Army are currently about 34 percent black. Army accessions are about 37 percent black; department-wide blacks are reenlisting at about 1.7 times the rate for whites. There are a lot of reasons for this, which we can talk about, but not in the amount of time we're allowed today. But this is, perhaps, the most significant effect from the point of view of representativeness.

The second most significant change in representativeness is the increase in the number of women. While the black increase was a divergence from the societal average, the increase in women does not constitute a rate of service anywhere near their proportion of the population. Gary is going to talk a lot more about that. Still, as we come out of 1979, the force has had a lot more women and the prognosis is that even more will be added, as shown in [Figure 23, page 271]. Converted to ratios, in the Air Force in 1985 one out of every six people will be a woman. People argue whether this is good or bad. The Navy and Marine Corps have legislation that restricts the assignment of women. To enable the Navy to recruit more women, Congress modified the law to permit assignment of women to some ships. But the Navy probably needs an even more sweeping change in legislation before large numbers of women can be used, and I'm not very encouraged that that change is going to come about.

Another significant change for women is the role that they have been assigned. As shown in [Figure 27, page 274], the traditional role is increasing, especially for enlisted women, but the big increase is in the nontraditional skills; and it is more difficult to recruit women for nontraditional skills. We have a lot of women who want to be clerk-typists, who want to be dental technicians, who want to work in the medical field. We're having more difficulty getting them to be tank turret mechanics and helicopter repairmen and so forth. [Figure 24, page 273], shows the distribution of women by skill both as a percentage of all women and as a percentage of all people in that job.

One point is important. Even though a third of our women are in the clerical area, this represents only 15 percent of the people who do clerical work in the armed forces. In the society as a whole, five out of every six clerical workers are women. In the armed forces the national percentage is almost reversed. Women represent a large untapped manpower pool in spite of all that growth. [Figure 22, page 271] shows the supply and demand for women. The lower line shows how many women we expect to recruit from the supply of 18-year-olds. The upper-line women represent a major source of future recruits, as Gary will point out in his presentation.

That completes our flash review of active force statistics. As for the selective reserve, I agree with many of Bill's points. I think the data show that he's correct. It's what you decide to do after you get the data that's going to make a lot of difference.

The active force has gotten smaller because we have changed force structure, *not* because we couldn't recruit to it. We've figured out ways to be a little more efficient. The opposite, though, is true in the selected reserves. The reserves have gone down in this period because of recruiting difficulties. Gary is going to talk about some of the things that we're doing and looking at that will have some impacts on increasing the reserves. The reserves are the toughest part of making the All-Volunteer Force work.

Just to give you a picture of what happened in a qualitative sense: we changed the entire reserve structure when we went to all volunteers. [Figure 16, page 257] shows that the mental groups reversed predominance. Most of the Is and IIs that came in back in the 1960s came in to avoid the draft. Once we stabilized a volunteer force, however, trends in the reserve force became very similar to those in the active force, and that's going to be true for all the rest of the things that we look at.

The same trend is true for education, as shown in [Figure 15, page 257]. This is an area we feel is terribly important. We need to get more youth who have jobs or who are going to college involved in the reserve program, and we need to quit trying to recruit the same youth for the reserves that we are trying to recruit for the active forces. They can serve in only one place at a time. We are taking a lot more prior-service people. Those who have finished their active duty time are coming into the reserves, as shown in [Figure 12, page 252]. They're up now to about half of the reserve accessions. That's a highly important source, and they're very well trained; they're very good soldiers. The trends for blacks look about the same in the reserves as they do in the active force, and the same thing is true for women [see Figures 13 and 14, page 253].

The last thing we want to look at is the Individual Ready Reserve. This is the part of the force for which General Rodgers testified he wanted to draft. He didn't want to draft for the active duty force. He didn't even want to draft for the selective reserve units. His recommendation was that somehow we have to increase the Individual Ready Reserve. There's a lot of debate as to how to do that, and how much. But whether you want to use our numbers, as shown in [Figure 17, page 262], or the Army's numbers, we're way below what we need. And that's what's most important. We've taken some action in 1979 that has brought us back up. If we could continue those actions, we might be very able to close the gap between what we have and what we need.

The dearth in the Individual Ready Reserve is a result not of any plan, but of the residue of our other actions. The reason there was such a sharp decline is that the volunteerism worked for the active force. People are serving longer and more of them are reenlisting. When the things we're trying to accomplish in the active force are working, the result is that there is no one left, or very few left, for the Individual Ready Reserve.

Some people have talked about drafting for the reserves. Gary and I suggest that we try volunteering for it first. Until very recently one couldn't even reenlist in the Individual Ready Reserve. If you were willing to stay and serve, we said, "We're sorry, you've got to get out. Our computer pushes you out the back door." We're changing that. We're working on it, and we're starting to test programs that will work in that area. We are beginning to test direct enlistments in the Individual Ready Reserve. A recruit signs up, goes into training, and then may elect to serve on active duty, in reserve units, or in the Individual Ready Reserve.

Taking all these data in consideration, I conclude that we're certainly not without problems. We have quite a few problems. Last year was a tough year, and this year is going to be tougher, but basically our conclusion, as Bill indicated, is that the All-Volunteer Force is, in fact, working.

GARY NELSON. I'm going to address the question: Will the All-Volunteer Force Work? And I'd like to begin by defining my terms.

An optimist is one who thinks that the All-Volunteer Force will face problems in the 1980s, and a pessimist is one who believes it will have trouble surviving the 1970s. By this standard and as of this date, December 1979, Dick Hunter and I are raging optimists on the subject. The All-Volunteer Force has had real successes in the 1970s. It faces some real problems in the 1980s.

First, population. We're all aware that a decline in the pool of prime, enlistment-age youth will occur during the 1980s and extend into the early 1990s.

Second, a recruiting dip. Recruiting for the All-Volunteer Force has declined significantly in the past four years. This casts a shadow on the prospects for the future, even in the short term.

Third, quality differences. There are sharp quality differences among recruits by service. These differences I don't believe can be said to be related to differences in requirements.

First, some numbers with respect to population. Our prime recruiting pool is males, age 17 to 21 years. This population hit a peak at 10.8 million in 1978. It is now beginning to decline. It will decline slowly over the next few years, but will then accelerate. We'll be 15 percent below our peak pool by 1987, 17 percent below by 1990, and something over 20 percent below by the trough, which is in 1992. Also, the effects on recruiting may be greater or less than the percentage changes in population. So clearly this presents a major management problem for the military forces in the 1980s.

There are a number of options available. There are basically two strategies when you're faced with a declining market like this. One is that you look for ways to reduce demand. What that really means is higher reenlistment rates and lower attrition rates—that is, more people reaching the point of reenlistment before leaving. Another example would be to have fewer total military personnel.

The second kind of strategy is to enhance your base by bringing people into the supply side of the market that weren't there previously. The biggest component of that increase, I think, is women. There are also the possibilities of relaxing physical and mental standards and taking older people to broaden the supply of male enlistments.

Apparently the best ways of adjusting to the population decline are (1) reducing first-term attrition and (2) increasing the utilization of women. Attrition soared with the introduction of the All-Volunteer Force, to the surprise of all those people on the Gates Commission who, like myself, had some responsibility for looking at retention in the All-Volunteer Force. I think that the basic reason for it—and there are a lot of reasons for it—is that with the All-Volunteer Force we changed philosophies. We went more to a volunteer-in, volunteer-out philosophy. If a guy was unhappy and not performing, we let him out. And as a result, the attrition went way up, from a base of about 25 percent of people not completing their terms prior to the All-Volunteer Force, to 37 percent with the 1974 cohort. What is being done now is basically to bring that attrition rate back down. The goal of the services is to bring attrition below 30 percent for the 1979 class. Basically we've cut attrition by about one-fourth. This is important because a reduction of this size *would* cut the requirements for new accessions by 10 percent, which is a substantial percentage of the decline in population that we're going to feel over the next ten years.

Attrition is a very tough problem. We could have a whole conference just on that, and let me say that we understand that there is an optional attrition rate. We don't know what it is. It's obviously not zero; there are people you recruit that you want to get rid of. In my own mind, it's obviously not 40 percent. We need to steer for something in-between. I understand that the services are meeting the goals of the current program. I suspect that this, in fact, will be accomplished.

The second strategy for adjusting to the population decline is use of women. In the pre-All-Volunteer Force, women were about 1 percent of the enlisted force and a somewhat larger percentage of the officer force because of nurses. Current plans would expand that to 12 percent. This goal is on track. It will be met by 1984 and that will have substantial effects on requirements for male enlistment.

I don't have any idea of the maximum number of women in the services. Let me say that there are limitations in recruiting of women both for jobs in nontraditional areas and for jobs in traditional areas. There are problems created by service in combat units, because of the need to provide a rotation base. But the track that the services are on now would result in a steady increase. Perhaps even further increases would be possible after 1984. Basically, the net effect of these two changes—and we lay it out in our paper —is that this would offset almost entirely the effects of the population decline in the 1980s. And as a result, I think that these policies will in fact take care of that.

The second problem, however, is one that's somewhat more serious because it's less well understood, and that's the dip in recruiting. Between 1975 and 1979, male high school graduate enlistments in the armed forces declined from 243,000 to 191,000. During this time the population actually grew 4 percent. What we find is that the enlistment rate of this group declined by 24 percent. This caused shortfalls in 1979, and will cause big problems for 1980 and the years beyond. There are a lot of factors involved here, and several that we can measure. And being an empiricist, I deal with factors that I can measure. First, unemployment. The year 1975, which was really the best recruiting year of the All-Volunteer Force, was also one of very high unemployment in the civilian economy. Between '75 and '79 the unemployment rates for American youth, males ages 16 to 19, declined from a little over 20 percent to 15.7 percent, an overall decline of about one-fourth. Based on the enlistment supply studies that I have seen and many of you have seen, we do project that this has led to a reduction of between 5 and 12 percent in recruiting of male high school graduates.

The second factor responsible for the drop in enlistments is military pay. Pay for enlistees has declined relative to nearly all nonmilitary pay indices. This is for two reasons. Military pay is linked to civilian pay, and during the last four years we have seen some technical changes in federal pay and the imposition of pay raise caps that have led to federal pay raises less than what surveys would indicate to be a comparability increase. That's about a 6 percent effect. The second factor, I think, is just as important, and that is the fact that the white-collar pay indices with which we link military pay have been growing much less rapidly than pay for total private-sector earnings, particularly blue-collar earnings. We find that military pay in this period grew 24 percent; average private-sector earnings, 36 percent; and blue-collar pay indices of various kinds, over 40 percent. Supply studies done in the post-All-Volunteer Force period have tended to arrive at pay elasticities of about 1.0: a 10 percent increase in pay leads to a 10 percent increase in enlistments. The Gates Commission used 1.25 on the basis of a number of studies done in the pre-All-Volunteer Force period. If we use the more conservative number, 1.0, I would say that this elasticity, coupled with these trends in pay, indicates a decline in enlistments due to pay of 9 percent if you look at total private-sector earnings and about 12 percent if you adopt an index that gives a greater weight to blue-collar earnings in this period. We now find, for instance, that the average E-2 in the military is paid less than the minimum wage.

The third factor I'd like to mention as responsible for the drop in enlistments is the elimination of the GI Bill, which was replaced by a far less valuable educational incentive. This was done for a reason. In my own view, and I think in Dick Hunter's view as well, the GI Bill was not an efficient recruiting incentive. It involved deferred income for individuals who had very high discount rates. This was income that would be four or five years in the future. It also was a noncash benefit, which meant that the per-dollar value was less than for cash. People got less than full-dollar value for this benefit. But even considering this, it was still a benefit, a large benefit, and there was a lot of money spent on it. And even if you account for a high discount rate, for a low valuation of this benefit, and for the fact that only a fraction of the maximum funds were utilized, we still arrive at a 4 to 10 percent decline in male high school graduate enlistments and perhaps more, from the elimination of the GI Bill.

There are other factors contributing to the reduction in enlistments. Let me cite them. First, reduced recruiting resources, although in our view the decision to cut down was not necessarily unwise. Second, the institution of large-scale CETA programs, offering jobs to youth. And, third, growing federally sponsored scholarship programs in the domestic sector. These constitute a kind of GI Bill, but in this case it's without the GI.

The cumulative effect of the three economic factors we have cited—reduced unemployment, retarded pay growth, and elimination of the GI Bill—indicates a reduction in enlistments of between 17 and 30 percent. By our calculations this trend could be reversed. A fifteen percent increase in the calculated present value of military pay and benefits would probably increase high school graduate enlistments by about 15 percent. The estimated cost would be far less than $1 billion, provided it was concentrated on junior personnel; was paid in large part to high school graduates, in enlistment bonuses or other ways; and was tilted in favor of the Army and perhaps the Marine Corps, the two services that have had the greatest problem attracting quality enlistments.

In summary, we believe that by reducing turnover rates, and hence demand for new enlistments; by slowly increasing the utilization of women, and therefore supply; and by reversing the trend that has sharply eroded the financial incentives the join the military, the All-Volunteer Force can be sustained into the 1980s. If you don't believe me, I have a chart [see Figure 1, page 357]. As a matter of fact, this is Rick Cooper's chart, which has to do with the supply and demand for young men in the military. The top line show the number of 19-year-old males as a three-year moving average. The chart goes back to the post-Korean War days of 1954. The second line is male total accessions in the military. A third line could have been included to show the number of eligibles—somewhat below the top line. We found that in the '50s and '60s, because of requirements and because of the total population, a very high percentage of the population was going into the military. The '70s were very favorable to recruiting. The ratio of eligible to total male accessions which was about 1.5 to 1 in the 1950s (two out of every three eligible men) climbed in the 1970s to about 4 or 4.5 to 1 (one out of every four or five men entered the military). And this ratio declines in the 1980s because of the reduced requirements for male accessions. This figure in the 1980s and in the early 1990s is no lower than it was in the beginning years of the All-Volunteer Force, when we were able to meet and maintain strength in every year. And so, on this basis, we say that the population decline is not an overwhelming problem, and that we think that the prospects are pretty good. But we probably have to take action to bring about this favorable result.

Thank you.

III

DISCUSSION

Martin Binkin, Walter Oi, and Robert Tollison

THOMAS MOORE: Thank you very much, Gary. Now we'll turn to our discussants. Our first discussant of the morning is Martin Binkin of the Brookings Institution. He's a Senior Fellow there in the Foreign Policy Studies program, and has coauthored a number of publications on the All-Volunteer Force. Martin.

MARTIN BINKIN: This controversy between sociologists and their cult followers on the one hand and economists on the other reminds me of a story that has been making the rounds in the Pentagon. It must have been spawned by the sociologists. It seems that an Army doctor, a Navy pilot, and an economist in the office of the Secretary of Defense were standing in front of the River Entrance waiting for their wives to pick them up. Each had his dog with him. They got into a discussion about the relative merits of their canines, each claiming his dog was better than the others. The Army doctor says, "Watch, I'll demonstrate." He picks up the little black bag that doctors usually carry around, turns it over, and dumps out a pile of bones on the sidewalk in front of the River Entrance. Then he turns to his dog and says, "Stethoscope, do your stuff." The little dog jumps into the pile of bones, makes a cloud of dust, and in about 90 seconds the bones are in the perfect shape of a human skeleton. The Navy pilot says, "That's quite impressive, but let me show *you* something." He looks at his little dog and says, "Tailhook, do your stuff." And Tailhook jumps in among the pile of bones. In about a minute the bones are in the perfect shape of the carrier *Enterprise*. Whereupon the economist from the OSD says, "Very good, but let me show *you* something." Turning to his little dog, he says, "All right. Analyst, do your stuff." In half a minute Analyst seduces the two other dogs and makes off with the bones.

It's very difficult to comment in a meaningful way in ten minutes on the rich content of these two papers, particularly since we didn't get one of them until yesterday. So I will offer some general comments on the subject that I think are appropriate and that I hope will provide some food for thought.

I must say that in reading the two assessments—one regarding the state of the present All-Volunteer Force and the other regarding its future prospects—I was not really surprised at the conclusions that came out of either. Given that the views of the authors are so well known, their positions on the issues are quite predictable. Yet, reading between the lines, I sense a softening in both camps. Bill [King] no longer seems to be describing the All-Volunteer Force in the harsh tones of a sinking ship. And Dick [Hunter] and Gary [Nelson] no longer seem to be saying that it is a rousing success.

The truth of the matter is that it's neither. What it is, in my opinion, is a system that may not be working well—certainly not as well as its architects had expected or had hoped—but for the foreseeable future it may be the only game in town. I believe that it's time that we admit that maintaining a peacetime armed force of crack troops, two million strong, by voluntary means and under current manpower policies, may not be a feasible proposition. The nation does not appear willing, Iran notwithstanding, either to pay the social costs of returning to a coercive system of recruitment, or to pay the high financial costs of buying a *high-quality representative* force.

So where do we go from here? I think at a minimum the current dilemma should force us to undertake a reassessment—and I think it has already started—of our role in the world, of our commitments, our foreign policy, our defense strategy, and our force structure. As I say, this has already commenced. I think events in the Middle East, most recently in the Persian Gulf, have prompted a reappraisal of all of the above, including even our NATO strategy, the centerpiece of our defense policy.

Whether we should move toward a less manpower-intensive maritime strategy is also under discussion. But this subject is really outside the scope of this particular gathering, and should be left to others. But it certainly is an opportunity to be explored.

Lest I be misunderstood, I am not advocating in any way that we set our strategy according to our ability to recruit. That could be a fatal miscalculation. What I am saying is that a reappraisal might just indicate that our previous preoccupation with replaying World War II in Europe—which in the final analysis is the principal current determinant of the size of our Army and, more importantly, the only rationale for large reserve forces—is not only misdirected but puts too much on the shoulders of the United States vis-à-vis the nations that we are committed to protect, which, by the way, may be in less dire economic straits than we are.

Foreign policy consideration aside, I don't feel that we've done all that can be done to get the maximum payoff from the military establishment that we have. We continue to manage our manpower as we did in an earlier era, under conscription, when we viewed recruits as a free good. We've come a long way toward changing the face of the armed forces. Women have been integrated; civilian substitution has taken place. Although we haven't, I think, reached the limits of substitution, we can expect only modest changes from here on in those areas.

One area still ripe for picking is the experience mix of the armed forces. Despite the popularized image, the armed forces are no longer composed mainly of foot-slogging grunts and able-bodied seamen. Indeed, only about 15 percent of the enlisted forces hold these general military skills. The rest are highly (and I might add expensively) trained specialists, technicians, and craftsmen, performing duties not unlike those found in the private sector. Yet, an examination of our personnel inventories indicates that we are attempting to maintain an increasingly technological military establishment with a force, on average, not much older, and hence not much more experienced, than our forces in the 1950s and 1960s. It is not just our readiness that suffers. The emphasis on youth also exacts a high cost, because large turnover not only is financially expensive, but compels the armed forces to take in less-qualified members than necessary.

The services have many reasons for maintaining an inexperienced force, not all of which are directly related to national security. But those who value experience indicate that they are having trouble retaining qualified people. In large part, they are right, owing to the nature of the military pay system— a system rooted in paternalism and institutionalism, but one that is out of step with the competition.

Here the main culprit is the neutrality-of-the-occupation factor. By paying everyone of the same rank and longevity the same pay regardless of which service he's in, regardless of which job he holds, and regardless of supply and demand considerations, we wind up paying some people too much and others too little. I would submit that one of the most important things that we can do in the next few years to improve the state of our armed forces would be to sever the link between rank and pay and to tie earnings more closely to occupation. By violating the long-held tenet that all members of the same cohort make the same contribution to national defense, this proposal would fly in the face of the so-called institutional model and in fact would move us to an unprecedented degree toward its occupational counterpart.

But the fact remains that for 85 percent of the force the armed forces is truly an occupation, and I don't think appealing to patriotism or duty or honor alone could change that. Maybe the time has come to set the combat arms more distinctly apart from the rest of the armed forces, an idea that's been put forward by many others, including Bill Hauser. A more elite status could play to the concept of the calling as sacrifice and patriotic duty for the combat arms. This would in effect apply the appropriate parts of both philosophies—the institution on the one hand and the occupation on the other—to the appropriate parts of the armed forces. I realize that such changes are difficult to make, and the nation may well opt for maintaining the old traditions. But the opportunity costs of doing so are now very high, and, given the future prospects, are bound to grow even larger.

THOMAS MOORE: Thank you, Martin. Our next discussant is the Chairman of the Economics Department at the University of Rochester, a longtime expert in this area, the mover and shaker behind this conference, really —Walter Oi.

WALTER OI: Let me begin with a review of the Hunter-Nelson paper, and I will come back to Mr. King's paper at the end. When we look at the Hunter-Nelson paper, it is rich in statistical information The various charts and figures that Dick Hunter showed you this morning tell the story of the All-Volunteer Force in a persuasive way. I was, however, disappointed by their measure of the "performance" of the All-Volunteer Force. The main attribute of performance pointed to here was discipline, which has been better under the All-Volunteer Force than it was under the conscript army. Mr. Moskos has pointed out in his paper that the All-Volunteer Navy has a higher desertion rate, but this may be unique to the Navy. It certainly did not show up in the Hunter-Nelson data.

Gary Nelson emphasized retention and attrition issues. The paper was a bit confusing because of its organization. There are basically three main issues: (1) Has the All-Volunteer Force worked? (2) Will it work? and (3) How can we explain the recruitment dip of 1976? This last issue, the recruitment dip, is rather interesting because it provides us with the background to evaluate the second issue, "Will it work?"

Basically, Hunter and Nelson identify six factors that were responsible for this shortfall in recruitment. The All-Volunteer Force is evaluated in terms of its ability to recruit, which I think is an inappropriate criterion by which to judge it. They point to six factors. The first is unemployment, and second is military pay, which has behaved better than academic pay, but not as well as civilian pay. The third factor is the GI Bill. Here, I think, there will be considerable discussion from people who have studied these compensation issues. Harry Gilman and others have questioned the wisdom of payment "in kind" versus payment in cash. The fourth factor is the advertising and recruiting budget. The fifth factor, which I found rather amusing (and the authors treat it in the same way), is what I call "an anti-

Say's Law," namely, if you have too little demand and too few jobs, you're going to have even less supply, because people are not going to be offering their services to a depressed market. Finally, the last factor is a variety of miscellaneous things like a bad press and so forth.

Let me begin my comments with the issue of pay. One of the things that we emphasized at the very beginning of the Gates Commission study was the implicit tax that was imposed on the draftee. Sociologists, psychologists, and others object to the economists' preoccupation with pay, and they point to the fact that people do things for a variety of reasons. I agree that's true. But I do not agree with the sort of policy conclusions that are drawn by people like the Governor of California, who wanted to reduce the pay of the Chancellor of the University of California because he didn't want someone taking the job for its money. Marty Binkin has some very good suggestions about pay, and notes in particular that the military pay system has too little dispersion. Of course we're not getting enough high school graduates when they're paid the same wages as high school dropouts, who have shown that they do not have the perseverance to stick it out through high school and to knuckle under to the sort of discipline that one has to conform to in large organizations. In fact, when you ask, "Why do big companies pay higher wages than little companies?" I suspect that a large part of the wage difference is due to the discipline.* I would very strongly urge a change in the pay structure toward something like the British and Canadian systems, where there are skill levels within each rank so that you get considerably more dispersion into the military pay structure.

There is another element that deserves a comment. It is a point that was made by Bill Meckling during the course of the Gates Commission study and that was studied by the British in their decision not to go with bonuses. This is the issue of work incentives. I recently read a section of John Maurice Clark's *The Economics of Overhead Costs* that points out the difference between machines and men. It tells us why the costs of machinery tend to be overhead costs, because machines are homogenous and predictable. Humans, on the other hand, are not predictable. If you can show them the most efficient way to do a task, they will not repeat it steadily; rather, they have a tendency to monkey. You must design a pay system that will provide incentives and penalize poor behavior. If we go to a system of bonuses,

---

* [Post-conference note]: Large companies have enough trouble recruiting qualified workers. Their problem would be aggravated if they were forced to offer the same wage to all applicants, which is what we are asking of the armed forces. If they can introduce pay differences reflecting productivity differences, they can lower the total cost of acquiring and retaining qualified personnel. This consideration prompted my next remarks.

especially initial entry-level bonuses and reenlistment bonuses, we establish a system of pay that is something very much like an overhead cost—a lump sum payment. Once you have it (the bonus), you have very little incentive to perform properly. If we move from that sort of system to one in which we give pay for good performance and penalize bad performance, I think that the effectiveness of the force is going to increase. I think that we ought to give this more thought in designing the pay package.

Let me turn next to the organization and production of defense. Everyone points to the problem with the *reserves*. One of the more memorable occasions during the Gates Commission study was when we studied this issue and resurrected some of the previous reserve studies. I remember when Harry Gilman and I were sitting in a meeting learning about a British reserve system that at one time had recruited individual reservists called Ever-Readies. They were like our Individual Ready Reserve, namely "fillers" (as distinct from organized reserve units). The British defense establishment offered people a sum—I believe it was something like 40 or 60 pounds a year. It was a modest amount to compensate them for being on the rolls, for being an Ever-Ready reserve in the event of a mobilization. It was Cyprus or some other place that blew up, and the Royal Navy had to mobilize. At that point, one of the admirals said,"Let's call up the Ever-Readies," and the other admiral in charge of personnel said, "No. We cannot do that because if we do, we'll never get another one to sign up for the program again."

We have studied the force structure of the active duty forces carefully, but I do not think that we have given the same care to the study of the reserves, the unit reserve forces, the ready reserve system, or the necessity for the two weeks of summer training.* Pay goes a long way in answering the question, "Who is in the reserves?" You find that there are a lot of congressmen, federal employees, and others who get two paychecks during the two-week summer training. They get higher pay than private-sector employees, who must give up their vacation or regular paycheck to serve in the reserves.

---

* [Postconference note]: Around 1955, the Department of Defense conducted a careful study of the reserve forces, which was reviewed by the Senate Armed Services Committee. One of the main recommendations of that study involved a reduction in the size of the paid-drill force of around 30 to 40 percent. Congress rejected this recommendation, and the structure of the reserve forces has changed very little in the last 30 years. It is high time to review the effectiveness of the reserve force structure. Is it optimal to have an organized reserve unit that is the "twin" of an active duty unit? Or would it be more efficient to have to maintain a reserve force that can staff the training bases or highly specialized skills only?

Of course we get a lot of government workers in the reserves. We want to study the summer training requirement because it imposes a fairly severe constraint on the supply of reserves. By changing the nature of the commitment, moving more toward weekends or after-hours, more toward a moonlighting sort of job, we may be better able to adapt the reserves to the available supply of qualified personnel.

Finally, let me turn to the use of women and civilians. We must carefully study all of the substitution opportunities. Do women provide the least costly means of staffing the positions? Should the DOD move toward more civilianization at civil service ranks or, as Rick Cooper has emphasized, should it rely on more contract labor?

During the Vietnam War, we relied on contract labor. World Airways was clearly more efficient than military air transport (MATS). MATS planes were flying about two hours a day while World Airways planes were in the air some 13 to 14 hours. World Airways was clearly supplying freight and passenger service at a lower price.

We should obviously consider options like these. The British have always used civilians for emergency support and logistical supply to bring fuel, food, etc. to ships at sea. As we move into an era when young men are scarcer and their "price" higher, we ought to look to alternative sources of labor and capital to minimize the costs of producing defense.

In closing, I am concerned with Mr. King's statement that we want to put national defense into what the economists would call a general equilibrium model. I am an economist. I realize that economists' reputations differ. I was at the European econometrics meetings in Athens where Mr. Joffe, a Soviet economist, described a May Day parade. First came the tanks, then the weapons carriers, the little missiles, the intercontinental missiles, and, finally, at the end of the parade came a little truck with three little men on it. Brezhnev turned and asked, "Who are they?" The Minister of Defense replied, "Those are the economists. You wouldn't believe the destructive power that they can unleash." Yes, I am an economist.

Sure, there is a general equilibrium problem. We should try to mesh national defense with other priorities. But if we start to worry about this (and we have worried about it in the past), we are often led to silly policies. If national defense is used to help educate people, we end up drafting men into the army. There are lots of unperceived benefits—the value of military training and so on. We've told a lot of stories that will be retold with no references to the evidence. I am convinced about Bill Baxter's statement that the costs of educating everyone and eliminating all irrationality are too high. Astrology and theology will survive. I don't think that we want to put everything into one grand program. I personally like going at problems one at a time, and try to use good benefit-cost analysis to see if maintaining the current system is worthwhile. I insist that if we look at the overall performance of the armed services, there is much to be gained by reorganizing the production of defense.*

THOMAS MOORE: Thank you, Walter. Our last formal discussant this morning is Robert Tollison. He is Executive Co-director of the Center for Public Choice at Virginia Polytechnic Institute and has written extensively on the All-Volunteer Force.

ROBERT TOLLISON: In my comments, I will focus on the paper by King. Unfortunately, I find this to be one of the most confusing papers I've ever been called upon to comment on at a professional gathering. I have made no attempt to organize my remarks in any systematic way. As I flipped the pages of King's paper, I wrote down my thoughts, and I'm going to share those thoughts with you for whatever they're worth today.

Bill King's general concern is that he feels it is a mistake to view military manpower policy strictly in terms of a military draft versus an All-Volunteer Force. The draft presents certain other well-known problems. Therefore, the way to go is to a third alternative, national service, which is somehow different from the draft and the All-Volunteer Force. Undoubtedly, King has some sort of program of national service in mind when he makes this argument, but you'll find it nowhere stated in the paper.

Be that as it may, regardless of the form of national service that he advocates, I'd just like to stress, as my first point, that he's engaging in pure mythology to claim that national service is somehow different from a draft. Any national service plan that I have ever seen proposed embodies the draft as a central precept, that is, the involuntary taking of labor resources at less than their market value. Indeed, if anything, national service is the draft turned into a nightmare. It is the draft squared, the draft cubed, the draft to the n-th power.

This sort of system avoids none of the problems of the draft; it simply compounds them, imposing huge costs on society by creating inefficiencies

---

* [Postconference note]: I have long favored greater flexibility in training and job assignment. The typical high school graduate in the civilian labor market will hold many jobs before settling on a career. The same option is not provided to the recruit, who must select a military occupational specialty and stay there for some time before he can be reassigned, usually to a closely related specialty. Issues like these have to be studied, but another gigantic, multidisciplinary study team sprinkled with officers, enlisted men and women, and Pentagon bureaucrats, like the one proposed by Dr. King, is *not* the way to achieve efficiency.

in the labor market. And it would serve to finance an unwarranted expansion of the public sector at the expense of those so conscripted, presumably young people. Moreover, philosophically, national service represents, to me at least, a bizarre type of mentality. It suggests that young people are like machines or cattle on a ranch. That is, they are resources over which the state has a claim and can allocate to whatever uses it wishes to put them. The metaphor of a slave society is not too strong to apply to the thought processes of those who advocate such a program. Perhaps nonwhites in the South prior to 1860 felt that they were engaged in national service.

Dr. King next turns to an assessment of the performance of the All-Volunteer Force, and I have no particular quarrel with his summary here, since he has no doubt kept up better with these things than I have. I would note, however, that his argument that the All-Volunteer Force is not a good vehicle for handling national emergency situations amounts to an argument that such emergencies should be underpriced to the relevant decision makers. For example, without a market-clearing price for military manpower during a crisis, decision makers will be less constrained than otherwise in such a situation. To me, this implies that they will not husband their available resources very carefully in responding to a crisis. Men could be more easily traded for cannons in this type of world. Dr. King seems to think that this would be a desirable state of affairs, while basically I do not. I feel that confronting decision makers with the full cost of their actions promotes a more desirable form of behavior, and one way to look at this is in terms of restricting, or promoting less, knee-jerking in responding to foreign events.

At this point in his paper, Dr. King turns essentially to methodological considerations related to how one should study military manpower policy. I find his remarks in this regard especially confusing.

First, he is concerned about the personal motivation and values of researchers, and he sees them as important determinants of research outcomes. I don't see how you can make much sense of this argument. At a basic level, it is obvious that values guide research projects. The scientific method, for example, is a value. Beyond this, personal convictions would seem to be irrelevant in positive scientific analysis. If researchers advance their results in refutable terms, then the process of verification and competition in research will ferret out cases where values are overriding sound analysis. Moreover, the analyst who chooses to proffer value judgments rather than analysis will normally suffer a loss of brand-name capital as a consequence. If arguments or analysis are stated in a nonrefutable form, that is, in terms of shoulds rather than is's, then they're only personal convictions and should be so regarded.

So while I agree with Dr. King, if it is his point, that we need to be on guard to detect normative biases in scientific research, I do not think that this problem is nearly as difficult or as paramount as he makes it out to be. Most of the biases he sees in studies of military manpower policy, for example, are easily predictable by the cost-reward structures facing the individual analyst in question. We do not normally expect government agencies to produce unbiased research. Lord knows, we have enough uneconomic investment in water resource projects in this country to know better than to trust government agencies to do competent economic analysis.

In contrast to the approach of the economists, Dr. King offers the approach of the sociologist. For their part the sociologists are preoccupied, or at least seem to be preoccupied, with the old bugaboo about representativeness in our military forces. What these people never seem to realize is that representativeness is costly, and it is costly in a way that they would not normally be prepared to accept.

What I mean here is quite simple. Attainment of proportional representation of the population in the military, where soldiers are paid market-clearing wages, implies a blatantly discriminatory military wage policy. For example, the military wage offered to minorities who presently find the military an attractive occupation would have to be lowered, or the wages offered to other socioeconomic groups who find the military a less attractive opportunity would have to be raised. Such a policy would achieve proportional representation, but I've yet to meet a sociologist who's in favor of such a wage system.

My response to the call for a more representative army is the same as it was ten years ago: Who cares? I see no compelling reason to deny the imperative of comparative advantage in this occupation any more than in any other risky occupation in our society. Where is the outcry about the fact that the Iroquois are disproportionately represented among the workers who put up the steel girders for high-rise buildings? Where is the outcry about the lower income whites who work the coal mines in southwestern Virginia?

The latter part of Dr. King's paper is a plea for a comprehensive interdisciplinary study of military manpower policy. This is by far the worst part of the paper. It reads like an unfortunate grant proposal. Sprinkled throughout are all the right Washington buzz words: *group effort, pragmatic analysis, different analysis frameworks, multidisciplinary team, group consensus, relevance of policy makers,* ad infinitum. I must say that this kind of jargon approach is completely alien to my experience with research. Committees are among the most useless inventions of mankind, most especially so when one is trying to arrive at some sort of truth judgment on a matter of scientific interest.

My basic view in response to Dr. King's paper, and perhaps to a lot of the positions taken at this conference, is that there is not really a problem with the All-Volunteer Force worth talking about. All the other agencies of the government are working quite well with volunteer labor forces, and I see no reason to single out the military as a special case in this regard. While plenty of people seem to resist the idea of paying volunteer wages to soldiers, I submit to you that this not an argument about the efficiency of the All-Volunteer Force. It is an argument about wealth redistribution from soldiers to nonsoldiers, and national service—woe to us the day it would come—would generalize this wealth redistribution process to the status of economic warfare among the young and old.

THOMAS MOORE: Thank you, Bob. The authors of the paper will get a chance later this morning to respond to some of these remarks. Right now I would like to call a short break. We'll reconvene shortly for questions and comments from the floor.

IV

GENERAL DISCUSSION AND QUESTIONS
FROM THE FLOOR

THOMAS MOORE: Let me just take the chance to raise a question I'd like to hear somebody discuss at some point today or tomorrow. That is, why don't we use foreigners? Why don't we hire mercenaries abroad? It seems to me that there are many Mexicans who would like to have jobs in this country; the Vietnamese have proven themselves to be good fighters and presumably would fight at a reasonable price—the boat people and so on. In any case, it might fill any gap in our military manpower needs.

Now, who would lilke to make the first point? Yes, Lewis.

LEWIS GANN: I'm Lewis Gann. I am a Senior Fellow at the Hoover Institution. I am somewhat concerned with the tone of the discussion. The object of creating an army is not to be fair, it is not to be economical. It is to fight a war; it is to meet the enemy in combat and to smash him. Which kind of an army, a volunteer army or a conscript army, is likely to do the job better? That should be the objective of the discussion.

As a minor point, I am somewhat concerned with the notion of differentiating between combat units and rear units. If and when the Russians strike, their armored columns will be ranging behind the front maybe a hundred miles or two hundred miles. Helicopter forces will be attacking in the rear, and I would hope that even the cooks and the bakers will be able to fight and will be trained for combat functions.

RICHARD HUNTER: I think the answer to the question, which kind of army fights best, is a question of how well it's trained and equipped and led, rather than how it was raised.

MARTIN BINKIN: I might add to that. We really don't know how to measure whether a conscription army can fight better than a volunteer army. We have very few measurements of military effectiveness, and that creates an awful lot of problems for both quantitative and qualitative analysis. With respect to your point about the differentiation between combat and support, I think you're living in the past. The popularized image of warfare—giving the cook a rifle and sending him out to the front lines—has seen its better days. You're talking about Soviet armored columns coming through to the rear. You're going to give the cook a rifle against a Soviet armored column? The equalizers we're going to want to use are Tows and Dragons, sophisticated antitank weapons, which cooks and bakers are not capable of handling. So, while we have to be careful about how we distinguish between combat and support (and that's always a problem), it's not so much a problem when you differentiate by service. The enlisted Army force is primarily a combat force, whereas the Air Force enlisted force is not primarily a combat force.

WILLIAM KING: I would agree with Marty [BINKIN] on the issue he raised—that we really haven't answered the question of which is more effective. I don't think we know how to answer that question, and this is precisely why I was proposing that we address it in comprehensive terms. Unfortunately, I discovered this morning that that's impossible to do, so I guess we never will resolve it. It is unfortunate, because I agree it is a critical question.

BERNARD ROTSKER: I'm concerned about the political, and to some extent the bureaucratic, vulnerability of the All-Volunteer Force. My training is similar to Gary [Nelson]'s except I spent close to the last three years fighting the same type of battles from a service viewpoint. A great deal of the underway supply for the fleet is carried out by Navy ships manned by civilians. The problem, however, is that when you start to civilianize you run into manpower ceilings and salary limitations that prevent you from carrying out the program. Over the last month there was an attempt to increase military pay; and the Defense Department attempted to incresase components of the military by about $650 million this year. Both of those efforts went down to defeat.

I think we have to understand the whole volunteer concept is afflicted with political vulnerability. For instance, segments of either the administration or Congress can prevent the kind of flexibilities required to keep the concept viable and fresh. Could I ask Gary to respond to that based on his OSD perspectives?

GARY NELSON: Let me say that with respect to the volunteer force and to major policy changes necessary to sustain it, what is important is that there be a recognition both of what the problems are and of what the proposed solutions are. I don't think we've had this in either my years in the Pentagon or your years in the Pentagon, Bernie. Three years ago we made efforts to do something about attrition, and to increase the number of women more rapidly than was being done in the services. I think those have been successful, though I haven't seen the latest data. I didn't suggest further changes at that time because of difficult bureaucratic obstacles.

On the economic side, the thing that's of concern is not just the changes that have occurred in the past four years, but also the trend and the prospect that those changes would be continued in the future and probably would get much worse. Here I think we need to have a clear understanding. The course of action is there. The defense budget is big and is going up very fast, probably, in total amount, by more than ten times the budget of my agency (Office of Personnel Management)—more than a hundred times the budget of your agency, Bernie.*

Yes, I think we need to understand military pay. It involves decisions that are made outside of the bureaucratic framework, but probably made within the legislative framework.

I do not agree with Walter Oi on the question of paying by specialty, even from the standpoint of paying bonuses by specialty. We certainly differ in degree about the use of bonuses. But I really question how effective we are right now in using bonuses to recruit people where bonuses are paid only on the basis of occupation. This seems to me not to be very effective, based on what we would expect. We would expect the supply to a given occupation to be more elastic than the supply to a service. We don't seem to see the size of effects in response to bonuses paid to the combat arms, and I suspect it's because we're really not a very good match with the market. When people think about coming into the Army, they think of coming into the combat arms: they expect to have to fight. When they think of going into the Navy, they think of going to sea. Our efforts to recruit people by specialty, where we offer different pay rates by specialty, may not be a very successful way to recruit people today.

RICHARD GABRIEL: Rick Gabriel from Saint Anselm's College. I have a question or probably a point of ambiguity, I'd like to raise. Professor Binkin made a point, and Gary Nelson, Bob Tollison, and Professor Gann. It's true, in modern warfare, as tank armies crash 35 kilometers behind the front, that no cook is going to stop a tank. It's also true that support troops in the rear are going to get chopped up. So maybe the question concerning the volunteer force—and we haven't addressed it—is not who serves, or who lives, but, in the end, who dies? And if that's the question, then we have not really looked at a crucial aspect of this. And that is the notion of representativeness, which Professor Moskos will address tomorrow. There is a vital difference, it seems to me, between utilizing economic models to decide what pieces of equipment to buy over what other pieces of equipment and utilizing solely economic models, or mostly economic models, to decide who

---

* [Editor's note]: Bernard Rotsker is Director of the Selective Service.

serves and who does not, or in the end (in a modern war) who dies and who does not. Using economic models to decide who dies or not seems to me either (1) a delusion of the first order or (2) the grossest kind of immorality, in the sense that one begins to treat the life and death of people as if they were mere economic instrumentalities or, to use Professor Oi's analogy, one begins to treat and value people as if they were machines.

Thus I argue, or suggest, that we're perhaps looking at the wrong question. To ask whether or not the volunteer force can be made to "work" in terms of recruitment through economic incentives is overlooking a fundamental point, and I would address this to Mr. Nelson. Mr. Nelson, the reason bonuses do not work in the combat arms is because death is always an uneconomic choice. Fundamentally, no one, no matter how high you keep bidding up, is likely to volunteer if the probability that he will die is great.

GARY NELSON: I would think, Mr. Gabriel, that the essence of a volunteer army is that the people themselves decide who serves, not the government through use of economic models.

RICHARD GABRIEL: We can go around that by arguing in terms of representativeness that we may have structured the economy in such a way that blacks or the poor don't have an equal opportunity not to volunteer.

GARY NELSON: There's another interesting point which we have not talked about here, but which you address, and that is the case of who fights a major war. Who are the casualties of a major war? Will it, in fact, be the volunteers who serve in peacetime, or will it be the draftees that come in in time of war?

RICHARD HUNTER: Your best chance of survival may be to be as close to the enemy as possible.

RICHARD GABRIEL: My question concerns what, I think, Bob Tollison was saying. When you begin to address certain kinds of questions, I believe there are limits, very severe limits, to the utilization of economic models. Mr. Tollison did not see a difference between civilian and military occupations. I would submit that there is a crucial difference. No one is ever going to ask you to die for IBM. In the end, to quote Mr. Kipling, if there is a war, "we'll put you in your stall." And I think that limits economic models, as far as it addresses this question.

ROBERT TOLLISON: What would you propose, that we deny minorities an opportunity in this sector because they don't have opportunities in other sectors?

RICHARD GABRIEL: I'll expound on this a bit tomorrow morning. I would suggest that the burden of death be spread at least as equally as possible. Now, it's true that when not all serve there will always be some inequality. But as Mr. Cooper points out, it's a question of rates of inequality. As we've structured the All-Volunteer Force right now, and Professor Moskos is very clear on this, we know who the burden of death is going to fall on, and you delude yourself, sir, if you think that giving men the opportunity to die on a combat battlefield is in fact an opportunity. It is a problem.

DAVID HENDERSON: David Henderson, the Cato Institute. I just want to address what Richard Gabriel said. I think the point's already been made by Tollison. I just want to elaborate on it a bit more.

There are all kinds of risky occupations that we have people volunteering for. And, in fact, IBM, I believe, probably does ask some people to die for them. [Laughter] I mean, they are all over the world. I mean this literally. They are all over the world. They probably have private police forces somewhere. They probably take some chances in certain unstable countries. It's a matter of degree. Tollison's point, and the point of people opposed to the draft, is not that people choose to die. Of course they don't. They choose to take a probability of death, and they choose voluntarily.

ROBERT TOLLISON: There's also quite substantial evidence that where government has tried to impose quotas on the private sector, it has not even lived up to those quotas within its own agencies. HEW, for example, does not meet its guidelines for universities with respect to percentages of minorities and others that they are supposed to hire. You can wish any part of society proportionately represented, but it's another thing to have a government agency capable of carrying that policy out. HEW is not representative of the population.

WALTER OI: The Commonwealth of Massachusetts gave deferments to all members of the legislature and to the fellows of Harvard College.

THOMAS MOORE: Bill, do you want to comment?

WILLIAM KING: Yes, I think things like representativeness are only a way of identifying potential unintended consequences. I don't think representativeness per se is important. I don't think that attrition per se is important. The real issues, it seems to me, are those indicators of unintended consequences—or externalities, in terminology more familiar to my economist friends—in all the policies we have adopted or are contemplating adopting. For example, hundreds of thousands of young people have been turned back into our society as certified failures by the All-Volunteer Force, by the military. What are the consequences in the long run to us of that? Attrition, per se, does not bother me. These people [DOD] are competent and creative and they will come up with some way of keeping the numbers at about the right level. The question is, while we keep those numbers at the right level, are we also doing some things that we didn't want to achieve and perhaps don't even recognize in the short run that we are doing?

ARNOLD MOORE: My name is Arnold Moore. Dick Hunter said that two armies that were raised in a different fashion, one conscripted and the other volunteer, would fight identically. Perhaps that's the central issue. That's an empirical question. You asserted it as if it's obviously true. Yet I believe some people here in this room, although they haven't put it that way, are differing with you on precisely that point. And that, perhaps, is what ought to be the issue we're talking about here. You're assuming it anyway. I guess I would tend to do so, too, but I would do so out of ignorance. I don't know.

RICHARD HUNTER: You changed my intent somewhat. I wouldn't want to say that conscription has no effect. We've had volunteers and had draftees in armies before, and it's hard to tell them apart once you get them in there and out where the war goes on. I think the primary criteria are training, leadership, and equipment. These have the major impact on the performance of the force.

I'd also like to add that we must keep in mind when we discuss this, and when we start talking about war, about major columns coming through Europe and whether we're going to go nuclear, and all those kinds of things, that the peacetime debate we're having is a debate on how we're going to maintain our force prior to the start of a war. It is the prewar maintenance that is the dominant factor in the early days, the critical days of a war. But no one I know argues we could maintain a volunteer force during a massive war. When the clear and present danger comes, I think you have to move toward a more conscriptive force. You have to mobilize the economy. You have to take over the means of production and a lot of other things that Bernie Rotsker, Director of the Selective Service, spends his time worrying about. And he wouldn't have an agency if we didn't believe that that had to happen when a war came about. Gary. . . .

GARY NELSON: Let me add one point to the comparison of performance of the conscript army with the volunteer army. I think we need to define what we mean by a conscript army. If we're talking about the pre-Vietnam conscript army, for which we drafted about 100,000 people a year, with the first-term force consisting about equally of volunteers and draftees or people who enlisted because of the draft, the career force consists entirely of volunteers. By definition, people have had an opportunity to leave. The officer force, though mostly volunteer, is a mixture.

It's not clear to me there's a real difference in kind, though there is some difference in degree. We tend to look at the people who serve. There are some differences, though they're not overwhelming. I would argue, though I am not an expert on this, that the burden of proof should be on those who argue that there would be a major difference in the performance of similarly trained, similarly equipped forces that differed only in this way. There may in fact, be, but I don't know what it would be.

THOMAS MOORE: Arnold, have you finished?

I might just inject at this point that the mercenary forces such as the Gurkhas have proven very effective in the past.

CHARLES MOSKOS: I'm Charlie Moskos. I'm wondering for purposes of the topic of this session whether from the economists' point of view there is any fact other than a shortage in numbers that would disconfirm the success of the All-Volunteer Force.

THOMAS MOORE: Anybody want to comment on that? Gary?

GARY NELSON: Are you talking, Charlie, in terms of criteria, or are you talking in terms of actual force?

CHARLES MOSKOS: To the question "Is the volunteer force working?" is there any factor other than a shortage of numbers which would make you say that it is not working? The pause itself is more than pregnant.

RICHARD HUNTER: I think, Charlie, that the trade-off in the economic model you're talking about is one of cost versus quality. And you can arrange those things in different forms. One of the things I would emphasize is that it doesn't matter whether it's an all-volunteer or a conscription force, or what. The important factor is whether it is supported by the American people or not. I think that lack of support is what keeps us from having national service or the draft. They are simply not supported by the people at this time.

CHARLES MOSKOS: I'm thinking here, Dick, of a more academic point. It's an epistemological issue. Not about advocacy of one position—just a sheer social-scientific question. What would make you say the All-Volunteer Force was not working other than a shortage of numbers? Nothing? What would make you disconfirm it other than a shortage of numbers?

RICHARD HUNTER: Now that you've given me your question, and then explained your question, and now explained your explanation, let me say that at the beginning we mentioned our concern about the quality of the general human capital embodied in the people who came into the military, their ability to accept training and disciplne. Those are the kinds of measures that we would use.

CHARLES MOSKOS: If the attrition rates were over 90 percent, then, but you could always get these refilled, would you consider that a failure? No, you wouldn't consider that a failure, as long as the numbers were still coming in.

WALTER OI: If you had that situation, there would be a training pipeline at all times. How would you judge whether a police department was working? Or whether we had to conscript people into the police force? There you would say you'd want to look at reported crimes, and that's a funny number. I think the thing that we want to look at is whether or not the people at the top, who are in charge of determining defense readiness for the combat units and their support units, are comfortable with the situation. We have to judge on some evidence.

It's not a function of numbers. We never defined a strength shortfall with respect to women back in 1964. It's because the women were insignificant; we just forgot them. Now we include them in. We've assumed that they're perfect substitutes, which I contend is not accurate, and you contend is not accurate. But now we've changed the numbers, and I'm saying it's not a function of numbers. And that's where I think focusing only on recruitment goal builds in a political vulnerability (Bernie's term), and, that's not the right way to ask the question of whether the All-Volunteer Force is "working."

STANLEY HOROWITZ: I'm Stan Horowitz from the Center for Naval Analyses. What I want to say is similar to what I think Walter just said, which is to ask you what you'd like to do from a methodological point of view. I don't think that the economists and their critics really ought to differ much on this. But what you'd like to do is, you'd like to be able to measure the organizational effectiveness or readiness of units, and determine what kinds of people contribute marginally, and in what ways, to that effectiveness.

Now, people can say, well, that's pie in the sky. But it's not as much pie in the sky as it used to be. There's a lot of research going on in this area, or that will be done. And I think that as that work gets brought into this question—what kind of people you need and how best to structure the force—you can take these factors into account in determining what kind of people you want. No one can deal with the question: If we do not now have a reasonable mix of people in the services, how much, from the economists' point of view, would we have to pay to get them? It is possible that right now our readiness is too low, and that it could be improved by bringing in higher quality people. Then, I guess, I would say that the All-Volunteer Force isn't working real well right now. My solution, of course, as an economist, wouldn't be to throw it out, but rather to structure compensation in such a way as to get people to make it work. And I think that, really, your [Moskos'] proposal and your paper tomorrow are quite along these lines. You propose a particular policy to bring in these higher-quality people. And the evaluation of that policy as to the best way to bring in higher-quality people is the sort of question that's right along the lines of standard econometric analysis. I don't really see that there's that much difference in the schools here even though everyone seems to think there is.

PATRICIA DUIGNAN: My name is Patricia Duignan, and I have a question for Mr. Oi, or for anyone else on the panel. I'd like to hear the reasons that you believe women would not be good substitutes for manpower procurement.

WALTER OI: I appeal to the people who have studied this from other viewpoints, and I look at the cross data, the turnover rates, and so forth. I also look at Mr. Moskos' paper where he says, of course we're not going to expect women to perform the same functions, and so forth and so on. Okay? Right away it says right there they're not perfect substitutes.

PATRICIA DUIGNAN: But I don't understand why.

WALTER OI: Because we won't allow them into the combat units.

PATRICIA DUIGNAN: But isn't it true that there are ten combat support people for every person in combat?

WALTER OI: That's right, but we haven't treated women as equals for those ten jobs. If we had, why should we [DOD] place a limit of 12 percent for women? I contend that the reason is that the cost of women begins to rise very quickly, and because of that there is an economic argument for limiting women enlistments.

PATRICIA DUIGNAN: Why are women more expensive?

WALTER OI: Turnover, mainly. Women tend to stay shorter periods, and therefore you don't recoup your investment in training.

RICHARD HUNTER: It depends on how you want to measure expensive or not expensive, and turnover or not turnover. As an economist I want to get down to margin and measure it. And we felt for quite a while that women were less costly than men who had the same kinds of IQ and the same kinds of strength and the same kinds of whatever we want to measure that's necessary to do the job that you're specifically looking at. In some areas strength is a major factor, and I think that's one of the things, at least so far, that is a major concern in combat.

There's also a deep-seated sociological thing about the combat issue that's real. Once again I come back to the fact that society has to decide. CBS or one of the networks is going to give you a good close-up of a lady getting killed, you know, getting maimed in war. And then there's going to be an outcry to take them out. I know that can happen because it already happened to us on 17-year-olds in Vietnam. Fortunately by the time the bureaucracy functioned they'd all turned 18, so we were right. [Laughter] Such a change is going to occur. If we committed our Army divisions today —and I think Max will back me up on this—and then, after they got there, decided that the women couldn't do the things that they were assigned to do in training, we'd have a serious problem. They hold key jobs, NCO jobs, officer jobs. They're an important, integrated part of the force. They do those jobs very well, and at that margin I think they are pretty interchangeable. Women lose more time for medical reasons than men do, but this is mainly because of the time women must take off for pregnancy. Men lose more time because of drug problems than for any other reason. So different problems come to bear in the two sexes. They trade off in different ways.

On the other hand, civilian society hasn't got around to paying women the same as men, so, like blacks, women are attracted by the relatively higher pay, and therefore they come in. But a lot of them want to work in the traditional skills. They want to come in as dental technicians or medical persons or clerical workers, and they're not as ready to come in to do the combat jobs that are now open to women.

ANTONIA CHAYES: Antonia Chayes, Undersecretary of the Air Force. I had a bit of a problem, Professor Oi, with your substitution statements, in addition to the women. But let me just start with the women.

The fact is that the cost of recruiting women is less and the cost of retaining them is, I believe, not higher. I think that in cost-effectiveness terms, they are proving themselves out, and that is why all services are relying on them to a certain extent. The fact is, we don't find large numbers of women to fill the technical areas, neither enlisted nor officers. It's very hard to find women engineers. This, I think, is a product of our educational system and cultural bias. You know, it's the old math-anxiety syndrome that has been studied elsewhere. I think that when you have 12 to 18 percent women, as we have in the Air Force, you're not looking at ceilings, you're really looking at sensible projections of what our people think they can get in terms of the interest of women in joining the armed forces, and that averages out. I think that if it turned out to be a higher number of volunteers, the services would take a higher number. There are many, many noncombat slots, and these are being redefined all the time. In other words, when I came into the Air Force, women were excluded from missile silos on the grounds that that was a direct combat job and was, therefore, restricted under the law. They were excluded from other enlisted occupations under the law. The law has been looked at, and the combat exclusion is now much narrower. We now have women pilots in many aircraft, though not fighters and bombers.

So I think the substitution notion of women is a valid one. Pregnancy causes attrition, yes. But Article 15 much less; women are not as much disciplinary problems, and there are not as many taking drugs. In the end, yes, there are problems, and there are limitations but they are just ones of reality.

Also you talked about civilianization. There are standards, and we have had a long-standing struggle with determining the appropriate mix of civilian and military people. I'm not sure we're correct, and probably Marty Binkin would like to comment on this since he has a big stake in the subject. It has been a running battle between the services and the Office of the Secretary of Defense as to which occupations could be made civilian and which ones ought to be on a sort of stand-by basis for wartime and made military. That battle, in addition to the civilian manpower ceilings, has, I think, limited the number of civilians. I think we probably could go somewhat further—that's always been my view—but not a lot further under the current political environment, which in a way has ended the debate between the services and the Office of the Secretary of Defense.

Likewise we have supported increased use of contract labor, not because it was a way to get around the end-strength restrictions, but because we have found that we run up against political brick walls as soon as any area gets heavily contracted. When there's a loss of civilian personnel, you hear from Congress about that. So you know that the analysis is good, the criteria developed in A76 are really quite refined, and the study has been done, I think, very carefully. But there is a political limit. So I think all of these substitutions are being studied and are being annually readdressed. But there are a number of constraints that make them difficult. There is no easy solution for the success of the All-Volunteer Force.

COMMENT FROM THE AUDIENCE: I happen to identify with those who've said we're focusing too much on numbers, but I do want to bring the discussion back to numbers. I'd like to read two quotes that I can't resolve. So I'd like the people here to resolve them for me. One is by John White, who said, "In the 1950s the potential supply of young men was only double the DOD demand. In the '70s the potential supply is five times the demand. A favorable ratio is projected to continue through the '80s, in spite of a projected decline of 15 percent in youth population, a very favorable picture." You repainted it here for us. And then we've got Bill King quoting Johnston and Guy, who estimate that "the active-duty military will have to recruit one out of every three qualified and available male youth until 1980," and that "this proportion increases to forty percent of the qualified and available pool in the '85–'89 period. When reserve requirements of 100,000 annual non-prior-service accessions are taken into account, the ratios become forty percent for '65–'80 and fifty percent for '85–'90. This means that by the late 1980s the military total force will be faced with the problem of recruiting one of every two qualified and available males in the population."

Now I can't resolve White's extremely rosy picture on the one hand and the extremely grim one that Bill King takes from Johnston and Guy on the other.

GARY NELSON: There are two ways of doing these ratios. One way is essentially to take the total population and reduce it by those who are not eligible under pretty strenuous standards—category Vs, people who are in institutions, people who cannot meet medical standards. That, in fact, is what we did. Basically, we're looking for the ratio of the number of males we have to take to the total population who can meet those standards. The other approach is to look at the qualified and available population, considering many more people as ineligible. This approach also happens to take out all the college population. The logical extreme is also to take out all those people who have jobs, so you are left with those people who are unemployed.

I've never felt comfortable with this latter approach. I've always tended to use the broader kind of approach. But that's the difference between the ratio of four to one and the ratio of two to one. I think it's largely the college population.

AUDIENCE: I could account for everything except perhaps that.

WILLIAM KING: Are the reserves factors in your research?

GARY NELSON: Yes, they are.

WILLIAM KING: That's another possible difference—the definition of qualified and available. Johnston and Guy basically did their study under the aegis of the Department of Defense, and at that time that seemed to be the number that was being focused on. Of course, I checked out the validity of the number when I did my report, but I accepted the Department of Defense statistics. Now, apparently, they have switched to another concept. I just wonder, why?

RICHARD HUNTER: One reason is because I came to work for the Department of Defense. I sat down and figured out what I thought would give us a better picture of what was there. But we look at both sets of statistics, and both are real and important. What's really important is the trends, what's happening.

People who go to college aren't going to go into the military, most of them. A few do. Also, the people who have jobs are less liable to enlist, and this is especially true when beginning military pay is below the minimum wage. These things are relevant, and you really are drawing out of a certain segment of the population. You can measure that on either set of statistics you want. I don't know whether one is rosier or less rosy than the other. It's a hard job to recruit. And it's harder in the Army than it is in the Air Force. The basic draw that we come to, the basic answer that we come out with, is that for *either* set of statistics it's possible to continue to operate a volunteer force, whereas it was numerically impossible in the mid-50s to do so, at the force levels being maintained then.

AUDIENCE: Well, it seems to me that the gap between numeric possibility and the political and bureaucratic problems Gary admitted to a while ago when Bernie Rostker raised them lies at the heart of the problem. That's a big gap, and we're really in a race between demographics and our ability to fine-tune a system with bureaucratic and political adjustments. This cannot be lightly dismissed. It's going to call for more genius than we may have.

GARY NELSON: In terms of the specific measures that I talked about which I think would help sustain the volunteer force in the 1980s, the system really has incorporated those actions on attrition and utilization of women. I spoke of the five-year defense plan which has been in there for a couple of years, and I think those things will be met. The other concern, which is an economic concern, is, I think, in a different environment. It's not a case of whether the Air Force happens to agree or disagree with the Office of the Secretary of Defense. It's rather a question of whether this country or this administration would really request larger funds for first-term military personnel. And that, I think, puts it right in the middle of the political environment. There are lots of ways to do things. I don't know what will be the outcome.

RICHARD COOPER: One of the things that has troubled me very much in reading the papers is this grand distinction between the economists and the rest of the world. Bill King talks about how all the economic models are based on the assumption of economic rationality on the part of everyone. None of our models has ever made those assumptions. What we assume is that people are rational *at the margin*. And there is a lot of evidence over the hundreds of years since Adam Smith to indicate that this is true. What we have tried to do as analysts is to look at data; we've tried to measure things. There are certain variables we can measure better than others. We can measure pay better than others. But most of us who have worked with supply equations—and there are a lot of people in this room who have— recognize how well or how badly those equations sometimes do. We try to use these equations for general kinds of insights, not to the exclusion of everything else. I think the notion that it's economists on the one hand and the sociologists on the other is a great mistake. I think what this really is doing is changing the tone of the debate.

When I first got involved with the All-Volunteer Force issues back in 1973, the big issue was quantity. The Army wasn't meeting its recruiting goals. We dispelled that notion and showed the reasons for what had happened, and what we could do. The next thing that came up was cost, and we showed that that was really a nonissue. The point is that each time an issue has come up, it has been shown to be wrong. Because of this, opponents of the All-Volunteer Force have come more and more to focus on the less quantifiable parameters because they are less refutable. I mean, you can sit and argue for days or weeks or months on philosophical grounds. Hopefully we're collecting data that will enable us to answer more of these things. But I think an awful lot of what's gone on is really based on conjecture, and what we really need to do is to get better numbers. We've seen numbers decried here. I think we need *more* numbers.

WALTER OI: I think we've been amazingly accurate in the predictions of what happened. And I think that when you say we've estimated a lot of bad supply equations—

RICHARD COOPER: I didn't say that, Walter. I didn't say we'd estimated bad supply equations. I said anybody who has estimated those equations feels uncomfortable with some of the numbers because we know how soft some of them are.

WALTER OI: I realize that, but I'm amazed at how well the reenlistment stuff is shaping up. That's what I find remarkable—how accurate you guys have been—which I think is rather striking. Some of the analyses do seem to be working.

WILLIAM KING: Rick, I think I would certainly agree with your comments. As I point out in my paper, I think there is a tendency to confuse measurability with importance. When we quantify things, they have a power that goes well beyond things that may in fact be very important but are hard to quantify. If we could separate those things, measurability and importance, I think we would be in almost perfect agreement, as we find most of the time when we get into this. But I think this missing of issues because they are hard to measure is a natural tendency of most of us who are trained in analysis. If we can't measure it, we aren't comfortable with it and we tend to dismiss it. In doing so, we implicitly give it low importance, when in the kinds of systems that I deal with, difficult-to-measure parameters may, in fact, be the most important things.

DAVID HENDERSON: David Henderson, Cato Institute. Richard Hunter said something earlier that no one challenged, and I was a little surprised. He said that no one is talking about having an all-out war with an All-Volunteer Force. Now, I'm not clear on that. He could have meant one of two things. One is that people aren't going to go for it as voters, and he might be right. The other is that economists don't argue for it, or there aren't other people arguing for it.

Well, I am one of the people who argue for it. In fact, the economic argument against the draft is stronger during war than during peacetime. The implicit tax is higher. You're not just taking a couple of years of people's lives with a small probability of dying. In very many cases you're taking their lives themselves. And so I think that, if anything, if I had to choose between having a draft in wartime and having a draft in peacetime, and I could only choose one of them, I'd choose a draft in peacetime. Of course, I wouldn't choose that either, but if it were a forced choice, that's what I'd do. And I know there's one person in this room who agrees with me—Bill Meckling. When I first met him, Bill told me that during the Second World War he opposed the draft throughout the war. I think we shouldn't let that issue go by. There's a real issue there.

RICHARD HUNTER: I guess I was speaking from what I viewed as Department of Defense policy and the Washington debate that's going on. There's an implicit assumption, and in most cases an explicit assumption, that we're going to call on Bernie Rotsker (Selective Service) as soon as we think we're in a really major war. You also have to define what you mean by war. We're talking about massive numbers of divisions crossing some Eastern European country's border, violence, and maybe or maybe not tactical nuclear weapons. That sort of thing.

DAVID HENDERSON: So you're talking about what you think is going to happen, not what is feasible.

RICHARD HUNTER: If that sort of thing happens, and we are then in what I classify as a struggle for the survival of our society, you kind of throw up your hands and you tax everybody 100 percent.

DAVID HENDERSON: Not everybody. Every young male.

RICHARD HUNTER: You say in fact tax everybody 100 percent and assign people to go work in factories where they didn't want to work before. All kinds of things can happen. You can even go out and not pay people money. That happened during periods of threat in some countries. The more serious the threat is—the more likely it is to destroy the society—the more you throw out all the rest of your social institutions and fight for survival. That's the kind of context in which we feel that you would have to mobilize not just for the military but for the whole society, the whole production capability.

GARY NELSON: You know, I've always thought that in the case of a total mobilization there would be a very good ex-ante case of market failure —that there would be no market, no real probability of a market wage being set that would in fact produce the very large number of people you would need in the short term. You simply couldn't do it. I've become very comfortable with the notion of not worrying about how to do it, and, instead, just going ahead and conscripting.

DAVID HENDERSON: What about the fact that in both the First World War right from the start and the Second World War after 1942 they didn't allow volunteers? They never gave it a chance.

GARY NELSON: That was because the cost of failure was unacceptable.

DAVID HENDERSON: Well, you're saying why they didn't give it a chance.

GARY NELSON: The cost of failure to execute the war properly was unacceptable, and you wanted to mobilize the whole population base. You didn't want to waste time trying to sort out and manage and do all those things. That's my perception of it.

DAVID HENDERSON: Well, you have to sort in any case. The point is, those people were volunteering.

RICHARD HUNTER: You didn't want the whole New York Police Department to volunteer and leave. You wanted to pick some people and leave some here. You wanted to manage the manpower force of the United States.

DAVID HENDERSON: Well, can I ask you this question, then? Are you saying that you think it's infeasible, or are you saying that people think it's infeasible to have a volunteer force during war-time?

RICHARD HUNTER: I'm only saying that, as I understand the plans of everybody involved in the debate and the Congress and the administration, the assumption is that this is a peacetime program and that normally in peacetime in our nation's history we have worked with volunteers. Congress, in its power to raise armies, and maintain navies, has done it through volunteers. And every time we've gotten involved in a major war, we've moved to some kind of conscription—and some kind of more or less management of the civilian manpower force. As I see history, that's the context of this issue. I think that if a massive war started this morning, none of us would be here. We would all have been called out. We would start immediately figuring out ways to mobilize the entire society. And Bernie's budget would go up faster than the whole rest of the country combined by a hundredfold.

THOMAS MOORE: We're really running out of this morning's time. I'd now like to let Bernie Rotsker have the last word, since this is his job.

BERNARD ROTSKER: Just to answer some specifics, I think the developing position in the Defense Department would be to continue a volunteer system, as long as it could be sustained, and certainly over the first several months. Conditions in World War II were different. The Selective Service System was truly choosing people with an eye to maintaining a home base, and volunteer rates were much higher than could be absorbed. This questioned the sustainability of the domestic infrastructure, so the system really was sorting out who could go. It was selective in a way that we don't understand today. The question envisioned by selective service today would be the equalization of the burden. We would be going to a random selection process in which we did not recognize occupation deferments. It's a very different concept than was exercised in World War II, and really comes out of the social experience of the Vietnam era, when there was a severe tax on the system in that the bright, and the wealthy, did not go.

(VOICE FROM THE FLOOR): Would you allow the purchase of substitutes?

BERNARD ROTSKER: It's not for me to allow the purchase of substitutes, but right now that certainly has not entered the debate. I think the notion is much more that of spreading the burden without any reference to a market solution, or any reference to the kind of problems that developed for the British at the end of World War I, where the elite, the intellectual leadership of that country, was largely decimated. This was one of the main reasons for a selective service with continued student deferments during World War II. But there is no plan for continuing deferments under any resumption of the draft that I know of.

THOMAS MOORE: Well, we've had a very lively morning. Thank you.

PART 2

The Law and Military Conscription

INTRODUCTION

William Meckling

WILLIAM MECKLING: I think we ought to start as promptly as we can.

Let me say that there are a number of people in this audience who were involved in the great Gates Commission, whose study led to the elimination of conscription. Two of those commission members are Milton Friedman, whom you'll hear from tomorrow, and Allen Wallis, Chancellor of the University of Rochester, who is here. Walter Oi, whom you heard from this morning, was in charge of demand, and Harry Gilman, who for some reason I can't fathom has been quiet so far, was in charge of supply.

Walter Oi mentioned this morning how accurate those numbers turned out to be, and nobody feels happier about that than Harry and I and the other members of the commission staff.* Most of you don't remember, I think, how big a problem it was trying to get some notion of what kind of pay raise would be necessary to get the number of volunteers the military said they had to have when we couldn't even determine what fraction of the force at that time actually were true volunteers. This was because there were a lot of so-called volunteers we knew were draft-induced. In addition to trying to estimate the elasticity of supply, we had to estimate how many volunteers were already in there. I have the feeling that in the end Harry Gilman pulled those numbers out of a hat, but they turned out to be pretty accurate, as a matter of fact. We were very happy, at any rate, that they came out as close as they did.

This afternoon we're going to hear from a somewhat different fraternity, one that also was quiet this morning—the legal fraternity. We have two distinguished lawyers, Philip Bobbitt of the University of Texas Law School

---

* [Editor's note]: William Meckling was the Executive Director of the commission staff.

and David Landau of the American Civil Liberties Union.

Our first speaker of this afternoon, Philip Bobbitt, is here because he was coauthor of a book with Guido Calabresi of Yale entitled *Tragic Choices*, which, I believe, included a chapter on the draft. Phil's topic this afternoon is "National Service: Unwise or Unconstitutional?"

V

First Paper:

NATIONAL SERVICE: UNWISE OR UNCONSTITUTIONAL? (Summary)

Philip Bobbitt

PHILIP BOBBITT: National Service is propounded on two bases. First, it offers an ameliorative adjunct to the draft. Our military requirements don't dictate wholesale conscripting. But if it's unfair to draft only a few young men into the armed services this unfairness can be alleviated by drafting everyone and augmenting military tasks with civilian ones. Civilian tasks suggest a second basis on which National Service is offered: it can solve a number of social problems by employing unemployables to accomplish what otherwise would be left undone. Actually, these two ideas are descendants of a common reality—the inequality arising from the modern necessity for highly differentiated mass manpower.

In a paper of a good deal greater length, I have tried to show the implications of this argument for National Service schemes. Insofar as they are proposed as ameliorative adjuncts to the draft, they will exacerbate the very difficulties such schemes are devised to solve; and insofar as National Service is a means of accomplishing other than draft-related ends, a social action scheme, it is unconstitutional. This afternoon I will have time only to go over a very brief summary of just the first part.

To see how National Service proves unwise as a draft palliative, it is necessary to understand that the same tensions are responsible for the suggestion in the first place as well as its ultimate unsatisfactoriness.

There are three paradigms for the way in which a statutory allocation of goods can be made—the pure market, the political agency, and the lottery. Each of these approaches has its peculiar advantages and shortcomings in the context of the draft.

Market mechanisms, of which our current All-Volunteer Force is, of course, an example, confer several benefits. The principal benefit, which the perhaps misleading term "volunteer" seeks to exploit, is the lack of overt coercion. Particularly when certainties of death and injury are being allocated, an apparent absence of coercion acts to absolve society from committing any particular person or group to a horrible fate.

There are also, however, disadvantages to the market mechanisms. Once particular category levels are determined, we face the fact that markets make statements about relative value that, in the circumstances of risking life and well-being, we may find intolerable. It may be perfectly all right to say that a doctor is more valuable to society than a mechanic, though in my experience the similarity in their work seems not to have escaped the attention of either, but when we find we are forced to pay several times as much to induce the doctor to risk his life as we are to bring about the induction of the mechanic, we may discover the comparison is a bit too vivid. By what justification, after all, do we accept a market's valuing of utility when it is life we are apportioning?

The greatest shortcoming of the market as a draft mechanism is, of course, that it is dependent on the existing distribution of wealth. We must face without excuse the fact that the measure of desire has a different significance depending on the wealth of the chooser. A $10,000 salary isn't much of an inducement to a very wealthy man. Forgoing it is a measure of his desire vis-à-vis a poor man's only in a very relative way. Indeed, insofar as the current voluntary system is financed by an accurately gauged inclining income-tax system, as one fears it is not, we have a system much like that of the Civil War, in which the rich are hiring substitutes to serve for them. Such a system, from the perspective of each participant, is often said to make those who do not choose to participate better off while not making anyone else worse off. If the poorer person chooses to enlist while the wealthier man does not, this simply means the poor person thinks he's better off in the army than out of it.

There are several replies I find convincing to this argument. But the one I choose to make has nothing to do with protecting the poor per se or protecting them from their choices, but rather with protecting society's interest in not conceding, to say nothing of exploiting, the fact that some of its members can be made better off, even at the risk of their very lives, by the inducement of a relatively slight wage.

Finally, the market presumes that relative desire, even warped by the existing distribution of wealth, is the sole criterion for deciding who serves in the military. But, of course, this is quite risky where civic duties are concerned, and the more so the more perilous the duty becomes. For the true volunteer, who would enlist when there is real danger, will often be someone society wishes to preserve rather than sacrifice. In other words, the market, when it is allocating incommensurables like death and great suffering, does not discriminate between persons whose social utility to society is not reflected in their relative desire to avoid harm. Cowards may die a thousand times, but they at least have the comfort of expecting frequent resurrections.

Political approaches, on the other hand, remedy each of these shortcomings. When draft deferments or exemptions operate to exclude farmers, geniuses, congressmen, or engineers, it is because these are felt to have a greater social utility at home. And, although the system of college deferments may have operated to the benefit of the middle class, a political approach can, *in principle*, avoid dependence on the prevailing distribution of wealth. Furthermore, since conscription does not have to bid for the service of the numbers it needs, the explicit valuing of each additional life is avoided. Thus the superiority of using political agencies in the draft is a result of their ability to reflect nonwealth comparisons and to enforce general social standards which the pure market does not incorporate. We can decide to use criteria such as health and age as standards by which to allocate wartime service at the very time we decide that wealth or race or class or alienage should not be used as an allocative principle. We can defer the conscientious objector even though he couldn't buy his way out. We can exempt the great research chemist, and we can draft the heart surgeon when no monetary inducement would succeed.

But this flexibility and this insensitivity to wealth distribution account also for the shortcomings of the political approach to the draft. By abandoning the market, we give up an efficient mechanism for measuring individual desire. We are more apt to draft the pacifist and leave the militarist at home. At the same time, the standards, meant to reflect individual social utility, impose a demand for information that is quite unnecessary in the axiomatic determination of utility which the market provides. This unsatisfiable need for information accounts for many of the shortcomings of the political process as a means of procuring military manpower: its high cost, its bureaucratization, its manipulability by lawyers, its personal intrusiveness, its susceptibility to corruption, and its bias.

Apart from the information gathering necessary to effectuate politically determined standards, there are problems arising from the standards themselves. In addition to the cost of determining such standards, we must bear the cost imposed by having to name which persons the society considers more valuable than others. Also, since these standards originate in society, they are likely to reinforce whatever social discrimination currently exists. Since the meting out of infantry assignments is more painful than not getting an invitation to a coming-out party, this reiteration of preferences must be counted as a grave shortcoming of the political approach in this area.

These shortcomings are avoided by the third paradigm of social choice, the lottery. Because lot systems represent choices not to choose, they require neither elaborate information nor definable neutral principles. In a lottery, either all have an equal chance at the good or the bad, as the case may be, or payoffs are distributed in equal amount to all group members. Lot systems, however, display defects at the allocative level that resemble both those associated with markets and with political approaches. In the market, it was difficult to reflect these differences among individuals which were not expressed in their choices. In the political process, individual desires are difficult to give weight to. Lotteries, whose virtue is, after all, their blindness, are insensitive to both individual and collective preferences. It's not just the "dove" who is drafted while the "hawk" stays home; it's the nearsighted research chemist approaching a breakthrough who happens to be a dove, and the crackshot with a particular taste for the bald eagle who happens to be a hawk. In addition to the high cost of this randomness, I am inclined to think that lot systems exert pressure to lower force levels, because they highly dramatize the initial, "first-order" determination.

As a result of the shortcomings of each of these "pure" approaches, they are never used in the paradigmatic way. Instead they are combined, piggy-backed one onto another, to mask the shortcomings of each and take advantage of the benefits of the mixture. It is scarcely conceivable, for example, that our country would employ a lot system to draft individuals into military service without appending some political agency to circumscribe the eligible pool—by excluding, for example, the handicapped. Two features of such allocation devices—their mutual compensation when used in combination in this way and the competition of values underlying them—together account for the use of mixtures of approaches in nontrivial allocations.

Beyond such mixtures, or combinations of mixtures, there is a more subtle type that one finds with respect to particularly precious allocations, and the draft is, after all, one of these. This is a mixture of mixtures, or the alternation of mixtures. It is the intricate strategy of successive changes demanded by the irreducible shortcomings displayed by even the richest static mixture. When the cost to social cohesion and society's values of choosing a single, though mixed, approach becomes sufficiently high, this strategy becomes worthwhile.

Many of you have been to other conferences on the draft before this one. Why, you may ask yourselves, do approaches to such allocation change? Why wasn't the last change enough? It was not mindlessly made. It was the outcome of rational responses to pertinent criticism preceded by lucid debate, or at least as rational, pertinent, and lucid as policy discussions usually are. Conferences were held, and the critics of the then-existing system described its fundamental flaws in generally accurate detail, acknowledging the flaws inherent in the proposed reform. Indeed, when the reform had become the system, it was eventually conceded to have the shortcomings its critics had predicted, and to degrade those values they had sought to protect.

Does this mean that the adoption of reform was a mistake? If it was not, why do we move restlessly from one system to another, from one concept to another? And if it was, why has each system in turn proved inadequate? The answer, as described in the book alluded to by Mr. Meckling (*Tragic Choices*), is that society may limit the destructive impact of these very difficult choices, of allocations like the draft, by choosing to mix strategies over time. By this alternation endangered values are reaffirmed while the cost to other values is initially postponed.

This phenomenon may be observed in an historical account of the draft in this country. For while the methods of making the first-order determination of the number of soldiers needed has remained relatively stable, virtually all of the classic approaches I have described have, in various arrangements, been used in successive cycles as devices for resolving the issues raised by forcing some people to fight while leaving others safe at home. And none of these approaches has survived the war in which it was used. In the paper that I am summarizing, there is a history, taking each of the successive draft acts, showing how we moved from a relatively pure market to a lottery, back to a complicated political system with deferments and exemptions, to a lottery again, and back to a volunteer force, each in turn. Because the underlying conflicts are not amenable to amelioration even by enriched mixtures, we go through these cycles.

I imagine it is obvious to my listeners what point I shall assert by way of this background. It is that National Service is nothing more than a scheme that uses a political mechanism as an added component to enrich the current arrangement of approaches that make up the military draft. By greatly expanding inclusiveness, so that everyone within a specified age group is drafted, it is thought that the draft's threat to egalitarianism can be ameliorated. No privileged undergraduates, no crafty lawyers, no victims. This, I submit, is what many had in mind when National Service enjoyed its vogue in the mid-1960s. And a similar idea can be detected in President Carter's statement in March 1977 that Universal National Service with nonmilitary options should be considered if a military draft becomes necessary. This sort of mixture enrichment will create benefits for a time by adding a component to the process, much as the lottery was piggybacked to a market mechanism in the 1970s or onto a political agency during the draft of World War I. Since the added component is chosen to compensate for a perceived weakness in the status quo, typically by marrying a variation of the pure approaches, the new mixture achieves an amelioration through complexity for a time. But because the underlying conflicts are not really ameliorable, this benefit will not last.

And so it is with a National Service modification of the military draft. Some mechanism must be established to determine who is going into the Army and who, say, into the Peace Corps. The report of the Committee for National Service suggests that it could be done through random selection, which means a lottery. This reflects, I think, the deep appeal of National Service as an ameliorative to the draft. And yet a truly random system could hardly be universal. There may be many social welfare tasks for the handicapped and the frail to perform, but we would, I think, be daunted by the prospect of including them in a pool from which combat soldiers are to be randomly picked. Furthermore, should we have a conservation corps from which forestry students are virtually excluded, owing to the small probability that a lot system would put them there, or a home medical extension service that for the same reason excludes persons who've had nursing training? It is difficult to believe that the awesome logistical and training task of deploying four and a half million teenagers will be rendered more tractable by refusing to pay any attention to the abilities, training, and interests of those employed. Far more likely, at least initially, is the use of an accountable political agency to direct persons into various options. Yet it should be obvious that the very use of discriminating criteria to make these judgments will provoke the sorts of conflicts that National Service was designed to alleviate. And this is not happenstance. Because National Service simply replicates the draft dilemma, one can predict the ontogeny of its programmatic development, and I will do just that.

First, a proto–National Service will employ market mechanisms. This will be the nonmandatory volunteer superagency, of which the current VISTA and Peace Corps programs are very small models. The use of the market in this context will arouse considerable criticism once the quantity rises above the present small numbers involved. But I doubt we will have much time for this reaction to develop, since, if I am correct in thinking of National Service as a creature of the draft, there will be collateral, irresistible pressure to replace the market apparatus of National Service once the military draft is reinstituted. It's not every family, after all, that can afford to have a child languishing at substandard VISTA wages waiting for the military to fill its calls.

So we will then see a political approach used to compel service, and to distribute the "volunteers." After a time, the shortcomings that were so evident with the political approach to the draft during the mid-'60s will become apparent. I'm inclined to think that after the initial benefit, a

National Service component to the draft will actually enhance those conflicts of values which the draft dilemma has already exposed for us. Thus we may then see the use of lottery mechanisms, at least to vary the mixture within the overall system. This will have the various advantages mentioned above, but it will confer, at a high price, that simple egalitarianism that is the refuge of a society that does not wish to make interlife comparisons when life is at stake. When we finally become aware that we have only thereby perfected a system for the indiscriminate imposition of inequality, we will have completed the cycle.

If this projection of the history we have yet to live is correct, I am justified in concluding that National Service, as an ameliorative to the conflicts of values generated by military service, is unwise because it is ultimately ineffective and, indeed, destructive of those values.

Owing to the shortness of time, I can give you only a couple of my conclusions, and these without really any argument as to the constitutional questions presented by National Service. There are a number of these questions, and I hope that perhaps in the question period you will ask me about them.

The one I'm most anxious to persuade you about is the global objection. This objection is not based on sex discrimination, right to privacy, the "takings clause" of the Fifth Amendment, due process, or equal protection issues, all of which, like the Thirteenth Amendment, are in fact involved in justifying any National Service scheme. My objection, instead, is one that no modification of a National Service scheme will cure. It is that Congress does not possess the constitutional power to create a large civilian conscripted work force.

The argument that leads me to this position is a very simple one. If Congress is to provide for a compulsory National Service, it must do so pursuant to some constitutional authority to regulate behavior. The very broad delegation of power to Congress to tax and spend for the general welfare will not apply in the context of forced behavior as it would if the plan were purely voluntary—that is, if the National Service scheme simply placed the government in the marketplace to compete with other employers. Since the spending authority conferred by Article 1, Section 8, of the Constitution is not sufficient with respect to a compulsory National Service, what other constitutional power, express or implied, can we find to support such an exercise of authority? In my paper, I consider two in some detail, and it is my conclusion that there is no such authority. It is my view that there is no power delegated to Congress to draft a civilian work force, so long as its sole object is not to raise an army.

I would like, after giving you a summary of one half of a paper and just barely a taste of the other half, to conclude with something that relies on both halves and is not just a summing-up. My paper, of which I've given you, I assure you, a very merciful abbreviation, has two main parts. The first is a discussion of the socioethical processes of the various allocative devices that National Service might employ in a role that supplements the military draft. The second is a canvass of the constitutional objections that a National Service plan might encounter if its purposes were not largely military.

From each of these parts I should like to draw a lesson. A great many absurd and fatuous claims are made for National Service. I will rely on your skepticism to puncture them, and not go into them here. My conclusions are cautionary lessons, and there are only two: One: Don't create a revolutionary army of young persons who will be embittered by having been forced to waste their youth in useless pursuits, and whose frustration will be compounded by the guilty knowledge that others who are not made to sit out their lives are forced to risk and sometimes lose them. Two: Don't allow a benignly packaged National Service plan to be a Trojan horse for a coercive plan. The dynamics discussed in the first part of my paper would, in such a circumstance, be peculiarly situated to exploit the subterfuges and constitutional deceptions alluded to in the second part. By such irresistible, yet moderate evolution we as a people would be much changed, the Constitution would be much changed, and both I think, for the worse.

WILLIAM MECKLING: Thank you very much, Phil, and congratulations on doing that in the 20 minutes allotted.

Our second speaker this afternoon is David Landau, who is National Staff Counsel for the American Civil Liberties Union. He is also Vice-Chairman of the National Committee Against Registration and the Draft and has recently spent a great deal of time in Congress on the issue of the recent attempt to introduce registration, and is the author of *Civil Liberties, National Security, and the Draft*.

VI

Second Paper:

CIVIL LIBERTIES, NATIONAL SECURITY, AND THE DRAFT (Summary)

David Landau

DAVID LANDAU: In the initial introductions this afternoon we were introduced as part of the legal community, and, as a lawyer, that makes me an advocate. That's what I'm here today to do—to give the advocates' view of this issue. And I would suggest that it's the advocates' view, as much as the analysts', to use Professor King's distinctions, which determines the resolution of these issues.

I've been pleased to note that there's been a general sense here that the draft is not feasible at this time. The question I would like to answer is, *why?* On September 12, 1979, the House of Representatives overwhelmingly rejected draft registration. The vote was 252 to 163. Despite a well-organized campaign by Congressional supporters of the draft, most members of Congress, I believe, had little choice in the matter. In the few months since the draft had resurfaced as an issue, a nationwide antidraft movement had sprung up. In less than three months a national coalition was coordinating local coalitions and groups all over the country—in every state, in every major city, and in smaller communities—groups like Mothers Against the Draft, religious organizations, and civil rights groups, and even Ronald Reagan. The vote on draft registration was, I believe, a reaffirmation of what was, up until the post-World War II period, an historical fact: Americans find wartime institutions, including the military draft, unacceptable in peacetime.

For this nation, war has usually been a last resort, when our security was significantly threatened. War demands special sacrifices from the citizenry.

For thoses who are drafted into the military, their individual rights must be curtailed to maintain discipline and order and they must face the ever-present peril of serious injury and physical and mental disability, and even loss of life. For civilians, national security institutions such as the intelligence network and the military establishment take precedence over all else. Inevitably, individual rights of the general population are impaired. Those are some of the inherent evils of war. Americans have demonstrated a willingness to accept such a way of life when there is a declared war, or when there is a consensus that the nation is faced with an imminent threat. Americans have also recognized, however, that because national security institutions and the military establishment are intrinsically antidemocratic, they ought to be tightly controlled in peacetime.

Daniel Webster was probably our earliest and most famous spokesman to apply these principles to the military draft. In his famous speech in 1814, following which the draft was not enacted by Congress, he said: "The question is nothing less than whether the most essential rights of personal liberty shall be surrendered and despotism embraced in its worst form. The people," he proclaimed, "have not purchased at a vast expense of their own treasure and their own blood a Magna Carta to be slaves."

It wasn't until after World War II that the draft was authorized in peacetime, because early in the postwar period there was still a consensus that the nation was faced with an imminent threat to its security. Then, as the years progressed, the wartime national security state became a habit of mind for this country. At the same time, the theoretical foundation of this way of life—that is, the consensus of a direct threat to the nation—eroded.

The Vietnam War was the breaking point. Because the military establishment and national security state were in place and operating, the government did not have to obtain the consent of the American people to fight a war. The American people began to rebel when they discovered that a war was being fought when our security was not significantly threatened and that their rights were being curtailed and their friends and children being killed. The system responded as if it were in a declared war, and attempted to silence the opposition and maintain order and discipline. Intelligence operations expanded. Law-enforcement agencies disrupted political activity. And, in the end, the distinction between war and peace, which are in large measure marked by the size of the national security establishment, became blurred.

By 1972 the national security establishment was being dismantled and the draft ended. This year, however, Congress debated whether to take the first step toward reinstituting this system—draft registration. Others have called for stepped-up intelligence operations, both at home and abroad. While proponents of the draft attempted to prove that the United States is threatened they were unable to convince the American people that the threat was sufficient to justify the inevitable curtailment of individual rights and liberties that result from a draft. The American people, in the end, applied a test similar to the one that the court employed in judging governmental abridgment of civil rights. There must be compelling proof that such measures are necessary. In the case of national security, this burden of proof is particularly heavy, because, as I have discussed in my paper and will briefly summarize, the erosion of democratic principles is so great.

I would like to discuss two facets of this erosion and of the impact of the military: the first is the impact of the military draft on individual rights, and the second the impact of the military draft on national security.

Captain Howard Levy was an Army physician stationed at Fort Jackson, South Carolina. During his off-duty hours he became active in the local civil rights movement. His civil rights activities led him to speak out against the war in Vietnam, particularly because of its adverse impact on minorities. Captain Levy was dismissed from the service and sentenced to three years' hard labor. His crime was making public statements against the war to enlisted personnel. These statements were found by the Army to be "conduct unbecoming of an officer and a gentleman." The Supreme Court of the United States upheld Levy's conviction for uttering such statements.

Roger Priest was a seaman apprentice in the Navy stationed at the Pentagon in the spring of 1969. On his own time, and with his own funds, he published a newsletter that he distributed to active-duty military personnel in the Pentagon. The newsletter contained strong protests against the war in Vietnam. Roger Priest was convicted of "disorders and neglects to the prejudice of good order and discipline in the armed forces," and the United States Court of Appeals for the District of Columbia Circuit affirmed the conviction.

There are many other examples, and I've outlined some of those in my paper. The point is that all of these men were punished for the expression of their personal political beliefs. They were not saboteurs or espionage agents engaged in covert activity. Many others in the country shared their views. Had they been civilians, they clearly could not have been punished for such speech, because the Supreme Court has repeatedly held that speech, including disrespectful and contemptuous speech, and even advocacy of violent change, cannot be prohibited unless it is both directed to inciting imminently lawless action and likely to produce this action. But the Supreme Court has also held that military discipline requires a different standard. Freedom of speech generally and freedom of speech in the military are two entirely different concepts. According to the Levy case, the military has broad discretion whether to permit or punish political speech. Moreover, a variety of speech-related activity, including political association, can be prohibited by the military. The Navy was permitted to ban personnel from associating with the Ku Klux Klan during off-duty hours. Symbolic speech, such as the wearing of buttons and patches, is made impossible by dress regulations. Political campaigning may be banned. And military personnel can even be sanctioned for the speech activities of civilian friends. For instance, David Cortright was in the Fort Wadsworth Army Band during the Vietnam War. When the band paraded on the Fourth of July, his fiancée (along with the wives of four other band members) attempted to march with the band while carrying an antiwar placard. As a result of this incident Cortright was transferred from New York to Texas.

In addition to free speech and political association, a variety of other constitutionally protected activities are substantially eroded when one enters the military. A citizen who enters the military cannot elect his or her own employment free from government interference, despite the right of choice guaranteed under the Constitution. Although the military does make a good attempt to provide job skills to enlistees, there is still no contractual obligation. For example, a radio operator enlists because the Army promises to teach him computer skills. The enlistee receives the training and is a computer operator for six months. Suddenly the Army transfers him to a radio-listening post at the outer rim of Turkey. He has very little recourse.

Recently we have been reading about cases in which people are fraudulently induced into the military and receive little training. Investigations are proving that the Army is finding excuses to renege on its promises and its advertisements.

Besides the lack of a right to contract, military personnel are forbidden by statute from collective bargaining. Working conditions can be negotiated only on an individual basis. In contrast, the right of civilians to band together and improve conditions and bargain on equal footing with employers is unassailable.

Beyond the employment aspects of the military, controls extend to every phase of private life, from appearance and dress to personal relationships. In fact, the military still regulates marriages of personnel stationed overseas. And the right to marry, of course, has long been recognized as one of the most fundamental rights of individuals.

The military domination of most aspects of personal life is, I think, typified by the Army's drug abuse program. This program authorizes warrantless drug inspections without probable cause. Everything from personal possessions to the body itself may be searched without suspicion of drug abuse. A United States Court of Appeals has upheld this search policy as reasonable. Now, as long as a particular search is ostensibly under the drug rehabilitation program, it cannot be challenged in court. I believe the Army's drug abuse program has many of the characteristics which distinguish the military judicial system from the civilian judicial system.

Because of the vast restrictions upon every aspect of a service member's life, the military, out of necessity, has established an intricate system of enforcement which, other than the court-martial proceedings, operates mostly outside the framework of the Constitution. In civilian life, state and local courts punish relatively limited types of behavior, deemed by society to threaten other individuals' life or property, by fine or imprisonment. The military, on the other hand, has an entire hierarchy of procedures, replete with varying punishments, to punish violations of the Uniform Code of Military Justice.

The best-known of these military proceedings is the court-martial. The court-martial can impose the severest penalties available in the military—a dishonorable discharge, confinement at hard labor, and even the death penalty. Although service members facing court-martials enjoy many procedural rights guaranteed by the Constitution, such as the right to counsel and the right against self-incrimination, the most basic right guaranteed to criminal defendants in civilian courts is denied service members—the right to a trial by a jury composed of one's peers. The court-martial is an ad hoc court composed of at least five officers. One-third of the court-martial members may be replaced by enlisted men, but this is not comparable to a civilian jury representing a cross section of the community.

There are a number of other types of punishment or punishment proceedings in the military which have a range of penalties and a range of due-process protection: the special court-martial; the summary court-martial; and the Article 15, which is the nonjudicial punishment. Article 15 punishments are much less severe than court-martial punishments. The significantly lower penalty means less due-process rights. Article 15 is a summary punishment without any kind of adversary proceedings.

Although the actual sanctions for nonjudicial punishment and summary court-martials are not so severe, the effect of these proceedings has more subtle implications—too many Article 15s and summary court-martials may result in a less-than-honorable discharge. And, of course, less-than-honorable discharges impose lifelong disability upon veterans. In the past, we have seen less-than-honorable discharges given for a variety of character and behavioral disorders, even homosexuality.

The military, then, not only has a well-developed system of punishing what we commonly know as criminal behavior, it also has an intricate system of punishing any aberrant behavior which it deems injurious to military discipline. Most of the behavior resulting in other-than-honorable discharges could not be punished in civilian life.

Neither this discussion, nor the somewhat more lengthy one in my paper, is intended to challenge the appropriateness or necessity of current military regulations. Most of us in this country believe that a military is necessary, and that a military requires discipline and order in terms requiring restrictions on freedom. Whether all the existing types of restrictions are necessary is the subject of another conference, and military rights have come a long way in recent years. Yet we must recognize that full democratic rights, full constitutional rights, do not, and probably never will, exist in the military.

The restrictions I have outlined may be necessary and acceptable to the military, but we have never tolerated this type of control on the civilian population. Indeed, only during World War II has the abrogation of the constitutional rights of American citizens ever been sanctioned by the Supreme Court. In that case a divided court upheld the forced internment of American citizens of Japanese ancestry. But even during the war these cases were few. In 1946 the courts struck down martial law in Hawaii which required civilians to be tried by military tribunals. Later the court overruled President Truman's seizure of steel mills during the Korean conflict. In peacetime, the Supreme Court has taken an extremely narrow view of the circumstances in which constitutional rights may be summarily restricted by the executive branch. And it has steadfastly refused to expand this view.

When Richard Nixon engaged in domestic-security electronic surveillance on American dissidents, the Supreme Court invalidated it. And other federal courts have frequently invalidated other aspects of the Nixon national security program.

The principle that emerges from all of these cases is that except when the nation is faced with an imminent threat to its very survival, individual rights are to be given the widest possible leeway. But, as the Supreme Court has said, "It would be indeed ironic if in the name of national defense, we sanctioned the subversion of [one of] those liberties . . . which make the defense of the nation worthwhile." Just as the courts have been vigilant in refusing to sanction the infringement of civil liberties in peacetime based upon claims of national security, the American people historically have also resisted this type of infringement by the government. Service in this country has always been voluntary. In a sense, patriotism in this country has been voluntary. The Department of Defense recognized this in its report on the All-Volunteer Force when it said that "the concept of a volunteer force is fundamental to the American ideal of a peacetime military."

Coercing people into the military, imposing a military life upon citizens, significantly erodes their indivdual liberties, and this kind of erosion cannot take place, and will not be acceptable to the American people, unless they recognize that it is absolutely necessary.

The impact of the draft on conscripted citizens is sufficient to bar its imposition in the absence of compelling justification. But since the draft is an integral part of the national security state, it also has a broad adverse impact on our society. Unless the nation is imminently threatened, an institution which out of necessity cannot adhere to fundamental democratic principles will create hostility in the general population. It breeds contempt of government for abridging citizens' rights and engenders militant opposition which is not afraid to take direct action against the system. The government, in turn, cannot permit this disruption. It therefore not only must enforce the system against those who resist it, but must take costly steps to prevent disruption and in some cases even to silence its critics. The case of Dr. Benjamin Spock and Reverend William Sloane Coffin are the mild cases. Then there is the case of Daniel and Philip Berrigan who went around destroying draft files in draft board offices. Hundreds of similar raids by others damaged or destroyed thousands of draft files. Damage costing hundreds of thousands of dollars occurred. As antidraft activity like this intensified during the Vietnam War, it became one of the excuses for widespread political surveillance and disruption programs. The CIA was forced to investigate to determine if these groups were being run by foreign governments. The FBI had to investigate criminal violation of the draft laws. The Army looked into the potential of such groups for disrupting the war effort.

Some of this surveillance was legal, but much of it was not. The prosecution of Benjamin Spock was necessary because his political opposition to the draft and the war threatened the entire system. Because the draft, in the absence of an imminent threat to the nation, fermented widespread hostility, particularly when draftees were used to wage an unpopular war, law enforcement and intelligence agencies were drawn into the political arena. Powers that are intended to weed out saboteurs, espionage agents, and criminals were directed at antidraft and antiwar activists. When these powers go unchecked, as they have been for the last thirty years, law enforcement and intelligence agencies tend to operate outside the Constitution, thereby stifling dissent. The illegalities and abuses of the past, from the FBI's COINTELPRO [counterintelligence programs] operation to the prosecution of Benjamin Spock, were not isolated incidents. An entire bureaucracy was established, involving hundreds of officials, aimed at thousands of people. It is one thing for this type of national security state to exist during a national crisis, such as World War II. It is an entirely different matter when it operates during peacetime. One of the lessons of the Vietnamese War is that the American people will not tolerate the constitutional infringements during peacetime, and the imposition of the draft at this time would be one of these.

Citizen reaction would be more violent that ever before. Even now, thousands have already vowed not to register should draft registration begin, and others are building their case files for conscientious objection. So, even though we wouldn't be fighting a war, a peacetime draft would place us in a situation which could erode our individual liberties as if we were fighting a war.

The recent vote on draft registration reaffirmed the principle established long ago: our founding fathers constructed a system of government so that the federal government would be under the control of the people. The Bill of Rights is a series of restrictions on the government's ability to abridge the rights of the citizenry. And, as Daniel Webster recognized long ago, the military has profound ramifications on society. To impose a draft as less than a last resort to preserve the existence of our nation would subvert the very principles upon which the nation was founded. In so doing, the security of this nation, which in the end lies in our adherence to these principles, would be undermined. I believe, therefore, that a peacetime draft should be rejected.

WILLIAM MECKLING: Thank you, David.

VII

DISCUSSION

Antonia Chayes, Phelps Jones, and John McClaughry

WILLIAM MECKLING: Our first discussant is Ms. Antonia Chayes, Under Secretary of the Air Force.

ANTONIA CHAYES: Lawyers don't joke, and this leads me to the conclusion that lawyers are essentially humorless. However, we are a very precise profession.

As far as I can tell, no one has talked yet about the law and military conscription, though I've heard two very powerful arguments for the policy of the All-Volunteer Force. So I'm going to address that.

I'm not going to address the issue of National Service because, in my view, it's too expensive, there's too little support for it, and so it isn't even an issue. It's a very interesting thesis by Professor Bobbitt, but, again, it is not the subject of this panel. There really are two issues, though, that he raises in his paper. First, is the draft constitutional? And second, is non-military National Service constitutional?

In my view, it is completely clear that a draft is constitutional, certainly in war. I don't think anybody questions that. The issue was settled in 1918 in the Selective Draft Cases, where the Supreme Court said—and I quote— "As the mind cannot conceive an army without the men to compose it, on the face of the Constitution the objection that it does not give power to provide for such men would seem to be too frivolous for further notice." The Supreme Court has chosen not to address that issue again.

There have, however, been a number of attempts to raise the issue of the constitutionality of the draft in *peacetime*. For instance, there was the 1954 case in the Court of Appeals. In that case, the Supreme Court chose, through the denial of certiorari, not to address it. In the *Bertleson* v. *Coony* case, the Court of Appeals for the Fifth Circuit stated, "This power exists in peacetime as well as in war. The power is plenary. It is not for the judiciary to review the legislative branch on the question of what military strength is necessary for the safety of the nation, nor how the forces shall be raised, nor of what element they shall be composed. Congress is expressly authorized to declare war and provide for the common defense. These powers necessarily carry with them the power to say who shall serve in the armed forces and in what circumstances."

And I think the cases really have been quite consistent. The issue of nonmilitary National Service, however, seems a little more complicated. Again, I don't think this is the crucial issue here. I would argue that if, as Professor Bobbitt claims, compulsory National Service were a way of making the draft more equitable—and I think his thesis on this point is very interesting—one could argue, under the necessary and proper clause, that it was an adjunct to that very power. I'm not at all sure, however, that I agree with his argument on the commerce clause [see pages 59, 314] because there could be an interesting economic justification for National Service that involved some impact upon the economic structure of our country. Again, I think that's an interesting academic question, but it isn't really the question before us. It's certainly worth some scholarly effort.

I think Mr. Landau's argument that the curtailment of civil rights is enough to make military service somehow less constitutional is not persuasive. In view of the cases, it just does not stand up. He paints a grim picture, a parade of horrors, about the curtailment of civil rights—unfairly, in my view. I think that it is clear, and we would not deny, that the armed forces are inherently antidemocratic—that military discipline is not compatible with the full range of civil rights enjoyed by the rest of the citizens of this country. That is one of the reasons why, at least in the Air Force and elsewhere, we've talked about the X factor, something that deserves extra compensation, because of that very curtailment. In the military there is coercion. You don't have the freedom of movement. You can't unionize. It is the view held by the Department of Defense that unionization is incompatible with the conduct of military affairs. Drug searches are tough. But on the other hand, Mr. Landau hasn't mentioned those cases which have prohibited certain searches and seizures as being excessive. The fact is, he also hasn't mentioned the constitutional rights that *are* preserved in the military—the reach of the *O'Callihan* and *Relford* cases. Not only do military personnel have access to civilian courts; the military must essentially justify the necessity of court-martial through the military justice system. I think that all of these are interesting questions.

I could go on citing a number of other cases which show that the picture isn't quite as grim as Mr. Landau paints. He raises a lot of free speech cases that came in in the climate of Vietnam, which was rather hysterical. But the constitutional climate does change. The climate today is different, with respect to the Iranian students. You have that case, as compared to *Korematsu* and the Japanese exclusion cases in the middle of World War II.

But none of that really says anything about the constitutionality of the peacetime draft. None of these cases say more to the fact that we ought not have a larger armed force than we need to maintain national security. Those of us who have been working on those problems, like Gary Nelson and Richard Danzig, and so on, certainly don't want a larger force than we can pay for or take care of.

There is another strictly legal question which has to do with conscription that we've not yet discussed from Professor Bobbitt's paper, one that I think raises a lot of questions. And that is the constitutionality of an all-male draft. I think this raises policy questions, and I would argue that an all-male draft for combat positions is probably, for the moment, constitutional. But I would submit that any draft limited just to men is not, even in face of the fact that during the Vietnam period a total of 11 out of 12 courts in which the constitutionality of the draft was challenged found that the draft law was constitutional. I think that the law and equal protection standards now applied have really changed that a great deal.

Congress has never felt any need to discuss its motivation for limiting the draft to males, and several reasons have been advanced as justification. If one begins to look now at the nature of the armed forces and the kinds of positions that women hold in the armed forces, everyone isn't just given a rifle and rushed off to war. There are not only cooks; there are a lot of computer operators and radar experts and intelligence people, all of whom are essential. If one then looks at the composition of the armed forces, women as volunteers have held and continue to hold 95 percent of the available types of positions in the Army, and over 98 percent in the Air Force. In essence, they are limited only by the combat restriction. Under the new constitutional test of *Califano* v. *Westcott* and *Orr* v. *Orr*, which Professor Bobbitt states correctly, the substantial relationship standard does not apply.

So I think it is quite clear that a more rational basis is now required to justify an all-male draft. The rational basis of equal protection under the law is a minimal standard. There would have to be a substantial relationship between the classification—the exclusion of females—and the objectives to which such government action was directed.

That raises some very serious problems about any decision to reinstate the draft, and any calculations that might be made in support of that position. Probably the very least you can expect is that a draft mechanism, once started, would grind to a halt until the case had been litigated all the way through the Supreme Court, and I would expect that Mr. Landau would be among those arguing the case.

I am left with the conclusion that legality isn't the issue here. I don't know whether, having stated that a non-all-male draft in peacetime is clearly constitutional, this country would support an Israeli-type conscription. Having heard Phyllis Schlafly fight the ERA on the grounds that women would be drafted, it might come as a great shock to her to find that women are going to be drafted, if there is a draft, *without* the ERA.

I guess my real question is whether *either* a coed draft, found now to be constitutional, *or* National Service is necessary or wise. Is National Service worth the resources? I've seen it talked about at anywhere from 20 to 30 million participants, when a lack of resources or an unwillingness to spend our resources is a major cause for the faltering of or predicted negative trends in the All-Volunteer Force. I mean, 20 to 30 million young people does seem like overkill unless there's a compelling reason.

With respect to the draft—and I pose these questions really to tomorrow's panelists and discussants—is the draft more equitable than National Service? How would Charlie Moskos handle a large coed pool? What policies of exemption and deferment would we need? Is it likely to be more representative or less representative? Is it cheaper? Will it produce a better, more effective peacetime force? Will it solve the problem of retaining mid-level experienced supervisors? Or is it going to increase our losses? Is Congress disbelieving of the trends we were talking about this morning? Or do most of the people addressing the subject believe that a draft really will cut personnel costs? Have they discussed this subject with [Richard] Cooper? The question I have is, why, when we're going to a 6.9 or so percent real growth and close to $158 billion in the Department of Defense budget, is it not possible to get even $650 million for compensation adjustment? Do we have to hit rock-bottom first? And if we hit rock-bottom first on the All-Volunteer Force, what's going to happen? What system will we then institute in the terrible cycle Professor Bobbitt tells us about?

Thank you.

WILLIAM MECKLING: Our next discussant is Phelps Jones, who has retired from a distinguished military career and is currently Director of National Security Affairs for Veterans of Foreign Wars.

PHELPS JONES: Like Mr. Landau, I shall be an advocate, though I'm not an attorney. I'll do the best that I can to practice the English language and to practice common sense.

I take as my thesis something that George Will said to a luncheon audience in Washington not long ago. He had seen a tombstone in a rural graveyard in Great Britain on which were inscribed the words, "I told you I was sick." My thesis is that the All-Volunteer Force is sick, and that we certainly must display the political wit and wisdom in this country to turn this around.

In my judgment—and I've argued this point on a number of occasions—the All-Volunteer Force is comparable to prohibition, prohibition being the noble experiment, the All-Volunteer Force, of course, being the inevitable experiment. Mr. Nixon, in my recollection, was the first to raise the notion of an All-Volunteer Force, in October 1968, as Mr. Humphrey was closing the gap in his campaign against him. The Gates Commission—of which a number of distinguished members are here—finished its deliberations in 1970, in effect stating that the United States could move to an All-Volunteer Force if the right benefits package was offered. But the supreme political fact, I think, was the 1972 election, in which Mr. Nixon won 49 out of 50 states, running in the national security area on a platform of détente and no draft. I think that message (49 of the 50 states) has been carried to both our major political parties.

In the brief remaining time that I'm going to be with you, I'm going to focus on the Army, because as the Army goes, so goes the All-Volunteer Force. The Navy has problems with desertion; sea duty doesn't have the attractiveness it had in yesteryear. The Air Force, as Secretary Chayes knows full well, has a problem with pilot loss, though they're coping with it and I understand that it is starting to turn around. The Marine Corps, like the Army, has serious recruiting problems and problems of desertion. Its commandant recently felt moved to consider a self-imposed, 10,000-man cut in the Marine Corps.

Since 1973 we've tried to keep about two million people on as volunteers in essentially a marketplace environment. This is some 600,000 less than fiscal year 1964, which was, of course, a pre-Vietnam year.

I picked up another point from one of Charlie Moskos's papers that I mentioned to him beforehand. (In terms of the character of the enlisted structure, once again I will be referring only to the Army.) In 1964 some 40,000 young Americans entered the enlisted Army ranks with some college background. In 1970, the comparable number was less than 5,000.

The character and structure of the Army was changed in another important respect—in the number of marrieds. The number of young married soldiers has just about doubled, with a grave effect on readiness. We also find that about one-third of all new enlistees fail to complete their initial enlistment and that the desertion rate is more than double that for the pre-Vietnam force. This finding depends on how you measure desertion rates, what your starting point is, but using the pre-Vietnam or peacetime period seems fair to me. In the recruiting year just ended—1 October 1978 to 30 September 1979—the Army fell a little more than 20,000 short of nonprior service people, or about 17,500 men and about 2,500 women.

Today young black Americans constitute 36.9 percent of youngsters coming into the Army (and once again, I'm speaking only of the Army). This carries two points home to me: Can we really look at these young people as true "volunteers"? I suggest we cannot. And I would further suggest that a political time bomb is ticking. A casualty list, if we responded to hostilities in the Middle East, for example, might be so blatantly disproportionate in terms of blacks that we would have a true social horror on our hands—a point, incidentally, not lost on Jesse Jackson.

Women have been and are being used in ever-widening roles, and properly so. But I think the dew is starting to come off the rose. Six years ago the reenlistment rate for Army women was 67 percent. Three years ago it was 54 percent. Now it's fallen to less than 50 percent or half.

As we've all read, and it makes rather melancholy reading, recruiters in both the Army and the Marine Corps have been under extremely intense pressure, and have resorted to illegalities to achieve their numbers. There's been widespread evidence and allegations, in any event, about getting young recruits to lie about illnesses, cheat on entrance exams, forge signatures, and fake birth certificates and educational records. In the Army alone, 165 recruiters have been suspended and 9 face court-martials. Recently, a little better than 3,000 recruits were dismissed early for physical reasons—including asthma, epilepsy, and the like.

As for the issue of deployment and pregnancy, I'm not competent to know, nor am I really interested in discussing, its social or ethical ramifications. But during the year 1978 there were 50,000 women soldiers in the Army—about 15 percent of its manpower base. Of that number, 7,832 became pregnant, and often, of course, the father was a soldier. The women went in three major directions from there. A little better than 2,000 left the service; a little better than 2,600 had abortions, and a little better than 3,000 had their babies and stayed. When both parents are soldiers, this, of course, affects readiness and affects it very severely.

If our active duty forces are having the problems I've indicated, our reserves, of course, are in a recession. The selective reserves—Army Reserves and Army National Guard—are about 150,000 under wartime needs. The Individual Ready Reserve, individuals who would replace combat losses, are about a half million short.

The government is, naturally, taking a number of administrative actions to correct this shortfall. The first is to lower standards. As of last February, a young person attempting to enter the service had to score about 50 on the armed forces qualifications test. On the first of October it was lowered to 16. Recently, 1,500 young enlistees were sought for the Individual Ready Reserve—the replacement pool I mentioned—and they got only 342, which averaged out to be 17-year-old high school dropouts.

Next year we will need about 180,000 Army recruits, as compared to the little better than 158,000 the Army sought this year. I think a case can be made for registration, and a solid and a serious case. Assuming a NATO scenario, we need to get people to their units about a hundred days faster than the Selective Service System can deliver them now, and we would need about 100,000 in 60 days; 650,000 within 6 months. There's a tremendous human and strategy cost of being 70 days late. Some people seem to think that the Royal Navy and French Army are still out there. In World War II, it took us 8 months before we could commit Marines at Guadalcanal, and just a little bit better than 11 months before we could put our Army forces into North Africa.

Our buffer of earlier committed allies is over. And as far as my organization goes, we find it very distressing that the poor and the nearly poor are defending all of us. We don't believe our long history of nineteenth-century volunteerism is relevant today.

So, we have no buffer of time and no buffer of earlier committed forces. By a margin of about 100, the House of Representatives overturned its House Armed Services Committee on the notion of draft registration. The committee voted 30 to 4 in favor of it, having earlier blocked Sonny Montgomery's effort to get conscription for the Individual Ready Reserve. In this particular case, the right and the extreme right libertarians made cause with the ACLU, and were a potent force indeed. There were some curious political marriages at the time. Phil Crane, Jack Kemp, Ron Paul, and others found themselves with Father Robert Drinan, Les Aspin, Pat Schroeder, and Ron Dellums. Jake Javits, I guess, gave the definitive explanation of what happened. He said that "the mothers of America won't stand for it."

Well, I don't know what the mothers of America will or will not stand for, but in 1978 a little better than 2 million young Americans turned 18. Looking to the future, to 1992, that figure falls to a little better than 1.6 million, a loss of 400,000. The administration, in my judgment, has waffled on this and waffled on it very badly. President Carter, speaking last May to Kentucky coal miners, who are always a good audience before whom to sound resolute, stated that the United States might need draft registration as a precautionary measure. He backed off from that, as we all know. On the fourteenth of May, Speaker of the House Tip O'Neill stated that he favored registration, if not conscription. Then he, too, backed off.

It's been rather difficult for both civilian and military leadership, and the Department of Defense ought to read the tea leaves on this one. There is some support for registration, if not a draft, but I would be the first to concede that that support does not extend down to people of the age who would face registration.

I think we're starting to see a change here. On the eve of the no-registration vote the *New York Times*, with which the Veterans of Foreign Wars finds itself in rare agreement, did call upon members of the House of Representatives to exhibit political valor. So did the *Washington Post*. Incidentally, there was no monument to political courage that I could spot that time. Every member of the Joint Chiefs of Staff, present and past, at a minimum favors registration.

My principal conclusion is that "the Emperor has no clothes." We can gimmick this thing around for a while by choice of station, by bonuses, or by extending contracts, which, as Mr. Landau accurately indicated, no service can be certain to meet. In far too many cases the needs of the service must obtain. We can recall young retirees. We can recall veterans only—I'll leave it to you to figure out how popular that one is to veterans' organizations. (I call it the "Son of Amnesty.") We can do all these kinds of maneuvers if we care to, but the problem is still right there before us: today's All-Volunteer Force, despite an admirable effort by the uniformed services, finds itself economically, educationally, and racially unbalanced, and now they're also starting to come up quite short on numbers.

The All-Volunteer Force has brought us from the time of our national nervous breakdown in 1972 up to the present. I would hope that we will continue to have a serious national debate and have at least the political courage at the start to register, count, and classify our people.

Thank you very much.

WILLIAM MECKLING: Our last discussant is John McClaughry of the National Council Against Compulsory Services. He is chairman of that council and has been involved in antidraft activity for some time, having written the antidraft plank for the 1964 Republican platform.

JOHN McCLAUGHRY: Professor Tollison proved this morning how easy it is to develop a stimulating discussion of a paper with which one fundamentally disagrees. I do not have that privilege, inasmuch as I largely agree with the two papers presented in this session. Therefore it will take a little more ingenuity to develop a stimulating discussion here.

I think Professor Bobbitt does us significant service, not as an economist or a lawyer, but perhaps as a social critic, in pointing out what I might call the escape syndrome—the idea that compulsory National Service is a route to escape from the problems that face the All-Volunteer Force.

I'm reminded of another area in which I work—the urban renewal program. The urban problem in 1948 was defined as blight. The cities were ugly, the buildings dilapidated, and the answer was therefore urban renewal. The result, of course, was that those blighted buildings were bulldozed down and carried away, and shiny new buildings went up in their place. It was not until some time later that people began to wonder what became of the inhabitants of those blighted buildings. How did they fare under this "new, improved" regime? We then discovered there was a whole new group of problems connected with that "solution," which, at the time it was initiated, did not seem to be characteristic of the problem.

We have here, it seems to me, a progression from a concern, a quite proper concern, with the All-Volunteer Force, to the idea of compulsory National Service as some kind of solution. Professor Bobbitt has shown, in rather excruciating detail in his printed paper, how the solution threatens—I would say in a very short time—to become much more of a problem than the initial problem that stimulated its appearance.

I think his paper also shows rather inescapably that it is impossible to have a National Service program which is both universal and voluntary. Somewhere in our society there will be somebody who won't go; I suspect there will be a lot of such people. The advocates of compulsory National Service have got to face the hard question, after leaving aside all the wonderful benefits to society of this corps of tree planters and social reform advocates: What about the guy who won't go? Does he go to the Gulag? Does he lose his driver's license?—an idea seized upon by the Potomac Institute study. How is society going to pinch him for his recalcitrance and mean-spirited resistance to the presumed greater good? At some point, everyone who advocates compulsory National Service has got to come to grips with the question: What about the guy who refuses to go?

It seems to me that, as Mr. Landau has pointed out, once you get into this cycle—conscription, objection, evasion, illegal act, prosecution, incarceration, martyrdom—you don't get out of it unless you abandon the one principal idea that caused the problem in the first place: that government is forcing people to do something against their will in circumstances which they do not regard as legitimate.

Professor Bobbitt has also made a trenchant point that I think is all too often passed over by those who see the compulsory National Service as in some way ameliorative of the shortfall problems of the military draft. That is the problem of deciding who among the universal victims will be assigned to fight the nation's battles, and who will be left over to perform the unessential, but supposedly socially desirable, tasks that so animate the backers of compulsory National Service. There's going to have to be a channeling mechanism. Among all the crack-shots and flower sniffers, not to mention the glue sniffers, who are going to get dragged into compulsory service, somebody's going to have to shoulder a rifle and slog around in the mud. And to find out who that person is among this universe of people, all of whom are under the threat of compulsion, is no small task, as the Selective Service System discovered in years past.

Bobbitt also raises, I think, a very important question that goes far beyond the immediate boundaries of compulsive National Service, and that is the question of the omnicompetent Congress and the omnicompetent federal government. I had a professor of constitutional law some years ago who happened to be in the Supreme Court chamber at the time that the court handed down the *Jones and Laughlin* steel case in 1937. Chief Justice Hughes read the opinion, which, as many of you know, represented a drastic reversal from previous decisions of the Court limiting the commerce power of the federal government. In *Jones and Laughlin,* the Court decided that the commerce power extended very, very broadly into matters that *affected* commerce, whether or not they were in fact *in* commerce. In that case, the Chief Justice read the opinion, which was clearly divided, and at the end of the opinion Justice McReynolds, one of the stalwart conservatives on the Court, raised his hands and his eyes to heaven and said to all who were present in stentorian tones, "The Constitution is gone!," put his hands down on the table, and sat there sobbing.

While we're probably not going to be treated to that kind of performance by the present Court, at least in view of the recent books and articles that have described their behavior, I think that starting with *Wickard* v. *Filburn* and going on to *Jones* v. *Mayer,* the open housing case, Justice McReynolds was rapidly spinning in his grave. And if compulsory National Service is by some unfortunate twist upheld by a future Court, I'm sure that rotations of Justice McReynolds could become a national energy resource if propely tapped.

I do think Professor Bobbitt is a bit brief in his discussion of the Thirteenth Amendment which, if it says anything, says that people cannot be dragged away to do what the government wants them to do, or what any private party wants them to do, unless they are being punished for a crime. It seems to me that if the Thirteenth Amendment does not absolutely ban a peacetime nonmilitary draft, it is no good at all and ought to be eliminated at the first of the many constitutional conventions some people are proposing.

Finally, I think it is a very important issue whether the taking-of-property concept applies to the taking of people's labor. Especially when you compel a man to perform service, you are, arguably, taking something that belongs to him—his time, his labor, his sweat, his brains. The Founding Fathers, going back to the time of John Locke, certainly considered a man's time and labor to be his property. James Madison believed that even a man's opinions are his property, and should be treated as such. We have our copyright law and our patent law based on that eighteenth-century notion. If convicting a man to, or requiring him to, engage in labor at the bidding of the government, absent the war power, is not some kind of taking of property, it's hard to see what is. Unfortunately, on the other hand, the courts have recently been very lenient especially at the state level, in interpreting the taking of property with respect to real estate in zoning and planning cases. So one can only imagine what might happen when that gets to a high court.

I compliment Mr. Landau for a very clear, well-organized, and well-researched paper. I think he does us a service in pointing out that military service not only is a risk of life and limb and a lost opportunity reflecting economic cost to the individual, it is also a practice which forces people into an environment where their civil liberties are in some cases quite seriously abridged, and where their due-process remedies are occasionally few and far between.

It seems to me that he is also making a very good point about the effect of enforcing conscription on society. The cycle I mentioned—policing, record-keeping, snooping, prosecutions, incarcerations, martyrdoms, and so on—leads to the kind of society we had at the tail end of the Vietnam War, a condition I think most of us would happily forego in the future. Nonetheless, I must say that I think Mr. Landau's paper insufficiently appreciates that service in the military is a qualitatively different kind of life than service in a service station or even at the Hoover Institution. (I may be wrong about the latter.) There is a certain requirement about the military that it be an organized fighting force to defend the country and protect national security. In those circumstances some liberties are going to have to be taken, if I may make a small pun. In that case it is the liberties of the people in the service that are going to have to be curtailed.

But I think Mr. Landau does us a service by pointing out that the due-process issues inside the armed forces deserve continuing vigilance on the part of those who believe in civil liberties. But I also think that it is a little fatuous to believe that, at any time in the future, life in the military is going to be on equal footing with civilian life with respect to civil liberties.

In wrapping up, then, let me say that it seems to me that Mr. Binkin made an exceptionally good point this morning that carries over into this discussion as well. And that is that perhaps it is time that we began to reassess the strategic role of our armed forces to decide what kind of threats we are really going to have to meet in the future, because without doing that we're going to be unable to make a fair estimate of what kind of price we are willing to pay to use the power of the state to compel people to do things which may in many cases be against their will. Unless we go back to that kind of fundamental starting point, it seems to me that we are going to miss an opportunity to do something creative here—to design armed forces that meet our requirements and at the same time preserve a society in which people wish to protect their country and are eager to give it voluntary service while at the same time being unwilling to yield their liberties to a state that commands them to do as it desires.

VIII

RESPONSES

Philip Bobbitt and David Landau

WILLIAM MECKLING: I think we will take a break now. I'm going to give Mr. Bobbitt and Mr. Landau a chance to say a few words before we get into the general discussion, as they did not have much of an opportunity this morning to respond to the discussants' comments.

PHILIP BOBBITT: I have struggled with what seems to be an irresistible impulse to drag the discussion back to National Service, and like people who wrestle with their conscience, I've won. There is a latitude to the word "discussant" that I had not encountered before coming to this conference and that I now appreciate.

With respect to Under Secretary Chayes's remarks, there are a great many interesting constitutional issues raised by National Service. Sex discrimination is certainly one of them. It is my view that an application of the substantial basis test would permit an all-male draft in the context of a combat army. But its importance for me is that such a test would not permit an all-male National Service, and that if National Service is used as an ameliorative adjunct to the draft, it would require one portion drafting just males and another portion, the National Service portion—the Peace Corps, VISTA, Conservation Corps portion—drafting males *and* females. This, in turn, raises a great many constitutional problems about the right to privacy.

Another interesting issue is the commerce clause issue. On that I will say that we would not have the very detailed list of things that Congress may regulate in Article 2, Section 8, of the Constitution, nor would we have the phrase "power not delegated to the United States," if simply ordering someone to show up at a certain place to begin work amounted to a regulation of commerce.

My third point is to give you the overall architecture of the paper I've written for this conference, which, I'm afraid, it is unlikely you will ever read in detail. My argument is, first, that National Service is unwise merely as an adjunct to the draft. In the second half of the paper, I refute the literature that supports National Service on the basis of social goals—a literature that is increasing, I think, as the Vietnam War recedes further and further away from us and the draft becomes less and less likely to be reissued at any time soon. It is my feeling that if National Service is supported on the basis of rehabilitating people who can't find jobs, taking care of jobs that ought to be done but that somehow we value just a little less than the minimum wage, and so forth, it is unconstitutional. It will be apparent to all of you that the 1918 case upholding the Training Act is of no relevance to that argument.

In my talk I have given you three bases for choice, in statutory form. The market, which Professor Danzig tells me has brought me out here; coercion, which compelled me to make this reply; and mere chance, to which I gather I will be subjected in the question period.

WILLIAM MECKLING: And now David.

DAVID LANDAU: I just have two points. First, the issue has been raised, both by the discussants and by others during the break, about the so-called legal questions revolving around the draft. While I did not discuss the case law in the classic sense and whether or not the Supreme Court would eventually uphold a peacetime draft (which, incidentally, I believe is an open question in terms of whether they've ever decided it before), I was talking about constitutional policy. I think that it is part of our obligation to talk about the impact of the draft on individual liberties, the individual liberties of both the draftee and society. And so, in that sense, talking about constitutional rights is a legal question. And the legal questions, I think, were examined by me and by Professor Bobbitt.

The second point concerns individual rights in the military. In my own presentation, I stressed that the kinds of restrictions I spoke about are necessary for the military, and I do recognize that military life is fundamentally different from civilian life. But if we recognize that, and also concede the erosion of democratic rights that occur in the military relative to civilian life, the question is whether the government legitimately compels that kind of situation. When can the government legitimately compel a citizen to give up some of his constitutional rights as he would during a draft? And my answer was: not in peacetime.

IX

GENERAL DISCUSSION AND QUESTIONS FROM THE FLOOR

WILLIAM MECKLING: Now we will take questions.

COMMENT FROM THE AUDIENCE: I'd like to discuss Professor Bobbitt's points, if I might, for a moment.

It's true that I think National Service probably would be found unconstitutional unless linked to Congress's power to raise and maintain an army and navy. But I think you leave an erroneous impression if you simply state it that way. In other words, there have been a number of opinions—at least two that I know of—by competent lawyers which state that they feel the court would find that National Service could be linked to the raising and maintaining of an army and navy, and, if so, would be found constitutional.

PHILIP BOBBITT: Now, usually the way I hear it is, someone says, Why do you want National Service? And the reply is: We'll get all these people out of the ghetto and put them into Wisconsin; and we'll get all those people out of Wisconsin, and put them into the ghetto; we'll employ a great number of people who are doing nothing now except listening to disco music and so forth to take care of the elderly, moving bedpans and that sort of thing. And then you say: What's the constitutional power for this? And the reply is: Well, if we can get Congress to say in a preamble that we're really doing this to make us feel better about the draft, then we can do anything, because the Supreme Court will leave it up to Congress to make the final determination.

Now there are two possibilities, it seems to me. One is that the Court will do that, and I think that's likely. That is, I think the Court will defer to Congress's justification in this area. If Congress says this is really necessary for us to raise and support an army, the Court will, as with other constitutional questions, leave that final determination to Congress. That does not mean, however, that it's constitutional. Congress can err constitutionally, just as the Court can. The other possibility is that we'll be treated to an open sham, and the Court will look through it. I hope the Court will look through it.

CHRISTOPHER JEHN: I have a question for the lawyers on the panel. As I understand it, the congressional power to conscript is viewed as being conferred by the congressional power to raise armies. As an economist, I don't see the necessary connection there, and wonder whether anyone has made the argument that conscription is not necessary for raising armies— that there are other ways of doing it, like paying people. Has that argument ever been made? Or, if it were made, what do you think the outcome might be?

DAVID LANDAU: The argument that has been made by legal scholars is a textual constitutional argument, based on the debate during the Constitutional Convention, that the power to raise and support armies at that time did not include the power to conscript. The 1977 Selective Service Law case rejected that argument. But in 1971, Professor Friedman of Hofstra Law School reexamined those arguments, and, I think, wrote a very persuasive article which said that, indeed, the Founding Fathers never intended to include the power to conscript. They were afraid of the federal army, just as they were of Britain's federal army. He argues that they intended the power to raise and support armies to be from the state militias only, and that that was what that clause meant. Professor Friedman takes a very narrow view of the power to raise and support armies. This same argument was made in a number of ACLU briefs during the Vietnam War, and, as Secretary Chayes properly pointed out, the Supreme Court declined to take the question on. So, when I say it's an open question, it really is an open question. Still, other scholars have responded to Professor Friedman and reexamined history itself, so it's a debate that is continuing and will go on.

ANTONIA CHAYES: Well, unless you consider an open question a question the Supreme Court has refused to hear by the exercise of its certiorari power, a further answer would be, I think, that the Selective Service draft cases of 1918 are dispositive. The Court there, in an additional quote (this was an argument of the plaintiff), said that "it must be assumed that the authority to raise armies is intended to be limited to the right to call an army into existence counting alone on the willingness of the citizen to do his duty in time of public need—that is, in time of war." The Court rejected this contention, saying that "the very concept of a just government and the duty of a citizen includes a reciprocal obligation of the citizen to render military service in case of need, and the state's right to compel it." I think that's dispositive. The Supreme Court has simply refused to hear the question since then. I don't know what more you can say in the way of its being open.

WILLIAM MECKLING: I think we have another Mr. Friedman.

MILTON FRIEDMAN: I'm not the Professor Friedman David Landau was referring to. I have a daughter who's a lawyer, but I'm not a lawyer.

I just wanted to comment on a side comment by David Landau. In referring to the fact that there was opposition to the registration requirement, he mentioned mothers against the draft, and so on, and ended up with "*even* Ronald Reagan." That "*even* Ronald Reagan" is very symptomatic of a great confusion among people about the philosophical underpinnings of opposition to the draft.

I should like to call to your attention that it was Senator Robert Taft who, in 1946, prevented President Truman from using the draft to conscript striking railroad workers. I point out that it was Barry Goldwater who was the first presidential candidate to come out against the draft in 1964 as part of his campaign. I point out that it was Richard Nixon who, as President, was primarily responsible for ending the draft and creating the All-Volunteer Force—for creating the Gates Commission of which you've heard something before. I note that in discussions on the All-Volunteer Force in the legislative hearings, one of the strongest opponents to *ending* the draft, one of the strongest opponents of an All-Volunteer Force, was Senator Edward Kennedy. It is the liberals—in the modern, corrupted sense of that term—who have been the main support for the draft. The belief in an All-Volunteer Force is a fundamental part of the belief in a free society, which is the belief of those of us who have been in favor of using a free market, and not government, to control economic activity. The proponents of Universal National Service today are exactly the same people who would like to have wage and price control, who would like to have central economic planning, who would like to have the government occupy a larger part of our lives. And so your comment, "*even* Ronald Reagan," is very much off-base. Rather it is to be *expected*, philosophically, that he would be among the first who would take a position against the draft.

While I'm here, I want to make one more statement in support of David Henderson this morning. I am also one of those who are by no means persuaded that there is any case for a draft, even in time of all-out war. And I just want to go on record as agreeing with him on that point.

LEE MAIRS: Mr. Jones brought out a rather descriptive statistic, which I think is somewhat misleading, when he said that the AFQT score required to enter the service has fallen from 50 to 17. Part of that—the change in the minimum AFQT score required to get into the services—results from better screening techniques. For example, the gentleman who has an AFQT score of 17 undoubtedly will also have, at least from the Navy's point of view, a high school diploma and several other qualifications that are better predictors of success in the service.

PHELPS JONES: Well, I'm instructed, of course, by the nature of your question. I tend to look askance at programs which are identified as "expanding Army service opportunities for young women." That means that the Army will now take high school dropouts with AFQT scores equal to those of males. But, once again, I thank you, and I have no particular argument with the point that you made. I think it is instructive that the scores go down. That is certainly one indicator.

DAVID HENDERSON: Thanks, Milton. Two things: One is, Mr. Jones said that it was 11 months after we got into Pearl Harbor before we got our people to Guadalcanal. I want to point out that that was *also* a period when we had the draft. So it doesn't sound like that's an argument for the draft. It was not a period when we had an All-Volunteer Force.

The other point is on Professor Bobbitt's paper. He said that the problem with the All-Volunteer Force is that it doesn't allow us to take account of societal values, of how much society values someone getting killed or whatever. Now, I take it that what you mean by society is a particular decision-making group in society. But what I'm wondering, if you do want that to be taken into account, is this: What if the majority of people disvalue a particular minority? What if they don't like that minority? Do you think that means the majority still has a legitimate claim to draft those people?

PHILIP BOBBITT: What I in mind was this: Taking not the All-Volunteer Force that we have, but taking the pure volunteer paradigm, we can't select out certain groups. Now, if we piggyback some political mechanism onto the pure volunteer paradigm, as we in fact do with the current All-Volunteer Force, that does allow you some selection. Now you asked me, would I like to use selection not just to remedy some obvious shortcomings with the All-Volunteer Force—like keeping, as someone said earlier, all the police in New York from volunteering at once, or something like that—but would even go so far as to allow a society to select out a few sacrificial victims whom it particularly despised and send them to the front? I suppose, putting it that way, the answer is that I would not like society to do that. But it's clear that if political mechanisms allow you to compensate for the market's shortcomings, then they do allow you that option. Fortunately, we have other political restraints.

DAVID HENDERSON: It seems to me, though, that if you're saying that there's some legitimacy to taking into account "society's" positive value of a particular person being in the military, then there's no particular reason to exclude "society's" positive value of other people, whom it *doesn't* like, being in the military. In other words, I'm saying that, philosophically, that is a reductio of your position.

PHILIP BOBBITT: Only if you assume that the only political value you can feed into discriminating classifications is a preference for one group over another. I assume that you want to feed in the efficiency of the soldiers who actually serve. Some of the criteria will be health, age, and physical ability, and all sorts of other preferences.

DAVID HENDERSON: No, I'm just pointing out that you're opening up a can of worms with that kind of approach, and it can lead to places you might not want it to lead to.

PHELPS JONES: The point raised [by Mr. Henderson] about my statement was incorrect. I said that it was 11 months before we could supply force in World War II. It was 8 months from Pearl Harbor to Guadalcanal, as he quite properly pointed out. My principal point there is that at that time we had earlier-committed allies who did, in fact, give us the luxury of time to build up our forces. We no longer have this luxury.

One point I neglected to mention in making my case for nonemergency registration was: In the event of a truly widespread emergency, just the act of registration itself could be considered provocative and might tend to induce the outbreak of hostilities or be one of the causes of it.

DAVID HENDERSON: Are you arguing against registration at those times?

PHELPS JONES: No, I'm arguing for nonemergency registration—not after mobilization day or a great crisis comes upon us, but during these piping days of peace, or whatever we're undergoing these days.

COMMENT FROM THE AUDIENCE: First of all, I just wanted to clear the record on something. The Armed Services Committee's vote was 30 to 5, not 30 to 4. In all deference to Mr. Aspin, he voted with Mrs. Schroeder against registration.

The decision as to whether to conscript, to draft, or to register people is not going to be made on the basis of whether the All-Volunteer Force is working, whether the numbers are good or bad, or whether there is a legal question or not. It seems to me that the real test of whether or not we're going back to registration and/or the draft is the perception of the American public as to whether we are "a strong country" or "a weak country." *That* will decide whether we need to go back to a system that is not purely volunteeristic. The courts, in that sense, or the law, will follow suit *after* the American public has made its decision. One of the things we're seeing now is that people like George Will and other journalists have decided to take on the All-Volunteer Force. I think this is going to provide a much more powerful force in terms of deciding whether or not we conscript than, say, whether the numbers are good or whether there is a constitutional question involved. I'd like to hear how you feel about that, as lawyers.

PHILIP BOBBITT: I don't think I agree with it. I think the initial position you offer is right. It is fundamentally a political question, to be resolved by the society at large. But law, as far as I understand it, is not a matter of formalities—just a few threshhold questions you have to answer before going on to the real thing—the media, policy analysis, or whatever. There is a kinesthetic effect between law and society at large. How people ultimately feel about the draft, and certainly about National Service, will be in large measure a result of the constitutional debate that is carried out about it. And that will be, in part, at least, a legal debate.

WILLIAM MECKLING: Would anyone else like to comment on that?

ANTONIA CHAYES: Only to say that there are a lot of other political issues involved than the perception of national strength. I think that the vote in the committee and the subcommittee is probably instructive in that there's a frank recognition that there are a lot of other issues. There's a real uncertainty as to what the reaction would be on the campus and how it might affect the political campaign. I think there'll be a different set of issues in 1981 than there are before November 1980, even if the fact of success or failure, the economic fact or the legal status, is just the same.

COMMENT FROM THE AUDIENCE: I think also that with the crisis in Iran it would be interesting to take the vote now as opposed to when we took it before the crisis. I think that there might be a difference in the way this amendment was voted.

PHELPS JONES: There are many of us who probably do the right thing for the wrong reason. Is that what you're suggesting?

RICHARD DANZIG: Richard Danzig, the Department of Defense.

I think that one of the particularly valuable things in Professor Bobbitt's paper for this audience, given the inclinations of a number of people here to put aside National Service as an issue for the moment, is the clear delineation of the mechanisms by which choice may operate: the political, the market, and the lottery method. I think the description in the paper is quite valuable—how people, over time, tend to gyrate between these three points, depending in part on their sense of the values at stake and in part on the psychology of the particular moment. The thing that particularly interests me, though, is whether there is some connection between those particular choices and the objective, external reality of the circumstances being confronted: either, for example, the size of the population you are drawing from relative to the size of the task that you've got at hand, or, as another example, what it is that you're asking people to do. As a further example, I note that this country has often drafted enlisted men but seems much more disinclined to use a politically coercive mode with respect to officers. There can be a lot of explanations for that. One explanation that might be offered is the nature of the work itelf. There might be some theory that the voluntary mechanism is more appropriate than either the lottery mechanism or the political mechanism when you're asking people to lead instead of follow, in theory at least.

The question I'd like to put to Professor Bobbitt is whether you think there are some external kinds of referents, and whether the discussion this morning or during the course of the afternoon suggests some objective referents which might lead you to think that one or another of those mechanisms is singularly more apt at the moment for recruiting our military forces. And I will just suggest, as grist for your mill, that a draft, a political mechanism, may be more apt than a volunteer mechanism if you have a war instead of peace. The risks people are taking are higher. As a last instance, as the demography changes, which mechanism might be preferable? From a philosophic standpoint, do you think that a smaller population relative to the task at hand argues more forcefully for a voluntary mechanism or more forcefully for a coercive mechanism? I know that's a long question.

PHILIP BOBBITT: In that case, I'll only answer part of it.

RICHARD DANZIG: That's the trouble with long questions.

PHILIP BOBBITT: I do think the nature of the good that is being distributed and the nature of the bad that is being distributed do, in large measure, govern the attractiveness of one or another of the variations and mixtures of allocations I've talked about. However—and I'll come back to the specifics of the draft in just a moment—that is only one factor that governs our preferences over time. You can see this in the differences among cultures in allocating the same kind of good. Other societies have played with the draft and with providing military personnel. The purchase of commissions, for example, would, I think, be intolerable in our society; it does not seem like an option we are likely to reinstitute no matter how many cycles we go through. Similarly, some societies quite recently have elected officers from the platoons and then shifted ranks after a certain period of time. That also seems to me most unlikely for us.

Why? Because, in part, it is the nature of specific good here if you're fighting a war, or preparing to fight one, efficiency has to have some paramount importance. But it also, I think, has to do with the nature of this society. We're much more pragmatic than other societies. We're much more egaliltarian in *some* senses of that term. The main principle, as I look at the shift in population, is the efficiency with which this or that wartime service or peacetime service is allocated. Efficiency considerations result in sex discrimination because of strength requirements for combat soldiers, not drafting the handicapped or the very old, and so on. That seems to me the paramount feature. And that's what allows professionals, like most of the people here, to reduce their numbers or to apportion them. Other societies might be uncomfortable with an analysis based on purely technical considerations.

RICHARD DANZIG: If I may comment, this strikes me as particularly interesting. If I read you right, what I hear you doing is advancing a philosophic or principled set of observations about the tensions between the three positions , and then saying that, because all three seem to you to have ineradicable, unavoidable difficulties, in the end you think the almost ideological preferences between the three poles will not determine the outcome, and ought not to, but rather efficiency or technological considerations ought to dominate. So that, in essence, if the panel this afternoon were representative of your view totally, its message would be a sort of surrender to the panel of this morning, saying that they ought to resolve the matter. Is that a misimpression?

PHILIP BOBBITT: Well, yes, but it doesn't go quite far enough. Though this society is particularly amenable to decisions based upon technical analyses, political considerations cannot be utterly erased. There is an irreducible core of values. Each of these options reflects a particular attitude about equality. I referred to simple, naïve egalitarianism in my talk this afternoon, such as that embodied to the greatest extent in the lottery. Then, formal egalitarianism—the market situation. You can make distinctions. Indeed, to function you have to make distinctions. Then, there's a corrected, or a qualified, egalitarianism, which you see in affirmative action programs, where you let the formal egalitarianism (market) device work, but then wait to see what results you get. If you don't like it, then you tamper with it. Because these values not only are always in conflict, but preferred by one system or another, I would be willing to surrender to the panel of this morning only if they, in turn, promise to surrender to another panel next month.

RICHARD DANZIG: Maybe, now that you've said that, some other members of the panel would like to comment on that.

WILLIAM MECKLING: No takers?

AUDIENCE: I'd like to speak to Professor Bobbitt again.

I don't want what I'm going to say to be interpreted as anything supporting National Service. That's not what I'm after. But you did, I think, misconstrue the current proposals for National Service at one point, as far as I understand them, when you referred to a lottery deciding who might be planting trees and who might not. A forestry major might be doing something else. As far as I know, the proposals we've got right now are the McCloskey and Cavanaugh proposals, and they would not use the lottery for that purpose. McCloskey would use a lottery to draw from the draft-vulnerable pool composed of those who had not opted for some form of National Service, if there were shortfalls. Cavanaugh would simply use the lottery to decide who was going to serve the nation in some capacity, civilian *or* military. That's a much different thing than the light you threw on

National Service in your talk.

PHILIP BOBBITT: The lottery mechanism I had in mind is contained in the report of the Committee for National Service, and it is one of many.

AUDIENCE: I have one question that is not directly related to the constitutional law question but has been bandied about a number of times by different speakers. That is the question of black people in the military, and the infeasibility of allowing a future military conflict to result in a high percentage of black casualties. As I understand it, black casualties accounted for about 40 percent of the Vietnam war losses during conscription. I'd like to hear someone who could quote directly what the figures are. I also know that the NAACP, and black veterans, and all of the members of the congressional black caucus have strenuously opposed registration and conscription, and that, as far as I can tell, almost all the leaders of the black community are very much in opposition to any form of conscription. I wonder if perhaps this is a bit of paternalism on the part of people like Senator Stennis and other members of the Armed Services Committee, who, after a history of not particularly progressive views on race, suddenly become born-again civil rights advocates. I wonder if, somehow, this isn't a ruse to cover up something else—that during the Vietnam War black people generally led the opposition to the war from within the military.

DAVID LANDAU: I'll make a comment. I'm not sure of the exact figure, but the figure for front-line minority casualties—which I think was much higher than the figure for minorities generally—was very high. And that percentage was higher, I believe, than the percentage of minorities today in the same category. I believe the last figure I saw was around 29 percent in the combat specialties.

I would associate myself with the remarks about race and Senator Stennis and Senator Nunn. It is difficult for me to hear, on the one hand, that there is a problem with educational and general quality of people coming into the armed forces under the All-Volunteer Force, and then to hear a little later that there are too many minorities and that it's unfair to place the burden of fighting our wars on minorities. I don't think the All-Volunteer Force should become a remedy for society's problems with unemployment and education, or whatever. But the draft doesn't fare much better in that category, and we can't go back to the draft, because opportunities for minorities are so much greater in the armed forces today than they were a couple of years ago.

PHELPS JONES: I'll comment very briefly there.

I mentioned the possibility of a large number of young black Americans winding up as casualties in some future conflagration. Certainly I don't believe I'm being paternalistic. There could be good reason to discontinue fighting in some future engagement. But I don't think we should furnish one in advance of actually fighting, by cruelly stacking, as best as we can foresee it, the pattern or structure of casualties. I would suggest that the Army and Air Force have probably done more for young black Americans than any comparable institutions in this country. Certainly I think they are far ahead of civilian groups, and the Navy and the Marine Corps have come along quite well in recent years.

WILLIAM MECKLING: Are you going to comment on this issue?

PHELPS JONES: No, it's a different issue.

WILLIAM MECKLING: Charles [Moskos], do you want to comment about these numbers?

CHARLES MOSKOS: On this point, I'd like to clarify the black casualty figures. In the Army, which had the highest black casualties—these were slightly lower in the Marine Corps and much lower, of course, in the Air Force and the Navy, where deaths in hostilities were predominantly those of officers—the figure was 13.3 percent blacks killed in action. Two points, I think, are interesting about that figure. First of all, it is a little higher than the percentage of blacks in the total national population, although that itself is not a completely known figure. Twelve to 13 percent is the best estimate. What I think is significant about that, though, is that even though the percentage of black casualties in Vietnam was close to the national proportion, the political fallout was high, and it would be compounded much more if we start talking about 30 or 35 percent casualties. A good message of the political fallout is that you think it's 44 percent when it's only 13 percent. Congressman McCloskey has also used that figure, 44 percent, which has somehow gotten into circulation. It's a tabulated fiction. Just imagine what would happen if the figure was in fact close to that.

WILLIAM MECKLING: Is this still on the same point?

RICHARD HUNTER: One thing that's important to focus on is what kind of draft you're going to have. If we have a draft like the one we talked about this morning, which is to draft people beyond those who already volunteer, and apply the rules that have been applied in previous drafts, where you can't turn down a qualified volunteer to get somebody you think might be more qualified, then that kind of conscription results in higher percentages of minorities than are produced by the current volunteer system. This is because we're turning down lots of qualified people right now in our effort to try to recruit more highly qualified ones. We would have to take those people. Then we would draw a random draft above that to reach our force levels. So it's not clear, unless you're talking about drafting the whole society—the universal military training idea—that you're actually going to reduce minorities in the draft.

AUDIENCE: Just a brief point. It's worth pointing out that Congressman McCloskey's National Service program would provide educational incentives for serving in the military as opposed to civilian positions. It seems to me that the poor minorities are going to go for educational benefits and therefore join the Army, and that this will be a direct incentive for a higher proportion of minorities to be in the Army, for the same reasons that they're in there today.

ARLEN JAMESON: This is a different issue—a legal question for Professor Bobbitt. What are the legal implications of discriminating by age in a return to the draft? That is, why should those people who have not been subject to the draft over the period of the All-Volunteer Force not be dealt with retroactively?

PHILIP BOBBITT: Dealt with retroactively? I don't see quite what you have in mind. Give me an example.

ARLEN JAMESON: I'll try to take it a bit further. We've talked about the changing makeup of families in the military. It is not unreasonable to ask what the legal implications are of limiting the draft just to 18-year-olds, as opposed to 25-year-olds or 28-year-olds who would have been drafted if the All-Volunteer Force hadn't been in effect.

PHILIP BOBBITT: You want to know about age discrimination, and whether or not it violates the "equal protection" clause?

ARLEN JAMESON: Yes, that's right. Not with regard to the very old. I'm interested in issues that deal with the ability to do the job and that sort of thing.

PHILIP BOBBITT: One of the things that differentiates the draft from National Service is that the government, in defending its classifications, has the handy tool of national security to satisfy the strictest constitutional test requiring a compelling state reason for the nation acting the way it does.

With respect to age discrimination, it's my guess that the courts would have no problem at all upholding it, simply on the basis that Congress and the Executive felt that some particular age group provided the best combat-ready force. And if some group had escaped the draft either by having lived in an era when we were not drafting anybody, or by being close to the vulnerable category but not within it, I don't think there would be any problem. Am I answering your question?

ARLEN JAMESON: You answered the question.

ERIC HANUSHEK: There is one issue brought up by Mr. Jones, and also brought up this morning, as a major criticism of the All-Volunteer Force as it's currently operating. This has to do with the size of the reserve force and the ability of our forces to respond during the initial phases of an emergency. A few years ago, when I actually looked at some of these things, it appeared more likely that you would run out of airplanes, bullets, and tanks and the like before you would run out of people. Therefore, I don't see why current "shortfalls" in the reserves are a major criticism.

Specifically, the current reserve "requirements" do not seem to be based upon a realistic estimate of the demands for manpower during the initial phases of a conflict. If there were an intense conflict, early replacement troops from the reserves would not be suitably equipped for battle. By the time we could produce equipment to replace that lost during the initial phases, we could also train new soldiers. This, of course, also says nothing about the state of training of current reserve units—a matter that seems to be open to some question.

PHELPS JONES: Well, I would think the administration certainly is moving quickly to get us more airplanes and tanks and jeeps and conventional things. It's awfully hard to forecast loss rates for different kinds of equipment over time. I know tables attempt to do this, but they're imprecise, at best. But even if we ran out of a certain line of equipment early in a future engagement, I don't think that provides us with a rational out for also accepting a perceived shortfall of manpower. Obviously, we should bring both up.

WARREN NELSON: To go back to the issue we were addressing earlier about the black casualties in Vietnam, in the first year of the war black casualties were 25 percent of those who participated. In successive years the percentage went down very rapidly, until, in the last years of the war, about 9 percent of Vietnam losses were black, compared with 13 percent of the youth population that was black. Remarkably, by the end of the war, total casualties were very much in line with the breakdown for the nation, and very conveniently so. Just under 13 percent of the dead for the entire war were black. The reason for the high 25 percent death rate for blacks in the first year of the war was the fact that blacks volunteered in abnormal numbers for the elite units within the Army (like the 82nd Airborne, for example) that were normally dispatched to trouble spots. Last year, when I checked these figures with a half dozen units, many of them were running better than 50 percent black. So, if we should go into another war tomorrow, more than half the casualties in the opening weeks or months of the war would undoubtedly be black. And there's no way you're going to change that, unless you change the fact that within the Army there are many elite volunteer units, which are the first to be dispatched and which have a greater attraction within the black community. Even if you go back to a draft, you're still probably going to have those units more than half black.

CHRISTOPHER JEHN: Let me just add a footnote to this discussion of black representation. It doesn't strike me that it would necessarily be so horrible if 40 or 50 percent of the casualties in a war were black, because, in this case, at least today, they would all be volunteers, which they weren't during Vietnam. Congressman Dellums, at least, has recognized this very explicitly in his arguments against a return to conscription and dropping the All-Volunteer Force. He has candidly recognized what Mr. Jones has recognized: that the military has, much more than almost any other institution in the country, provided opportunities for blacks that aren't there elsewhere. And if part of the price of that is higher wartime casualties, so be it. In the meantime, our blacks are much better off in the military than they are in the civilian sector. If anything, that's an indictment of the civilian sector, not of the military or the All-Volunteer Force.

PHILIP BOBBITT: I have a question. How do you account for the falloff in black casualties if both the original level and what you predict to be the subsequent level are attributed to volunteering in these particular elite units? How did it get down to 9 percent?

WARREN NELSON: At that time I was the UPI reporter at the Pentagon, so I wrote those stories, and got the figures, every six months. The figures dropped off dramatically when the percentage of blacks became an issue. I was never able to get an adequate explanation as to why the figures so suddenly dropped, markedly, below the national proportion. But the proportion of black casualties fell from the high figures of the early months because other nonelite, nonvolunteer units soon began to be poured into Vietnam.

MILTON FRIEDMAN: I want to get involved in an argument that came up between David Henderson and Philip Bobbitt about this analytical question of black overrepresentation.

There is nothing about a market system to prevent an All-Volunteer Force from not enlisting, say, all New York policemen. If you really want to make the kind of argument that David is raising, what you say in economic language is that in addition to the internalized costs and returns, there are some external costs and returns, and that it's appropriate for government, in hiring people, to take into account not only the internal but also the external costs and returns. That is, just as we think it may be appropriate to impose a tax on pollution, we might also think it appropriate to offer a lower wage in the military to New York policemen than offered others because there is an external cost in enlisting New York policemen. In the same way, if those who are worried about unduly black representation in the All-Volunteer Force are willing to carry their argument to its logical conclusion, they should be proposing that we offer a lower rate of pay for blacks to enlist in the Army than we offer for others, because the logic of their argument is that there's a negative externality in the hiring of blacks.

Mr. Moskos talks about sociologists versus economists. There is no such thing. As Frank Knight always used to say, there are two sides to every question—the right side and the wrong side. And there are two ways of analyzing a problem—correctly or incorrectly. There are no economic analyses versus noneconomic analyses; that's silly. There are just analyses. The claim is being made for this argument—I'm not for the moment arguing whether it's correct or not—that there is a negative externality in adding blacks as opposed to whites at the margin to the armed forces. If there is, it calls for offering a lower rate of pay, and, in that case, that would correct the problem of the negative externality.

PHILIP BOBBITT: Let me just ask one question. As an expert and as an analyst, what do you think of a wealth-neutral market? That is, do you think, using the system you just described, but with a considerably greater complexity, you could design a market that would not depend on the existing distribution of wealth? Now, of course, you have to redesign all the time . . .

MILTON FRIEDMAN: The problem with that argument is that you're asking, I think, the wrong question, because you want to avoid compensating for wealth with respect to the purchase of butter separately, with respect to the purchases of shoes separately, with respect to the purchases of hats separately, etcetera. If society believes—and again, I'm not asking the question of whether it should believe it or does believe it or saying what I believe—but if society believes that somehow or other the existing distribution of wealth or income is inappropriate, it ought to attack that on the level of the general distribution of wealth or income, not on the specific issue of armed forces.

PHILIP BOBBITT: But the society may not believe that it's the distribution of wealth that's unfair. Do you think it would be possible to have a wealth market that overcame the distribution?

MILTON FRIEDMAN: Of course it would be possible. It would be highly undesirable, in my opinion, but what you would have to do would be to impose a special tax, as it were, on the nonwealthy whom you did not want to join, and give a special subsidy to the wealthy whom you did want to join—exactly the same as in the black versus white problem. You see, what you're saying is that from your values of externality, you believe you ought to have a larger proportion of the wealthy in the army, and a smaller proportion of the unwealthy. Well, you can do that either with a carrot or a stick. And you can design either a set of carrots that will produce that end or a set of sticks that will produce it.

WILLIAM MECKLING: I'm going to take the liberty of chairman and generalize Milton's proposition, because it has a lot to do with the whole discussion of whether the All-Volunteer Force is working or not.

The issue is not whether volunteerism is working. The issue is whether the present system of pay and other emoluments in the military is providing the quality and number of true first-term enlistments that the country would like The issue is not one of volunteerism per se at all. The issue is whether the present set of emoluments is the right set given what Congress or the administration, or whoever it is that decides these things, really wants. Or, to put the matter in its most dramatic form: if you give me the right to decide on the pay scale and the terms of employment, I guarantee you I can get you any kind of military force you want up to the limits of the human numbers there are on the face of the earth. That's *all* there is to the idea of whether the All-Volunteer Force works or not, pure and simple.

Next question. [Laughter.]

WARREN NELSON: I'd like to return and harp on this subject again—the numbers of black casualties. And I'd like to thank Chris, by the way, for adding the point Ron Dellums has made, and a number of the members of the black caucus have made, that they're not concerned with the numbers or percentages of black deaths. Rather, they are concerned whether the person was compelled to go into that military unit or whether he went into it voluntarily. Nonetheless, I think that there is a legitimate political issue that will arise one, two, or three months into a war if the casualty lists come back and somebody does a calculation and we find that 60 percent of the dead are black. We lack general awareness of the huge percentage of blacks in the elite army units that are the first likely to be deployed. There is even a lack of awareness in the black community that the brunt of the fighting for the first few months, and only for the first few months, would be borne very heavily by the black community. I think this is something that we do have to address. I think it's something that a lot more people ought to be aware of.

MARTIN BINKIN: I have three unrelated points. First, to Mr. Jones.

That was an impressive list of statistics you reeled off. I don't know about the validity of all of them, but the one about the Marine Corps, I think, should be straightened out. It is true that the Marine Corps did propose a 10,000-man reduction. However, that was not proposed because of the quality of the recruiting.

PHELPS JONES: That is correct.

MARTIN BINKIN: That was based on a budgetary consideration, which, I understand, has since been turned around. And I think they will be only some 2,500 short.

PHELPS JONES: I hope I left the impression that the Marines were brought to consider this, and you are quite right in saying that it was not due to the quality of the force at all.

MARTIN BINKIN: A second point. I'm not here to defend Sam Nunn, but I think you have to be careful how you interpret what he has said about the racial question. Very carefully put, he has not said that he's concerned about the large proportion of blacks. He's concerned about the shortage of *middle-* and *upper-class whites*. [Laughter.]

Third, I believe that the racial question is one of the principal issues underlying the whole discussion, and it's one that a person is afraid to talk about in public for fear of being branded a racist. But, in fact, we are doing some of these things that you're talking about. I think we are offering whites higher pay, and we're doing it in a number of ways. Take, for example, the two-year enlistment in the Army. Offering a bonus to individuals, with the quality screens that are now set up, would eliminate most blacks from consideration. So I think that we *are* establishing policy to control the racial balance without doing it explicitly, and I for one feel that that's not a very attractive way to do that. I think that if, indeed, there are problems with the racial balance, that these should be brought up, discussed, and resolved on their merits.

WILLIAM MECKLING: Two of the panelists would like to comment.

DAVID LANDAU: I agree that race is one of the larger underlying issues that people do not like to talk about. I think that it's a very complex issue. I'd just like to bring up a point that raises some of these questions. We are obviously concerned largely about the percentage of blacks in the Army, but if you look at the percentages of blacks in the other services, particularly the Navy, you find they are much, much lower. I think we have to examine why. In part, one of the things that the ACLU has discovered is the parity program, which the Navy instituted after the racial disturbances on its ships. This is a policy in which, if there was one minority in a particular region during a particular recruiting period who applied for entry into the Navy and who did not score in the top level, they required three other minorities in that same region during that same recruiting period to score in that level before they would admit the person who did not score as high. The effect of that policy in different recruiting periods was to keep down the number of minorities. The reason for this, perhaps, may have been legitimate in that there weren't enough minorities rising up through the ranks, and this was part of the reason for the disturbances on the ships. But the effect of their remedy was probably worse than the original problem. I think they're now on the way to correcting that problem under the encouragement of Congressman Dellums.

There are problems like that in the All-Volunteer Force as a whole.

ANTONIA CHAYES: I would feel more comfortable if somebody who talked about the racial issue would at least express concern about the low participation of blacks in the officer force in all the services. It just seems conspicuous by its absence.

QUESTION FROM THE AUDIENCE: Hasn't that risen a lot?

ANTONIA CHAYES: It's rising, and there are steps being taken, but it's very low.

PHELPS JONES: Is that in the grades of captain and major?

ANTONIA CHAYES: Everybody has one black general. [Laughter.]

Of course, there are very fine recruiting efforts. I don't mean to belittle that. I've participated in them. But, I'd say that here seems to be a great concern on the racial side, and there doesn't seem to be *that other concern*.

CHARLES MOSKOS: I might add that the percentage of black generals in the Army is now 4.4 percent—a figure exceeding the number of blacks in this room.

ANTONIA CHAYES: That was something on which I silently commented.

WILLIAM MECKLING: Thank you. We will now adjourn.

PART 3

Invited Presentation

INTRODUCTION

W. Allen Wallis

W. ALLEN WALLIS: Our speaker this evening has a very distinguished career, even though he's young—by my standards anyway. As you know, he's the Principal Deputy Assistant Secretary of Defense for Manpower, Reserve Affairs, and Logistics. He took his bachelor's degree at Reed College in 1965 and then was a Rhodes Scholar at Oxford. He also took a Ph.D. at Oxford and then a law degree at Yale. He was with the Rand Corporation on foreign policy for a while, and then was clerk to Justice White. He then became a member of the faculty at the Stanford Law School, where, I understand, he's the leading authority on *Hadley* v. *Baxendale*, which I assume all you people are familiar with. It is apparently an important case in law of contract damages. He was a prime fellow in the Harvard Society of Fellows, and a Rockefeller Foundation Fellow in '76–'77. He then went to the Department of Defense, as Deputy Assistant Secretary for Program Development, and since last December has been in his present position. It is a great pleasure to present to you Secretary Richard Danzig.

X

DINNER SPEECH

Richard Danzig

RICHARD DANZIG: It feels very strange, to substitute for Robin Pirie.* I suppose it shouldn't seem that way—it's happened before. But I always feel in these circumstances like the fellow who plays a bridge hand with an expert looking over his shoulder. When he's all done playing his hand, he turns to the expert and says, "How would you have played it?" And the expert says, "Under an assumed name." I must say, if I had followed the advice of the creators of this conference, I might well have appeared and told you that I was Robin Pirie. They told me I could get away with it. Having decided not to do that, however, I must convey to you, truly, Robin Pirie's regret in not being able to be here. That annual bacchanalian orgy known as the Defense Department budget has a particular meaty and exciting quality this year with $156 billion on the table, and Robin was unable to tear himself away from that. Although, if he'd realized what a sort of Dionysian orgy this has turned out to be, I think he might well be very regretful about not being here.

He, like me, would have been particularly interested in being here, because both of us share an interest in what I would describe as cross-cultural experiences. And this conference, I think, certainly offers these. I was quickly exposed to such things coming to the Pentagon as a lawyer. Indeed, shortly after I met Robin Pirie and John White, the two people I was working for, the two of them got me in a room, chuckled together as economists, and, elbowing each other, said to me, "'Do you know about when the Devil and God had an argument about where the boundaries of their respective domains were?" And I, thinking this must have something

---

* [Editor's note]: Assistant Secretary of Defense.

to do with the strange world into which I'd become immersed—perhaps the boundaries between the Joint Chiefs of Staff and the Office of the Secretary of Defense—ever witty and clever, said, "No." And they said to me, chuckling and elbowing each other even more, "Well, the Devil said to God, 'Let's bring it to a court and have a legal case.' And then he turned to his assistant and pointing to God, said, 'Where is He going to get a lawyer?' " I thought about that one for a while, thought about why they thought it was funny, and decided I was being exposed to an intercultural experience.

This conference, I think, manifests that kind of experience. I was very struck by it as I listened to the speakers and comments. Having watched this event unfold before my startled eyes, it seemed to me that there really were three worlds in operation—a world of economists, a world of lawyers, and a world of military folk—and that they had periodic intersections (thank God!) and moments of genuine exchange and communication. There really were some fundamentally different views about how one structures the world, about the kinds of questions one asks, etcetera.

When I taught here at Stanford Law School a few years ago, a half-mile up the road, I was quite interested in the issue of question framing, an issue which occurs in some of the papers. Professor King, in fact, addresses it quite explicitly. At that point I wrote a paper on Felix Frankfurter's Supreme Court decision-making. In it I talked about how Frankfurter put questions. I might say, just as an aside, I think he put them in quite a loaded way. When I got done with this learned article, which I thought made a powerful intellectual point, a friend of mine from the University of Chicago—the large clique here that likes this sort of thing will be pleased to hear that he was from the University of Chicago (I will make appeals to the other groups in a few moments as we go along . . . though it's not clear to me that there are other groups, and they're certainly less vocal if they are here, but no matter)—said to me, "Your point about question-framing reminds me of the argument between a Protestant and a Jesuit over the propriety of smoking while praying. They fell to arguing this intensely, and each agreed that he would consult his superiors. When they came back, the Protestant said. "It's clearly impermissible." To this the Jesuit said, "That's funny, my superior told me the opposite." And the Protestant said, "He told you it was permissible to smoke while praying? What did you ask him?" And the Jesuit said, "I just asked whether it's permissible to pray while smoking."

That question-framing illustration, I think, summarizes much better the point in my article, and summarizes in a sense a major point that concerns me about the All-Volunteer Force and about the kinds of discussions that have gone on here. Early in the conference Charlie Moskos asked the panel of economists what their criteria would be—what would ever convince them that the All-Volunteer Force was or wasn't a good thing. How would one know if it had gone awry? What would matter? There was the usual exchange: that is, several minutes were spent asking what was meant by the question, and so forth. I keep thinking that we should have somebody here who is bilingual or trilingual who could facilitate a simultaneous translation.

I think this matters, because it gets back to a basic issue. General Max Thurman was talking about it after the sessions, at the end of the day. The issue is, what matters to you? There's a wonderful line of Nietzsche's I'm fond of quoting, the essence of which is that the commonest form of stupidity is forgetting what you're trying to do. And I have a feeling, with respect to the All-Volunteer Force, that different people, at different times, are trying to do different things. So if you asked people what it is that we need to do in the near term with respect to the All-Volunteer Force, they would point in different directions, in part because their disciplines, not to mention their temperaments and ideologies, suggest different directions.

Well, I will not try to give you some general theory about what we ought to be doing, in part because I think that probably the best advice I received with respect to this talk came from a well-wisher who came over to me just before I stood up, leaned over, and whispered in my ear, "Make it short."

Having been thus encouraged, I will, however, tell you that I think you can take a series of problems and with respect to each of them say, "If this were our criterion, if we were mainly concerned about this factor—representativeness, the availability of pretrained individual manpower, patriotism, or whatever—let's compare the kinds of proposals on the table as to their effectiveness against this or that." That seems to me to be a rational way of proceeding. Note, however, that though this seems to be a rational way of proceeding and my expectation is that all of you would sign up for it, it doesn't often happen. Indeed, it didn't happen often in the discussions today.

It doesn't happen in two respects. First, the problem is not often identified. Second, lots of people tend with, I think, alarming frequency to content themselves with stating the problem. Then, having gone through some demonstration describing how the All-Volunteer Force has this or that problem, they conclude, "In some manner or another, the All-Volunteer Force is not a success." They then, by some absolutely miraculous leap of logic, move on to the assertion that a draft is needed. It seems to me that it is incumbent on anyone who makes those kinds of statements (or uses them to support National Service) not to argue simply that there is or was a problem which should be documented, etcetera, but also to go on and say how it is that the draft or National Service would in fact solve that problem. (Some of Phil Bobbitt's comments, I think, were directed toward that in the course of his paper, and quite usefully so.) Moreover, in doing that, one would need to go on, in any intellectually respectable fashion, to say what other kinds of problems were created by that solution; what kinds of costs were being paid by choosing it, etcetera. When I do that—as I'm forced to do, by virtue of being, at the moment, neither a lawyer in the practicing mode nor an economist nor a military person, but instead, alas, a faceless bureaucrat—I find myself coming to conclusions that not only are usually more mixed and ambivalent than the conclusions reached in the course of commentary today, but also, I think, tend to have more operational bite.

I might quickly indicate to you that the bottom line of my conclusions, for the moment, is to make me a very active supporter of the All-Volunteer Force concept. I say "for the moment" because I can imagine circumstances in which the kinds of variables that matter to me might change.

Let me give a couple of examples, and then, in accordance with the good advice I've received, I'll stop. First let me take the issue of representativeness, which came up a good deal this morning. It is said—and I will take it for granted throughout this talk that the criticisms are right or at least have force—that the All-Volunteer Force has, let's say, too many blacks, too many people from lower socioeconomic classes, not enough whites, not enough people who are rich, and so forth. We would like more people who are very rich, or whatever, in the All-Volunteer Force. Taking the criticism as it exists, we need to ask, what's the alternative? And I think right away we see an intellectual fallacy frequently exhibited in these kinds of conferences. The alternative to an All-Volunteer Force—it must be immediately apparent to all of us—is *not* an all-draft force. It is, rather, a partial-volunteer force. In every kind of peacetime mobilization we've ever had (and I've never heard anybody suggest to the contrary in the context we're dealing with), the force that we've created is one in which we've taken qualified volunteers and then, after doing this, turned around and drafted to get our additional people. You could refute that; you could argue against it; you could say, "Let's refuse qualified volunteers because we want a draft." But I would first of all urge the people who want to point out a problem and say that they highly value this or that to also point out with some specificity what their solution is, and to note the costs of that solution. I don't think many of them would advocate turning away all or even most volunteers. Instead, if they were clear and explicit, I think, most of them would advocate a part-volunteer/part-draft force.

There's a problem with that solution. To begin with, even in a bad recruiting year, we wind up, like this last year, falling 20,000 short of our requirement. What is the proposal we hear? To draft 20,000 people? But the draft is a terribly broad-brush type of mechanism, as Dick Hunter pointed out in his comments today. It is a mechanism which draws everybody—poor people, people not terribly well educated, middle-of-the-road people, extremely talented people, extremely wealthy people, blacks, whites. If you have a draft that is really fair, the reality is that it's going to draw the kinds of people I've just described in a very broad-brush way and, in fact, not significantly change the representation of the force at the 20,000-draw level. Again I ask: What's the proposal? And what's the connection between the alleged problem and the recommended solution? Certainly, somebody can come along and logically argue that what he would like to do is refuse qualified black applicants who want to join the armed forces and instead draft white kids who don't want to join. But I don't think that's the proposal on the table. It is, by the way, something that the Navy did once when it constructed a parity program which ran for a number of years and which said, as was described today: we will not take significant numbers of minorities in special occupational fields where the minorities are already receiving their share of representation. But that's a system that we in the Office of the Secretary of Defense and people in Congress and in the Navy changed. We didn't think that system was fair, and I don't think anyone would propose it across the board for recruitment.

Well, they might propose a more *sub silentio* way of doing the same thing—a quieter, more veiled mode. One way to do that would be to raise qualification standards so that you'd take less of the current sort and draft more of the other sort. Well, that too, I think, is a very crude mechanism.

There is, I suppose, another way to do it, which would be to let our recruiter force ease up considerably; that is, practice, with respect to recruiting, a kind of benign neglect where we don't go out and actively look for volunteers, so that the number of volunteers decreases. Any way you cut it, though, in one way way or another you're turning away people whom we now consider to be qualified or allowing our recruiters not to make an effort to get those people so that we can draft people who are unwilling. And I think that unless we begin to turn away the unwilling people in very large numbers, we're playing with something that's extremely dangerous and difficult to see worked through. I make this point not to say that people shouldn't be concerned about representation and not to say that it's obvious that the All-Volunteer Force provides the "right" representation, but only to say that I think it's incumbent on all of us to think very carefully not just about the problems, but about the *alternatives* that are proferred, and how, precisely, those alternatives would supposedly generate a better world.

When I talk about putting questions and answering them, I only mean to say that I would hope that all of you when you hear this kind of argument in the future, or choose to make it yourself, would hold people to the key question. Not "Is the All-Volunteer Force a success or a failure?" Not, "Does it have a problem or not?" But, "How does it compare with its alternative?" If it turned out that the All-Volunteer Force was a wild success but that the draft was better, I'd be for the draft. To put the point in the extreme, it is not relevant to me whether the All-Volunteer Force is a success or a failure. What is relevant to me is, how does it compare with the other kinds of options in terms of costs and benefits? Now, I think that's a point we would all subscribe to but one we all tend to slough off.

Let me take another example: quality. I talked about representation of economic classes and so forth. You can run through an analogous argument with respect to the quality of people who are brought into the military. A reasonable argument can be made that we would like more qualified people, more people of higher quality, and let's say that that meant people who had gone to college. Of course, you could use the broad-brush mechanism of the draft to try to get such people. But I would remind you that there is strong pressure in society not to let the bottom-level people out of a draft world. If you start to fiddle with that and say, "Well, we'll only take the top half," you generate a lot of grievances. You generate a lot of people who are trying to cheat, to appear to be not as good as they really are—you generate the opposite of the present compromise problems. You get a compromising down, and something that's extremely difficult to deal with.

I'd point out also that there are other kinds of costs I care deeply about, as one who has some responsibility for the way the Pentagon runs its manpower system. The costs I'm speaking about are beyond the costs of drafting people—even high-quality people—who are unwilling to serve. Of course, I worry about the higher implicit tax on them. I worry about their probably lowered performance as unwilling soldiers. I worry about their serving for shorter durations than volunteers, because when you draft people you draft them for only two years, whereas most of our volunteers sign on for three years or longer. I value longer service because it's expensive to train conscripts and then have them leave because they're not volunteers.

Putting all these points aside, something really concerns me that I have not heard mentioned here, because I don't think there's careful enough consideration of the alternatives. That is, that I think it is important to pay people in proportion to their worth, and not to get them at no cost. This is because when it receives people at no cost, the military, like most institutions when this happens, tends to treat them as if they were virtually of no worth. It treats them as being virtually of no worth in a hundred ways—in the kinds of experiences they receive, the barracks they live in, and so forth. Beyond that, the military tends to misuse draftees in an efficiency sense. Tales of military misuse of quality conscripts are probably as old as the military itself

—like the recruit who speaks German and gets sent to Korea, or the qualified electrician who gets stuck painting or peeling potatoes, or the Harvard B.A. who's the company clerk. It's wonderful to have a Harvard B.A. as your company clerk if you're company commander but it may not be wonderful for the Harvard B.A.

From the standpoint of the way the military works, the incentive to put quality people in the "right" place—to be efficient in the use of people—tends to diminish dramatically with a draft. I care very much about that. I want to introduce more such incentives, more such efficiencies, into the military constellation. When I analyze my gut reaction to the All-Volunteer Force, I see it as prompted, in significant measure, by this kind of efficiency incentive. That is important in the context of other kinds of issues that have been raised.

Let me take a third issue: pretrained individual manpower. It's been suggested (and this is rightly said) that we have too few people in the Individual Ready Reserve. The Individual Ready Reserve [IRR] is the primary pool of those individuals who have already been trained and who have an obligation in the event of mobilization. People have said that, because of the low number of such reservists, we ought to have either a draft for the active force or a draft directly into the IRR. A draft for the active force would in the end generate more people for the IRR, because conscripts would be in the active force for two years and then come out and still have four years of individual obligation as Individual Ready Reservists.

I've got a lot of problems with these two proposals. Particularly there are a lot of problems with the notion that it is desirable to draft directly into the IRR. By our estimates, this would require spending about half a billion dollars a year to train people for six months. They would have no significant unit experience and yet be set loose on the world for some five and a half years after that, during which time we would *count* them as mobilization assets. I have a real problem with how their skills would erode during that time; with whether we'd retrain them; and with the value of that kind of activity, as well as with its intrusiveness.

The point I stress tonight, though, is that, as the Individual Ready Reserve system presently operates, the waste associated with it is mammoth. Because we have significant shortages, we in the Department of Defense have turned to that system and have started to make improvements in it. We're concerned about not having more people coming in, and we have to stop the waste, because we cannot easily offset it by drafting more young people.

When I say "improvements," that may conjure up in your mind a variety of extraordinarily subtle constructs that we have generated. But they're not subtle at all. For example, it used to be that everybody who left the service with residual obligation went into the stand-by reserve—a less-accessible pool of people—*not* into the Individual Ready Reserve, unless they specifically requested to do so. The Army and our office finally came up with the none-too-brilliant idea that we would make the presumption that people went into the IRR instead of the less-accessible stand-by reserve, unless they specifically requested the opposite. The net effect was 50,000 more people in the Army Individual Ready Reserve over this last year.

It happens that it is impossible to volunteer into the IRR. The only way you can get into the IRR is to have been in something else to begin with. Having been trained in another mode, one could then choose later to go into the IRR.

Now suddenly we have a flurry of proposals, some from military people and some from people in Congress, to draft directly into the Individual Ready Reserve. To that, we at the Department of Defense say wait a minute. In the past it has never been possible even to volunteer into the IRR, and suddenly we're leapfrogging to the notion of the draft. You can open up the volunteer possibility and see what it gets you (it's not going to get you tens of thousands of people, though it will get you some).

It is a logical leap of extraordinary proportions to say that the All-Volunteer Force is failing and then point to the Individual Ready Reserve, which you couldn't even volunteer into under the All-Volunteer Force, and say that we need a draft there. That's not fair to the All-Volunteer Force. It turns out, also, that we've always expected 70 percent of the Individual Ready Reservists to be available in the event of a mobilization. So, some people ask, why not the other 30 percent? The answer is that we don't really keep track of their addresses, we don't do physical checkups, and so forth. I think that it's profligate—it may even be perverse—to say, "Gee, we need to draft people and obligate them to serve in our mobilization system," when we don't think we can locate one-third of these people who are *already* obligated.

These kinds of inefficiencies abound, and the prod to correct them is the existence of the All-Volunteer Force. Even if I knew for certain that two, three, or four years from now the draft would return because of demographic changes or because Congress wasn't willing to pay the bill, I'd still value those two or three years with the All-Volunteer Force because of the efficiencies they would generate between now and then. In this respect I would second the comment one speaker made earlier today when he said that there is really a competition between the kinds of efficiencies we can achieve (our capacity to make the system work well) and adverse demographic trends. His was, I think, quite an accurate and perceptive comment. I think that there is a lot that we can do, and should do, along efficiency lines.

Let me give you a fourth example: the Army Reserve. The selected reserve in general—that is, the number of people in our units—is well under strength. The Army Reserve is 25 percent below our peacetime objective, the National Guard 17 percent below. We now have to ask ourselves: How is it that a draft, if we're talking about an active force draft as we've always known it, is going to be able to generate more people for the selected reserve? One of the answers I frequently get is, "Well, we'll exempt people who go into the selected reserve." That's fine, and it's a logical policy; I can make sense of it. But don't tell me, on the one hand, that you're going to exempt people who go into the selected reserve and on the other tell me that you're going to generate a draft system which will be better than past systems because it won't allow any exemptions. In spite of its contradictions, that is a not-infrequent pairing of arguments. People say, "Ah, we'll improve the representation in the active force." But if you're going to exempt people who go into the selected reserve, you will have created a loophole a mile wide for the privileged in society to self-select themselves into the selected reserve. Whereas I can think of ways of plugging the loophole, the problem is an obvious one, and I haven't seen people really come to grips with it in ways that satisfy me.

Most fundamental, though, is the issue of efficiency. Our problem with the selected reserve is *not* a lack of recruits. Contrary to popular impression, we have almost as many recruits for the selected reserves—Army, Navy, Air Force, Marines, and National Guard—as we had all through the draft era, and even before the draft. We're not lacking recruits. We could easily fill those units with the numbers of people coming in.

Our real problem with respect to those units is *attrition*. We did a study of the people who had access to their reserve components in the summer of 1974—just that quarter, a three-month period. We found that 60 percent of them were gone three years later, and only a tiny fraction had moved into the active force.

What happened to the rest of them? Why did they leave? We're not sure; there are hard problems with respect to the reserve. We've asked ourselves, does the training make sense? Do these people really have a role? How do we integrate their mission in a way that's meaningful to them? I would suggest that we have to come to grips with these hard problems, and I don't claim that we're doing a great job of it. The coming to grips, however, is provoked, even forced, *by the existence of the All-Volunteer Force*. If you throw away that prod, you throw away something terribly useful. You don't, in my opinion, want to "paper" over reserve problems by pouring people who don't want to be there into the selected reserves. In my opinion, such nonvolunteers make the selected reserves weaker during the period of the draft by virtue of their deep desire to avoid doing as much as they possibly could do. You don't want those people in those units, engaged in exercises that aren't meaningful to them. The trick is to take the people who *do* want to be in the reserves, but whom we're now losing as though through a sieve, and make the exercises meaningful to them in a variety of ways.

I could make a similar critique of proposals to register people rather than improve the efficiency of the Selective Service System we now have so that it would be able to deliver in the event of mobilization. I think that is a very correctable problem. It requires some efficiency and some imagination, but I think we can generate, and are in the process of generating, workable solutions.

Let me take a last example that's of a very different sort: patriotism. It's been suggested that one of the advantages of a draft would be that in some way it would improve the psychological milieu of society as against the psychological milieu that exists with the All-Volunteer Force.

There are two modes to this quite genuine concern. One is that it is really desirable to have people feel at least a residual sense of obligation. Even if you are not drafted, the argument goes, it's good for you to realize that you might be because that will enhance your interest in the military, in international affairs, and in related subjects; and it will be psychologically useful in terms of the attitude of the citizenry. A second argument is that it's desirable to have a draft because it brings people into the military who by definition don't want to be there, but many of whom find that it is a positive experience and leave to create a constituency for this institution in the world at large. I think that there is something to these arguments. I don't want to demean or dismiss them.

I will note three problems, however. First, these arguments tend to belittle the role of the All-Volunteer Force along precisely these same lines. For instance, our advertising to bring people in results in attracting a substantial number of people who, declining a career in the All-Volunteer Force, nevertheless leave to create the same kind of a constituency out there in society that's claimed for the draft. I'm concerned that comparative analyses of these two methods apparently aren't being done.

Second, I would reiterate the point about numbers I made earlier. If you're talking about drafting 20,000 people, it's not going to make much difference. If you're talking about drafting 200,000 people, you're talking about a very different system than people have imagined up to now. You're talking about *turning back* volunteers. So when a draft proposal is made, I want to know what's being proposed: numbers, concrete kinds of impact, exemption policies, and so forth.

Third, I think there is another point that stems from the numbers. People who advocate a draft sometimes act, I think, from a feeling of nostalgia for what existed in the fifties. The numbers suggest to me that they are trying to re-create a world which simply can't be re-created in the present.

The roots of this impossibility are in the numbers. In the Korean War period, in the early 1950s, we were taking more than one out of every two able-bodied males. That created an impression about the nature of military obligation in society at large and about an infusion of people with military experience into society, an impression that I think has real positive effects. Today the population has gone up. If you're talking about a modern draft, you're talking today about drafting a considerably lower percentage of the available pool of young people to fill your numbers—you must be more selective. Today 2 million young men and 2 million young women turn age 18 every year. What proportion of these young people are you going to draft? Putting the women aside (something that you may not in fact want or be able to do), if you draft 20,000 out of that pool of 2 million men, you're talking about only one in a hundred. Even if you're talking about drafting ten times that number—200,000 people—you're talking about taking only one in ten.

Now the attitudes of people who are drafted when they are one in ten are going to be considerably different, it seems to me, than the attitudes of people drafted at a level of one out of every two, as in the past. I would suggest they will reflect more a sense of grievance and less of a sense of patriotism than people who were drafted when we were taking one out of every two to reach the same manpower levels. The impact of young people returning to society in these circumstances is also going to be very, very different. My main point is that I think people ought to be extremely precise about how they talk about the payoffs we're going to receive from a draft in terms of patriotism or any other named goal. I worry about a natural propensity people have to focus on the simple question of whether the All-Volunteer Force is a success or a failure. It's too easy to list a number of problems that arise in the All-Volunteer Force and then say, "Well, therefore we'll draft."

I could go on with this theme indefinitely, and those of you who know me know that I have on other occasions. Accordingly, I will stop with two simple observations.

First, though the thrust of my comments tonight have been antidraft, I do not want to suggest that a draft is inconceivable to me or even, in the longer term, necessarily undesirable. My judgment at present is that it is not a good thing to have, that it would be a mistake. I believe that we benefit substantially from having an All-Volunteer Force. Of course, that could change. It might turn out that society is not willing to pay the bill; it might turn out that the quality of our recruits, or something else, changes so dramatically that we can't make it work under that kind of circumstance. I don't want to predict the future. I can't predict it.

What I think is so important is that, before we move from any type of system like the All-Volunteer Force, we look very carefully at what we might be moving *to*. You look before you leap. The value of a conference like this is precisely the degree to which it looks. What I'm worried about, perhaps, is a propensity we all have to be tempted to take the leap without looking very carefully.

The second thing I want to leave you with is a recollection from my Stanford Law School days, which may be very appropriate in the light of the fact that the person who so kindly introduced me said that I must have been one of the informants for Woodward and Armstrong. When Justice Douglas was in his prime, he used to relate how his father, who was an itinerant preacher, would meander around the Northwest from one congregation to another preaching sermons—rather like this one, though I expect not quite on this subject. One day Douglas's father arrived in a largely empty church, mounted the podium, and looked down to see one person out in the audience. As he peered out over the pulpit, he said to this guy, "Do you really want me to go through with this?" And the guy looked up at him and said, "Well, preacher, I'm just a lonely cowhand. I don't know much about these things, but I can tell you this: If I went out to the field with food for 40 horses and found just one, I wouldn't let that one go hungry." Well, Douglas says his father thought about that and decided he was going to give a full-blown sermon. So he got up there and preached a sermon, led hymns, gave prayers, and so forth. At the end of all this he very proudly marched back to shake hands with his congregation of one. When the cowboy shook his hand and started to wander off into the sunset, Douglas's father just couldn't stand it and yelled out to him to come back. He came back, and the preacher asked him, "Well, what'd you think of that?" And the cowboy said, "Well, preacher, I'm just a lonely cowhand, but I can tell you this. If I went out to the field with food for 40 horses and found just one, I wouldn't dump the whole load on him."

I say all that to emphasize restraint. I won't dump the whole load on you tonight, mainly because I have the feeling you would respond like 40 horses and pull me off the podium. I appreciate what you're doing here and urge you onward in your labors. And I apologize for Robin not being able to be here.

Thank you.

PART 4

Equity and the All-Volunteer Force

INTRODUCTION

Martin Anderson

MARTIN ANDERSON: The most controversial of all the issues involved in any discussion of the All-Volunteer Force or the draft is the question of equity—particularly who it affects, how much, and what it costs them. Today we have two papers, the first by Dr. Richard Cooper and the second by Charles Moskos. Dr. Cooper was formerly Director of Defense Manpower Studies at the Rand Corporation, and is the author of what is perhaps the most comprehensive review of how the All-Volunteer Force has worked since 1971. He is currently the Director for the Economic Studies Group at Coopers and Lybrand.

XI

First Paper:

MILITARY MANPOWER PROCUREMENT: EQUITY, EFFICIENCY, AND NATIONAL SECURITY (Summary)

Richard V. L. Cooper

RICHARD COOPER: Before starting, I'd like to say that I've been involved in many different conferences, either attending or giving papers, and I wish to express my thanks to Walter Oi for putting on one outstanding conference here. It's been a real pleasure, and it's been well-run. As a participant, I've been greatly enjoying it.

The title of my paper has changed from what appears in your program. After the initial outline came out, Walter wanted me to focus it a little bit more broadly, so the new title is: "Military Manpower Procurement: Equity, Efficiency, and National Security." I'll try to touch on each of these issues.

Once again the possibility of conscripting young men, and possibly young women, into the nation's forces is emerging as a major public policy issue. This renewed interest in the All-Volunteer Force, or AVF as it is known, and alternatives to it, including a much more comprehensive national service program, can be seen in the media, the military, and Congress. Indeed, it's been noted that formal legislation was recently introduced to reinstitute peacetime registration. That was defeated recently on the Hill.

It's useful to go back and think about how conscription has taken place over time. Historically, the decision to implement conscription has been driven largely by so-called military necessity, not only in the United States but in the other English-speaking nations of the world as well. This was true for the United States in the War of 1812, when the attempt to implement conscription nationally never was successful, and for the Civil War, World War I, World War II, the Korean War, and really throughout the postwar period. It was true for the British, the Canadians, and the Australians in both world wars. When the "necessity" was evident, conscription was implemented, though usually only after a very lengthy and protracted debate.

During the last quarter of this century, the problems have been more subtle. They have involved a different kind of necessity, not one of an ongoing or imminent war, but rather one of preparedness. The concern for national security is thus still key. But so are concerns about other aspects of military manpower procurement policy, most notably its fairness, or equity, and its efficiency.

What I would like to do, then, is to address military manpower procurement somewhat along the lines that Richard Danzig talked about last night —that is, to discuss manpower issues in the context of alternatives as they relate to three concerns: national security, equity, and efficiency.

There are really three main types of military manpower procurement systems, and there are perhaps an infinite number of variations on each. One, obviously, is volunteerism; the second is universal service of some sort; and the third is selective service. The last two, of course, are both forms of conscription.

Selective service and universal service differ in that under universal service, everyone, or virtually everyone, in the eligible age population serves. This is the prevailing system in Switzerland, Israel, and other small countries around the world. Selective Service is any system in which only a portion of the population serves. What I would like to do here (and I've done this in my paper) is to talk very briefly about the viability of some of these alternatives. I think we'll find that the United States has a choice, really, between only two policies.

But first let me note that, the way I see the policy environment today, there are two critical factors with respect to military procurement policy. Number one is what our defense requirements are likely to be. Over the next quarter of a century, barring some major unforeseen circumstances, I see these are being in the neighborhood of, let's say, 2 million members. Whether it's 1.5 or 2.5 million is not, I think, the point. The point is that it's neither 500,000 nor 6 or 7 million.

The second critical factor with respect to military manpower procurement is the population base that the military has to draw from. Traditionally, the military maintains an up-through-the-ranks system, but some military jobs are very physically or otherwise demanding. The military has typically recruited from the population of young males and, to an increasing extent in recent years, from that of young women, as Dick and Gary pointed out yesterday.

It's useful to think of the military's manpower requirements in the context of the 18- or 19-year-old male, or male and female, population. That currently is about 2.1 million 18-year-old males. By the mid-1980s it will drop to about 1.8 million, get as low as 1.6 million by the early nineties, and then pick up again in the late nineties. But, again, the point is that our relevant population base is much larger than the 400,000 or 500,000 new recruits the military needs each year to man its 2 to 2.5 million-man force.

Simply as a practical matter, this rules out universal military service and universal military training. So neither of those really represents a viable option. In my paper I go into greater detail on this point, and I'd be glad to entertain questions about it.

A slightly different option that has received increasing attention in the last couple of years is the notion of universal national service. I think I have to agree with Toni Chayes that this is certain not to happen soon. Still, I think it's useful to trace some of the reasons why it's not going to happen soon. As envisioned by its supporters, a national service draft would serve two principal purposes. It would help supply the manpower needed to staff the nation's armed forces, and it would provide a means for utilizing the remaining young men and women in nonmilitary functions.

I see five or six major problems with universal national service and I'm going to mention three of them here. First is the equity of such a proposal, which was alluded to yesterday. How does one allocate manpower between the military and nonmilitary aspects of service, or determine which kinds of nonmilitary service will be utilized? For example, it's certainly hard to argue that cutting down a tree as part of the Forestry Service program in Wyoming is the same thing as cutting down a tree on the border between North and South Korea. Such questions raise profound equity concerns.

Second, it would be enormously expensive to undertake these kinds of projects. My guess is that it would take in the neighborhood of $30 billion for one year of a national service program which utilized both men and women, though the numbers could be as low as $20 billion or as high as $50 or $60 billion. Either way it's enormously expensive.

Third—and this is something seldom given much consideration—a national service draft would be likely to displace many currently employed workers, who are typically in the less-educated and the less-employable category, because national service tasks would require less experience. So in many ways national service would probably exacerbate some of the basic concerns, like unemployment, among that population. Well, the list goes on; there are numerous reasons why a national service draft isn't going to work.

I think the choice really boils down, over the next quarter century, to volunteerism versus some sort of selective service draft. And a selective service draft could be like the one we've had in the last 20 years, though perhaps of a different shape. But that is the choice. Because not all young men and /or women are going to serve in the armed forces, the question is: Will they serve through compulsion or through voluntary means?

What I would like to do, then, is to evaluate those two possibilities in two major senses: How equitable are they, and how efficient are they? I will focus mainly on the question of equity, although I'll also talk a little about efficiency concerns.

The equity issue became very important during the early 1960s and continued to be prominent throughout the sixties, because of the population dynamics that I mentioned earlier; whereas in the mid-fifties immediately after the Korean War, we conscripted roughly one out of two, to two out of three, young men into the armed forces. While not universal, this was approaching some form of universality because of our smaller population base. By the 1970s the issue was very different and it will continue to be different throughout the 1980s. Roughly one out of every five young men —or if you want to count it in terms of young men and women, one out of every ten—would have to serve. This raises the whole equity issue.

In looking at this issue, we want to focus on two main features. One is the burden of conscription, and the other is the selectivity that results. There have been numerous studies on the fact that individuals subject to the draft are forced to bear a burden that other members of society do not bear: low pay, risky jobs, personal hardship, disruption of lives, arduous working conditions, etcetera. The list goes on and on.

The impositions of these burdens, however, does *not necessarily* constitute inequity. Society frequently imposes burdens on its members: we have to pay taxes; there's the right of eminent domain, prohibition of illegal acts —things of that sort. So the notion of burden-sharing is common in any society. The issue of inequity does arise, however, when these burdens are distributed *selectively*, and such was the case with the postwar draft. When only some in the cohort are forced to serve, the question becomes, who should bear that burden?

I would argue that no matter how fair the selection process is before the fact, it has to be inequitable after the fact. If you're going to line five people up and pick out just one to bear the burden, that's inherently inequitable.

Let's think a little bit more analytically about what actually happens as a result of this. The Gates Commission was really the first to take very explicit note of this extra burden, and captured it by calling it a conscription tax. Though it had been talked about in the literature earlier, it was first brought to full public view by the Gates Commission. Although this "tax" never appeared on any income-tax form or in the accounts of any government agency, it was nevertheless very real for those forced to pay it.

There are numerous studies that have tried to measure the conscription tax, and they all come out with essentially the same message. The burden is substantial. The financial burden alone—the fact that young men have been forced into the military at a salary less than they could earn in the civilian sector—has been estimated at being between $2,000 and $4,000 during the period of the postwar draft. Military salaries are typically about 50 percent less than salaries that can be earned on the "outside." In fact, if you aggregate it in total, the conscription tax appears to have amounted to between $2 and $3 billion in 1964 alone—better than one-fifth of our total manpower costs that year. The message is that this tax is substantial.

As I said earlier, this impression of burden is not intrinsically unfair; it becomes unfair when it is selective. This raises the question, then: Who serves when not all serve? Or, as Charlie Moskos puts it in his paper: Who serves when most do not serve?

Folklore is replete with story after story about the extremes to which some young men have gone to avoid induction. There were cases of young men purposely maiming themselves or spending thousands of dollars on lawyers. There was a lot of extra orthodontic work done. In fact, Baskir and Strauss guess that between 50,000 and 100,000 people fled this country during the postwar draft. Part of that was, of course, associated with Vietnam, but a large part was associated with the draft itself.

One reason young men found so many ways to avoid induction is that the Selective Service System itself institutionalized many ways of avoiding the draft. The system was faced with the problems I mentioned earlier: how to pick one out of every five, or one out of four, or one out of six. Deferments and exemptions were provided. Initially there were deferments for hardship cases and for college students, and later these were expanded and hardship deferments liberalized. Deferments were given for post-graduate study, and for marriage and fatherhood. In short, draft avoidance became as much a part of *official* U.S. policy as the draft itself.

Not surprisingly, "who serves when not all serve" turns out to be the poor, the undereducated, and the black, although I would like to emphasize that when people from all walks of life did, in fact, serve, it was these poorer segments of society that were overrepresented.

We hear a great deal today about the overrepresentation of blacks in the armed forces, despite the fact that, throughout the postwar draft period, blacks served in numbers roughly twice the proportion of whites, according to their relevant population bases. The only reason black participation was as low as it was during the fifties and sixties was that the vast majority of blacks didn't qualify for military service. That's no longer the case. Now the majority are qualified.

Many of the inequities that led to the poor bearing a disproportionate share of the burden can be attributed to the specifics of the postwar, pre-lottery draft. Although not as blatant as the draft during World War I, when individuals were classified and inducted according to their "value to society," there were still numerous ways of avoiding induction during the postwar draft, ways that served to benefit largely middle- and upper-class white youth. Despite the draft reforms that were implemented in the late sixties, including the lottery and the closing of many loopholes, there still turned out to be ways that young men could avoid military service. In fact, some analyses I've done show that a young man living in one of the highest income areas in the country stood only about half the chance of serving as did a young man in a middle-income area and only one-quarter the chance of serving as did a young man in a low-income area. So getting rid of all the draft loopholes still did not solve the equity problem.

This should not be viewed with surprise. As long as there is an incentive to avoid induction, people will avoid it, and the ones who will be successful are the ones who have the most to gain. So the main difference between a volunteer force and a conscripted one today is not in who serves, but rather the fact that, in paying a "fair" wage to youth, the All-Volunteer Force has not discriminated against the poor the way that the draft did.

That pretty much summarizes the equity side of the issue. Since we're running short of time, let me just touch on the efficiency side.

The draft is a very inefficient way of administering military manpower. It encourages the military to use too much manpower, especially too much junior personnel, and encourages people to spend large sums of money on draft avoidance. My guess is that the total of all these costs due to inefficiencies amounted to as much as the country spent on total manpower during the period we had the draft. Basically, then, all the draft does is to hide resource costs from public view.

Let me conclude by saying that I've been struck in the All-Volunteer Force debate by what would seem to be a tail-wagging-the-dog situation. Yes, there are problems with the current volunteer force. But, as Bill Meckling pointed out, the question is not whether an All-Volunteer Force can work, but whether *this* All-Volunteer Force is working and will work. There are problems. There's a shortage of doctors and we're having some problems with the reserves. Also, there are problems in society as a whole—for instance, youth unemployment. But the draft is a very inefficient way of dealing with these problems. Using it, you can gloss over some of them, but you create others. In short, with the draft, you're painting with a very-very broad brush which creates numerous, numerous problems. As a practical matter we have a choice between selective service and an All-Volunteer Force, which compels us to think about three things. Number one, can we meet national security needs with an All-Volunteer Force? The answer has certainly been yes for six years. Number two, which alternative is more equitable? I think the case is clear: the All-Volunteer Force is more equitable. And, number three, which is more efficient? I think that's equally clear: the All-Volunteer Force is more efficient.

So, I would argue that, looking ahead, we have really three options: (1) making the volunteer force work; (2) letting it go as it is and not worrying about the population decline, and other problems, in the next few years, thereby letting military capability and the quality of the force erode; or (3) reinstating an active selective service draft.

MARTIN ANDERSON: Our next speaker is Charles Moskos, professor of sociology at Northwestern University. I think it's probably safe to say he's published more in the field of equity and the armed forces than anyone else I can think of. His publications include *The American Enlisted Man, Public Opinion and the Military Establishment,* and *Peace Soldiers.* I might also add that at one time he was a draftee in the Army (combat engineers).

XII

Second Paper:

SERVING IN THE RANKS: CITIZENSHIP AND THE ALL-VOLUNTEER FORCE (Summary)

Charles C. Moskos, Jr.

CHARLES MOSKOS: I'm very appreciative of this opportunity to be a kind of Daniel-in-a-lion's den, but I do see so many familiar faces around. I'm reminded of the line of Claude Rains in the movie *Casablanca*, when toward the end of the movie he told the police inspector to round up the "usual suspects."

My remarks today are going to consist primarily of three elements. First, I'm going to argue that the All-Volunteer Force army is not representative. Second, I'm going to ask, does this make any difference? And third, I'll suggest what we might do about it.

But before I begin, I want to say that I'm on the side of the All-Volunteer Force. It *must* work.

The major pitfalls of the All-Volunteer Force are not found in the declining pay rates vis-à-vis civilian salaries for the lower enlisted ranks, in the declining youth cohort of the 1980s, nor, indeed, in the efforts of service recruiters, who I think have accomplished a task of immense proportions. Rather, the major problems with the All-Volunteer Force are found in the redefinition of military service in terms of a cash-work nexus. This redefinition was given powerful expression by the Gates Commission on the All-Volunteer Force, and has contributed to moving the military from what I have termed an institutional model to one resembling more that of an occupation.

My remarks today are going to focus on the All-Volunteer Army, because one can say that, in general, the Army has faced the most severe difficulties in the all-volunteer era, the Air Force the least, and the Navy and Marine Corps somewhere in between. There is a kind of domino theory going around that states that if the Army topples over, the other services will quickly follow. I'm not really persuaded that that may happen. I do think that the Air Force stands out, almost *sui generis,* and that it may be able to maintain its recruiting goals even under *the present all-volunteer framework.*

In most of my analyses I try as best as possible to use pre-Vietnam peacetime data rather than late sixties/early seventies draft data. I think it's a common mistake—one which underlies many studies on the All-Volunteer Force—to compare our force in the present all-volunteer era with the so-called draft army of the early 1970s. That was the worst time in modern American military history. Everything had to get better from the tail end of the Vietnam War on, so the more relevant comparison in terms of organizational relevance, I think, would be between one peacetime era and another peacetime era.

In my own work, I focus heavily on the educational composition of the All-Volunteer Force, with particular emphasis on non-prior-service (NPS) males, who constitute over 80 percent of all accessions. In 1979, for example, 3 percent of the NPS had some college background, which contrasts with 40 percent for the 18- to 20-year-old civilian male population. You can see the table in my paper for more detail on this. In 1979, 55 percent of NPS males in the All-Volunteer Force were high school graduates, versus 40 percent among the 19-year-old males. Perhaps most dramatic, however, 41 percent of non-prior-service male accessions were high school dropouts, as contrasted to 20 percent in the 18- to 19-year-old civilian population.

There is simply no question that the educational unrepresentativeness of the All-Volunteer Force is sharp. Even if you look at the 1964 figures, the All-Volunteer Army is recruiting a lower proportion of high school grads, and people with some college background, than is found in the 18- to 19-year-old male population. These data should be assessed in the context, of course, of dramatically rising levels of education in the civilian population as a whole from 1964 to the present.

Much has already been made here about the rising rate of black accession, now pushing 40 percent of non-prior-service accessions in the Army and lesser rates in the other services. In all services, by the way, the black proportion exceeds that of the national average. We haven't heard about the Hispanics, about whom data are harder to tabulate, but they are becoming another increasing component within the All-Volunteer Army. We are now encountering problems with commanders telling their troops not to speak Spanish while on duty and then getting slapped down for making these kinds of edicts.

It is easily argued, I think, that well over 40 percent of our entering accessions today come from minority backgrounds. Yet at the same time—and I might immodestly take credit for uncovering this fact—it must be stressed that the educational level of our black soldiers *exceeds* that of our entering white soldiers. Indeed, the Army may be the only arena in American society where educational levels of blacks exceed those of whites, and by a noticeable margin. For example, in 1976, 65 percent of blacks entering the Army had high school diplomas as contrasted with 54 percent of white male accessions.

The introduction of women has, of course, been one of the most important, and generally positive, results of the All-Volunteer Force. I think the argument can be strongly made that the margin of success the All-Volunteer Force can boast has come from the introduction of women, virtually all of whom until recently had to have a high school diploma to enter. This requirement has now been changed. That is, rather than raising the standards for males, we're lowering the standards for females.

A crucial issue remains: the prohibition of women in the combat arms. A congressional statute prohibits women from duty on combat aircraft and warships, and the principle of the statute has been codified in Army regulations prohibiting women in the ground combat arms. Ironically, it would be easier to get women into the infantry than it would be to get them aboard a warship, simply because of an Army regulation.

Yet, removing the ban against women in the combat arms cannot be viewed as a solution to all-volunteer recruitment. There are already indications that the pool of highly qualified women is being tapped close to its maximum, and, more importantly, it's simple-minded in the extreme to believe that women will show any greater eagerness to join the combat arms than men. For certain, a fraction of Army enlisted women are capable and willing to be assigned to combat units, even leaving aside the normative and cultural problems that exist in this area. But to allow women the choice of whether or not to volunteer for the combat arms would lead men to ask for the same prerogative, including the option of not serving in the combat arms. If regulations were changed so that women could be compelled to serve in the combat arms, as is presently the case for men (that is, all men today are at least *liable* to serve in the combat arms), the end result would almost certainly be a sharp drop in the number of women who would volunteer to join the Army in the first place.

It is this major dilemma, I think, that precludes the utilization of women in the combat arms for the foreseeable future. And lest we forget, in January 1943, when the Army was having difficulty recruiting women during World War II, it lowered its standards. You can read about this in Madie Treadwell's study, *The Women's Army Corps*. "Lowering standards" soon became a euphemism for not requiring a high school diploma, so it sounds like history repeats itself. The problems we encountered by lowering standards for women in 1943 were so severe that before the end of the year the old standards were restored.

Another phenomenon in the recruitment of the All-Volunteer Force has been the sharp change in marital status in the junior enlisted ranks. At the E-4 level in the Army, for example, this has increased from the pre-Vietnam level of 25 percent married to a present 41 percent married. This trend is contrary to the national pattern which is clearly in the opposite direction. I might add that the military mobilization and effectiveness problems now encountered due to unsophisticated families, single parents, child abuse, spouse beating, and all the rest, are very, very apparent today. In this area, I'm always indebted to the work of Cecile Landrum who has done, I think, path-breaking research on the issues of the young family in the all-volunteer context. It's also important to note, however, that even though the census data show a broad trend toward later marriage in the population at large, there is a kind of deviant white population that is marrying younger. It is also true that while there are fewer high school dropouts today than over the last couple of decades, there is a deviant white population in this category as well. There are more white high school dropouts at ages 14 to 17 today than there were ten years ago. Many of these data are presented in my paper.

What I'm arguing here is that we are witnessing two kinds of white population in America: one that is middle class, at least in its aspirations if not its background, with a trend toward later marriage and higher educational levels, and a smaller, deviant segment tending to be high school dropouts with earlier marriages. It is in this *latter* white group, as well as in the minority groups, that the All-Volunteer Army is overrecruiting. Indeed, in some sense I'd say that whites coming into the Army are even *more* unrepresentative of the general population than our minority soldiers. Another way of phrasing this is to say that only 30 percent of non-prior-service male accessions entering the Army are currently white high school graduates. Other studies show that within a high school graduating class, those most likely to join the Army do come from the lower reaches of their classes, so that even a high school diploma is not an indication of middle-class background.

Certainly the lower ranks of the peacetime Army were never a mirror image of America's class system, but it's undeniable that the All-Volunteer Army is much less representative of the American middle class than the pre-Vietnam Army

Rick Cooper makes a statement in his book on military manpower, and I quote, "The evidence presented here thus shows that the American military has not been, nor is it becoming, an Army of the poor or of the black." I think the data quite refute that kind of observation. The All-Volunteer Army *is* becoming an Army of the poor and of the black. Whether this makes any difference is another question.

First we got to the point of answering the question, Is the All-Volunteer Army unrepresentative? I'm arguing, yes, it is unrepresentative. If we can get that question out of the way, we can go to another question: Does it make any difference if it's unrepresentative? And that's what I now want to address.

All measures of soldierly performance—such as enlisted productivity, number of disciplinary actions, and attrition rates—show clearly that, in the aggregate, high school graduates significantly outperform high school dropouts.

The difference between attrition rates for high school graduates versus dropouts is really quite dramatic. The graduate is twice as likely to finish his or her enlistment as is the dropout. Yet, despite the overwhelming evidence that the higher the quality, the better the soldierly performance, it is too frequently argued there are many menial tasks to which bright soldiers are less suited than the not-so-bright. Congressman Aspin has seriously proposed that the services recruit more heavily from the less-intelligent precisely in order to fill menial jobs. One is reminded here of *Brave New World,* where Alpha, Beta, and Gamma ratings are assigned to people on the basis of their intelligence and where the more intelligent are purposely assigned to the more skilled jobs. Of course, we do enough of that anyway. Now, some say, we should make it a policy.

The proposal that we recruit less intelligent people to fill our menial jobs has the apparent attraction of making a virtue out of a perceived necessity. But the idea that it would actually work is patently contradicted by the facts. The evidence is unambiguous that in measures of enlisted productivity, higher-educated soldiers do better in low-skill jobs as well as high-skill jobs. Much of Rick Cooper's work has demonstrated that.

Most discussion about the representativeness of the All-Volunteer Army centers on the very heated issue of racial composition. This is most likely an effort to scare people away from raising the representation issue, and I appreciate Martin Binkin's remarks yesterday that we have to look at this kind of question.

It is true that the rise in the number of blacks reflects not only the large increase in the number of blacks eligible for military service, but also the unprecedently high unemployment rates that characterize our society's minority youth community. Nevertheless, to look at the racial composition of the Army solely in terms of the social forces impinging upon, or internal to, the black community should not preclude attention to lack of participation of our white middle-class and even black middle-class population.

To what extent the changing racial composition of the Army reflects white reluctance to join a truly integrated system is not known. I am personally unpersuaded that a significant number of middle-class white, or members of the middle-class of any race for that matter, would be more likely to join the Army if it were lily-white under present recruitment incentives. Probably what would happen if the Army were lily-white today is that we'd simply have 30 percent fewer soldiers because *there wouldn't be* any blacks.

We must, I think, be alert that it would constitute a setback of historic proportions if the Army were to back away from racial integration under the guise of equal opportunity.

The issue of black overrepresentation in the Army raises many political questions. I refer here to a letter by Congressman Fauntroy to the *New York Times* in the wake of the Andrew Young affair, in which Fauntroy argued that, based on history, a U.S. involvement in a Middle East war would involve a disproportionate impact on black military personnel and that the resulting overproportion of casualties they would suffer would be "outrageous." This is the kind of thing one can expect. To hide our heads in the sand and think such an eventuality is not going to have political consequences is, I think, deceitful. This *is* going to become an issue.

The military has always recruited large numbers of youth—white or black—who had no real alternative job prospects. A recently advanced view that the armed forces should serve as an outlet for other unemployed youth is, while seemingly persuasive in the short run, deceptive on several grounds. It fails to take into account the preponderance of disadvantaged youth in low-skill jobs who have marginal, if any, transferable ability to other civilian employment. Moreover, with such a large proportion of volunteers, both white and black, failing to complete their enlistment, the All-Volunteer Force is producing large numbers of what are, in effect, two-time losers. We've already released 700,000 attritees, if such a noun exists, back into society since the end of the draft.

Whether a soldier drops out or is forced out of the military is a personal matter. But if the attrition rate begins to overtake the success rate, we will have to begin to wonder not about what has gone wrong with a specific soldier, but about what is happening to the military institution as a whole. The rising minority composition of the Army actually reflects a pervasive shift in the social class origin of men in the lower enlisted ranks. Whatever success the military has had as a remedial institution for deprived youth has been largely due to legitimization of the armed forces on other than overt welfare grounds. In other words, those very conditions peculiar to the armed forces that have served to resocialize poverty youth toward productive ends depend directly upon the military *not* being defined as a welfare agency or an employer of last resort.

By no means does being middle-class necessarily make one braver or more able. There are many outstanding soldiers in the All-Volunteer Force of modest educational attainment. However, our concern must also be with the chemistry of unit cohesion, which requires an optimum blend of talents and backgrounds. Starting with World War II, the distinctive quality of the enlisted experience came from a mixing of social classes and, starting with the Korean War, from the integration of races. This gave poor youth an opportunity to test themselves, often successfully, against more privileged youth. Such enforced leveling of persons from different social backgrounds had no parallel in any other existing institution in American society, and was *the* fundamental fact underlying the enlisted experience at that time. It also is a state of affairs that began to disappear during the Vietnam War, when the college-educated avoided service, and has all but disappeared in the All-Volunteer Army.

The choice in this conference has too often been couched in the wrong terms. We talk about a draft army versus a volunteer army, when the real issue, I'm arguing, is a representative versus a nonrepresentative army. In the classic fourfold table, you're going to have *volunteer* and *draft* on one side, and we can put *representative* and *nonrepresentative* on the other. For instance, we've had representative draft forces. Our force in World War II came close to that, and we had one during the late 1950s, when the "Depression Babies" were maturing. We've also had unrepresentative draft forces. The Vietnam period certainly produced one of these. And now we have an unrepresentative volunteer force.

I'm arguing that we can also fill that fourth cell, which is a representative volunteer force. I think, too, that it's naïve to think there's going to be an agitation to restore the draft because some politically articulate people are excited about getting a lot of poor people into the Army. Quite to the contrary, that's the reason we're *not* going to go back to a draft. The draft failed during the Vietnam era not because it was unrepresentative, as everybody seems to think, but precisely for the opposite reason. It tried to *become* representative. That's when it collapsed.

One of the crucial aspects of combat groups is the effect of social composition on combat performance. A summary of years of research has shown that level of schooling is the strongest predictor of effective combat performance. Studies for the Army during the Korean War also show that educational background is positively correlated with combat effectiveness. All such evidence serves to confirm the observations of both commanders and noncommanders from the draft period of the importance of the college-educated in enriching the skill level of military units in peacetime as well as in war. Some recent studies of the All-Volunteer Force based on survey data also show tremendously high levels of alienation and disaffection within the All-Volunteer Army in comparison not only with civilian groups but even with World War II groups. One such study found that there was only one World War II group which approached the All-Volunteer soldier in job dissatisfaction and that was a *prisoners'* detachment during the war.

Today, if our forces are to fulfill their function of military deterrence in the post-Vietnam context, representation concerns are still germane. I'm not arguing here that the makeup of the enlisted ranks be perfectly calibrated to the social composition of society. I am asking what kind of society excuses the privileged—indeed creates policies to excuse the privileged—from serving in the ranks of the army? It's a social reality that without some kind of coercion, the combat arms and labor-intensive jobs will always draw disproportionately from poorer and lower-class youth. But to foster policies that *accentuate* the tracking of lower-class youth into such assignments is perverse. If participation of people from minority or blue-collar backgrounds in military leadership positions is used as a measure of the democratic character of our military, and properly so, it's even more important that participation of the more advantaged groups in the rank and file also become a measure of representational democracy. Econometrically-based analyses tend not to ask these kinds of questions, but we must.

I think we're ready for our third point: Now that we've determined it *does* make a difference, we need to ask what can be done about it.

These debates should not be constrained by an assumption that tends to dominate our conversation, and that is that tinkering with the status quo forces us to bring back the draft. I believe that the draft is inadvisable at present. For one, there's the cohort problem I've already mentioned: Who serves when most do not serve? To maintain some legitimacy, most have to serve in a draft, and a consensus must precede a draft, not come afterwards.

Restoring the draft will create turbulence in our society. I even think that draft registration is not advisable because, contrary to what my good friend Phelps Jones has said, I believe registration would give us the worst of both worlds. It would make no real difference in military preparedness and still get us into all the trouble that goes with a draft. Any kind of compulsory scheme is going to involve turbulence on the campuses. Many will attempt to avoid it, or get out of it, and that will bring other problems in its wake.

Another option, and one that will be increasingly mentioned in the near future, is to considerably reduce the size of our forces. Alan Sabrosky has written on this. However, I think that, unless accompanied by a major retrenchment of America's defense commitments, such a resolution of our problems with the All-Volunteer Force would only compound an already "hyper" atmosphere prevalent in all our military units. Already, too much is being asked of too few people in too little time.

A major reduction in our force levels would have to accompany a redefinition of America's military purpose. We ought to give this consideration. But, in any event, whether our military force is large or small, it must always answer the test question: Is this the best we can have?

Granted conscription is not feasible, and a major reduction of our force doesn't seem to be in the offing, what management steps could we take to improve utilization of manpower within the all-volunteer framework? Here we run into the difficulty that comes with most proposals along these suboptimal-approach lines: they do not really address the core issue— getting qualified young men into the combat arms. Neither lowering physical or mental standards for men, nor increasing the number of women and older people, nor greater reliance on civilian personnel answers that question.

In the All-Volunteer Army today there is a discontent among enlistees with no counterpart in the peacetime draft era—what I call "postentry disillusionment." In our all-volunteer recruitment efforts, a consistent theme has been the self-serving aspects of military life. The irreconcilable dilemma however, is that many military assignments, and by no means exclusively in the combat arms, require skills that are not, and cannot be, transferable to civilian occupations; and it's precisely in such military occupations that recruitment shortfalls, attrition, and desertion are most likely to occur.

One of the principal Gates Commission recommendations—large raises in military pay for enlisted personnel—was the major inducement for people to join the All-Volunteer Force. This turned out, however, to be a double-edged sword. Youth surveys show that whereas pay motivates less-qualified youth—high school dropouts and those with poor grades—to join the armed services, it has a negligible effect on college-bound youth. So the central issue remains: Is there a way, short of direct compulsion or unrealistic cash inducements, to attract a broad cross section of youth into the combat arms and related tasks? Or, put somewhat differently: Can we get an analogue of the peacetime draftee in the all-volunteer context?

I believe that the answer to this question is yes. One step would be a two-year enlistment option restricted to the combat arms, low-skill clerical duty, aircraft security guard positions, and labor-intensive jobs. The *quid pro quo* for such assignments would be general service educational benefits along the lines of the World War II GI Bill: a college education or vocational training in exchange for two years in the combat arms or its equivalent. This would be a way to attract highly qualified soldiers who could learn quickly, serve effectively for a full tour, and then be replaced by similarly qualified recruits. Because there would be no presumption of acquiring civilian skills in the military, the terms of such short service would be honest and unambiguous, alleviating a major source of postentry discontent in the All-Volunteer Force. Also, the added costs of postservice educational benefits should, in part at least, be balanced by lower attrition, reduced combat arms bonuses, and, most likely, fewer dependents for lower-ranking enlisted personnel.

To go one step further, the military could set up a two-track personnel system, recognizing a distinction between a citizen soldier and a career soldier. The career soldier would be assigned and compensated in the manner of the prevailing system. The citizen soldier, however, would serve a two-year term in labor-intensive positions with low active-duty pay; he would have few if any entitlements (for example, no marriage entitlements) but would have deferred compensation in the form of generous postservice educational or vocational training benefits. This would need to be linked with the reserve obligation, without which I don't think there's any way of salvaging the reserves.

Notice that in my remarks I am not innocent of financial inducements. I'm not saying that we're going to wave the flag and have everybody run in and join the Army. I'm talking about financial inducements of a different kind—but not the cash-work kind of financial inducement. Our immediate goal is to *break* the mind-set that sees the All-Volunteer Force in terms of a cash-work nexus.

Regarding the military as an occupation raises many other nagging issues about the future of the armed services. The All-Volunteer Force, as presently constituted, excludes enlisted participation by America's future leaders in government, business, and the intellectual community. Will enlisted service become viewed as a place for those who have no other options? Will career military people, as is already becoming apparent in the Army, acquire an increasingly distorted view of American youth and American civilian society in general? Rotating participation among middle-class youth would leaven the enlisted ranks and help reinvigorate the notion of military service as a widely shared citizens' duty. Notice that from my perspective the low cohort is a good, not a bad, thing. It's only bad if you take a labor-economics viewpoint. It's a good thing if you taken a voluntary service viewpoint, because it means a higher proportion of our youth would be serving, thus giving more legitimacy to the program as a whole. This would prevent the Army being labeled a recourse for dead-end youth, an unfair characterization which is hard to escape unless enlisted membership reflects a true cross section of American youth.

I'd like to take just a moment to digress somewhat on retention issues, which I think, by the way, are not directly related to recruitment issues. Many of these issues would still be with us, even if we did have a draft. For skilled technicians, for instance, we may have to think of some other kinds of schemes, like preservice education or higher salaries.

Today Congress has to concern itself with governmental policies which undercut the All-Volunteer Force and the notion of citizen service. I refer to the $4.5 billion presently given to college students in the form of federal grants or loans. In fact, it's surprising, given the current debate on providing governmental relief for middle-class families with children in college, that no public figure has thought to tie such student aid to service obligations on the part of the youth who benefit. It might be decided that no able-bodied person who has not performed national service should be eligible for federal student aid, CETA funds, or youth-training programs. Many of these programs already have a "need" criterion, but they don't really stand up to inspection. For instance, Basic Educational Opportunity grants, which next year will allow students $2,700 a year, are applicable to *two-thirds* of American families.

An overriding strategy should be to make governmental subsidy of youth programs consistent with the ideal that citizen obligation ought to become an essential part of growing up in America. The cupboard of those who view military manpower sheerly as an exercise in labor economics is bare. There are no more ideas in that cupboard. We must now go, I think to the public—to Congress—and admit candidly that the All-Volunteer Force is in trouble. Already the credibility of the Department of Defense is low with Congress precisely because we've been saying that everything is fine with the All-Volunteer Force. Quality is linked with quantity: the definition as well as the machinery of military selection needs overhauling. To realize this would clarify the military's role by emphasizing the larger calling of national service.

Thank you.

XIII

DISCUSSION

Richard Gabriel, Patricia Munch, and Alan Sabrosky

MARTIN ANDERSON: Thank you very much.

I think there's no question that we've had two very interesting and very stimulating papers by Professors Cooper and Moskos. There might be a few questions later on. We have three discussants and what I'd like to do now, if we can take the next thirty minutes at ten minutes apiece, is to move on to them.

Our first discussant is Richard Gabriel, who is professor of politics at St. Anselm's College.

RICHARD GABRIEL: It's interesting for me to be here—I'm one of the few political scientists in the group, as opposed to sociologists, economists, and lawyers.

What I'd like to do, very quickly, is to make a few comments about the two papers that were presented, and then suggest an idea that I think we really should have looked at in some detail, especially as there isn't a paper on the subject.

Let me begin by noting that Professor Friedman yesterday kept me up all night by asking me a simple question: Are there any approaches which are *not* at base economic? After staying up all night and thinking about that, my answer is: There had better be. This is because in any decision we're talking about the authoritative allocations of value, and in that sense we run the risk of falling into what I call the "Eichmannism" trap—of the value-free technician who will serve any master.

I think Professor Moskos's paper does us a service by reminding us that there are other criteria for determining values and decisions. One of those I would like to remind you of—and I think Charlie Moskos hits on this when he talks about representativeness—is *the* very basic question of warfare in a democracy: Who dies? That is what warfare is all about.

Moving on quickly to Professor Cooper's paper, again I note that reliance on economic models and analysis tends to miss a fundamental point in the debate on the All-Volunteer Force. And that is that certain social institutions address communal goals which have always been regarded as not being subject to strictly rational economic analysis, but rather accepted as costs borne out of special obligations related to notions of special law or the good of the folk, communitas, tribe, or society. In these instances the application of economic analysis doesn't help us much in answering the crucial question, Who dies?

Consider, for example, some of the other weaknesses of pure economic analysis that emerge. The argument about conscription being a tax seems to me to follow a pattern of economic analysis. It asks the question, "Who serves?" and ultimately, "Who dies?" and then says, "Well, we can frame that in dollars and cents terms." So, we say that just because we can do that we'll treat it as if it were a tax. Then the analysis proceeds, the words "as if" drop off, and what started off as an analogy ends up as a fact. The result, I believe, is that we end up attributing a pseudo-accuracy to economic models that do not exist. We forget the Humean injunction that logic compels logic; it does not compel reality. And as Professor Moskos noted to Professor Oi yesterday, a model that is not subject to specified conditions of disproof has only heuristic value. I have no objections to looking at the world *as if* conditions of economic equity, or whatever, obtained. I do have problems when we begin to forget the "as if" and suggest that the compulsions on our models are compulsions on reality.

My second point on Professor Cooper's paper relates to the dichotomy between efficiency and equity, and to the basis of choice. I have to ask: So what? We have a wide range of such programs, ranging from aid to the crippled, to aid to the aged, to public transit, where we have recognized that they are important enough to the common good that the question of efficiency must be temporarily laid aside.

The question of the draft and equity is a question of degree. I suggest to you that if we are going to resolve the question of equity versus efficiency, we should at least try to resolve it in terms of equity. That way, at least, the casualty rates of the poor, black, and cumulatively disadvantaged in any future war will not be as appalling as I believe they will otherwise be.

Finally, in response to Mr. Danzig's injunction last night that the volunteer army is a good one because it provides a spur and we need the time for change, I would say that we have had seven years. We have had the Gates Commission report, and the one thing that strikes me about that report is how wrong it was. Many, if not most, of the assumptions it made about supply and demand, about the kinds of people we could get, and about one-dimensional economic stimuli attracting multi-dimensional men like doctors and lawyers have not really worked out. The tendency has been not to reexamine our principles or promises, but rather to look for an economic "fix" and argue that if we add more dollars and more incentives we can make the All-Volunteer Force work.

Those are my comments on the papers.

Let me do now what I would like to have done if I had presented a paper: let me give you what my "bag" is.

My "bag" is this: The wartime goal of troops—and I'd like to remind you that the function of an army in an industrial democracy, as opposed to a totalitarian state or an emerging state, is to be a fighting mechanism, as Professor Gann reminded us yesterday—is to close with the enemy by combat maneuvers and destroy him. In my mind that means that Robert McNamara was wrong when he once suggested that if you take the 46,000 parts that comprise a Ford, no matter where you assemble it, or who assembles it, you end up with a Ford. If you take the 900 men needed to comprise a battalion, even if they have a high skill level, you do not end up with a battalion. A batallion is cemented together by other factors that are noneconomic and value-laden, that are essentially social, behavioral, and above all psychological.

What I'm suggesting to you is this: At the point that we went over to the All-Volunteer Force we adopted certain modalities, values, norms, and behaviors extracted directly from economic models and applied them to the military structure. As we began to apply the economic criteria of these models, like cost-effectiveness and the assumption about prices as economic stimuli, very gradually we began to erode the institutional supports binding the military force together under the terrible stress of combat. The result is that the ambiance and values of economic modeling have penetrated an organization—the military—whose effectiveness does not depend upon being rational and bureaucratic, but upon being premodern and predicated on the kinds of social actions Weber talks about.

What has happened, in my mind and my analysis, is that a series of structural changes has precipitated a series of deficiencies in the Army. If I had time, I could draw those specific linkages for you, but I don't. But I'd like to point out that if you analyze armies historically, and look at the U.S. Army today, a number of statistics indicate very clearly that that army will not fight. Personnel turbulence is too high, especially among officers who do not know their men. The up-or-out policy has turned our officers from leaders into managers. Let me tell you, you cannot manage men to their death: they will not go. Drug-use rates are ridiculously high. Twenty percent of the troops admit to the use of hashish at least five times a week;

9.5 percent of the troops are confirmed alcoholics; and 25 percent of our combat forces under the age of 21 are classified as problem drinkers. Trainability is a horror: 59 percent of the troops are in Category III-B or below.

When the Army did a 12-volume study on trainability, it found that out of eight basic tasks on its new readiness test the Army-wide average was 1.8 per MOS [Military Occupational Specialty]. The MOS shortfall is 42 percent, and 29 percent of our tank gunners cannot lase, fire, and track their guns. AWOLs and desertions are high. Attrition rates are ridiculous. Discipline is shot. A troop charged with drug use still has a 93 percent chance of getting an honorable discharge; and 95 percent of those charged with desertion stand a chance for an honorable discharge.

What we have done is to begin to dismantle the institutional supports which make an army in the field effective as a fighting force. And the primary stimulus for that dismantling has been the emulation of economics—the absorption of the values, behavior, and ambiance of economic modeling.

In my view, focusing on the man in combat as economically one-dimensional is wrong. We have asked the wrong question. The question is: What makes an effective *combat* force? That is the question to be addressed, and whenever we wish to make a change in what we know or in our models of a combat force's effectiveness, we must ask: Is the cost-effectiveness, in terms of dollars saved, worth it in terms of the trade-off we make in combat effectiveness?

As an example, this query was put to a member of the Department of Defense testifying before the Senate: "You want to rephrase DOPMA [Defense Organization Planning and Mobilization Act] — you want to change the Army Officer Corps in its structure and function. I have a question. Have you done a study and an analysis on what this will do to combat effectiveness and the ability of troops to maintain cohesion?" The answer from that official was that that was an irrelevant question.

So I suggest the following. I suggest that we follow the advice of Isaac Bashevis Singer. He said: Never debate; go on and raise another point. We need to rework the question. In my view, we must develop a model and a definition of what makes an army combat-effective. I think we can do that. Then we must use that model as a standard with which to analyze and decide whether to adopt certain economic or cost-effective policies. It will do us absolutely no good if the army we commit to the field is cost-effective, cheap, and even representative but ends up in the enemy's camps. Thank you.

MARTIN ANDERSON: I think you may have stimulated some questions. Our next discussant is Patricia Munch, who is an economist at the Rand

Corporation. This year she is on leave from Rand and is a National Fellow at the Hoover Institution.

PATRICIA MUNCH: I won't pretend to answer the questions raised by the previous discussant.

The authors of these two papers differ substantially on everything—their facts, their criteria used in evaluating them, and their policy conclusions.

I'll deal first with the disagreement over the facts—over the extent of change in the socioeconomic composition of the services with the move from the draft to the All-Volunteer Force. To some extent this difference is due to selection of different bases for comparison. Charlie Moskos focuses exclusively on the Army and uses educational attainment as a measure of quality. If we base the comparison on all four services—as Rick Cooper does—and use aptitude test scores rather than educational attainment as the measure of quality, the apparent change in socioeconomic composition of the military is reduced.

However, I do not wish to argue that there has been no change in socioeconomic composition. If there had been a free market for buying deferments, one would expect to have seen no change in socioeconomic composition with the shift to the All-Volunteer Force. To the extent that there was a market, but a less than perfect market, one would expect to see a change. So the change in socioeconomic composition is really only a measure of imperfection in the market for deferments.

Assuming that we could agree on the extent of change in representativeness of the force, what would that tell us? Charlie Moskos concludes that "experience to date has shown that the market system is not the way to recruit an all-volunteer army," that "surveys show that pay motivates less-qualified youth . . . to join the armed services while having a negligible effect on college-bound youth," and that therefore the All-Volunteer Force has not failed in general, but has failed selectively to attract more qualified personnel. Charlie interprets the evidence as a differential response to the same stimulus. Implicit in this conclusion, however, is the assumption that the All-Volunteer Force introduced an equal change in the incentive to enlist for all groups in society—that is, that the differential response is due to different elasticities of supply for the different groups. But you cannot measure supply elasticities without knowing the change in wage rates; and no evidence is produced to show that the All-Volunteer Force increased military pay by the same amount relative to civilian pay for all groups. I have no evidence on that point, but strongly suspect that the relative pay increase was larger for the less-skilled. Not surprisingly, their response was greater. In the absence of information on relative pay changes for different groups, then, we cannot conclude that the supply elasticity of more educated personnel is lower. We certainly cannot conclude that it is zero and that the desired degree of representativeness could not be achieved by *some* change in pay.

We also cannot conclude, as Charlie does, that the desired increase in high-quality recruits could be obtained at less cost by offering educational rather than cash inducements. The cost of using educational incentives would certainly be higher, if only because educational incentives would not be attractive to those smart enough to be considered desirable for purposes of representativeness but too smart to want to go on to college—that is, those who would value the benefits of a college education at less than even its discounted cash value.

Before leaving this question of relative supply elasticities I'd like to point out that even if the All-Volunteer Force experience did demonstrate lower supply elasticities for those from higher socioeconomic groups, that would imply that the implicit tax on those groups imposed by randomized conscription would correspondingly higher. In other words, there is a one-to-one correspondence between the budget cost of achieving a representative force and the discrimination implicit in a conscription tax. The higher an individual's reservation wage to induce enlistment, the higher the tax if forced to enlist.

Assuming there were agreement on what the evidence showed about the representativeness of the All-Volunteer Force, the next issue is, so what? Is this good, bad, or indifferent? Or by what criteria should we evaluate it?

Both authors recognized two criteria—efficiency and equity—and on both they differ in their conclusions. Again, this is partially due to different assumptions. On the efficiency question, Rick Cooper is concerned with the efficient use of resources from the standpoint of the economy as a whole, whereas Charlie Moskos focuses exclusively on the Army. Focusing as he does just on the Army, his conclusion is inescapable: the All-Volunteer Army would be better served by attracting more high school graduates, or, even better, college-bound youth—that is, a more representative cross section of American youth. I cannot disagree. The Army would be better served, but at the expense of the rest of the economy.

It remains to be demonstrated why one should be exclusively concerned with maximizing the productivity of the Army. Even if national defense receives a very high weight in some societal objective function, the Army is only one input to the production of defense, and it is not clear that you would increase total defense productivity by transferring skills and manpower to the Army enlisted force from, say, weapons production in the civilian sector.

Charlie Moskos's concern for representativeness is based more on consideration of equity than that of efficiency. Equity is roughly defined as an equal sharing of the burden of defense. It is further defined as equal representation of different socioeconomic classes in the military. I have to take issue with several key assumptions underlying this notion of equity.

First, the notion that enlistment in a volunteer force is an assumption of a burden is a misuse of words, at the very least. The enlistee who enlists voluntarily, by revealed preference, prefers this choice to his alternatives. In no sense is it burdensome. The use of the word "service" to describe enlistment in a voluntary military is a misnomer, an unfortunate carryover of concepts from the draft era. Volunteer military service is no more a service than being a college professor is professional service.

Second, the notion of representativeness by socioeconomic class seems to me totally without merit. In what sense have I discharged *my* duty more if someone else with my income and education enlists than if someone five-foot tall enlists? Equality of distribution by class may make sense if all in a class are affected, but not if only some are. This point has been made by others with respect to the cohort as a whole. It applies equally to specific classes within the cohort.

Third, the assumption that equal conscripted time in the military implies an equal burden across socioeconomic classes is only one quite arbitrary definition of equality. As I said before, to the extent that military service is nonvoluntary, the tax imposed by conscription differs among individuals depending on the difference between their military and civilian wages and on their preference for civilian life. Randomized conscription at equal wages is a higher tax on those with higher civilian alternatives. It is equality by one criterion, but discrimination by another.

Fourth, the suggestion that if educational or monetary inducements were successfully used to increase enlistment of more qualified personnel, the burden would thereby be spread more evenly—is simply false. The result of such a system would be to transfer income to middle-income, high-quality individuals, not away from them. Prior to tinkering with the system, these individuals' military alternatives were dominated by their civilian opportunities. Now you improve their military opportunities such that these opportunities dominate their civilian alternatives. These individuals are thereby better off overall than they were prior to the subsidies introduced in the name of equalizing the burden. Incidentally, so also are college professors, due to the increase in the demand for their services. This transfer to middle-class youth and college professors is achieved at the expense of taxpayers in general.

Finally, even if one wants to ensure equal contribution to the cost of defense, there is a tendency in discussing a volunteer versus a conscripted army to ignore the fundamental point that everyone can gain by separating the issues of income distribution and production. We can distribute the burden of paying for defense in any way we like through the tax system. This can be a head tax on the whole population, on 18-year-old men, on 18-year-old men and women, and so on. Given the selected distribution of the burden, *everyone* is better off if we use the market to select those who will produce the chosen level of defense at lowest cost—that is, those who have a comparative advantage in this occupation due to their skills, preferences for risk, or other factors.

If everyone can gain from using the market to procure defense, why is there any talk of returning to a draft? Apparently only for the same reason that income distribution effected through the political process is often done in kind rather than cash: simply that it is politically easier to achieve because the true distributional impact is concealed.

MARTIN ANDERSON: Thank you. Our third and last discussant is Alan Sabrosky, associate professor of politics at Catholic University and coauthor of *The International Security Review*.

ALAN SABROSKY: Since this seems to be one of those occasions when I have a very hard taskmaster in terms of time, I'm actually going to make a serious effort to keep my comments within the ten-minute framework. I'm also happy that some of my predecessors have managed to blunt some of the effect of the teeth of the lions, so perhaps as I go through what I have to say some of your appetite will already have been assuaged by my colleagues.

A friend of mine once told me that when you get a sociologist, an economist, and a political scientist together to discuss a question like this, the sociologist always asks, Is it equitable? The economist asks, Is it cost-effective? And the political scientist tends to ask: Can it fight?

I suspect all of these concerns are justifiable. Since I am a political scientist, however, my inclination obviously is to phrase these questions in terms of the ability of the military institution to function as a politically reliable and militarily effective instrument of policy. That is simply a tendency my ten years of enlisted service in the Marine Corps has reinforced.

I'm particularly intrigued that in this conference we seem to be discussing both the feasibility and the desirability of the All-Volunteer Force. Those were also the two major issues talked about earlier in the 1970s when we began addressing the question of whether we should move to an All-Volunteer Force and wondered if it could succeed. For a period of a few years in the mid-1970s, the question of the desirability of an All-Volunteer Force almost appeared to be considered moot. It seemed to be assumed not only by supporters but also by most of those thinking about the volunteer-force concept that if we got the numbers we needed, the force would be working. I think Charlie Moskos's question yesterday—whether it's possible to disconfirm the success of the All-Volunteer Force so long as we *are* getting the numbers we need—did not receive an adequate response, which suggests that this attitude is still prevalent.

I'm going to take this opportunity, as the final discussant on the final panel of the conference, to address some of the issues raised in both Cooper's and Moskos's papers which touched on some of the core issues in the All-Volunteer Force we've been dealing with here. Rather than burden you with descriptive statistics on any of these points (I assume everyone has either been listening or has read the papers, or both), I'm simply going to talk about some of their implications for the All-Volunteer Force that we have.

I think we ought to examine more explicitly what considerations are truly to be taken into account when we appraise, at the beginning of the 1980s, what we are to do with the All-Volunteer Force. There are some obvious issues: quantity, quality, turbulence, and attrition.

First, quantity. Sure, if you break up the All-Volunteer Force into the active force, selective reserve, and Individual Ready Reserve, you can paint a very different picture in each one of those cases.If you focus explicitly on the active force, you can say, yes, the All-Volunteer Force is succeeding. The only problem with this is that when you consider the *total* force concept, which presupposes that all three components—active, selective reserve, and Individual Ready Reserve—are maintained with levels of sufficiently qualified personnel to allow them to perform their designated missions, you cannot in fact say that the All-Volunteer Force concept has succeeded. One part has succeeded reasonably well; a second part, marginally well; and the third part, not at all. I have rarely seen a tripod stand on one and a half legs.

Second, quality. We've seen changes in the quality of the All-Volunteer Force. What we essentially have, particularly in the ground forces (in the Army and the Marine Corps) is a situation in which less-sophisticated, less-qualified personnel are having to deal with more sophisticated weapons technology. The question is whether or not that is a concern if, having begun to regress to the mean of category III-B, we are reducing the net effectiveness of the armed forces simply by increasing the discontinuities between sophistication of personnel and sophistication of the weaponry they need to use.

An equally important element of quality—since no one, I think, is ever terribly satisfied with looking at a high school diploma or other mental-group ranking as the sole indicator of quality (we use them as surrogates because we have little else)—is the important question of motivation. We need to ask not simply whether a person is educated, or even intelligent, but whether he *wants* to be a soldier or sailor or air person or Marine. Does he want to do it? Can he perform? If you consider the mixed conscript/volunteer force during the Vietnam War, you do find significant increases in educational attainment and mental-group ranking, owing to the conscription of college-educated individuals and an increase in their numbers entering the reserves during this period. But they were also the focus of most of the political opposition to the war within the military and one of the principal sources of disciplinary problems. I would suspect that highly intelligent, well-educated individuals who saw the reserves as a means of avoiding active military service, and whose political predispositions were not supportive of the military policy, could not be considered to have produced a quality force, *whatever* their level of academic attainment or mental-group rank.

As far as personnel classes are concerned, attrition and turbulence were once very bad, though clearly they are down now. I think Charlie Moskos may even have understated the case at one point when he said the thing was so bad in the early seventies that it had to get better. For a year or two there —around 1972 or 1973—we weren't at all certain things were going to get better. There were some very clear arguments in many circles, from such people as Dave Landau and Dave Cartright, that the situation in many of the units in the armed forces was in fact extremely precarious. The worst years for the Army were the last years of its experience with a conscript force—1971 and 1972. The worst years for the Marine Corps were 1974 and 1975, when the desertion and unauthorized absence rate for a time soared to over 300 per thousand. And we've already heard described the situation for the Navy, which has become progressively worse over time.

Nonetheless, things seem to have gotten better, though they have *not* improved following any clear pattern. There are some interesting trends, but they are independent of the manpower procurement system. That is, the fact that you happen to have volunteers or conscripts doesn't necessarily mean that that should produce differential rates of attrition or differential rates of disciplinary problems within the military itself. These things are a function of the way personnel are managed in the military; they involve the motivation of the personnel and the degree of discipline, training, morale, and leadership. To attribute a specific degree of first-term attrition or disciplinary problems to the manpower procurement system, be it volunteer, selective service, or something else, I think substantially misperceives the problem.

Another problem is obviously cost. I was intrigued by Rick Cooper's analysis suggesting that a volunteer system is actually more cost-effective than a selective service system. Whether it's true or not, I think that our major concern with the high absolute cost of manpower today means that there's a reduction in resources available for training and operations. In the case of the Marine Corps, for example, whereas all individuals graduating from basic training were once sent to advanced infantry training at

Camp Lejeune or Camp Pendleton, today that is not the case. Only those going into the infantry are sent on this way. The reason for this, I was told last October at the recruit depot in San Diego, is that there simply isn't the money and resources anymore to do more than that: it costs too much to recruit personnel, it costs too much to train them, et cetera.

Third is the question of equity and representativeness. I've always been intrigued when this issue is raised because there is a clear historical linkage between the equity or representativeness of a military institution on the one hand and its combat performance on the other.

The American military has never been representative of the society. In fact, I would suspect that with rare exceptions, such as ancient Greece and contemporary Israel, military institutions are rarely representative of their societies. Does that lack of representativeness or lack of equity in the institution mean it cannot perform well? I would suggest not. Certainly the fact that many elite military institutions and organizations in history have been noticeably *un*representative and noticeably *in*equitable in terms of selection and recruitment suggests that the notion of equity, whatever its political utility or political significance in the United States, isn't necessarily a *military* consideration that ought to be taken into account.

The obvious question we raise is, Why should equity or representativeness be a military consideration? Why is the question of equity, and specifically representativeness, important to us? Obviously, as I think everyone here recognizes and as several presentations have pointed out, it reflects the disproportionate representation of blacks in the American military and, specifically, their concentration in the ground combat arms. There are three concerns here that people often talk about. One is that it is wrong for those who have been historically most disadvantaged to have to defend the society, if a term as light as "disadvantaged" can even be appropriate for describing two and a half centuries of slavery. But there's a more important concern, the political one: What happens if you *use* such a military establishment and begin finding casualties proportionate to representation in the military as opposed to society—if you have infantry units coming back with 35 percent to 40 percent black fatalities? Is this politically sensitive? *Very.*

The real question concerning representativeness, however, is one that very few people talk about in a public context, and that is reliability. The crux of the problem is a concern that black soldiers in the future would have a greater loyalty to the black community than to the Army if a recurrence of the "long, hot summers" of the 1960s should once again require the use of federal troops to restore order. I think most sociologists and economists would recognize and agree that problems in many of the urban ghettos in the United States today are not significantly better than they were 15 years ago. For example, there is an unemployment rate approaching 45 percent to 50 percent in cities such as Washington, D.C., among teenage black youth. Crime rates are high. There are increasing numbers of single-parent families. None of this suggests a significant amelioration of the problem in the near future. The obvious concern with troops from this background is: Could you trust the unit? Personally, I think one could, if cohesion is high, and if there is good leadership, good morale, and good discipline.

But all of that, I think, touches the heart of the problem—and that's the question of the cohesion of the institution. Cohesion in our forces today, I suspect, no matter how one defines it, is certainly not what we might expect and certainly not what we might wish. Turbulence is down, but in part this is due to a reduction in stress and in the demands of training. That is, the military institution has in many respects decided that high rates of disciplinary problems and high rates of desertion and unauthorized absence are unacceptable, and one of the ways that problem can be dealt with is simply to reduce the demands placed upon personnel. We've found that less stress generally means there will be fewer people engaged in acts of noncompliance.

Motivation in the forces is clearly down, as Charlie Moskos and others pointed out. Not only is the institutional ethos in the All-Volunteer Force more occupational; I suspect that most of the minor remedies proposed to deal with the problems of the All-Volunteer Force only tinker with the system and reinforce the occupational image while adding to its cost.

In sum, when we look at the future of the All-Volunteer Force I think one of the things that we clearly ought to do is to recognize that the situation is difficult and that it's not appropriate to finesse it simply by focusing on the political sensitivity of making significant reappraisals of the institution. In the trade-off, it's a question of capabilities versus compulsion. That is: What do we need? How many people do we need in the military, and, specifically, in the ground combat arms, to fulfill our missions and requirements? And, are volunteers militarily preferable?

I think that if you look at the relationship between missions and requirements, as was briefly pointed out yesterday, the requirement to maintain, for example, 24 divisions in the Army's active and reserve structure is basically predicated on a single mission requirement: that the United States could wage a protracted, high-intensity war against the Soviet Union in Europe. This is an interesting idea, though not one which I consider terribly likely. I suspect that the notion that we ought not think about such things— that we should allow force requirements, and therefore manpower requirements and the demands on the system, to be dictated by modern counterparts of cavalry generals and battleship admirals—is not terribly appropriate, and that a smaller, more highly disciplined, and professional force that will allow us to fulfill our missions is certainly feasible.

Finally, we need to ask: Are volunteers militarily preferable? Personally, I think so. Theoretically, I think that volunteers can be disciplined and trained more rigorously, and with less public opposition, than can conscripts; the finding that disciplinary problems increased as we moved to a voluntary force may have been an anomaly. And potentially, I think that using volunteers would cause less public opposition, particularly in very difficult conflict situations in the Third World, than would be the case if we used conscripts.

In view of these considerations, I think the All-Volunteer Force can be retained, at reduced levels, and with a more effective force.

MARTIN ANDERSON: Thank you.

XIV

GENERAL DISCUSSION AND QUESTIONS FROM THE FLOOR

BERNARD ROTSKER: I'd like to make a personal observation to strengthen the comments of the last discussant, though they hardly need strengthening.

I've just spent the last two and a half years as Principal Deputy Assistant Secretary of the Navy for Manpower and Reserve Affairs, and was struck by the fact that so many of our military problems today have nothing to do with our manpower procurement mechanism.

It is almost an historic accident that high attrition came at a time we were in an all-volunteer force. I would suggest that this is much more related to the conditions of military service today, which are vastly different from what they were in the late sixties and early seventies. Our fleet today—and I speak from my personal experience in the Navy—is roughly half the size of the fleet that existed ten years ago, and is being worked at unprecedented levels of operations and inspections.

If you look at things like attrition in the Navy, they are almost totally related to the power plant—to boiler technicians and machinists mates, who are all tied into the inspection schedules, 80-hour-plus work weeks at sea, 60-hour-plus work weeks at shore, and career force personnel shortages resulting in abnormally large requirements in the first-term forces. This results in a lack of leadership for the first-term force, feeding back upon itself through attrition.

Neither can the fact that career retention is severely down be related to the procurement policy for initial first-term personnel. We used to talk about a lock-in into the career force after the first enlistment, but then it went out to eight years, then ten years. Today we're losing sizable numbers of careerists at the twelve-year point, and I would submit that that's much more related to the conditions of service than to any procurement strategy that we have.

I have one specific question for Charlie Moskos, and I would also like to make an observation.

I'm prepared to agree completely that in the matrix that Charlie has proposed the optimal world is one of a representative all-volunteer force. But I would also like to suggest that in Professor Gabriel's sense Charlie's cupboard is bare, more bare than the economists' cupboard. He proposes a two-year enlistment with a strong educational component that would be grabbed up by middle-class people who would make the military truly representative. During the last year, in fact, that idea has been tested out by the services, and has been found to be wanting. Also, tests in the reserve forces in the early seventies in which reduced commitments were tried out did not bring in the middle class to anything like this extent.

The whole question of educational benefits, I think, deserves a great deal more study. If you look at the actual figures for the reduced program, the VEAP [Veterans Educational Assistance Program], you'll find it was the lower mental groups with *less* education that took those benefits while they were in service, not the higher mental groups. Similarly, if you look at the GI Bill, you'll find that it was not the mythical veteran who came out of World War II and went to Harvard who exercised those benefits when the bill was changed. In fact, that was one reason why the bill was changed. Instead, you'll find the persons in lower mental groups getting ripped off by programs of dubious quality. There have, for example, been studies of the off-duty education program, and it has been severely criticized for a lack of quality control. This is a problem that neither the Veterans Administration nor the Department of Health, Education and Welfare has been able to control, and the Office of Management and Budget was quite insistent on control whenever the Navy did in fact propose increased educational benefits.

So I think that the burden of proof is clearly on Charlie [Moskos] to demonstrate that a two-year enlistment with a strong educational component is a viable alternative.

MARTIN ANDERSON: Is that your question for Charlie? [Laughter.]

BERNARD ROTSKER: Yes, thank you.

CHARLES MOSKOS: I might preface this by saying that Bernie Rotsker made the interesting point yesterday that the U.S. Department of Labor will not give credit to employment counselors who place a youth in military service. An element of my proposal is that we have to really do something dramatic: to change this we'd have to restrict all or a great part of the Department of Health, Education and Welfare's $4.5 billion now allotted for student aid to those who perform national service. This was a crucial part of my proposal—something that would be on the 5:30 news; something that would make headlines in the newspapers: "Youth Plans Will Change."

What we have now are projects being developed in the Army which offer educational and other kinds of bonuses. Whereas these are steps in the right direction, they don't change the mind-set of today's high school youth. They're still unknown by most people. One almost has to walk in the recruiting door before you know that they exist.

Even at this level—with the more generous programs now being implemented—you have to be a Philadelphia lawyer to figure out what bonuses come with which requirements, they're so complicated.

All of that is not going to work. What will work is going to have to be shy of going back to the draft, but something ultra, ultra dramatic.

Why do I argue that educational benefits will attract middle-class kids? One is that experiments which have been done heretofore have not really been recruiting programs. I know there are pros and cons, but the very fact that they were experiments meant that they were not widely known and did not become part of the mind-set of high school seniors or their parents. There was a surge of high-quality recruiting in the last quarter of 1976 to make the deadline before expiration of the GI Bill. So at a point where people could vote with their feet, they did vote with their feet.

At the very time that the Vietnam GI Bill expired—and that was a very stingy GI Bill, I might add—we began exponentially expanding these Department of Health, Education and Welfare federal education grants. Let me also say that these need-based programs never stand up to inspection. I have a small survey, taken at Northwestern University, which is at least suggestive of youths who would be the hardest group one could consider trying to recruit: the top 10 percent of their high school class, upper-middle class, 1300 on the SATs, one-third Jewish, 80 percent going on to graduate school. I got the idea to do this survey after a hand poll at the University of Chicago, that seat of libertarian economic thinking. I asked a sample of 300 kids if they would join the Army either in the couple of years after graduating or during their tour at Northwestern University. One hundred percent said no: 0 percent would join. Then I asked, would you join the Army at $1000 a month? Two percent said maybe. Would you join at $2500 a month? Eleven percent said maybe, or that they would be likely to do that. Would you join the Army at $5000 a month? And close to 40 percent said they would join. Then I asked if they would join the Army for four years of tuition plus a $500 a month stipend—the amount allowed by the GI Bill of World War II. And the response was almost identical to that for the *$5000-a-month salary.*

The point is that there is something else operating here with that kind of reward, even though anybody knows that when you make $60,000 a year for two years you can save up a lot more than if you're just on this kind of tuition-plus-stipend system. The *tuition* in the tuition-plus system is crucial in this, rather than just a straight stipend as in the Korean and Vietnam programs.

We've already dribbled away $4.5 billion for people who don't serve, and now people can rip the system off four times: (1) they don't serve; (2) they get a government subsidized loan; (3) they don't pay it back; and (4) they go work for HEW. We've created a system which discourages the military as an opportunity for gaining educational benefits.

This does not, of course, address the retention question—how many of those who go in for two years become careerists—which requires a different kind of and more imagination. I think most of the beauty in my proposal comes from the all-win situation in that it would not distinguish between category III-As and above, as we're already offering modest educational benefits to certain selective groups with either high school diplomas, or category III-As or above in the Army. These benefits would be across the board, and everybody would at least get an equal crack at them.

These are the kind of data I refer to. We have to get the HEW money to become an issue. There's already been talk of a tax credit: Moynihan's proposal last year of a $500 tax credit for middle-class families to send their kids to college. Maybe in an election year it will pass.

Again, my point is that by doing that, we'll dribble away billions of dollars for a purpose counterproductive to service recruitment goals.

BERNARD ROTSKER: I would find that hardly sustaining, Charlie.

RICHARD HUNTER: Five hundred dollars a month is more than we are now paying a recruit while he works for us. We've only recently been trying, and unsuccessfully, to get E-2 pay for *trained* people, *up to* $500 a month. You're proposing to give them $500 a month for four years at school for serving only two years. so you're really giving them $1000 a month— doubling the current pay and throwing tuition in on top of that. That might attract some people we're not now attracting. [Laughter.]

CHARLES MOSKOS: Dick, talk to any high school seniors. They just don't know about these programs. That's the real issue. There has to be a national educational campaign to let our target people know what's available. Something very dramatic is going to have to be done to save the All-Volunteer Force. Just tinkering is not going to do it.

RICHARD HUNTER: I don't think we're tinkering. I think what we're doing is working. I'd like to reactivate Richard [Danzig's] statement from last night: we don't want to leap before we look, and I think what we're doing now is looking. This is productive.

Richard [Gabriel], you brought to mind something that I hadn't thought of since I passed age 40. A little over 20 years ago, when I was in flight training, our boss, who was a commander, came down, lined us all up and said, "Everybody dies. All of you are going to die. The question is when and why." He then had us count off in threes and hold hands in a circle. And he said, "If you become an aviator, a Naval aviator, one out of three of you, one out of each of that little triangle, is going to die before you reach age 40. If you're fortunate enough to have a war, two of you will die. And in old age that poor fellow who's left will have to know that he was denied the opportunity of giving his life for something worthwhile." You see, that's patriotism.

RICHARD GABRIEL: That's really not patriotism.

RICHARD HUNTER: I assumed that I was not going to reach age 40, and I structured my life-insurance programs and all those things based on that assumption. [Laughter.] The day I reached age 40 and it came to mind, I went back and checked my flight class. He was off by one person. Two-thirds of us are dead. That's part of patriotism.

So I'm going to be one of those old guys who's going to have to worry he's not given his life for a useful purpose, although sometimes I'm not sure but that I might get killed in the storm around this issue. [Laughter.]

The question you raise that I think is most important is whether the All-Volunteer Force will fight or not. Again, I have a little political science background as well as a little economics background, and even have a wife who's a sociologist who keeps me honest. But my political science background tells me that every generation, all the way back to Cicero, has wondered about whether the youth of its generation would fight: World War II people weren't glorious like the men at Verdun, who weren't as brave as those who charged up San Juan Hill, who weren't anything like those brave souls at Gettysburg; and those boys at Gettysburg just didn't compare to the brave boys at Valley Forge. It's the past wars that are glorious; a current war is fought by the scum of the earth for whom you have to have sabres to beat them up to the line. That's why officers have sabres, so they can keep the troops up to the line.

I think the current force *will* fight if we have to fight. I think the current generation is as patriotic as any generation I have met. I have seen that in my visits to the campuses in the last month, with the problems in Iran.

The issue in manning the force comes down to a lot of things we've talked about. I would only ask: How do you come back to structuring the alternatives against what we do? I think we ought to focus this debate on that, instead of the way it's been going.

ALAN SABROSKY: Two quick comments, if I might, on that.

One, when you talk about these historical analogies—every generation saying the previous wars were the hard ones and now you've got the trash of the world, et cetera—now, occasionally, that's true. In the late 1930s people said that the French soldiers weren't as good and efficient, and not as likely to fight, as those in World War I. And, you know, they were right.

RICHARD HUNTER: Well, at least the French officers weren't brave enough to keep fighting. They decided to compromise. They decided to live instead of die.

ALAN SABROSKY: Sometimes when you make these selective comparisons, unfortunately, you find that armies do occasionally collapse internally. We had a case in 1975 which ought to have been instructive to us.

RICHARD HUNTER: We had the case in the United States in 1967 to 1970 where we collapsed and quit fighting a war. We quit.

COMMENT FROM THE AUDIENCE: We had the draft then.

ALAN SABROSKY: More to the point, though, I think it's not so much a function of what we're talking about today—individual patriotism or individual competence—but whether or not our forces are *collectively* efficient and reliable. My concern is less with individual skills, intelligence, or even individual patriotism, than it is with whether what we are doing to recruit, maintain, and manage our forces is in fact producing a collectively efficient military institution. As for individual efficiency and reliability, I think I would agree with you. But as for collective efficiency and reliability, I have very serious reservations, and I think Charlie Moskos's work shows that very clearly.

RICHARD HUNTER: I agree with you, Alan. My concern is not for the United States military. My concern is for the United States society. That's the issue. If the glue's there, we'll stick it out. But with the attitude, you know, of fighting inflation now but taking it out of somebody else's paycheck, we can't even close a military base around here when we don't need one.

RICHARD GABRIEL: I want to make two points. One goes back to Charlie's point about the extent to which the society has rigged the rules to make recruitment of the better classes less likely. I think there's one additional indication of the extent to which the rules were rigged, and perhaps the general who's in charge of recruitment who is here could respond to this. It's been my understanding that the extent to which recruiters are allowed into certain kinds of high schools to recruit is very limited. For example, all the schools in Manchester, New Hampshire, which is a working-class mill town, are open to recruiters. But in the suburbs—Bedford, Derry, and so forth—which contain what we call Boston Farmers, the middle-class schools are closed to recruiters.

Now I've been told by the Association of the U.S. Army—though I do not have any hard data on this—that only 37 percent of American high schools are open to recruiters. I don't know if that's true, but *if* it's true, it's some indication of the extent to which our society is rigging the rules to keep the All-Volunteer Force from working.

Dick, I don't think we really disagree. We've been around this barn a lot of times, but I think it's interesting to point out that your concern is mine: *Will* that force *fight*? I also agree with you that there is a whole range of problems inflicted on our force that are not really connected with methods of acquisition. I'm not suggesting that a conscript army would be better than the All-Volunteer Army—at least not *a priori*.

Two years ago I raised three questions with Bill Hauser: Do we know the requirements of an ideal soldier? Do we know the requirements of cohesiveness and battle effectiveness? The answers, two years ago, were *no*. And, correct me if I'm wrong, but the answers today at the Army Research Institute are still no. All I am suggesting is that perhaps we've utilized the single cost-effectiveness mode of analysis for too long. What we must now begin to do, I think, is to recognize the sterility of a single factor analysis which results in a picture of a uni-dimensional man, *homo economicus*, or, as I prefer it, *homo lupus*, and begin to reverse the equation. This is essential in my view because the indicators of incohesion and potential combat ineffectiveness are there.

What I suggest is this: Let's first design a task force to answer those three crucial questions I asked Bill Hauser. Then, when we have our models, let's use them as a basis for analysis. Then, whenever the economists want to make a change on the basis of dollars, we will at least have a standard for the other side of the equation to use as a comparison. If it is true that saving a few bucks does not affect battle effectiveness or cohesion, then by all means let's save them. But if it is equally true that saving a few dollars means spending lives on beaches, then, I say, let's spend the dollars.

Let's at least raise the question. Let's follow the advice of Isaac Bashevis Singer, and stop the debate in midstream, because it's not going anywhere. Let's restructure it and rephrase the question. Let's look at the All-Volunteer Force in terms of what it's *supposed* to do—*fight*, be an instrument of collective social violence. In my view, right now it can't do that.

ARLEN JAMESON: I just want to make a comment I think goes to the heart of the problem, and that is peace. When you talk about readiness, and about the problems of training to a razor-sharp edge, you have to realize that it's like being on a football team or baseball team that trains week after week with a coach who says, occasionally, that he *thinks* there's going to be a game; but it may or may not come up. Soon the conditions of those practices are bound to decline. I think that talk about unit cohesion being important doesn't get us anywhere. It's a leadership and conditions-of-service problem I think Bernie Rostker is talking about, and there's apparently a lack of reality here, a scarcity of people who've been out talking with those units around the world. I have a hard time tracking what is said here about unwillingness to fight versus what is actually the case. I think it's a disservice to say these things until you can really demonstrate them.

RICHARD GABRIEL: What you've been talking about is one person's impression. I would say statistically, however, that if you talked to a few great officers in the Army today, you would find you are in the minority, by a factor of five to one, on that kind of question. People are very, very concerned at the senior NCO level, at the field grade level, and at the company grade level about whether these men will fight. Remember, you also have to talk about Air Force versus Army. We've been concentrating here on the Army, because this is where most of the problems are. I think all of us agree that the situation in the Air Force is qualitatively different. Steven Westmark at West Point did a correlation study on survey data concerning alienation of volunteer troops and their performance in peacetime, and found a high correlation between the extraordinary degree of alienation among many of our all-volunteer soldiers in combat units and their performance. You just can't talk around it.

ARLEN JAMESON: The Marines I've seen coming out of Iran and talking about it don't give me the sense they're not willing to fight. I don't think there's any indication of that at all.

ANTONIA CHAYES: I think you glorify the Air Force a bit too much. Yes, we do have quality recruits, but we're losing pilots and we're losing experienced supervisors.

I would put the problem a little differently from Dirk [Arlen Jameson], but I think the game analogy is an interesting one. The fact is, if we are at peace and it appears that we are not going to war or not participating in any regional conflict, we've got to recognize that we are going to be moving towards the occupational model. It's very hard to keep an institutional model together for a game that isn't played by a generation of military personnel. For that reason I think that your solution, Charlie—and it's a solution I like very much—is, despite your analysis, a recognition of the occupational model. Even though you deplore that model, I think you have to go the next step and recognize our military personnel are a very precious trained resource that we have to *pay* for because they have other occupational choices.

I think also, Professor Gabriel, though I'm very much moved by what you say, that it is very hard to achieve unit cohesion when all you do is exercise year after year after year. That's a game that never gets played. (Not that I'm advocating war, mind you.) [Laughter.]

RICHARD GABRIEL: Sure, I understand that. But armies in history have remained at peace for enormous periods of time. The Roman army remained combat-effective for a hundred years, as did the 435-year garrison of Britain.

One other point: you wanted some evidence that they will not fight. I'll cite one piece: a CBS poll taken last year at the tip of the lance in the Berlin brigade. Fifty-three percent of the troops said they would not follow their officers or their NCOs into combat. Agreed, that's only one unit, but I suspect it's a very deep feeling in the Army.

ANTONIA CHAYES: They hadn't heard the fire.

RICHARD GABRIEL: They may run when they do.

COMMENT FROM THE AUDIENCE: It is true we need to look at cost-effectiveness, but the other side of the equation is whether the force is effective or not. I'm a labor economist, and I don't think my cupboard's quite bare either. In most occupations it's very easy to tell whether someone's effective or not: You observe that the person hasn't been fired, so you assume he's doing what's required of him. What you seem to be saying is that there is no similar standard for evaluation in the military. What I'd like to know is what would you accept as evidence short of fighting a full-scale war and winning it, that our troops *are* effective?

CHARLES MOSKOS: They do quit. It's called attrition.

AUDIENCE: The fact that they quit doesn't mean they weren't effective. It just means they didn't want to be there.

CHARLES MOSKOS: People are also fired from the Army and, by and large, the reason a soldier is booted out of the Army is that he isn't being effective. The command structure combines to make these decisions. Whether the guy quits or gets fired, or whatever, it's very much correlated with educational background. There's no way of turning it around. All of the services report the same finding: a person with a high school diploma does twice as well in terms of completing his service. You can't just talk around a finding like that.

AUDIENCE: Okay, fair enough. But, of those who are left in the military, are they worth anything? You're suggesting that maybe they aren't.

RICHARD GABRIEL: My guess is that many of them are, of course, but also that many of them are not.

AUDIENCE: What's your evidence?

RICHARD GABRIEL: One of the pieces of evidence I have about those who remain in the Army is that 20 percent admit to using hashish five times a week; 28 percent admit to hard drug use; 9.5 percent are classified as alcoholics; and 25 percent of the combat force under 21 are problem drinkers. The 12-volume Army readiness study showed that trainability is so bad that out of a maximum score of 8, the average soldier scored *1.8*. Twenty-nine percent of the tank gunners cannot lase and fire their gun. I could go on *ad nauseum*.

AUDIENCE: I believe you read those statistics to us earlier.

RICHARD GABRIEL: That's correct. I tell you that these units will not fight; at least they will not fight well.

I'll give you another indication. Two years in a row we've placed *last* in the European tank competition. What other indications do you wish to have? The troops cannot fire their guns; they will not follow their officers, they admit openly that if we get hit in Europe, they're going to take care of their families first. If you will not accept all that as an indication of poor effectiveness, I don't know what will convince you. I have no other data except those.

RICHARD COOPER: I think there are a couple of points here. First of all: this selective use of statistics. From what I've seen, the poll referred to was widely discredited regarding the people they interviewed, the questions they asked, and the kinds of numbers they got. Several detailed studies were done just this last year concerning drug and alcohol use in the military, and the numbers you cite are way too high. More important than all this is the question, What are you going to do to solve the problem? It's what I was referring to earlier—the tail wagging the dog. What are we going to do? Conscript everybody to solve all these problems? You are sadly mistaken if you think that going back to a conscript army is going to solve these problems. My basic point is the one that Al Sabrosky and Bernie Rostker made earlier, and that is that, indeed, there are ways we would like to improve morale. In many units morale is down, but I'm not convinced that it's any worse than it was 15 years ago. In any case, that's a leadership problem; it's a management problem. The Army and the other three services are trying to work it out, and I think if there are ways that we can try to help them do a better job, it's incumbent on us to do that. But you're certainly not going to solve it by going back to the "good old days" and drafting a big chunk of American youth.

ARNOLD MOORE: Two brief comments. First, I've heard there was a survey—I believe it was at Oxford—in the late thirties in which "the best and the brightest" in England said they wouldn't fight; later they fought. I'm not certain about the details of this incident.

My second, more general, comment is that it seems to me that we've been talking proxy issues for two days. Finally the smoke screen starts breaking a little bit—we begin to try to talk about the real issues—and a new proxy is introduced without its being recognized. And that is the question of whether the services are representative. The issue is usually put in terms of demographic matters. I think that what's behind that is really something quite different, and that is: Are the services representative of the ideas, notions, and values of the society to the extent that they will fight a war which the society wants them to fight? That's quite a different question from the question of whether they're demographically representative, and I think it is important in raising this issue and trying to solve it that we be careful not to get drawn off into worrying about demography, which I think is a false issue.

ALAN SABROSKY: The question I'm curious about, because it comes up sometimes in other discussions, is: Do you really think that in anything except a garrison state or a militarized society you will ever have direct congruence between the values of a society as a whole and the values of those who comprise its military, particularly its professional military? I find very few cases where, in fact, that does occur.

ARNOLD MOORE: No, I wouldn't think you would have strict congruence, and I don't think Charlie Moskos suggested that you should have strict representativeness either. But it seems to me that you need enough congruence, and that that's where the question of reliability comes in. My guess is that what happened in Vietnam is that there was no popular support for the war and the military therefore had a hard time fighting it.

ALAN SABROSKY: That may be part of it, but, you know, there are two parts to the question. One is whether or not the people in the military reflect the values of the society, and the second is whether or not they support its ultimate ideals and goals. I can see that the second one is terribly important —the ideals and purpose for fighting. I was curious because there's a distinction here that I have a great deal of difficulty with, because it's really hard to get a grasp on those data.

DAVID HENDERSON: David Henderson, Cato Institute. I wasn't going to comment on this, but I'll just do so briefly here. Do we want or need our garbagemen to have the same ideals as the society as a whole? Why do we need people who specialize in a particular task or occupation to hold the ideals of the average person in society?

In Richard Gabriel's comments, he criticized the notion of using incentives. Now, it seems to me that's not an issue. You can't have anything *but* incentives. Even people who advocate a draft are advocating a system of incentives, only the incentive is different. If you don't join we're going to put you in jail. And if they put someone in jail and he escapes, he's still borne a cost. So we still have incentives.

The real question is: What is the *best* way of designing our incentives? Is it to use the market, in which people can voluntarily choose whether to take a pay offer? Or is it to use a method of imprisoning people? There are, I think, very good moral arguments in favor of using a market, as well as very good efficiency arguments. Gabriel says that people who talk about a conscription tax are using an analogy. They aren't using an analogy at all. It's not "like" a tax: it *is* a tax, and a very inefficient tax. It takes people who have other alternatives and makes them work at something they don't want to do. By the way, the correct measure of the conscription tax is not the difference between what you earn in the military and what you would have earned if you had worked in a civilian occupation. The correct measure—if you could measure it—would be the difference between what you earn in the military and what you would have to be paid in the military *to join it voluntarily*. In many cases that amount would be a *lot* higher than the pay you would have earned in the civilian sector. This is because there are all kinds of things in the military which have a high disutility associated with them. One very important one is the prospect of getting killed.

ROGER FOLSOM: I have a couple of comments on some of the data Charlie Moskos used—the various educational measures and so forth. So many of his statistics, though not all of them, compare the quality of enlistees with the quality of enlistees in previous periods. But at the same time he makes the comment that attrition is much higher now than it was then. If that's true, this seems to be a comparison of apples and oranges. In other words, if your policies now let in a lot of low-quality recruits and then you roll them out again, attrition is high. But you *expect* it to be high. That tends to bias the comparison with attrition during other periods and exaggerates the decline, if any, in quality of our forces.

CHARLES MOSKOS: That's the very point.

ROGER FOLSOM: The fact that those who turn over quickly are of low quality doesn't mean that those who stay in are of low quality. They might be, but not necessarily.

RICHARD COOPER: Roger, let me comment on that. What happened in the Army especially, but in the other services, too, during the early years of the All-Volunteer Forces was that an explicit policy decision was made to cut down on the number of mental category IVs, which many would argue was a surrogate for cutting down on the number of blacks, and accepted large numbers of non-high school graduates instead. All the evidence shows that non-high school graduates in categories I–III have much higher attrition rates than high school graduates in category IV. So, it's not a question of low quality or high quality, as Patricia rightly noted. In fact, I can make a case that the quality of today's recruits is much higher than the quality of personnel during the draft. During the 15 years preceding the All-Volunteer Force, category IV rates were about 24 percent. Today they're about 6 percent. What happens when you turn off one spigot and still want to fill the basin? You've got to open another one. In this case, opening the other spigot was letting in people in categories I–III (non-high school graduates), which is one of the fundamental reasons we have a problem. The Army and the Marine Corps both recognize the quality issue as an important problem and have tried to deal with it. This last year was a tough recruiting year, and I think 1980 is going to be one also.

So I think you are right, but for a slightly different reason than what you said.

ROGER FOLSOM: I didn't mean to imply that. All I'm saying is that you need to make sure you're not comparing apples and oranges. Only if the ones who come in and go out quickly do not differ substantially in measured characteristics from those who come in and stay in, will your comparison make sense if your attrition rate is different in different periods. Otherwise your comparisons will be biased.

CHARLES MOSKOS: There's something else to be considered. Rick Cooper's own studies, which tried, very insightfully, to break down military tasks into high-skill, medium-skill, and low-skill categories based on a measure of enlisted productivity for those presently in the military, shows quite clearly that on those measures high school graduates always do better than non-high school graduates and that higher mental groups tend to do better than lower mental groups.

ROGER FOLSOM: I would certainly agree. I've seen smart and I've seen stupid, and smart is better. [Laughter.] But the question is, as was pointed out already in several contexts: What is the correct allocation of smart to stupid people? "Less-smart" people is perhaps a better word.

CHARLES MOSKOS: Then you slide into a Brave New World, where you put the less-smart people in the low-skill jobs.

ROGER FOLSOM: Yes. I think that's not a bad choice considering the alternative, which is to put the physicist to digging ditches.

CHARLES MOSKOS: That's where the issue becomes joined to the question of what we need. Richard Danzig mentioned today the hypothetical case of the Harvard B.A. becoming a company clerk in a combat area unit. That company clerk, by the way, was me. I was a Princeton B.A., but it is the same kind of thing.

RICHARD DANZIG: No, it's not the same kind of thing. [Laughter.]

MARTIN ANDERSON: It's been a very fascinating and lively discussion. At this point we should ask if anyone has a question.

ROGER FOLSOM: Let me throw out one quick point about comparability, and that is: I want to remind everybody that in World War II the Air Force was part of the Army. Consequently, when we're making comparisons about the quality of troops today versus Army recruits in World War II, we need to make sure to have purged the Army Air Corps from our data.

CHARLES MOSKOS: Nobody has done that. We're comparing 1964— the peacetime draft—with the 1970s All-Volunteer Force. Nobody's gone back to World War II.

MARTIN ANDERSON: Perhaps we could get a comment as to whether we should combine the Army and the Air Force.

CHARLES MOSKOS: That's one way to go back to the institutional model.

ANTONIA CHAYES: We'll take over the Navy pilots.

MARTIN ANDERSON: Does anyone have a real question?

QUESTION FROM THE AUDIENCE: This really is a question for Mr. Moskos. I'd like to know if you're aware that the attrition rate at General Motors for 18-year-old employees is 60 percent or 70 percent. Also, would you be as upset about those 18-year-olds dropping out of an occupation as you are about the attrition rate in the military? Would you want them to have to stick it out?

CHARLES MOSKOS: Your statement assumes that General Motors and the Army are the same.

AUDIENCE: That's my other question.

CHARLES MOSKOS: I disagree on that fundamental assumption. General Motors and the Army are *not* the same kind of organization.

AUDIENCE: How do they differ?

CHARLES MOSKOS: How do they differ?

AUDIENCE: I propose that the main difference is that General Motors pays better.

ALAN SABROSKY: If you made the argument about *Chrysler* and the Army you might have had a better one.

MARTIN ANDERSON: That's all the time we have for this third session. Thank you all for an interesting and lively discussion.

PART 5

National Service, the Draft, and Volunteers: A Debate

INTRODUCTION

Albert Rees

ALBERT REES: Welcome to the last session of the Hoover-Rochester Conference on the All-Volunteer Force. I've attended almost all of this conference. In my view, it has been an extremely productive and useful discussion of the issues in which all positions have been well and eloquently put forward, and I commend the Hoover Institution and the University of Rochester for their planning of this conference. I can say this without blowing my own horn, because, although the Sloan Foundation is listed on the program as a sponsor of the conference, the role of the foundation is strictly that of providing a portion of the funding that has made the conference possible.

I might just say, for the benefit of Under Secretary Chayes, that economists are also sticklers for accuracy, and I should therefore point out that Mr. Alfred Sloan's middle initial was P, as in Peter, and not T, as in Thomas, as the program has it.

Our session this afternoon is a debate on national service, the draft, and volunteers. And it's my great privilege to chair this debate between two very distinguished Americans. I will not give them elaborate introductions. That would be presumptuous. You all know them.

Congressman Pete McCloskey has been for many years a leader in the House of Representatives, the body in which it sometimes seems to those of us on the outside to be increasingly difficult for anyone to offer any leadership. We're all indebted to him for the constructive role that he's played there.

Professor Milton Friedman won the Nobel Prize in Economic Science. Quite apart from his scientific contributions, which are enormous, he is very well known for his defense of the free-enterprise system, and his defense of freedom, even more broadly defined.

The format of our discussion this afternoon is that each speaker will make an initial 20-minute presentation. Following that, each will have 10 minutes for rebuttal. That should take approximately an hour. After that we will have discussion from the floor.

Congressman, would you please be our first speaker?

XV

ARGUMENT FOR NATIONAL SERVICE

Pete McCloskey

PETE McCLOSKEY: I can't think of a better arena or a more worthy antagonist to present this argument before.

Let me say at the outset that I know of no one in the United States who wants to return to the draft if the All-Volunteer Force is working. The problem has been that over the last year, discussions with noncommissioned officers and enlisted men have led to a growing perception in Congress that the All-Volunteer Army is not working—that the quantity and quality of recruits do not measure up to the tremendously demanding tasks that we place before our military forces.

At the outset, let me say that the purpose of a military force is not to make war. I'm afraid that we came out of World War II and the Korean War with the idea that Americans should fight, and would fight, anyplace for any oppressed nation or on behalf of any country where we perceive that freedom is in jeopardy. You may recall Jack Kennedy's words when he was inaugurated, that we would fight any foe, we would go to the assistance of any friend, to preserve liberty. The acclaim with which those words were received by the American public is not surprising when you realize that back in the early sixties we Americans had the view that we fought only just wars, that we fought only for good causes. Then we were led into the morass of Vietnam and, I think, through a tragic era. It's been my opinion that had Jack Kennedy not been assassinated in November of 1963, we would have been out of Vietnam within two years, and never have been involved there. But through a succession of circumstances we became involved.

I think public opinion may be as erroneous today with respect to our responsibility and our nation's need for an armed service around the world as it was in the early sixties in the belief that somehow, whenever we went to war on behalf of any nation opposing a communist adversary, this was correct. When public opinion strongly favors isolationism on the part of America and strongly opposes any use of military force, that is precisely the time we ought to have a considered and restrained debate on this subject.

Now, what is the purpose of an armed force in the 1980s and 1990s? It is not to make war. It is to preserve peace. But its readiness to fight a war is a deterrent to others who might try to terminate peaceful circumstances.

We've had five ambassadors assassinated in the last 15 years. We've seen a number of embassies under attack. We seek peace in the world through commercial and trade transactions in nearly every country of the world. There are American personnel, American property, and American investments around the world. I think all of us would concede that it is our desire that the commercial transportation and communications networks continue to grow, in hopes of a world peace in which the nations of the world are commercially interdependent.

But under those circumstances we can be prepared to see actions like that of the Ayatollah, actions like those in Afghanistan, in Africa, in Latin America, where American people and property assets are going to be threatened if we do not have a quality army able to respond. I think everyone would agree.

Now, if a volunteer army works, we would expect to have the quality and caliber of recruits capable of manning sophisticated weapons systems, capable of manning sophisticated communications systems, capable of guarding nuclear warheads with all of the responsibilities that entails, capable of coolness under fire, of the ability to face hostile crowds in riot situations without losing their control—without losing their *cool*—like the young Marines guarding those embassies under assault. Had any one of those Marines not been intelligent or not been cool, had he let loose a burst of machine-gun fire into the crowd, we could have had an incident which would have provoked a war.

I think all of us would agree that we need a quality army—in terms of fighting capacity and ability to deter aggression—in this time of peace. Yet what is the record of the last year? We have had an insufficient number of young people volunteer for all branches of the service over the last four calendar quarters. In a test run in Germany last May, of 450 infantry soldiers, it was found that only 7 of those 450 young men could read at the ninth-grade level. We have had to drop our training manuals from the twelfth-grade level to the eighth-grade level, and now to the fifth-grade level. We're using comic books to train people to military proficiency because the level of the recruit has become so low. In fact, it appears that no reasonable young man will volunteer for the combat arms today, if he can get into school or get a job.

I've asked the following question here at Stanford; I've asked it at Foothill College; and I've asked it at 12 of the 24 high schools in this district: How many of you will volunteer for two years of combat readiness training if I tell you what you're actually going to go through as a combat-ready soldier and if we double the current pay, from $418 a month to $836 a month? I have yet to have the hand of a young man on the Peninsula who is willing to volunteer if we double the pay.

The Army contends that if we increase pay, which is one of the alternatives, we can attract the proper number of the proper quality recruits. If that were so, I think we would be prepared to raise the pay by some reasonable amount. But the fact is that there is no indication that such a raise in pay will attract qualified people for this onerous duty of citizenship. And if that is the case—if we cannot get the proper quantity and quality of people—what, then, are the alternatives for the United States?

Well, there are two alternatives. At the present time, the right number of people are in the armed services, but we're approximately 600,000 people short in the reserves, the units that would have to flesh out the army in the event of an emergency. I might point out that the reserves are as crucial to our combat readiness and our deterrence policy as are the right number of weapons and the right number of radios and of ships and aircraft to transport troops into combat. This is because anyone who might want to test us would know that the reserves who would have to flesh out our troop units, 30 days or 60 days or 90 days after hostilities commenced, are just not there today.

We find young people all over America today who are willing to say, "Yes, if we are threatened, if the Ayatollah should lead us into war, we would be the first the volunteer." But the present problem stems from circumstances that differ from those of prior wars, including Vietnam and World Wars I and II, in that six months of careful, hard, arduous training must elapse before any young person has a reasonable chance of surviving in combat. To prepare a combat-ready army, this training must be done in time of peace.

Now the argument has been made, particularly on the campuses, that constitutionally we do not have the power to force people into voluntary service in time of peace. That was destroyed by the Supreme Court in the sixties in the Holmes case, and in others, in which it pointed out that it wasn't merely a power but a duty of Congress to raise an army. When you go back to the Constitutional Convention debate, you find that it was clearly understood that the country couldn't wait until a war started to raise an army. It is in time of peace that the army must be trained and must be ready, particularly in this day and age where war could break out in 24 hours or, at the most, 30 days.

Now, who should serve in this army, if you concede that we have one and need one? At the present time, if we went into combat in Eastern Europe or in Germany, over half of the front-line infantry casualties would be black or Mexican-American. These two minorities during the Vietnam War made up about 17 percent of our population, yet in the rifle companies they furnished over 40 percent of those killed in action. Why? Because the draft had an exemption for college students: if you were able to get into college, you could avoid the draft. Those who couldn't get an education, who couldn't get jobs that justified being exempted from the draft, were drafted. When the services pick who is going to man what, of course it is the people who have the worst education and are the least able to handle the more sophisticated jobs who get the jobs in the rifle companies. If any of you saw the troops who had manned the North Korean DMZ jogging with President Carter a few months ago, when he jogged three miles with the troops of the Second Infantry Division, you couldn't have failed to notice that over half of those troops were black.

Now what kind of a country do we want to be? An affluent all-white or white-controlled nation whose most arduous duties of citizenship are borne primarily by the minorities and poor?

The quality army that I think we need cries out for a cross section of America. People say, "Well, we're likely to get into war when we have a draftee army," but I think not. I think it's just the opposite. I think we're far *more* likely to get into war if the sons who are going to be killed in that war do *not* come from the best families of America, are not the sons of the university professors, the bankers, and the businessmen of America. Only if the rich as well as the poor are serving in the military will we see the whole country involved in the decision whether we go to war or not.

Now, the libertarians say, "Well, that's against our liberties." But the courts have spoken time and time again on that subject: if you're to preserve liberty, someone has to be ready to fight. It's never been conceived a denial of liberty to say to a young person, "One or two years of your youth will be spent in service to your country if the need is there." Take jury duty. We don't like jury duty. It's involuntary servitude. Anybody who's spent eight weeks sequestered in a jury on an antitrust case or a criminal case at $5 a day, denied his livelihood, denied the ability to meet with his family, considers that an involuntary servitude. Yet we feel that the constitutional guarantee of a fair trial entitles a person to be tried by a jury of his peers, and, consequently, we impose that duty on ourselves in order to ensure justice. Similarly, it does not seem to me unwise or unfair to insist on a duty of young people, as a price of the privilege of being American, to serve their country.

Now, what does that mean with respect to the draft? At present, we need only about 400,000 young people out of the 4.3 million who turn 18 each year. If we take men and women, we need only about one out of ten. If we take just men, we need only about one out of five. None of us wants to go back to a straight lottery draft. How can we maintain morale in an armed force made up of one out of every five or every ten unlucky enough to have his or her number selected, while the other four, or the other nine, are back drinking beer on the Stanford campus? How would *you* feel if you were unlucky enough to be selected by a lottery draft?

A second alternative to the general draft is a draft for reserves only. In a draft of all young men, in which we'd probably lose 40 percent as mentally or physically unfit, we might be taking one out of three and could draft everyone into the reserve. If we drafted for four to six months of military training backed by three or four-and-a-half years of combat-ready reserve status, we would then have spread the burden fairly. We would have drafted all qualified young men, and at least would have fairness under draft conditions.

The third alternative is the program that I propose. This program would give an 18-year-old four options.

1. He could be drafted; or, to avoid the draft,

2. He could enlist for two years, and, if he did, we would give him four years of college benefits; or

3. He could agree to enlist for six months, followed by five-and-a-half years of combat-ready reserve state, to get one year of college benefits; or

4. He could volunteer for a year of civilian service in any of a number of agencies—federal, local, charitable—where service is performed (Peace Corps, fire-fighting, hospital work, and so forth) if he didn't want to volunteer to serve in the military. Many thousands of young people do this already. So the bureaucracy need not be excessively increased to administer the program. The selective service mechanism would make the assignments, and work would be at subsistence pay.

Frankly, today we have a lack of spots for young people who want to take a year off from their education, training, or work experience, so I think in general it would not be harmful to young people to serve in a volunteer capacity. If a young man were in the Mormon church, for instance, which sends 20,000 young men overseas for two years, and wanted one of his two years to go for community service, such as the Peace Corps performs, rather than evangelical work for the church, that would qualify. If someone wanted to work on the skyline in this county, protecting against fires or maintaining trails under the auspices of a local organization, that would qualify.

Only if a person did not choose one of the three alternatives to the draft would he then be subject to the draft, and under those circumstances, the burden would be spread fairly.

In an article in *Newsweek* magazine Mr. Friedman has said that whatever system we have must be *perceived* as fair. I can think of no fairer way than to flesh out our Army with a cross section of America, reluctant citizen soldiers. I find this national youth service program far preferable to a professional army in this day and age.

Let me conclude by saying what the state of Congress is on this subject at the present time. Last year the House Armed Services Committee voted 31 to 4 to move back the draft by instituting registration. And the Senate Armed Services Subcommittee voted 4 to 3 to install registration. When it reached the House floor, a number of us who felt we were going to have to look at the draft counted noses and found that the House broke down to about 30 percent who favored a return to the draft, 30 percent who opposed the draft under any circumstances, and about 40 percent who said, in effect, "Well, we may have to go back to some form of compulsion to have a competent army, but we need more facts before we do it." On that basis, the so-called Schroeder Amendment, as drafted by Leon Panetta of Monterey and myself, proposed that we have a six-month study and defer registration until that study was returned. When that proposal was taken up in conference, the Senate caused the period to be reduced from six months to three months. So in February of next year we will have a report back from the administration on alternatives to the draft and on alternatives to returning to combat-ready status. That vote will come before us next spring. I hope that debates like this will continue up to that point, because it's going to take some courage on the part of politicians to address this issue, and courage comes more easily when you have an enlightened public.

Thank you.

XVI

ARGUMENT AGAINST NATIONAL SERVICE

Milton Friedman

MILTON FRIEDMAN: I want to start by expressing full agreement with Congressman McCloskey about our objectives. Unfortunately, we need to have an army, and we need to have a good army and an efficient army. There's no dispute on that, at least between him and me. There may be some other people who will dispute that, but between the two of us there's no dispute about that.

The problem is not one of objectives. It is, on the one hand, a problem of methods and on the other hand, a problem of the effect of the methods applied on the rest of our society.

We need an effective military for a democratic and free society. We do *not* need a military that would be effective for a totalitarian society, and that is a very, very important and basic difference. I know that Congressman McCloskey agrees with me on that, too. We disagree on what techniques will achieve the most effective military force for a free and open society.

Unaccustomed as I am on this kind of issue to quoting the *New York Times*, I have in front of me an Op-Ed column that brings out some of these issues in a very effective way. The column is entitled, "Why Not Draft the Next Congress?" and I hope you will pardon me if I read a few excerpts from it.

> The All-Volunteer Congress has proved to be a failure. Its cost is extremely high, and there is not a proportional representation of minorities. There are also many doubts about the honesty and intelligence of the recent volunteers. Many of Congress's recent failures are owing to the low

quality of its composition. A change is needed. This country can no longer afford the high cost of the volunteer system. Nor can it tolerate the low level of performance and reliability. Conscription appears to be the only way to get a decent Congress at an affordable price. . . . Some people object to the idea of conscription in itself. But rather than being a moral evil, Congressional conscription should be seen as giving an opportunity for service to the middle-aged. The draftees would have the chance to serve their country and be a part of an important process, and would also learn a lot in the process. Can we allow our national interest to be determined by an overpaid, racially unbalanced, and psychologically unstable pack of volunteers? Our national interests can only be served by a balanced selection of people from all parts of society.

I've read only a small part of this piece, but I recommend the whole of it to you as an extremely effective document for bringing out the implications of departing from volunteer service.

The plain fact is that maintaining an armed force of 2 million people in a democratic free society is a tough job. It's bound to be done imperfectly. It's bound to generate difficulties. As was brought out very effectively in Professor Bobbitt's paper, the farther grass always looks greener. Every system that you adopt is going to have some evils. It's going to have some problems.

The All-Volunteer Force, as it is now being implemented, has some real problems. There's no doubt about that. Congressman McCloskey pointed to some of them, though I think on the whole he exaggerates them. It has some real problems, but so, in my opinion, does a draft—far *worse* problems. Universal national service has some real problems that I'll come to, in my opinion *far worse* problems.

The danger is that we tend to run from the evils we know to those we don't know. We see the system we now have, where the problems have emerged and are visible, and are tempted to move to another system, for which the problems are in the future.

This is the *normal* political operating mechanism. Why do we have so many bad laws? Because legislators invariably tend to point to real evils, describe fine objectives, and then enact programs that are not well suited to respond to those evils or achieve those objectives. There's a strong tendency on the political level to operate in terms of what ought to be done, and to brush aside the more fundamental question of how do you do it.

The national service rhetoric, which Congressman McCloskey adopts, has a great deal of appeal. It *seems* very reasonable to say that all young men owe their country service. But I hasten to add that its appeal is always in general terms and not in specific terms. On this I quote from Professor King's paper given earlier at this conference, expressing a favorable view toward national service: "I am not certain that any *particular* national service proposal would, in fact, be superior to the All-Volunteer Force or to the draft." I believe that what you will find, if you take all the people who have expressed preferences for national service, is that each one has a different plan in mind. And none of them likes the other fellow's plan. There may be a good deal of support for national service *in general*, but there is very little support for any particular program.

Part of the appeal of the idea of national service is due to an intellectual confusion between two very different systems. One is universal military service, such as exists, for example, in Switzerland and in Israel. If you have a country which needs the service of all young men, and maybe young women, for its defense—essentially all able-bodied citizens—then a reasonably equitable and fair way to impose a tax on the people is simply to require everybody to serve, to see that everybody is trained, to see that all are available to come to the defense of their country.

But that is *not* the situation in the United States. As Congressman Mc-Closkey pointed out, we need at most to recruit something like one out of every five young men, or one of every ten men and women. I say "at most" because I believe that a superior policy of manning our armed forces would place less emphasis on obtaining people averaging 18.569 years of age. Together with retaining people over longer periods, such a reform would reduce substantially the number of people that would have to be recruited each year.

Be that as it may, for purposes of argument let us take the numbers that are now cited: at most we have to recruit one out of four or five males, or one out of ten young people. Under those circumstances, universal *military* service is simply not a feasible proposition. It would be necessary to train 2 million young men a year and 1.5 million of those would be irrelevant. Nobody really proposes that we require 2 million men a year to undergo military service in order to be able to get 300,000 or 400,000 men a year.

Universal *national* service is a wholly different thing. Universal national service is not universal military service. It is a system under which every young man or every young man and every young woman, depending on how it is done, is required to put in a year or two of so-called compulsory service in forms designated by somebody-or-other.

I'm going to come back to that in a moment, but I may say that Congressman McCloskey's own particular scheme is a rather backhanded way of reintroducing a lottery draft. It's not really universal national service. It's mislabeled and misrepresented, as he puts it forth. He talks about people volunteering. That's Orwellian language. Voluntary under his scheme is *compulsory*. In a speech he gave at the Commonwealth Club on August 12, 1979—and I was glad to see he did not repeat that part of his speech in his comments today—he said, "We are now paying approximately 58 percent of our defense budget for manpower as against only 23 percent by the Soviets. We clearly cannot afford to spend more than the present 58 percent for manpower costs. If the volunteers are not of adequate quality and quantity, we do not have the option of paying more to get good-quality people and adequate numbers of them."

I assume that the reason Congressman McCloskey did not repeat that is because he now realizes that those numbers are utterly irrelevant to the issue of the All-Volunteer Force. Of our current manpower costs, roughly 90 percent is going for people who would not be affected by the issue of whether you had an all-volunteer force *or* a draft. The All-Volunteer Force issue is concerned with *first-term enlisted people*. In 1978, the latest year for which I have figures, out of $60 billion total military payroll costs, only $5 billion was going to pay people in the first two years of service, and another $5 billion to pay people in the second two years of service. So the total expenditure figure for manpower costs he quoted has no relationship whatsoever to the issue of All-Volunteer Force. If Congress had not exempted itself from its truth-in-advertising legislation, we would have a case to bring before the Federal Trade Commission for misleading advertising.

In any event, the cost argument is also irrelevant for a different reason. The proposal he makes would cost a good deal *more*, not a good deal less, than the present volunteer system. What he proposes is to cut in half the pay of the lowest-paid people in the armed forces. Those are the people who are now being attracted into first-term enlistments. That would save only about $2 billion. But he also has to handle all of those people who volunteer for national service. To administer them, he has to set up a mechanism and a bureaucracy to handle them, and he has to *pay* them. Estimates of these additional costs of his proposal vary from something like $2 billion to $40 billion, depending on what fraction of young people volunteer for national service options. So his program would cost more, not less, than our present program.

I must say that I was amused by the conclusion that Congressman McCloskey reached in his talk I mentioned, and I would be interested to know whether he still regards that as his proposal. He said, and I quote, "I urge reinstitution"—note, *re*institution—"of the principle that all young men, people, at age 18 be asked to volunteer for the service of their country in a capacity of their choice, granting special benefits to those who choose to volunteer for the most arduous type of service." But that is a *precise* description of our present All-Volunteer Force.

What is our All-Volunteer Force? Perhaps they don't do a very good job of making it known, but the military does advertise that all young people, at age 18, are asked to volunteer for the service of their country in the capacity of their choice. Moreover, the military recruiting people give special bonuses for volunteering for the most needed branches of service. So what Congressman McCloskey was summarizing was a need for the program *we now have.*

If we go beyond his proposal and consider national service in general, I submit to you that it solves no problems that we now have with the All-Volunteer Force and creates vast new problems. If we're talking about a comprehensive universal national service—if it's something more than a back-door approach to a lottery draft—we'd have to handle 4 million people a year, men and women. If we suppose a two-year tour of duty, that means *8 million* people to administer. Who allocates them to jobs? Who decides what they do? Who determines their training? What power to put in the hands of people who would seek it!

Note also that none of what those people would do would be useful work: it would all be make-work. If you tried to have them do useful work, the trade unions of this country would be down on you like a ton of bricks. It would be work which some people believe *other* people ought to be paying for, because the whole purpose would be to enable a group of administrators to direct young people into activities that young people did not want to engage in. If they wanted to engage in it now, we would already have a system of universal national service. Right now every young man in the country, and every young women in the country, has an opportunity to volunteer for a whole variety of tasks, paid and unpaid, and that is equivalent to a system of universal national service. But, unlike Congressman McCloskey's proposal, it is a truly voluntary system of universal national service, not a compulsory system.

I must say that we don't learn very much from history, and I really cannot do better than to quote Senator Robert Taft, who, in discussing the issue of the draft before World War II, said,

> The principle of a compulsory draft is basically wrong. If we must use compulsion to get an army, why not use compulsion to get men for other essential tasks? Why not draft labor for essential occupations at wages lower than the standard? In short, the logic requires a complete regimentation of most labor, and the assignment of jobs to every man. This is actually done in the communist and fascist state, which we are now apparently seeking to emulate.

In light of that comment it is interesting to consider who has favored and who has opposed the idea of using compulsion to man our military. With respect to the draft in the United States, the situation is quite clear: in the main, conservatives have been opposed to conscription, whereas liberals have supported it. The wartime draft was barely passed. In 1946, Robert Taft, all by himself, prevented President Truman from using the draft to return striking railroad workers to their jobs. Barry Goldwater in 1964 came out in opposition to the draft. President Richard Nixon and his Secretary of Defense, Melvin Laird, were the main movers in ending the draft in 1973. The one exception is that of Adlai Stevenson, who in 1956, under the urging of John Kenneth Galbraith with respect to the only issue on which he and I agree, came out in opposition to the draft.

In the congressional debates on the All-Volunteer Force, one of its main opponents was Teddy Kennedy. If you look at the overall record, you will see that those people who have opposed the voluntary force have generally consisted of two very different types: one group, the strong military types under the influence of some of the professional military, and the other what we now call, in our debased language, liberals.

If you look at the record in the United States, the first extensive treatment of universal national service was by Edward Bellamy in 1888, in his book *Looking Backward*, which is a socialist Utopian novel. Ever since, universal national service has been supported primarily by modern liberals, by people who believe in a collective society. It has tended to be *opposed* by people like myself who believe in a *free* society, who believe that individuals should separately be free to choose their activities in accordance with their values, and that if some of us want to hire others of them to do certain jobs for us, we have to pay them what it takes to get them to do it for us and not impose it on them by force directly or indirectly.

My general conclusion is that universal national service would be a monstrosity. If adopted, it would undermine the basic foundations of this free society, and it is something that we should avoid like a plague.

I do not believe that Congressman McCloskey, if he really looked seriously at the consequences of what he proposes and what would develop out of his proposals, would like what he found. This is an experience that has happened over and over again. The proponents of plans like this almost invariably turn out to be the people who later are the very ones who least like the Frankenstein they have created. I believe that Congressman McCloskey would find himself one of that group.

XVII

REBUTTAL

Pete McCloskey

PETE McCLOSKEY: When I was first training here at Stanford to be a lawyer, and later in my first years of law practice, some very great legal scholars and lawyers told me: If you've got a good case, argue the facts. If you've got a bad case, hold up the opposition to ridicule. The first point of my debate, you will note, Mr. Friedman has not addressed at all. He has devoted the whole 20 minutes of his opening statement to the Frankensteinian problems that a national youth service might present if in time of peace we required compulsory service in a free society.

He points out, very properly, that we once passed a draft law in 1940 and then renewed it in 1941 by a single vote. But we did that only four months before Pearl Harbor, and as a result of the fact that we *had* had a peacetime draft, that we *had* had compulsory military training in time of peace, probably several hundred thousand young Americans weren't killed who might otherwise have been killed in World War II.

He quotes Mr. Taft's position, but that position was then, as it is now, in the minority. I think the *other* view—which George Washington expressed after we had won the Revolutionary War but were in danger of being taken back by the British because under the Articles of Confederation our original 13 colonies didn't have the power to raise an army, and which called for acceptance of the principle that in order to hold off foreign aggression every young person of 18 sharing the privileges of this country should cheerfully serve in the military—is more viable.

Mr. Friedman has an axe to grind here. He has properly pointed out the deficiencies of Congress, but let me recall for you that he was a member of the Gates Commission that recommended the All-Volunteer Army, and that the All-Volunteer Army was a mechanism proposed and supported strongly by President Nixon as a means of quieting public concern over *Mr. Nixon*'s conduct of the Vietnam War. The campuses of this country, if you will recall, were in an uproar between 1967 and 1972, and it was very helpful to Mr. Nixon's policy to continue the bombing in Vietnam while also quieting down young peoples' concern over being drafted.

I also ask you to weigh the validity of the Defense Department's arguments today that the All-Volunteer Army is working against the recollection that it was this same Defense Department that argued then that we needed to be in Vietnam—that "with one more division" we would win in Vietnam—and was the author of a long line of pronouncements that no one could believe because the Executive branch of government, like Congress, tends to exaggerate its successes and not admit its failures.

The key question in whether we go back to a draft or not is not the question of national service versus a draft for the reserves. The key question is whether or not the All-Volunteer Army is working. And I submit to you that when, in his opening argument, a gentleman takes 20 minutes and doesn't even address whether the All-Volunteer Army is working, it is an attempt to divert attention from the weakness of the argument he would have to make to defend it.

Because clearly the All-Volunteer Army is not working. If no reasonable young people on the San Francisco Peninsula will volunteer, can you say that it's working? Can we afford an army made up of more than half by minorities in this country? Should we have an army made up only of those who can't get into school or get a job? These are the real issues that face debate in Congress. It's fine to hold the problems and the costs of the alternatives up to ridicule, but the responsibility of the country and its elected representatives is to provide for the common defense, and the questions are: Do we need a quality army? Should it be an army made up of reluctant citizen soldiers? Or should it be made up only of those who are so poor and so ignorant that they can be conned by a recruiting sergeant into enlisting?

Mr. Friedman also doesn't address the recent recruiting scandals. Perhaps you're aware that in Tennessee and Texas, Oklahoma and North Carolina—the great bastions of volunteerism—where young people have traditionally come forward to volunteer, we're practically indicting most of our recruiting sergeants for misleading the people that they ask to enlist or for faking the test scores, because you're not supposed to get into the Army unless you can read at a ninth-grade level, and the pool they have to draw from simply can't do that. What does that indicate about 443 of those 450 soldiers who were tested? It means that somebody lowered the recruiting standards or faked the results in order to draw people into the Army.

The real question is whether the All-Volunteer Army is working or not.

Because I was one of those who opposed Mr. Nixon on the Vietnam War, the Executive branch of government invites me every year to address the War College, which is made up of colonels and lieutenant colonels who have been selected as possible candidates for our Joint Chiefs of Staff. For the last five years in private sessions I have asked those gentlemen (and sometimes a woman is admitted): Is the All-Volunteer Army working? The answer has invariably been nearly unanimous: one or two vote yes and 200 or so vote no. The consensus is that the All-Volunteer Army is not working and cannot work

Perhaps you saw the interview last fall on KQED television of four 19-year-old PFCs down at Fort Ord—two white PFCs, one black, and one Puerto Rican. They were asked: Do you think we can make this army work? Do you think we can have a quality army that can fulfill its mission without going back to the draft? All four of those young men said they felt we would have to go back to the draft.

Based on the quality of recruits, the conclusion invariably reached by colonels, by captains back from Germany—by officers and enlisted men alike—is that we need to go back to the draft, that we haven't got the quality soldier we must have to meet our needs. You may say, "Well, then, why isn't the Army saying so?" Because, presumably, it's the same situation we had in Vietnam: the professionals said we were winning and the young people said we were not. Who do *you* believe when the Secretary of the Army says that the All-Volunteer Force is working and his own people in the lower ranks say that it is not? I submit to you that you will get the truth about the quality of an army far more reliably and quickly from the officers and enlisted men than from the generals and the civilians in the Pentagon Mr. Friedman is quoting.

Let me now read to you from a letter a lady wrote me after this debate began last year.

> Dear Representative McCloskey: The *Akron Beacon Journal* published your feelings on the future of the draft, and I felt compelled to write to you because, although I am against the draft, I know that it is probably the only solution for the armed services. My husband is a staff sergeant in the U.S. Army, with 14 years of service. I have seen the Army up close in the 11 years that we have been married. Everything that you have mentioned as being wrong with the All-Volunteer Army is in fact true. Today's Army is made up of minority groups, of people who don't want to work but want to draw a paycheck, of unemployables, of misfits, of social outcasts. Nobody who can get a job as a civilian goes into the low-paid Army.

I ask you in this room, isn't that our experience? If anybody can get a decent job, does he go into the Army today? I continue with the letter:

> We returned from a tour of duty in Germany a year ago, and what I saw there scared me a lot. On any given day of any given week, we would not have put 50 percent of our troops into combat. My husband is an old Army and Vietnam veteran. He likes the Army the way it used to be. He doesn't understand today's Army. We have seen a lot of 10- and 12-year men get out because they wouldn't have their families around the situations that exist on bases today. I can confirm your belief that the military is greatly out of shape and would be slaughtered, just like the divisions sent against North Korea at the beginning of that war. It scares the life out of me that my husband would have to lead and depend on the men in his company. They would be worthless.

Now, whom do you believe about the quality of today's Army? Do you believe the academics on the college campuses? Do you believe the generals in the Pentagon? Do you believe the servants of the White House?—all of whom have something at stake in saying that the All-Volunteer Army is working? Do you believe the well-intentioned men who back in 1972, faced with the Vietnam War and the need to maintain a public opinion which would support that war, chose the All-Volunteer Army as a means to quiet public opinion so that they could continue the war?

I submit to you that the issue in doubt here is whether the All-Volunteer Army is working, and that no one should make the argument that we should continue the All-Volunteer Army without being able to defend the quality and the quantity of those troops. Mr. Friedman's omission of this issue—his deliberate decision not do that, in my judgment—makes his arguments worthless.

I probably won't have time to respond to Mr. Friedman's rebuttal, but I will point out to you that he has denied me the opportunity to rebut the one single argument that would justify the position he takes—that the All-Volunteer Army is working. If it is not working, it's the duty of Congress to proceed in a fair way to meet the problems this country faces.

I stress again that it isn't that we want a larger army. It's that we want a *quality* army. It's not that we don't want minorities in the army. It's that we want *all* citizens, from every walk of life, to share the most onerous duty of citizenship. I think we all have a duty to serve our country, and it's not a duty that we should ask only our poor and our minority to bear. It's a duty that ought to be shared by Stanford students and MIT students. The Army ought to be a cross section of the *best* in America, not the worst. We're going to *need* that kind of military service in the next 20 years—not a huge force to fight aggressive wars, but a force that is small, tight, competent, and that we know is capable of going into combat on 24-hour notice. We don't have that today, and we must do whatever is required to get it.

XVIII

REBUTTAL

Milton Friedman

MILTON FRIEDMAN: If I can exercise unusual restraint, I'll be glad to give Congressman McCloskey two minutes of my time to answer his question.

The question of whether the All-Volunteer Force is working is a meaningless question. We must ask, compared to *what*? The burden is on *him* to demonstrate that some alternative he has to propose will do better and will correct the difficulties he sees with the All-Volunteer Force as well as or better than proposed changes in the method of recruiting the All-Volunteer Force.

Is the All-Volunteer Force working? If I compare it with the draft, most certainly it is.

Personally, I do have an axe to grind. He is absolutely right. I have been opposed to the draft for at least 30 years, well predating the Vietnam War. If Congressman McCloskey would like some textual reference, I'd be glad to give him some from that fount of all wisdom, my book *Capitalism and Freedom.*

So, of course, I do have an axe to grind. But, as he himself pointed out, the effect of a draft was disastrous when we had the draft in practice. It was because of the draft that we had the uproar on the campuses. I believe that the Vietnam War would never have taken the form it did if we had not had a draft at the time, but I'm not going to go into that.

I want to go back directly to his question: Is the All-Volunteer Force working? I ask, with respect to *what?* There is no doubt that the officer corps has always been a voluntary corps; there are no shortages in its recruitment. It's fascinating to me that when people talk about whether the armed forces are working they tend to leave out 50 or 60 percent of the armed force—namely, the career force and officer corps.

If we come down to enlisted men, what are the facts? The facts are that there are defects in quality and quantity, yet all four services of the military have been able to come within a few percent of achieving and maintaining their stated force objectives.

Congressman McCloskey unfortunately was not able to attend our sessions yesterday and this morning, or he would have known that everyone here is up to the neck with figures on both sides of the question of whether the All-Volunteer Force is working. But the principal facts are that we have been *able* to achieve our quantitative objectives; that on the qualitative side, the average scores for the four forces put together *compare* very favorably indeed with the average scores under the *draft*; and that, though there is a real problem in the case of the Army, a large part of that problem arises out of the unwillingness of Congress to implement the pay scales that were recommended by the Gates Commission. The pay now of the lowest-paid units in the force—the first-termers—is about 10 percent less than the minimum wage. And I use the minimum wage only as a benchmark. I'm not in favor of the minimum wage. In fact, one of the ways to get more people for the All-Volunteer Force would be to raise the minimum wage, because that would render more people unemployed and would drive them into the armed forces.

The facts are that the Gates Commission did recommend a pay scale, and Congress has not been willing to make that pay scale effective. Initially the pay of first termers was raised substantially, and you did get recruitment. Now the pay has been allowed to erode relative to pay scales of blue-collar workers in general.

I do not believe one ought to put on the military all of the sins of the whole society. Congressman McCloskey referred to the use of comic books to train the military. I was shocked a while back to get a comic book on economics that was being used in colleges in the United States. Unfortunately, our educational system has been failing in the civilian world as well, and there's a good deal to be said for putting emphasis on *that*.

Regarding the problem of attracting college youth into the military, Congress, in its wisdom, has for some time been bribing college youth to stay out of the military—providing, as Charlie Moskos pointed out, something like $4.5 billion a year in grants for higher education to induce people to go to college instead of into the military. Again, you ought to be consistent and put the two together. One of the best ways to improve the quality of people in the All-Volunteer Force would be to do as Charlie suggests: make any receipt of higher educational benefits contingent upon serving in the armed forces.

So the point is that the armed forces have problems, of course. But all of those problems are soluble far short of the radical kind of proposal Congressman McCloskey proposes, by regular means. I wonder, if you went around and asked Stanford students whether they would volunteer to drive garbage trucks at $400 a month, or even at $800 a month, why it should be surprising if they didn't volunteer. Is it socially desirable that they should? Are you really saying that it's desirable that the police force of every city be a replica of the civilian population? If not, why should the armed forces be a replica?

We have officers, specialized people, in the armed forces. We ought to have more horizontal recruitment—also one of the recommendations of the Gates Commission.

I'm going to close with one more comment, and let Congressman McCloskey reply, by telling you a little story of an experience I had when I was on the President's Commission for an All-Volunteer Armed Force. It concerns the attitudes of the top people in the military and why they favor the draft.

They've always been in favor of a draft because it's the easiest life for them. They press a button and say to the Selective Service, send over another hundred thousand people. It doesn't cost them anything. There they are.

During the Gates Commission we were interviewing the various Chiefs of Staff, and, as it happened, General Westmoreland made the statement, "I do not want to command an army of mercenaries" (Congressman McCloskey referred earlier to mercenary soldiers). And I said to General Westmoreland, "Tell me, General, would you rather command an army of slaves?" He sat back in his chair and said, "I don't like to hear our patriotic draftees referred to as slaves." I said, "Well, General, I don't like to hear our patriotic volunteers referred to as mercenaries." I then went on to say, "'You know, after all, General, I'm a mercenary professor and you're a mercenary general. And both of us are being treated by mercenary physicians."

There's nothing wrong with mercenaries: they're simply professionals. It's just one of those antics with semantics. But it would be very easy if I were a top military person to be attracted to a draft because it's a system under which we can use force to compel people to serve rather than having to make service something that young men *want* to engage in.

So in answer to your fundamental question, the All-Volunteer Force is on the whole working—imperfectly, not as well as it could or should perhaps, and certainly not as well as it can be made to if we improve the operation of the All-Volunteer Force itself.

Now your obligation is to tell us how the particular difficulties of the All-Volunteer Force today would be cured by a specific alternative that you have to propose, and, in particular, by a return to compulsion.

XIX

CROSS-REBUTTAL

Pete McCloskey

PETE McCLOSKEY: Let me point out that the very problem that you recognized in your *Newsweek* article, which I mentioned in my opening statement, you have chosen not to reply to. You say that, quantitatively, we have met our goal. But you concede that we are 600,000 men short in the reserves. When we set the 2.1-million-man goal for the armed force, it was based on a total force concept: that it would be backed up roughly by 1.3 million ready reserves ready to flesh out our combat divisions if we went into combat. You, and the Secretary of the Army, dismiss as almost irrelevant the fact that 600,000 of those reserves aren't there. And I think you'd concede that of the other 700,000, there aren't more than 100,000—some of the units of the Air National Guard—that are combat-ready.

As a matter of fact, those Army generals that you defend so strongly are saying that if we went to war in Iran tomorrow, we'd have to call up Vietnam veterans because of the lack of reservists. Can you image the kind of rebellion there would be in this country if, because we were unwilling to ask people who haven't served in combat to serve, we called up Vietnam combat veterans? I can think of no greater admission of the All-Volunteer Army's failure than the statement that in 1979, because our reserves don't exist, we would have to call up Vietnam veterans in order to fight another war. I don't think those people would fight. I think they would justifiably decline to be called up.

You have also not addressed, in either of your sessions, this serious question about the reserves. Most battles in history, and most wars, have been lost because of the lack of a proper reserve. It was generally the side which could throw a reserve into action that ultimately prevailed. Our lack of a sufficient, qualified reserve is no minor administrative failure. Every advocate of the All-Volunteer Army can see that the reserve is simply not there today.

You say that my plan is compulsory. It is true, under the plan, that if a person does not volunteer for two years of service for the reserve, or for a year of civilian service, he would go into a pool subject to being drafted. But at least he would have had the opportunity to avoid that.

The point of Professor Moskos's you made, that by paying $4.5 billion in college benefits we are paying people not to go into the Army, I think is a good one. I think it would be perfectly appropriate to cut out all educational benefits and give them solely to those young people who volunteer for the two years in the combat infantry units I propose. In one poll of, I think, 100 high school students in this area, 98 were opposed to the draft. But when it was asked, "All right, what if you have these four choices: two years in the military, one year in the reserve, one year of civilian duty, or the uncertainty of six years susceptability via the draft?," half of the young men said that, under those circumstances they would enlist in order to get the four years of college benefits. I think it's very possible that under this national service program you would get 400,000 enlistees and volunteers and would never have to move to a draftlike compulsion, and that, if you did, it would be to draft a fairly small number out of a fairly large pool.

Under those circumstances you'd also have a high-morale army. My concern is that without the concept that everyone should be obligated to share this obligation or this choice, we have the problem of a low-morale army. I feel that *without the reestablishment of a concept of duty* this country is in trouble.

And that's what I'm talking about: the reinstitution of the attitude that we all have a duty to our country. That is basically the underlying disagreement between Professor Friedman and myself. He feels that we've got to economically reward people to get a quality army, no matter what it costs, because that's the only alternative, whereas I feel that the duty to serve and the need to spread this burden fairly is something we ought to preserve in the history and the ethic of this country. That's essentially what he calls a monstrosity. It isn't the administrative burden of it; it's the fact that it's compulsion during time of peace. But it seems to me that the history of this country shows that, whether it was the militia on the frontiers or the draft before World War II, only when we restored a common sense of duty did we make it a matter of pride to serve in the service.

I think the concept of duty to one's country is an honorable concept. I don't make any apology to someone who has taken one or two years out of his life to serve his country. Frankly, I spent 18 months in the Navy as an enlisted man, 21 months in the Marine Corps as an officer, and a number of years in the reserve. I think that, when you look at that kind of military education, 18 months or two years is as valuable to anybody's future, in terms of training and perception of the rest of the world and the rest of humanity, as any two years of the college any of us went through. Of course, it's one thing to serve in a war in which you fight the wrong people in the wrong place for an ignoble cause and another to serve your country to discourage our ever having to fight again in a major war.

XX

DISCUSSION AND QUESTIONS FROM THE FLOOR

ALBERT REES: I'm now going to open up the floor for discussion.

DAVID HENDERSON: David Henderson, Cato Institute.

I have a question for Congressman McCloskey. Actually I have about nine of them, so I'm going to have to choose one.

How do you choose which information source to believe? You've told us that most of the people who are volunteers in the present military are dumb. You've told us that we can't trust the generals or the Department of Defense. And yet you're basing your case that the All-Volunteer Force is not working, in large part, though not completely, on numbers generated by that same Department of Defense or through interviews with four of these dumb first-class privates.

PETE McCLOSKEY: Is your question: Whom do I believe?

DAVID HENDERSON: How do you decide whom to believe? You seem to be very selective about whom you believe: you believe those who support your case and not those who go against it.

PETE McCLOSKEY: What I said was that, given the choice between elected officials, the Secretary of the Army, and his generals on the one hand, the PFCs, the second lieutenants, and the captains on the other, I would always believe the lower-ranking people. They have nothing to lose by stating the truth.

QUESTION FROM THE AUDIENCE: I have a question that probably is going to take about two minutes, and I want to put it out so that I'm not stopped in the middle of this great bout of democracy and debate. Because my question is not to the podium, it is to the audience, especially the young students in the audience. I want to pose a question for us to think about, and I encourage you then to bombard the chair.

First a statement. This "little" army that we're talking about is basically an army of *2 million* people today. We've heard that there aren't enough people in the reserves, though we're talking about some 700,000 people in the reserves—almost another million people. That's almost 3 million people in the army. What kind of battle is an army like that going to fight? Why do we even *need* such an army? What kind of a war is it going to fight but a *world* war?

So my point is that, in this great democracy, we've got to *question* what this army's going to be used for. Do we have any interest in the wars that are going to be fought, because I don't think we're going to get it from the top. Congressman McCloskey, for instance, tells us that we've got to protect American economic interests in Iran. But *do* we? I'm proposing that we should *ask* this question. I would ask Congressman McCloskey whether it is really in our economic interest to protect the Shah? *Why* should we fight in Iran right now?

For that matter, Milton Friedman is another person we're not going to get an answer from. He talks about fighting for democracy—a person who went into Chile and advised Pinochet.

ALBERT REES: You may ask a question, but not make a speech which is not relevant to the subject of this debate. This is a debate on a very well-defined topic—whether or not we should have an All-Volunteer Force. If you want to ask a question that's relevant to that topic, please ask it. [Applause.]

AUDIENCE: The question for the people in America is: Do we have an interest in even *going* into the army? We don't want to talk about how we're going into the army, but why we *should*. Why should we fight in Iran? Do *we* own oil wells in Iran?

QUESTION FROM THE AUDIENCE: I have two questions. Question One: Is Professor Friedman aware of the fact that many democratic societies such as Switzerland, Holland, Israel, and Sweden have the draft without incurring any deficits in their democratic integrity?

My second question is in relation to his point that we need to ask whether the All-Volunteer Force is good—good in relation to what? Is he aware of the fact that if war comes we'll have to fight the Soviet Union, which has a mass-draft army, with all the advantages that go with that?

MILTON FRIEDMAN: Let me go to the first question.

Somehow or other I'm afraid you mustn't have been here when I was speaking, because I started out my comments by pointing out the difference between the situation in a country like Switzerland, Holland, or Israel and in a country like the United States. I said that I had no objection, in principle, to universal military service if that was what was required to defend our country. The situation in Israel, in which every citizen is asked to serve in the armed forces, is wholly different from the situation in the United States. For the United States, the question is: How do we get one out of five or one out of ten young people to serve in the armed forces? I do not believe that universal military service in a small nation like Israel is in any way antithetical to democracy or freedom. But I believe that using compulsory means to man the armed forces when only one out of every five or ten has to serve is very *seriously* antithetical to human freedom and democracy.

On your second point, of course, I'm aware that the Soviet Union is a major potential foe. But that does not mean to me that we can most effectively protect our system against the Soviet Union by adopting the method which the Soviet Union has adopted. Compulsion is universal in the Soviet Union, for civilians as well as military persons. In our society, voluntary cooperation is a fundamental, basic principle.

I might point out that, with respect to your first question, Congressman McCloskey cited George Washington. I agree with George Washington's initial statement. He was talking about universal military service at a time when the population of the United States was so small that we were in the position that Israel is in now. That's a very different circumstance from the situation we're in now.

QUESTION FROM THE AUDIENCE: This is for Congressman McCloskey. Why do you include women in your national service bill? And do you foresee roles for women in combat?

PETE MCCLOSKEY: On the first question. I would like to see the Equal Rights Amendment adopted. If women have equal rights, I feel that they ought to have equal obligation. As a matter of fact, in many of the jobs in the service today women are serving as well as or better than men. We are getting a better quality of education in women volunteering than we are from the men.

To your second question: for reasons, I suppose, of my own background and chauvinistic attitude, I would prefer that women not serve in front-line combat units. This has also been the Israeli experience. They tried for a while, but felt that they didn't want to have women in the front-line combat units. If we fight a major war, certainly women, in any civilian capacity, are going to be injured as much as in the front-line units. In fact, the casualties in any European war involving nuclear exchange might very well involve casualties to rear echelon units that are as high as those in the front-line units. But I would prefer not to have women put into the combat infantry, into the front-line forces. As I say, that's a preference.

If you take the constitutional argument that women have equal rights—given that you get them—you can scarcely argue that they should not have equal obligation. I would prefer that that amendment pass, and, if it does, it will impose equal obligation.

SCOTT OLMSTED: Scott Olmsted, Stanford Libertarians.

As a libertarian, I believe that every individual owns his own person, his own body, and has the right to exercise sole dominion over it so long as he respects the equal rights of others to do the same.

I'd like to ask Professor Friedman if he agrees with this moral constraint (the moral principle of self-ownership). And I'd like to ask Congressman McCloskey what moral, not legal or constitutional, principle he holds that is different from this one that allows some persons to force an occupation on other persons and does not allow them control over their own bodies.

MILTON FRIEDMAN: I have a little difficulty replying to this, because obviously I regard myself as a libertarian. But I believe that "libertarian" covers a multitude of sins.

I do believe that people own themselves. But I believe there are dfficult problems of interrelations among people, and that to state the moral principle that people own themselves is not an immediate formula for giving practical answers to practical questions about how you resolve some difficulties.

For example, consider the case of a country like Israel. Does a libertarian who believes people own themselves also believe that it is inappropriate in a society like Israel for people to follow a policy of requiring everybody who lives in Israel to serve in the military? You and I would say, as libertarians, that if we had a large number of small countries like that, some of which did require military service and some of which did not, and if people were free to move among them or to choose among them, then there would be nothing wrong in any individual entering into an agreement with the community in which he lives that he will go along with adopting that rule. But, unfortunately, these are hard problems. There aren't a large number of small countries with these differences. And thus, while my moral principles, I think, are identical with those you express, they don't provide me with an immediate answer to many of these very difficult questions. Interrelations among people present strictly individualistic decisions.

As you know from what I've written, I believe that the argument of externalities is a cloak for covering up many government interventions that you cannot really justify on those grounds. But that doesn't mean there aren't some real cases of that kind.

ALBERT REES: We have a second question on the floor from Mr. Olmsted: What moral, as opposed to legal or constitutional, principle does Congressman McCloskey hold that is different from one which allows some persons to force occupation on other persons and does not allow them control of their own bodies?

PETE MCCLOSKEY: I believe in liberty so strongly that I would agree with Patrick Henry: Give me liberty or give me death. But I would consider that the real prospect of having to live under the yoke of a system of government which denied me liberty of speech and liberty of religion and liberty of where I lived and where I worked, which the communist system imposes, would move me to give up the liberty of my body for one or two years when I am young. It is a liberty well worth giving up in order to preserve those greater liberties.

MILTON FRIEDMAN: But you, and others, are free to do so without imposing a plan like you propose. The difficulty with this issue is that these are hard questions. I don't mean to say that they're easy. But you talk as if what you've just said is an argument for either a draft or universal military service. It is not. It is only an appeal to your fellow citizens that they should accept certain jobs at lower pay than they otherwise would accept.

PETE MCCLOSKEY: But since that appeal plainly isn't working, and no reasonable young people will volunteer, we then have to devise—

MILTON FRIEDMAN: But (a) it is working, and (b), if you think it isn't, the alternative along your lines is for *you* to go on the stump as a recruiter for the military.

PETE MCCLOSKEY: Let me be very honest and put this question to you. As I say, I've spent much of my life in the military, but I know of no one at age 18 today who is going to volunteer, and certainly if I were 18, and if you were 18, we wouldn't volunteer to spend two years in the desert or in the jungles or climbing mountains—cold, wet, and miserable, or tired, hot, and hungry. What reasonable person is going to volunteer for that?

QUESTION FROM THE AUDIENCE: Why did you do it?

PETE MCCLOSKEY: Because at the time, 1945, when the choice existed for me there was a war on, and the concept was prevalent that every young person who was healthy had a duty to his country. Also, if he didn't volunteer, there was a draft behind him and he was going to get drafted. [Laughter.] No one would question that many of the alleged patriotic volunteers who left Stanford to go into the Air Force, the Navy, or Marine Corps didn't do so, in part, because the draft was in the background.

That is precisely the program I propose—a draft in the background—so that if there are insufficient volunteers, we will have the means to defend this nation.

MILTON FRIEDMAN: Let me just say one thing. The fact is that people are volunteering for the kind of jobs you're talking about at pay scales today that are lower than those recommended by the Gates Commission. The fact is that for a couple of years immediately after the institution of the pay scales recommended by the Gates Commission we did not have any shortages.

Economics is a serious subject, and one of the things we've learned in that subject is that if you want to know how people behave you *don't* ask them. You look. The doctrine of revealed preference in economics is a fundamental doctrine, and it is no good going around and asking. If you ask people foolish questions, there's only one kind of answer you're going to get.

PETE McCLOSKEY: But, may I ask this, because I think it focuses on the point of debate, Mr. Friedman. Have you asked about the quality of these young men? In your debate you said we're getting the quantity, and we might be. But a third of these young men are leaving during their first enlistment. Have you made any personal inquiry to find out if the quality of the army is what you would like it to be?

MILTON FRIEDMAN: The quality of the Army is not what I would like it to be. I would like it to be a much higher quality army.

PETE McCLOSKEY: Then it's not working, is it?

MILTON FRIEDMAN: That isn't the question. In politics, you don't beat a candidate without a candidate, and it's the same thing here. We have to ask, "not working relative to *what*?" I would say that if the quality is not as much as you and I would like, the way to improve it is to make the incentives better—to offer more—and those incentives don't have to be monetary. They can be nonmonetary. People could be offered greater opportunities within the service to choose their activities, to go where they want, and so on. Contrary to what you might think, I'm told by people in the military that it's precisely the dangerous and dirty jobs that are the easiest to fill.

QUESTION FROM THE AUDIENCE: My question is for Congressman McCloskey.

A great many of our ancestors fled Europe to avoid the draft. Do you think they had a duty to serve?

PETE McCLOSKEY: Those ancestors who fled the wars of Europe were fleeing nations that made war through the whim of rulers that fought for glory, that fought for territory, that fought for a lot of different things that do not relate to our need for the military today. I quite agree. Our ancestors fled circumstances in their countries that were repressive, that were repugnant, that led the common man to be buried in wars fought by kings.

Once you concede that we need an army, it ought to be a quality army.

COMMENT FROM THE AUDIENCE: A great many of them fled specifically to avoid the draft.

PETE McCLOSKEY: I accept that. But that isn't the case today, is it?

MILTON FRIEDMAN: No, but let me ask you a different question along the same lines, because I think the question of foreign policy is relevant. I don't think they're independent.

I think we will have a better foreign policy, in which the public at large will play a better role, if we have a volunteer force than if we have a draft.

I don't think there's anything wrong with people not being willing to volunteer for conflicts they don't believe in and which they think are wrong. [Applause.]

PETE MCCLOSKEY: I completely agree with you.

MILTON FRIEDMAN: But having a draft means that they are forced to serve in conflicts *regardless* of their attitude.

PETE MCCLOSKEY: Right.

MILTON FRIEDMAN: Personally, I am not even in favor of a draft in time of major war. [Applause.] If you have a conflict like World War II, which had widespread public backing throughout the society, I do not believe there will be any shortage of young people willing to volunteer out of a sense of patriotism to defend this country. That's a major reason why I'm in favor of a volunteer force.

PETE MCCLOSKEY: Yes, but the problem is that the next war is going to burst upon us like Korea. It isn't going to be like World War II or Vietnam. I think that when you mentioned the Vietnamese experience, you really made that point. Congress didn't declare war for Vietnam. We never had the American people solidly behind a constitutional declaration of war. And we only went halfway with the Gulf of Tonkin resolution. We authorized a president to undertake acts of aggression, and then slid into conflict over a period of some three years.

I also think that the draft is a mechanism by which young people can express their opposition to an unjust and improper war, and that this carries over into this argument. It's one thing to say nobody wants to be drafted to fight an unjust war. It's another thing to say nobody wants to be drafted to make sure that we don't have to fight a war. As I see it, *that* is the purpose of the draft today. The danger is that we will be led into a war because we are weak, or perceived as weak—not because we're overly aggressive the way we were in the sixties.

QUESTION FROM THE AUDIENCE: My question, Congressman McCloskey, is whether you think our ancestors who fled Europe had the same kind of moral obligation to serve their country as you did in 1945? I wanted to see if you could carry that to the European situation.

PETE MCCLOSKEY: The European situation then compares with the recent situation in Vietnam. In the European case, however, wars were fought every year for centuries using the common man as fodder. Such wars were properly resisted.

I agree that a war in this country should be fought only if the American people, by majority vote of their representatives in Congress, declare war. My proposal is to cover our manpower requirements in the case we have a sudden case of *that*. This is an entirely different situation from the European situation you used as your precept.

QUESTION FROM THE AUDIENCE: I have a very short question on the same, or a similar, point.

Congressman McCloskey, do you not think that the best way to spread and protect the principles of freedom is actually to practice them at home and not just to preach them?

PETE MCCLOSKEY: I quite agree with that. But protecting freedom does require the maintenance of some kind of army. There is no lack of people around the world who would take our freedom from us if we didn't have an army.

COMMENT FROM THE AUDIENCE: If we reinstitute the draft and adopt the same totalitarian principles as the socialist and communist states, there's nothing to defend here anyway.

PETE MCCLOSKEY: If you look at the peace-loving European countries like Sweden, Denmark, Norway, and the Netherlands, you'll find that they all have compulsory service. It does not necessarily follow that a nation becomes warlike merely because it stands prepared to fight.

COMMENT FROM THE AUDIENCE: I'm one of the libertarians who do believe that involuntary servitude of any kind is bad.

Congressman McCloskey, you've brought up the race issue repeatedly and said, "No reasonable young man will volunteer for the Army today" and "The Army must be a cross section of the best in our society, not the worst." You made these statements in interesting proximity to other statements about statistics on the high proportion of black people in the military.

It's not at all certain that conscription will lead to a different racial mix than we have. I wish you had been here throughout the conference, because this is a point which a lot of interesting people addressed. If you a priori believe that a particular mixture is appropriate or desirable, you have to take certain measures in order to attain that mixture.

I'll now outline some appropriate measures that would actually bring about a different situation from what we have today, which I think is monstrous. One would be to exclude qualified black people who apply and say, "We don't want you. You're second-class citizens." Second would be to offer them a differential wage—a lower wage than white people. Then not as many black people would volunteer and more white people would volunteer. Third would be not to allow any volunteers whatsoever, but simply draft selectively on the basis of race.

PETE MCCLOSKEY: All three of those alternatives violate the Constitution.

AUDIENCE: They're also the only ways we could obtain the goal that you are proposing, and I think they're all evil and monstrous. If you don't like any of them, then you don't have any case whatsoever. I think that perhaps you should take a course in economics.

PETE MCCLOSKEY: I suppose this is a matter that economists are best suited to determine.

COMMENT FROM THE AUDIENCE: If you eliminate educational grants to get more people into the Army, then the rich boys will be in college and the poor boys will be in the Army. This is the old way, the way it was in Europe. I don't like it. [Applause.]

MILTON FRIEDMAN: The problem with what you are saying is twofold. In the first place, the facts are not what you say. Our present educational benefits are going to the wealthy. In my opinion, the governmental subsidization of higher education is a scandal because it taxes the poor in order to provide benefits for the middle and upper classes. Those are the facts.

The second problem with what you say is that, if you want to do what Congressman McCloskey wants to do, then that's what you have to do: you have to induce higher-educated, higher-status people to go into the armed forces, and the only way he has to do that is by paying them a higher wage. His proposal really amounts to giving higher military pay to people from upper-income classes than to people from lower-income classes.

PETE MCCLOSKEY: But, Mr. Friedman, don't you concede the validity of her statement? Under the All-Volunteer Army, as it is today, the rich boys are in college and the poor boys are on the front lines. That's *also* a fact.

MILTON FRIEDMAN: The rich boys are having to pay taxes to pay the wages of the poor, whereas under a draft, what you do is impose the cost on the poor, and the rich go scot-free and don't even have to pay to hire the poor as they do now.

PETE MCCLOSKEY: But you do concede her point, do you not?

MILTON FRIEDMAN: No. [Laughter.]

PETE MCCLOSKEY: Under your All-Volunteer Army, the rich boys are in college and the poor are in the rifle company. Isn't that true?

MILTON FRIEDMAN: Of course, that's true if we take only the enlisted forces and do not consider the officer corps. The rich boys in the military are in the officer corps.

COMMENT FROM THE AUDIENCE: Mr. Friedman, if the boys who are getting educational grants are in fact rich and do not need them, then you need more efficient people administering these things. That's right up your alley. You ought to be able to figure that out. [Laughter.]

MILTON FRIEDMAN: I have written extensively on that question and this is a wholly different question. Our present educational grant system is, in my opinion, a scandal. There is no way to correct it, in my opinion, except by much more fundamental measures than the kind of thing you're speaking of now. That's a different issue. It's not the present issue. The present issue is that, so far as the armed force are concerned, it is the same as in every other occupation in this country: low-paid people are doing low-paid jobs; high-paid people are doing high-paid jobs. [Laughter.]

COMMENT FROM THE AUDIENCE: Mr. McCloskey, I haven't yet decided whether or not I'm for the draft, but I do have a serious problem with your proposal. You have spoken again and again about the need for having a cross section of the society in the military. At the same time, though, I hear you use phrases like "the burden of the young people" and "the responsibility of the young men." Tell me, why must 18-year-olds bear the burden of responsibility for the entire population of the United States? [Applause.]

PETE McCLOSKEY: I can recall once in 1971 making an argument in Congress that we should not go to war without generals and Congressmen sharing in the assault wave.

The reason that the burden falls on the young is essentially that combat, unfortunately, is best borne by the young, not old. That is an unfortunate fact of the youthful physical condition and relative lack of fear of youth and the fact that the circumstances of combat are far more easily faced by the young. I can recall walking down a road at the age of 24 as a second lieutenant, looking at a 31-year-old captain, and thinking, "Why should that old man be subjected to this?" He was too old to be undergoing the physical arduousness of what we were then facing in the Korean mountains. That's the reason for preferentially using the young. It's not a desire to put the burden on the young. It's the fact that the young have the best chance of *survival*. The best fighting people are young. If we went to war anywhere in the world tomorrow, I would just as soon see a few of the politicians that ordered people into combat accompany them in the assault wave.

COMMENT AND QUESTION FROM THE AUDIENCE: My question is a little bit different. What bothers me is what the kind and size of army you're talking about will be, and has been used *for*. What bothers me are the Kent States, the Vietnam wars, the Korean wars, and—Milton Friedman will know about this—what happened in Chile with the institution of fascism at the hands of the CIA. All these things, you know, make me question what this army is going to be used *for*. Our army is in a desperate shambles, that's true. But that doesn't bother me at all, because, in fact, I should be forming an army against your army.

My question is, Which applications of this army are really for national defense and which for pure aggression? And who makes those determinations? Why are there U.S. troops in the Philippines? Why are there U.S. advisers in Chile? The question is: Why the hell should we join your imperialist army? And it *is* an imperialistic army.

MILTON FRIEDMAN: I want to answer this question. I believe you should have the freedom not to join the army. [Applause.] I don't agree at all with the implicit political judgment you have expressed, but I believe the great virtue of a free society is that it permits opportunity for people to have widely different views. I do not believe you ought to be forced under compulsion to join the armed forces. You ought to be free. But are you being consistent? Are you opposed to using force?

MARC STRASSMAN: My name is Marc Strassman, and I'm running against you for Congress, Congressman McCloskey.

VOICE FROM THE AUDIENCE: What's your name?

PETE McCLOSKEY: [He's] Marc Strassman, candidate for Congress.

MARC STRASSMAN: I'm running against you because I believe your position on this issue is intellectually and morally bankrupt. And that is because you're not addressing yourself to the premises of the entire constellation of the issue—which is why we even need an army and what we need it *for*, or, *who* needs the army and what they need it for. If we consider things in that context, it won't be so easy to justify the need for a technically proficient military that can work with forward-based computer assisted weapons,which is what it has to do if its real function is to serve the economic interests of specific American-based multinational corporations in foreign countries and not to defend freedom as such. I think you should address yourself to that point.

PETE McCLOSKEY: First of all, I welcome your running for Congress, because the most important part of our free process is full debate between people with different views.

We're working right now to get an initiative on the ballot so we can have a fair Republican presidential campaign in this state.*

MARC STRASSMAN: I signed that.

PETE McCLOSKEY: No matter what a view is, I think it contributes to the progress of this country, and, in part, I agree with you. I think that we should examine the purpose of the army and what the size of that army should be to accomplish those purposes. But as you point out, it is an army that is going to be asked to have great skills. And whatever the army is like, it should be made up of cool, competent people who can read. If the present army is not made up of such persons, as the evidence is beginning to indicate, we have to find a way of correcting this situation.

I'm not wedded to the idea of national youth service, but I am wedded to the principle that this country ought to have a competent army. I would much rather see an army of reluctant citizen soldiers made up of the rich

---

* [Editor's note]: This refers to the California State initiative for proportional representation in the selection process for Republican delegates in the primaries.

as well as the poor than what we've got now. That's what we're seeking to achieve, and I'm perfectly willing to hear any suggestion for alternatives as to how we can reach that result. I think you'd concede from the evidence today that we can't reach it through the All-Volunteer Army. And we aren't going to reach it through a straight draft with college exemptions. We can't do it fairly if we're going to draft only one out of ten for this arduous duty. I think the best result is some sort of compromise that picks up Professor Moskos's suggestion that perhaps the only educational benefits tendered by the government should be to those volunteers who seek to serve the government in this arduous capacity.

But I agree with you in that I think in the next debate in this election year we ought to force the presidential candidates to address the larger contexts as well as these more specific questions.

MARC STRASSMAN: I share your view that the army needs skilled, competent operators to use the sophisticated equipment it relies on. I think that we have to address what they're going to be doing with those men and that equipment.

I'd like you to address the question of what our needs are going to be for the armed forces. Assuming that we have a force capable of rapid deployment, its purpose, as I see it, is going to be to take over oil fields. I think we have to examine why we need that oil, who's going to benefit from our having it, and whether that's what we want to do as a *country*. We should decide on *that* issue *first*, rather than deal with the secondary issue of the draft.

PETE McCLOSKEY: You raise a very good point, and I think Mr. Friedman will want to address this also.

Let me just say that after 12 years of being in this funny business of politics, and particularly after following diplomatic negotiations and the posturing of national and international leaders and diplomats, I'm increasingly convinced that intergovernmental negotiations are not what's crucial to keeping peace in the world. There will always be leaders who *want* to go to war to satisfy themselves or some constituency, whether it be religious or economic. It looks to me that the most important building block of peace is the expansion of trade, commerce, and communications, and the export of values from one country to another. If you're going to keep up these commercial transactions, you're going to have to have airports, and ships, and you're going to have to have ownership of property. While it may be that we will be using our American military force to protect airports or 747s full of passengers, or embassies with our people in them, that is an understandable and appropriate use of military force in order to keep the world moving towards an economic exchange of commerce and trade that builds the basis for world peace. We've got to have a police force.

MARC STRASSMAN: I might agree with you if the economic exchange were on the basis of mutual respect and not exploitation.

PETE McCLOSKEY: I can tell you that the rest of the nations of the world are, hopefully, resisting any tendency to exploitation. In fact, the oil crisis, the mineral crisis, and the coffee cartel are all essentially the result of nations which have been exploited starting to resist exploitation by using the principles of economics and the free market Professor Friedman so capably defends.

COMMENT FROM THE AUDIENCE: At the end of the last draft here in northern California, half of the people who were called for induction failed to show up. When resistance reached that level, it became impossible to enforce the draft. It was only possible at that point to cover up the fact that the resistance had reached that level.

I also want to point out, Congressman McCloskey, that your program is not fundamentally different in the choices it offers. We've never drafted people who volunteered for the Army.

PETE McCLOSKEY: The resistance you speak of, though, occurred during the Vietnam War. The only way you could resist that war was to resist the draft. That's perfectly understandable to me.

COMMENT FROM THE AUDIENCE: That is true.

We had three large rallies last year here at Stanford against the draft and against your proposal. My question is: What are you going to do under your proposal with people like myself who are going to resist the draft on principle?

PETE McCLOSKEY: Given the principles you espouse, you would have the option of civilian service. We have *always* given the option of alternative civilian service to those who opposed the draft on religious grounds. Under my plan you would have that option. You could choose the year of civilian service and never come under any risk of being drafted. Also, if you *were* drafted, if you fell within that pool, and met conscientious objector criteria, you would be entitled to conscientious objector treatment.

COMMENT FROM THE AUDIENCE: I would refuse all of those.

PETE McCLOSKEY: As a conscientious objector, you would oppose that also?

COMMENT FROM THE AUDIENCE: Yes.

PETE McCLOSKEY: Then, under the rule of the Supreme Court in the Holmes case, you would be sent to jail.

COMMENT FROM THE AUDIENCE: Thank you.

QUESTION FROM THE AUDIENCE: You may have just answered one of my questions. I have a second one. Under your bill, Congressman Mc-Closkey, would conscientious objections to the national service plan be allowed or recognized?

PETE McCLOSKEY: Yes. You could be entitled to be a conscientious objector.

QUESTION FROM THE AUDIENCE: I'm sorry, I meant to ask whether conscientious objector status would be recognized for those who objected to the *civilian* plan options as well.

PETE McCLOSKEY: The first three alternatives are all voluntary. [Laughter.] It's the fourth pool, where you don't choose any of the first three and therefore would be draftable, that the conscientious objector status would apply to.

COMMENT FROM THE AUDIENCE: I'm only talking about the civilian services, about the people who object to the compulsion involved in that because of the draft being in the background.

PETE McCLOSKEY: The chances are that if you didn't choose one of the first three options, you probably still wouldn't be drafted under my plan. But if you were drafted and then raised the conscientious objection complaint, if you were successful you would be entitled to alternative civilian service. But the civilian service would then be compulsory for you, as it was in the sixties.

QUESTION FROM THE AUDIENCE: So there would be no conscientious objection for the civilian service options?

PETE McCLOSKEY: No. Conscientious objection would be relevant only to the fourth default option.

COMMENT FROM THE AUDIENCE: I'm sure you've read the decision in the Holmes case, which says that in time of peace alternate service can be imposed, even on a conscientious objector, to preserve morale in the armed services. I take it that the law would be the same under your plan.

QUESTION FROM THE AUDIENCE: I have a second question: If your national service plan is passed, how would the two parts—the civilian system and the military system—utilize young couples with children where both parents are liable for service?

PETE McCLOSKEY: We're trying to do everything we can to discourage 18-year-olds from being young couples with children.

COMMENT FROM THE AUDIENCE: There still exist a great number of people who *are* parents at 18, and they are parents at the time they would be liable to serve under your plan.

PETE McCLOSKEY: I'll have to think about that one. I honestly don't know what I'd do with an 18-year-old who became a father and then claimed that he shouldn't have to serve.

QUESTION FROM THE AUDIENCE: How about an 18-year-old mother?

PETE McCLOSKEY: I don't know that either. I'll have to think about that. I haven't thought that one out. . . .

MILTON FRIEDMAN: No—under my plan, there wouldn't be that problem for 18-year-old women. It wouldn't be a problem because under present circumstances women would not be drafted, and there would therefore be no reason for a woman to volunteer for one of the first three options. She would be home free. So the plan is not universal in any way, shape, form, or manner.

QUESTION FROM THE AUDIENCE: My understanding is that under national service, women would be required to serve. I have heard from a reliable source that an attempt would be made to station young mothers near their homes. Could you comment on that?

PETE MCCLOSKEY: One of the problems we've had with women's rights is that women get pregnant. I've forgotten what percentage of the women in Germany are pregnant, but it's substantial. It's a problem we haven't begun to learn how to cope with yet.

ALBERT REES: I'm very sorry we're not going to have time to get to all the people who want to ask questions, but I don't think we should impose any more on our two distinguished speakers. They've done very well under what were sometimes extremely difficult circumstances, and I want to thank them both very, very much.

PART 6

Complete Papers

XXI

THE ALL-VOLUNTEER MILITARY: VIEWPOINTS ISSUES, AND PROSPECTS

William R. King

My special delight in conferring here is founded not only on our topic, which I believe to be of grave national importance, but also only my appreciation for the other participants—an especially knowledgeable and prestigious group with whom I am proud to confer.

The Problems of the All-Volunteer Force

What I find perhaps most satisfying of all about this conference is the breadth of coverage of the topic. To indicate why this broad scope is of particular interest to me, I ask that you allow me to indulge myself by quoting from my testimony on the All-Volunteer Force (AVF) before the U.S. Senate Committee on Armed Services several years ago. At that time I said:

> The AVF has been operating under a combination of circumstances that could not reasonably be expected to be more favorable.[1]
> ... The current problems of the AVF translate into potential future problems that may be of significant impact on our future ability to maintain an effective defense establishment at reasonable cost levels. ...
> ... While many alternatives to the AVF, other than the pre-1973 variety of draft, are dismissed outright by some as infeasible, I have concluded that a program of national service could be developed and implemented in such a way that it would alleviate many of the problems of the AVF, substantially enhance the nation's ability to pursue a broad range of our national goals, and be reasonably economic.[2]

I believe that each of these statements could be made today with equal veracity, and my concern for our nation is profound because of this.

Our newspapers are filled almost daily with reports of the "failure of the AVF" in some operational sense of recruiting shortfalls or attrition levels with consequent predictions of a return to the draft. This is precisely the sort of simplistic "either-or" choice that I forecast we might be forced to make if we did not act to assess whether other, better alternatives might be available. It appears that much of the public, the news media, and some policymakers are convinced that the "draft versus AVF" controversy presents us with a dichotomous choice that should be made solely on the basis of whether or not the current system is working.

In reality it should be no such thing. First, we should recognize that in assessing the merits of *any* personnel procurement system—draft, AVF, or whatever—we should not be concerned merely with how efficiently it works, but *with its overall impact on our society*. The burdensome tax levied on those conscripted under the draft was largely ignored until the Gates Commission focused attention on it. The broader impacts of the AVF on society were given little attention until Janowitz, Moskos, and others performed analyses of the AVF that went beyond economic measures of performance.

Clearly the agenda of this conference indicates that its planners recognize the need to assess the AVF, or any alternatives to it, in broad multidimensional terms that incorporate the efficiency and effectiveness of its operation as well as its impact on our society. Moreover, the agenda includes consideration of national service, which, if broadly defined, opens up a wide range of alternatives to the draft and the AVF that is rich with potential for our nation.

I believe that the dichotomous debate that is reaching ever greater crescendo is a sterile one for our nation, because *both* alternatives have severe social costs associated with them. That is why I made the previously quoted statement to the Committee on Armed Services and why I have included a discussion of the potential of various national service programs in every public statement that I have made concerning the AVF.

I am not certain that any *particular* national service proposal would, in fact, be superior to the AVF or to the draft. I do know that the national service concept is broad enough to encompass a wide variety of specific arrangements, many of which would appear to have attributes that overcome many of the social costs of both the draft and the AVF.

I have feared the acrimonious debate over "draft versus AVF" that I predicted some years ago, and my prediction becomes more valid as each month and year pass. Our nation is in ever greater danger of wasting its energies debating which of two poor alternatives it should use to raise its military forces.

I believe that it may be an unnecessary as well as largely fruitless debate. We succeeded in dealing with some of the features of the draft that were most undesirable to large segments of our society when we instituted the AVF. Now, we are finding that some features of the AVF are equally undesirable to large segments of society. If we opt for a "quick fix" in returning to the draft as it was previously constituted, we shall probably begin the cycle anew and have gained nothing of permanence, while incurring great cost.

If, on the other hand, we use this opportunity to design, develop, and evaluate other alternatives—which I shall collect together and refer to broadly as "national service"—we may be able to fulfill our military personnel needs while simultaneously fulfilling other important national goals.

Thus, I find it especially refreshing that this conference's breadth of coverage goes beyond the question of how well the AVF is working to discuss what impact it is having and to consider national service alternatives to *both* the draft and the AVF.

The Performance of the AVF

One of my purposes in leading off this conference is to present an assessment of the performance and status of the AVF.

I shall not burden you with yet another statistical analysis of the AVF's performance. My analysis is comprehensively reported in my report to the U.S. Senate Committee on Armed Services.[3] Since there are Defense Department officials here who, I am sure, will quote these statistics on request, particularly as they reflect changes that have occurred in the recent past, I shall refrain from making an updated version of the statistical case that I have made in my Senate report and other meetings.

To briefly summarize the AVF's performance, let me make a number of assertions that are based on fact and analysis, but that clearly are stated in ways that are suggestive of my conclusions and value judgments. I do not believe that the essence of these assertions can be seriously challenged, except by those who find that very recent contrary data may suggest that a turning point has been reached, or believe that a just-instituted program will remedy the deficiency, or object on the basis of semantics. However, the implicit judgments almost surely will be challenged.

1. Within a range of error that would be considered acceptable in most fields, the active forces have been maintained at close to desired force levels during the AVF era just as they were in the draft era.

2. On the other hand, the reserve forces have not been so maintained and are seriously undermanned—a factor that can be directly attributed to the loss of the draft-induced reserve "volunteers."
3. Through the lowering of standards, and the use of monetary and other incentives, this general situation can probably be maintained for the immediate future.
4. However, as the inevitable consequence of smaller age-group cohorts, less attractive pay relative to civilian jobs, and other factors, it will become increasingly difficult to maintain desired force levels, even with reduced standards and incentives, through the 1980s.
5. In any case, the AVF is a peacetime concept that could not realistically be expected to serve as a basis for dealing with an emergency situation requiring significantly enlarged force levels.
6. Adequate reserves, a registration system, a "backup draft" and other support that was assumed to be an integral part of the AVF when it was instituted[4] are not a reality, thus calling into question whether the present-day AVF meets the minimal needs of our nation for defense over the long run.
7. The impact of the AVF on society and on our ability to meet our defense needs has not been adequately assessed, despite seven years of experience with the AVF and numerous studies that have been made of it.

Standards for Assessing the Performance and Potential of the AVF

I make these assertions to concisely summarize the state of the AVF as I see it. More importantly, however, I wish to use them as a basis for developing some more important themes related to our ability, both at this conference and more generally, to assess the AVF, its problems, its benefits, and the merits and demerits of alternatives to it.

I suspect that my seven assertions have already fomented the basis for controversy in this body. It is this potential for debate and controversy to which I shall devote my primary attention, for if the conference is to be productive, we must at least agree on what and why we disagree. Beyond that, it is my hope that I can establish a framework within which the *substance* of disagreements may be more clearly understood and, in some cases, resolved. In this sense, I have taken it on myself to explain, in advance, some of the disagreements that will inevitably arise at this conference.

I have adopted this goal because in my role as an assessor of the AVF, I have found how easy it is to become enmeshed in unproductive controversy.

After my Senate testimony in 1977, I was referred to on the floor of Congress, before it became fashionable to criticize the AVF, as the "foremost opponent." I have also been referred to, both on and off the floor of Congress, as a "draft advocate" and in some much more vitriolic terms.

I assure you that I am neither an AVF opponent nor a draft advocate. I am critical of the performance of the AVF in absolute terms, although I believe that the Defense Department did an admirable job, particularly in the early years, of instituting a radically different system of procuring massive numbers of military personnel. I am also critical of the shortsighted view we have taken of the AVF's future viability and its impact on our society.

These viewpoints and conclusions are considered by some, who see the world in much clearer dichotomous terms than do I, to represent both opposition to the AVF and advocacy of conscription. I am confident that this conference will not adopt such a simplistic view of this complex issue. To further that confidence, I shall attempt to provide a partial explanation for some of the controversy and misunderstanding that have characterized the issue and that we should avoid.

It is now much more fashionable to be critical of the AVF than it was when I first adopted that posture. However, the vitriol remains. The "AVF versus draft" issue remains as controversial seven years after it was implemented as it was at that time.

There are passionate "believers" on both sides of the controversy. To some AVF advocates, conscription is so evil that anything, particularly something with such an appealing, apple-pie name as the VOLUNTEER military, is preferable. Some draft advocates, looking at the old days of the pre-Vietnam draft through rose-colored glasses, do not see the inequities of taxation and the dislocations caused by forcing young men into contrived choices, such as the choice between college and military service or between fatherhood and the military.

One suspects that many such advocates assess these alternatives primarily from the perspective of their personal experience. It is easy to see how one who was forced by the draft into hard personal choices could become an ardent opponent of it and how one who served serenely in the pre-Vietnam draft era could support it.

Some champion the AVF because of their political beliefs and philosophies. There are those who abhor war so much that they wish to do away with its instruments altogether. Failing that, they wish to leave it only to those who will volunteer to perform this disagreeable function. To others, the idea of conscription is inconsistent with their interpretation of personal freedom.

On the other side, some draft advocates are strong believers in the sort of planned and controlled society into which the draft fits nicely. They do not like the inefficiencies and lack of discipline that they see in our modern democracy and they want a more clear-cut approach to military procurement, just as they yearn for the control of prices, labor unrest, and many other confusing aspects of modern life.

I believe that these different views can be readily understood or readily explained to, and perceived by, the informed sector of the public. It seems that much of the confusion in the minds of many informed people concerning the ongoing debate is generated by *serious analysts who appear to have substantial disagreements in the conclusions that they have reached concerning the AVF*. Since these analysts are presumed to be honest and competent, and since they all draw conclusions from essentially the same set of data, this dissonance is puzzling to many.

The fact is, of course, that both the analysts and the advocates, to greater or lesser degrees, produce conclusions that reflect their own personalities, backgrounds, values, and analytic frameworks. Mitroff has empirically demonstrated this in the case of the "Moon Scientists" of the 1960s,[5] and it is no less true of the "Manpower Scientists" of the AVF. Each analyst reaches conclusions that reflect the results not only of objective analysis but of the intricate processes that have structured his own personality, values, and framework for thinking. As Kaplan has said, "The problem for methodology is not *whether* values are involved in inquiry, but *which*, and above all, how they are to be empirically grounded."[6]

This differential effect of the analyst, coupled with the fact that various studies have different scopes and methodologies as well as different sponsors, surely serves to explain much of the dissonance in assessments of the AVF's past performance and future potential.

The Impact of Analytic Frameworks

The impact of the analytic framework of the individual or the group performing a study can be illustrated by comparing two analytical frameworks —that of the economist and that of the sociologist.

The economist's analytical framework is based in the marketplace. With its measurable quantities and prices, it is an idealized world in which "everything has a price" and in which the actors behave rationally as dictated by price and quantity variables.

The Gates Commission Report, which provided the rationale for the AVF, uses such a framework.[7] For example, consider the treatment of the concept referred to as the "hidden tax" paid by draftees—an important element in the commission's argument against conscription. This concept argues that draftees were required to pay a hidden in-kind tax because they were paid at lower levels than would be required to induce them to volunteer.[8] This aggregate tax was estimated to be $2 billion: $1.5 billion reflected an assumed difference between the military earnings of draftees and their potential civilian earnings, and $0.5 billion reflected the additional pay required to motivate these people to volunteer.[9]

This idea of a "hidden tax" is a theoretical construct that flows from the economist's idealized analytic framework. Certainly, it describes a valid consideration. However, in estimating it numerically, no consideration was given to: (1) the *real* alternative civilian job opportunities that existed for the majority of unskilled and inexperienced young people who were draftees; and (2) the benefits, in terms of job training and experience, offered by the military.

Certainly, many young draftees had very poor *real* civilian job prospects. During the draft era the demand for the unskilled and inexperienced was simply not great; nor is it now. Moreover, despite the fact that there may be some basis to question the real value of the job training and experience offered by the military, these benefits were unquestionably *perceived* to be very significant by the young men who are the best prospects for the military under either conscription or the AVF.[10]

Thus, in calculating the theoretical hidden tax levied inequitably on draftees, the economist's framework uses a series of other theoretical constructs that may not well reflect the real world as perceived by the "payer" of the tax.

Now consider a sociological analytic framework as applied to the AVF. Moskos, a sociologist, deals with the issue of the representativeness of the AVF using both objective empirical data and personal observation. He concludes:

> In comparison with the peacetime draft, . . . today's Army is much less representative—and becoming increasingly so—of American youth. . . . [A] more representative enlisted force will have beneficial consequences for the Army in terms of military efficiency, enlisted life in the ranks, and civic definition. Most troubling, even at present levels of quality and numbers, recruitment will become progressively more difficult as the cohort of eligible enlistees drops more rapidly over the next decade.[11]

In contrast to the sociologist's framework the economist's focuses on a limited number of measurable quantities, often measured only at aggregate levels, and uses theoretical constructs such as the "hidden tax." The economist tends to ignore or explain away phenomena that do not fit within his analytical framework.[12]

The sociologist's framework, on the other hand, allows for more subjective analysis and gives a broader interpretation to what are considered to be data. The penalty paid for this, of course, is that it may be even more value-laden and *less actionable*. What action is a policymaker to infer from evidence of lesser "civic definition," for instance? The economist's model tells the policymaker just what to expect and at what price, thus presenting a clear, if incomplete, basis for decision-making.

The Effect of the Analytic Domain

It is trite to say that analysts may well reach different conclusions when they study different things! However, as the public perceives it, this has been exactly what has been happening in the AVF debate.

Various AVF studies have defined the AVF in different fashions. Some, like the Beard (Reed) Report,[13] have focused attention on the active Army. An analyst might reasonably choose the Army on the theory that it has the most difficult recruiting job under the AVF.

Other studies have been broader in scope, but have tended to focus on a "worst case" analysis, wherever it occurs (recruiting and force maintainance are worst in the Reserves, the Air Force has had the most difficult situation for the recruitment of physicians, and so on). This approach is taken in an attempt to ferret out what is "really" happening, rather than to rely on the mass of highly aggregated, and therefore often misleading, statistics that the Defense Department usually makes public.

Still other analyses, such as the RAND (Cooper) Study,[14] focus primarily on the active duty force and are reported in the press and perceived by the public to say that the AVF is working well. Yet the author would quickly add that the reserve forces are an integral part of our defense under the "total force" concept and that by no stretch of the imagination could one argue that reserve force recruitment and force maintainance have been acceptable under the AVF.

Thus, in part, whether the AVF has worked or not depends on the domain that one assesses. It clearly has worked better in some services than in others (e.g., Air Force versus Army), better in some segments than in others (e.g., active versus reserves), and better according to some measures than others (e.g., recruiting versus attrition).

The Impact of Analytic Methodology

Closely related to the analytic framework is the methodology that is employed to gather evidence and to draw conclusions. This may be illustrated in the choice of the surrogates that will be measured and the base to which they will be compared.

For instance, one element of the representativeness issue is the educational level of the military. If one compares the educational level of the current forces with that of the draft-era force as a whole, the result obtained may be different from that obtained by comparing the present level with that of a specific draft-era group, such as those actually drafted, or draft-induced volunteers (who we sometimes forget existed), or the non-draft-induced volunteers.

Indeed, the meaning of some superficially clear measures is not at all clear. How is educational level to be measured? If one focuses attention on college graduates or "college-experienced" soldiers, one result is obtained. If one focuses on high school graduates, a different picture may emerge.

That different methodologies often lead to different results and conclusions is amply demonstrated by a review of the various studies of the AVF. For instance, Cooper uses aggregate income statistics for Zip-Code areas to conclude that "the increasing proportion of blacks in the force does not indicate that the AVF has resulted in an Army of the poor."[15] Moskos, on the other hand, studies a wide variety of social variables such as marital status and, using data on actual recruits, concludes: "It is undeniable . . . that the all-volunteer Army is much less representative of the American middle class than was the pre-Vietnam Army."[16]

These two analysts use different analytic frameworks, different surrogate measures, different levels of aggregation, and different methodologies to arrive at conclusions that most people would view as being antithetical.

Yet, it cannot be said that one is correct and the other incorrect. Both are correct conclusions *within their respective frameworks and methodologies*.

The Need for a Comprehensive Study

An analysis of various AVF studies leads me to conclude not that one is correct and another incorrect, but rather that *none is sufficiently comprehensive and multidisciplinary to deal adequately with this complex entity*.

A comprehensive study is necessary if we are to make rational and informed choices in this critical public policy area. Yet I believe that such a study is likely to be only one more on the long list of studies unless it meets certain criteria.

The Issue to be Studied

The issue to be studied must be clearly and broadly defined. This is best done in final form by those who will conduct the study in *close collaboration with those who will use its results*.

This posing of the question in operational terms that are agreed on by both analysts and policymakers is of critical importance. Again quoting Kaplan, "How we put the question reflects our values on one hand, and on the other hand helps determine the answer we get."[17]

For purposes of discussion, I should like to tentatively propose that the issue be: *How can we use the necessity of maintaining a defense establishment to best meet our national goals?* In other words, given that we must do it, how can we do it to best serve our national purposes?

I state the question in these broad terms because so large and complex an institution as the military will necessarily have impacts on many nonmilitary aspects of our society. This has long been recognized in a proactive sense. For instance, President Truman used military personnel policy as a spearhead in the drive for greater racial equality, and today development programs for weapons systems are assessed not only for their military effectiveness but for their economic impact as well. Likewise, the "unintended consequences" or "externalities" associated with our decision to move to an AVF are increasingly recognized.

The "given" element of the proposed issue statement is specifically intended to remove it from the domain of philosophy and morality. This is because I do not believe that we can resolve the ethical and moral questions within the time frame in which I consider it to be imperative that we resolve the AVF issue.

When viewed from this perspective, the critical question is not "How well is the AVF working?"; rather the salient questions are "What overall national impact is it having?" and "What overall impacts can be obtained from other alternatives?"

Who Should Conduct the Study?

Since I have argued that the conclusions reached in analyses of complex systems are affected by the analytic frameworks, personalities, and values of the analysis, the question of who should perform such a study becomes of paramount importance.

I propose that a multidisciplinary team be organized to address the task. The team must be consciously constructed to incorporate those who use *different analytic frameworks*. Indeed, it would probably be best to include a philosopher of science who can explain and interpret various frameworks and the nature of different varieties of evidence as they relate to the conclusions that may be drawn.[18] This study group must also include "pragmatic analysts," such as those who serve on the staffs of congressional committees, for it is they who can best assess the practicality and potential for implementation of various conclusions.

Probably no existing analysis group has the necessary resources and credibility to conduct such a study. Most certainly, a new "blue-ribbon commission" should *not* be the vehicle.

An Interdisciplinary Analytic Process

If such a study is not to deteriorate into controversy or into a series of fragmented analyses, the multidisciplinary group must be organized on an interdisciplinary basis. This means that every issue and subissue must be clearly defined on the basis of *group consensus*. Each hypothesis to be tested and each surrogate to be measured must be defined and agreed on. When such agreement cannot be reached, *alternative* approaches must be specified just as clearly.

It is critical in making choices concerning military manpower to define each subissue clearly, to assess the AVF's performance in terms of the definition, and to assess the importance that should be placed on the issue in making the policy decision.

If this process is truly an interdisciplinary one, it will obviate the difficulties that are inherent in a simple expert (or parochial group) who

> often makes *virtual decisions*, presupposing certain policies in his very formulation of the problem or in the tacit assumptions underlying his solution, and this intrusion is rationalized as nonexistent by the formula that as a scientist, he is only providing the basis for a decision which others, after all, must make. Thus the policy maker wills ends without scientific assessment of their conditions and consequences, while the scientist exercises power without corresponding responsibility, refusing indeed, "as a scientist," to assume responsibility.[19]

This process may be accomplished by reviewing how those who have discussed each subissue have explicitly or implicitly defined it, by collecting together the various definitions, by making them operational, by stating them in terms that can be measured, and by gathering objective data and informed judgments not only on the impact of the issue on society but also on the importance of that impact.

For instance, the representativeness issue can be *defined* in terms of a variety of factors such as race, sex, color, socioeconomic background, and so on. The *standard for comparison* can be the society as a whole, the cohort of military-age youth, or the military as it existed under the peacetime draft. The *impact* of representativeness can be assessed in terms of military effectiveness, the quality of life in the ranks, and the credibility of the military in the eyes of the public, as well as in a variety of other ways.

The *degree of impact* of such a factor as representativeness is admittedly hard to assess. Indeed, some have used that measurement difficulty as an excuse for ignoring the issue. In making this excuse, they unwittingly assign a low *importance* to the issue.

The *importance* of an issue and the *assessment of its impact* are two different things. An issue may be of high impact and low importance, or of low impact and high importance, or any other combination. *The difficulty that one may have in assessing an issue's impact has nothing to do with its importance.* If one dismisses an issue because it is difficult to assess, he is confusing impact with importance. Unfortunately, this sort of confusion has too often been characteristic of studies of the AVF.

An interdisciplinary analytic process, particularly one involving specialists in the *processes* of analysis (such as philosophers of science) as well as specialists in relevant disciplines, would be the best way of defining, focusing attention on, and resolving some of the methodological differences that have led to confusion with past AVF studies.

Maximizing the Potential for Impact

If the potential for acceptance and use of the conclusions of the study is to be maximized, the users must be involved in each stage of analysis, beginning with the operational definition of the issue to be studied. There is ample evidence that unless there is such involvement, the results are not likely to be accepted and implemented.[20]

In this instance, this means that congressional leaders as well as members of the Cabinet and of the Executive Branch must participate, at least on an advisory basis, in the analysis. This might be accomplished through an "advisory panel" that would be actively involved in an ongoing review of *both* the accomplishments and the problems of the study as it progresses. If, as is often the case, analysts allow the review process to focus exclusively on the accomplishments of an analytic endeavor, it will not provide the level of understanding and support that is necessary.

Conclusion

I have attempted to provide a summary view of the performance of the AVF, to explain some of the reasons why various analysts seem to have arrived at different conclusions concerning its performance and potential, and to outline a study that I believe might serve both to lay some of the AVF controversy to rest and to provide a basis for rational policymaking as we move into the 1980s.

Although this conference was not necessarily designed to do so, it might well serve to help resolve some of the AVF issues and/or to motivate such a systematic study. I look forward to participating with you in discussions of this critical national issue.

Notes

1. Opening statement of Dr. William R. King, "The All-Volunteer Armed Force." Hearing before the Subcommittee on Manpower and Personnel of the Committee on Armed Services, U.S. Senate, 95th Cong., 1st sess., March 2, 1977, p. 7.
2. Ibid., p. 6.
3. William R. King, "Achieving America's Goals: The All-Volunteer Force or National Serice?," Report prepared for the Committee on Armed Services, U.S. Senate, 95th Cong., 1st sess. (Washington, D.C.: Government Printing Office, 1977).
4. For instance, see President's Commission on an All-Volunteer Force, *The Report of the President's Commission on an All-Volunteer Force* (Washington, D.C.: Government Printing Office, 1970).
5. I. I. Mitroff, *The Subjective Side of Science* (New York: Elsevier-North Holland Publishing Co., 1974).
6. Abraham Kaplan, *The Conduct of Inquiry: Methodology for Behavioral Science* (San Francisco: Chandler Publishing Co., 1964), p. 387.
7. President's Commission on an All-Volunteer Force, *Report*.
8. Ibid., Chap. 3.
9. Ibid., p. 26.
10. "Good vocational training" is the most frequently mentioned benefit of military service *in all major categories*: college men, black noncollege men, white noncollege men, and young boys. See "Attitudes and Motivators toward Enlistment in the U.S. Army" (Princeton, N.J.: Opinion Research Corporation, April 1974), p. 8.
11. Charles C. Moskos, Jr., "The Enlisted Ranks in the All-Volunteer Army," Paper prepared for the Military in American Society Study, University of Virginia, Charlottesville, January 1978, p. 61.
12. For instance, see the Gates Commission's treatment of the issue of racial representativeness in which the following scenario is dismissed as having "no basis in fact": "The higher pay required for a voluntary force will be especially appealing to blacks who have relatively poorer civilian opportunities. This, combined with higher reenlistment rates for blacks, will mean that a disproportionate number of blacks will be in military service. White enlistments and reenlistments might decline, thus leading to an all-black enlisted force. Racial tensions would grow because of white apprehension at this development and black resentment at bearing an

undue share of the burden of defense. At the same time, some of the most qualified young blacks would be in the military—not in the community where their talents are needed" (President's Commission on the All-Volunteer Armed Force, *Report*, p. 15). This scenario that was so casually dismissed by the commission could be argued to be a reasonably accurate description of what has actually transpired.

13. J. L. Reed, "The Beard Study: An Analysis and Evaluation of the United States Army," April 1978.
14. Richard V. L. Cooper, *Military Manpower and the All-Volunteer Force*, R-1450-ARPA (Santa Monica, Calif.: Rand Corporation, September 1977).
15. Ibid., p. vii and Chap. 10.
16. Charles C. Moskos, Jr., "The Enlisted Ranks in the All-Volunteer Army," in *The All-Volunteer Force and American Society*, ed. J. B. Keeley (Charlottesville: University of Virginia Press, 1978), p. 52.
17. Kaplan, *Conduct of Inquiry*, p. 385.
18. For instance, see Ian I. Mitroff and Louis R. Pondy, "On the Organization of Inquiry: A Comparison of Some Radically Different Approaches to Policy Analysis," *Public Administration Review* 34, no. 5 (1974): 471–480.
19. Kaplan, *Conduct of Inquiry*, p. 401.
20. For example, see R. P. Schultz and D. P. Slevin, eds., *Implementing Operations Research/Management Science* (New York: Elsevier–North Holland Publishing Co., 1975), and R. Burton, D. Dellinger, and W. R. King, "Legislative Implementation of Public Policy Analysis," in *Implementation of Management Science*, ed. R. Doktor et al. (New York: Elsevier–North Holland Publishing Co., 1979).

XXII

THE ALL-VOLUNTEER FORCE: HAS IT WORKED, WILL IT WORK?*

Richard W. Hunter and Gary R. Nelson

Introduction and Summary

Seven years ago this month the last draftee entered military service. In that time we have been able to learn how well our nation will support and how well our government can manage an all-volunteer armed force. Although America has a tradition of voluntary military service, no nation had ever attempted to sustain a military force of 2 million exclusively with volunteers. From our experience in the 1970s we can also project how well the volunteer concept will work in the 1980s, when both demographic and economic factors appear certain to increase the challenge to a volunteer force.

Our efforts at this conference are to determine whether the volunteer concept has worked in the 1970s and whether it will work in the 1980s. Workability is different from desirability. It is not the authors' task to determine whether the all-volunteer armed force is superior either socially or

* This paper reflects the hard work and substantive contributions of a number of people. Captain Ronald E. Sortor, USAF, who did much to prepare this paper, and G. Thomas Sicilia, whose past creative efforts show up in much of the work reported here, deserve special mention. And because this paper draws heavily on the report *America's Volunteers,* (1978), we should like to mention the contributions to that volume of Lt. Commander John R. Thompson, Spec 6 Terryl L. Wisener, and Major Audrey V. Reeg, USAF. Mrs. Ethel Koger greatly assisted in the preparation of both works.

militarily, to the various forms of conscription the United States has used in the past, or whether it is the best of all possible forms of military personnel procurement. We leave such a determination to others. Our task is empirical—to present and examine evidence and to take projections on the successes and failings of America's volunteer forces.

For criteria and measures we turn first to the President's Commission on an All-Volunteer Armed Force, chaired by former Defense Secretary Thomas S. Gates. The commission set as the main objective of the All-Volunteer Force (AVF): to meet peacetime military manpower requirements without conscription. And, as a secondary but still important objective: to attract persons of adequate quality to meet the requirements of military jobs.

To these principal criteria we add two others: to maintain adequate reserves to meet essential mobilization needs; and to provide a standby Selective Service System to help mobilize the civilian population.

Our efforts for this conference have been principally directed at the first two criteria, which concern the active force, but we go to some effort to summarize what is being done to define and meet the mobilization manpower needs of the United States. The active force, for which our goals and objectives are carefully laid out, provides the best and the firmest basis for judging the successes and failures of the AVF.

Table I summarizes the experience of the AVF from 1970 through 1979. By the important measure of strength, the AVF is clearly successful The armed forces have been within 1.5 percent of strength in every year.

The Gates Commission expected that achieving objectives would be aided by accepting more qualified low-aptitude personnel and by reducing turnover rates and hence requirements for new enlistees. In fact, neither factor has had a strong influence on meeting strength objectives. Among recruits, the percentage of low-aptitude personnel, as measured by the proportion of mental category IV enlistees and non-high school graduates, has declined (see Table 1). Thus, by these measures, the quality of recruits has improved under the AVF. And, although overall reenlistment rates have risen, attrition during the first term of service has also increased; consequently, turnover rates have not markedly improved. Therefore the military services must continue seeking large numbers of recruits.

Each of these elements and many others are described and discussed in this paper. We do observe, however, that the AVF appears to be working and, in important ways, working better than was forecast.

The 1980s will undoubtedly offer a less favorable recruiting environment than the 1970s. The population of 17- to 21-year-olds, those of prime recruiting age, is now near a peak and will decline by 17 percent by the end of the 1980s. This, plus the possibility of greater competition for youth

TABLE 1
Summary of Data on the All-Volunteer Force

Strength	1970	1973	1974	1975	1977	1978	1979
Authorized strength (000)	a	2,313	2,190	2,127	2,093	2,085	2,056
Actual strength (000)	3,066	2,252	2,161	2,149	2,074	2,061	2,027
Percent achieved	a	97.4	98.7	99.0	99.1	98.9	98.6
Accessions							
Total (000)	643	485	423	458	411	332	338
Percent of objective	99	96	97	102	98	98	93
NPS (nonprior service) accessions (000)	624[b]	455[b]	395	419	388	312	316
Mental group IV (000)	141	61	39	26	20	17	17
As percent of NPS accessions	23	13	10	6	5	5	5
High school graduates (000)	448	301	233	277	269	240	229
As percent of NPS accessions	72	66	61	66	69	77	73
Reenlistment rates (percent)							
First term	14	24	30	37	35	37	37
Career	77	83	81	82	75	72	68
Total	30	47	52	57	54	55	53
First-term attrition (percent)	25[c]	32	37	35	35 [d]	30[d]	28[d]

[a] Congressional authorization for end FY strengths were not established until 1972.
[b] Includes 206,000 inductees for 1970 and 36,000 for 1973.
[c] Estimated rate for FY 1970, adjusting for past Vietnam early releases.
[d] Projections.

from private employers and educational institutions, will make recruiting more difficult.

Yet, despite the relatively more favorable recruiting environment of the past decade, the enlistment rates among male high school graduates have dropped 25 percent in the past four years. The second part of this paper explores the reasons for this sudden drop and weighs the policy changes, economic measures, and other factors that might correct this problem and offset the population decline over the next decade. (Table 1 summarizes the actual results for these measures.)

Since the AVF became a reality, many researchers, analysts, executives, and congressional leaders* have examined the AVF, commented on how it actually functions, and recommended improvements or alternatives to it as it is now operating.

When the Carter administration took office, the new Secretary of Defense asked the staff to conduct a thorough review of the AVF. Later Senator Nunn asked that the review include an analysis of alternatives to the AVF. The result of this review was published and sent to Congress in December 1978 under the title of *America's Volunteers: A Report on the All-Volunteer Armed Force*. The authors of the present paper were principals in the production of *America's Volunteers*. *America's Volunteers* was largely based on data through fiscal year 1978; this paper is based on data through fiscal year 1979, but draws heavily and expands on the material of the earlier report. Because the two additional years of data and experience have been rather unusual years, a number of findings in the earlier report have changed.

Has the All-Volunteer Force Worked?

The All-Volunteer Force has been in existence for seven years. The last draft call was made in December 1972 and the statutory authority to draft expired in June 1972. The return to a volunteer force was in keeping with the American tradition of using conscription only in time of war. To a large extent, it was the favorable supply-and-demand situation with respect to young men of military age that made the AVF possible. In 1955, the military needed 70 percent of the 18-year-old males; in 1979, the military required fewer than 20 percent.

The active force was originally perceived as the most serious potential

---

* Among them, to name a few: William R. King, Charles W. Brown, Charles C. Moskos, Les Aspin, Robin L. Beard, Robert Hale, Daniel Huck, Morris Janowitz, David Grismer, William A. Steiger, Sam Nunn, Martin Binkin, Shirley J. Bach, John D. Johnston, Jerry Reed, and Richard V. L. Cooper.

AVF problem. There were concerns that the active force might not be able to recruit enough young people, that the quality of accessions might drop sharply, and that the force would not be as representative of the nation as during the draft years. In the first years under the AVF, the active force received the bulk of management attention.

Following is an evaluation of the strength, quality, and representativeness of, first, the active force, and, second, the reserve force.

Active Forces

STRENGTH TRENDS

The transition to the AVF occurred simultaneously with the drawdown in active strength from Vietnam. The active force inventories were reduced from over 3.5 million officers and enlisted personnel in FY 1968 to slightly more than 2 million in FY 1979.

Figure 1 shows that most of the drawdown occurred between FY 1969 and FY 1972 (just as the AVF decision was being made) and that the

FIGURE 1

TOTAL ACTIVE MILITARY END-STRENGTH TRENDS

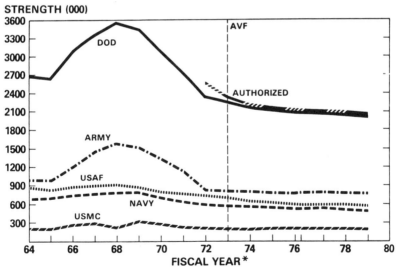

NOTE: The "Authorized" line shows the congressional authorizations since FY 1972. Active force personnel strengths were not specified by congressional authorization before FY 1972. Total DOD (Department of Defense) actual end strengths have been within 1.5 percent of the authorized level since FY 1974.

* Includes transition quarter between 1976 and 1977.

reduction was concentrated in the Army. Unlike those in the reserve force, the reductions in active-duty strength were not caused by inability to recruit, but by changes in force structure and weapons systems. In FY 1979, strength was again within 1.5 percent of the authorized level.

ENLISTED STRENGTH TRENDS

As shown in Figure 2, the enlisted strength trends are very similar to the total strength trends in Figure 1.

As with the overall strength trend, the major change in enlisted strength occurred in the Army, which had increased the most during the Vietnam War. The strength decreases in all services resulted, for the most part, from the post-Vietnam drawdown. The trends in annual nonprior-service accessions (NPS) are shown by service in Figure 3.

Fiscal year 1978 was unusual in that the requirement for accessions was very low. In FY 1979 the requirements for accessions were more normal but it was a difficult recruiting year. For the first time under the AVF, all four services fell short of their recruiting objectives. The problems surfaced particularly in the Army and the Navy. Overall, the shortfall was about 24,000, or some 7 percent of the recruiting objectives. Attrition and reen-

FIGURE 2

ACTIVE-DUTY ENLISTED END STRENGTHS

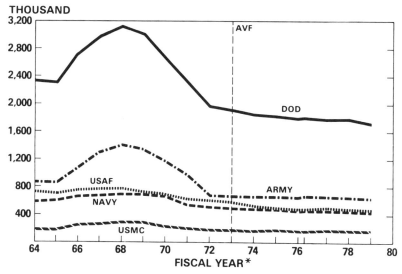

* Includes transition quarter between FY 1976 and 1977.

listments were fairly stable. Although there were more career personnel than ever before, career reenlistments continued to decline as shown in Table 2.

As a consequence of the recruiting shortfall and high career constant,

TABLE 2

DEPARTMENT OF DEFENSE
HISTORICAL CAREER REENLISTMENT RATES, BY SERVICE
(in percentages)

Fiscal Year	ARMY	NAVY	USMC	USAF	DOD
1971	64.6	90.0	81.8	90.9	78.2
1972	45.5	91.0	82.6	94.4	73.8
1973	63.0	91.7	81.7	92.7	82.6
1974	74.5	80.3	79.6	89.8	81.4
1975	75.4	80.5	73.1	89.6	81.5
1976	70.8	74.8	77.6	81.9	76.3
1977	69.5	68.1	71.6	86.2	74.8
1978	68.6	63.5	69.1	82.2	71.5
1979	66.4	62.2	51.9	81.5	68.2

FIGURE 3

TOTAL ACTIVE-DUTY ENLISTED NPS ACCESSIONS
(includes males and females, inductees and enlistees)

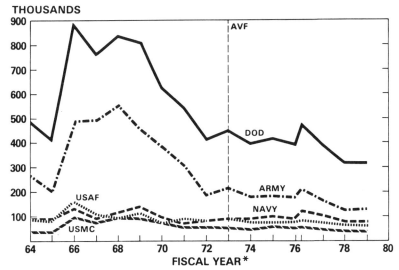

* Includes transition quarter between FY 1976 and 1977.

FIGURE 4
Active-Duty NPS Enlisted Mental Category I and II
Accessions as a Percentage of Total

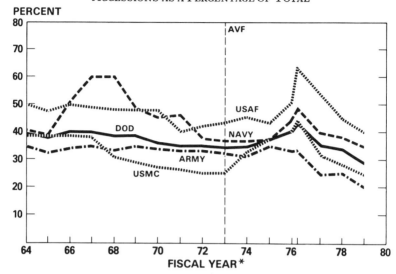

* Includes transition quarter between FY 1976 and 1977.

Active-Duty NPS Enlisted Mental Category III
Accessions as a Percentage of Total

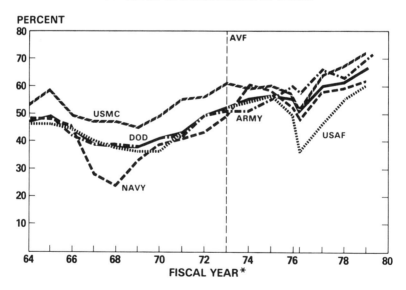

* Includes transition quarter between FY 1976 and 1977.

the strength of the active forces at the end of FY 1979 was slightly below the end strength set in the President's FY 1980 budget. But the FY 1979 shortfall of approximately 1.4 percent is hardly unprecedented. Similar small shortfalls have occurred in each of the last six years.

Since the shortfall in any year is included in the determination of requirements for the next year, these shortages are not additive. Even during the draft years, variance in strength of these magnitudes were common. For all practical purposes, the active forces may be considered "on strength."

QUALITY OF ENLISTED ACCESSIONS

Quality is difficult to define and measure in regard to people in general, and certainly it is no easier in regard to military personnel. Honesty, integrity, morality, commitment, and loyalty are all terms that would be associated with quality. Moreover, training and leadership, which are supplied by the service and not the individual, are usually thought to be critical determinants of the efficiency and dedication with which individuals perform. For the purposes of this paper, we are interested in recruit quality, with measurable attributes of persons who enter military service. Consequently, we focus on trends in individual attributes and not on the skill and

ACTIVE-DUTY NPS ENLISTED MENTAL CATEGORY IV
ACCESSIONS AS A PERCENTAGE OF TOTAL

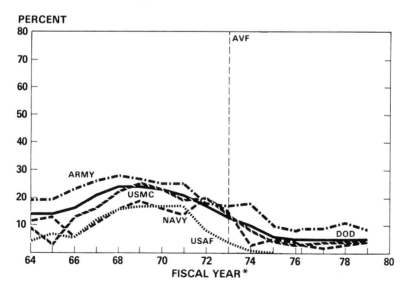

* Includes transition quarter between FY 1976 and 1977.

readiness of our military forces. The principal measurable attributes are mental aptitude and level of education.

Mental Categories

The mental quality of the enlisted force, as measured by scores on the Armed Forces Qualification Test (AFQT) and the Armed Services Vocational Aptitude Battery (ASVAB), has tended to increase under the AVF. Figure 4 shows the trends in the mental quality of military accessions during the AVF years. These upward trends were achieved in spite of general downward trends in youth scores on other tests administered to the general population, such as the Scholastic Aptitude Test (SAT), Iowa Standard Test, and National Merit Scholarship Qualification Test.

In FY 1964, one out of every seven active force enlistees ranked in mental group IV. During the all-volunteer years, this percentage steadily dropped, reaching the level of 1 in 20 in FY 1970. Although mental category IV accessions are easier to recruit, they are not able to complete training in many skills and are more likely to require more time to complete training in skills open to them than do those in categories I, II, and III. They have higher losses than other accessions at the same educational level. Training costs to replace losses must be balanced against the increased recruiting costs associated with recruiting those in the higher mental categories.

The trends in FYs 1976 and 1979 were relatively steady. Of importance is the decline in mental category IV personnel from 25 percent of accessions in FY 1968 to around 5 percent a decade later. This is significantly lower than the pre-Vietnam level of about 15 percent. Also the mental group III percentage increased from about 40 percent to about 60 percent of NPS accessions. These trends have to be viewed with some caution, as norming problems and possible compromise reduce the reliability of the data. Even so, the results do not support arguments of inferior quality.

As shown by the study of FY 1977 accessions for the *America's Volunteers* report (Figure 5), only a slight difference in score for those Army personnel scoring at the III and V/IV boundary levels would have greatly increased the number of IVs. There is some concern that the norming problems and compromise might increase the number of IVs significantly, especially in the Army. The more important information in Figure 5, however, is the inequality among the services. It appears that Air Force recruiting strategies may significantly reduce the supply of high-quality recruits for the Army.

These data must be put in perspective. The Army required 41 percent of the total NPS accessions and the Air Force only 21 percent. But both services received about the same amount (about 30 percent) of the high-quality personnel. The Air Force, however, took only 19 percent of the

FIGURE 5

Distribution of NPS Accessions by Mental Category in FY 1977
Normal Curve for Total
Military Eligible Population

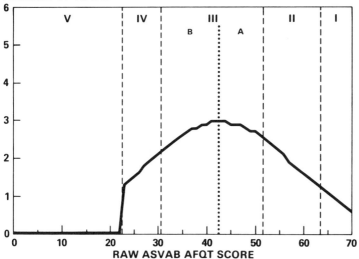

DOD Total Active Enlisted
NPS Accessions (FY 1977)

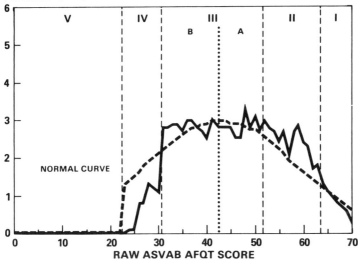

Army Total Active Enlisted
NPS Accessions (FY 1977)

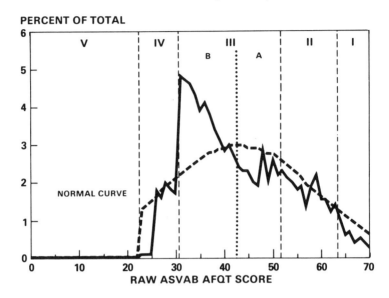

Navy Total Active Enlisted
NPS Accessions (FY 1977)

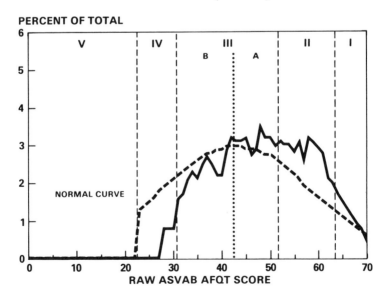

Marine Corps Active Enlisted
NPS Accessions (FY 1977)

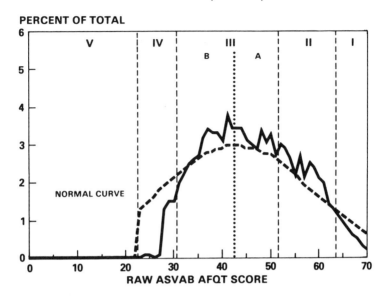

Air Force Active Enlisted
NPS Accessions (FY 1977)

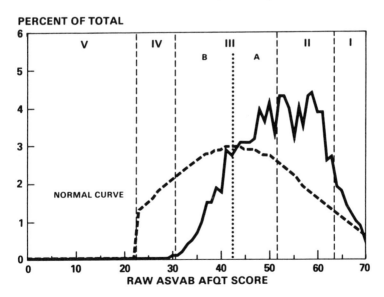

mental group III accessions (and most of these were III-A) and less than 1 percent of the total group IV accessions, as compared with the Army's 44 percent of the total IIIs (mostly III-B) and 73 percent of the IVs, as shown in Table 3.

TABLE 3

DISTRIBUTION OF NPS ACCESSIONS BY MENTAL CATEGORY IN FY 1979
(percent of DOD total)

Service	I	II	III	IV	Total
Army	28	29	44	73	41
Navy	33	30	24	17	25
USMC	9	11	14	9	13
USAF	29	30	19	1	21

Educational Levels

It is generally accepted that possession of a high school diploma is the best single measure of a person's potential for adapting to life in the military. High school graduates are more likely to complete their terms of service than are their contemporaries who did not graduate. Recruiting programs for the active forces have therefore concentrated on enlisting high school graduates. The outcome is shown in Figure 6. In FY 1979 the services recruited 73 percent high school graduates (229,000), as compared with 68 percent in FY 1964, the last pre-Vietnam year. That 73 percent is down from 77 percent (240,000) in FY 1978, in spite of an increase in total NPS accessions required in 1979. But remember that 1978 had unusually low requirements for accessions as compared with 1977, when there were 269,000 high school graduates.

To put these percentages in perspective, about 75 percent of the 18-year-olds have graduated from high school, but almost half of these enter college and thus are not prime candidates for enlisted recruiting. The remaining 18-year-old high school graduates (not enrolled in college) form the prime market for enlisted recruiting. There are about 1.7 million men and women in this group, or about 40 percent of the 18-year-old population.

The situation is complicated, however, by the requirement that nine out of ten service accessions must be men. In each 18-year-old cohort are about 790,000 men who are high school graduates not enrolled in college. In FY 1980, about 320,000 young men, or 40 percent of the cohort, must be recruited by the active forces, as well as about 50,000 women, or 5.5 percent of the 910,000 female high school graduates in the cohort not enrolled in college. Although there have always been some college-bound youth who have enlisted, the ratio of male accession requirements to non-college-bound young men is an accurate measure of the military's recruiting problem.

While the percentage of accessions who are high school graduates has increased only slightly over the pre-Vietnam period, the percentage of the total active enlisted force with a high school education (including certificates) has reached the highest level ever recorded. In FY 1979, 88 percent of the active enlisted force had a high school education or equivalent, as compared with 81 percent in December 1972, the time of the last draft call, about 75 percent during 1964, the last year before Vietnam draft calls, and 55 percent in the cold-war year of 1956. During the AVF period, the average educational level of persons entering active duty has been greater than the level of those leaving.

THE REPRESENTATIVENESS ISSUE

The armed forces have never been truly representative of American society, if the term "representative" means equal service by groups of equal size. Perhaps the closest they ever came occurred in the latter days of World War II, when some three-fourths of each 19-year-old cohort served. Yet, even then, as in the Korean and Vietnam wars, there were large disparities —between blacks and whites, rich and poor, the well educated and the badly educated, the very bright and the not-so-bright, and men and women in the burdens of combat and suffering. Just as black Americans suffered disproportionate casualties in the Vietnam War, whites suffered considerably higher casualty rates in the two previous conflicts.

Although mention is often made of the social and political demands for a representative force, most definitions are vague and ambiguous. This lack of consistency may, in part, stem from (1) the possible range of population characteristics for proportional measurement is virtually limitless; (2) the national civilian standard for comparison could be any one of almost limitless definitions. and (3) the number and type of "targets" in the military services are—again—almost limitless. Whereas agreement on these points conceivably could be attained through extended national debate, there is no doubt that vested interests would play a major role in the decision process. Consequently, a national consensus on the need for representation— much less on the specific details concerning scope, standards, and targets—is highly unlikely.

There is no denying that a large part of the public's acceptance of the military is affected by the composition of the forces. Yet the question of whether and how the composition should be controlled or influenced is open to conjecture. Nevertheless, it is the DOD's position that all qualified youth, regardless of their membership in an identifiable group, should be

FIGURE 6
Active-Duty NPS Enlisted High School Diploma Graduate Accessions as a Percentage of Total

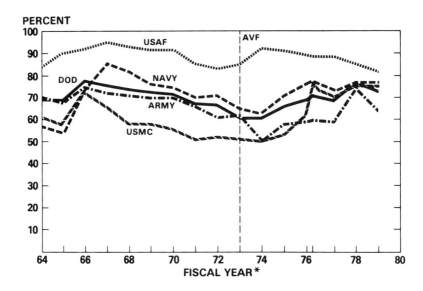

* Includes transition quarter between FY 1976 and 1977.

FIGURE 7
Active-Duty NPS Black Enlisted Accessions as a Percentage of Total

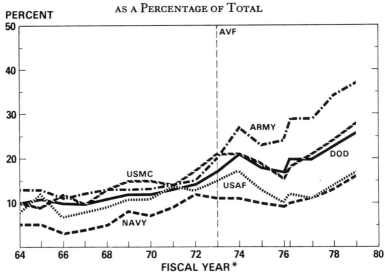

* Includes transition quarter between FY 1976 and 1977.

allowed to serve their country. And though some potential may exist for representation-related problems, it does not appear that they warrant any policy or procedural changes in current AVF practices.

There are other angles to the representation issue. Each of the following is discussed in Addendum A.

- *The distinction of black personnel by military occupation.* Do blacks serve disproportionately in combat and low-skilled jobs? Blacks in the Army, and to a lesser extent in other services, are spread proportionately across all occupations.
- *The geographic representation among recruits.* Does the South or any other low-income area supply a disproportionate number of recruits? Service preference does appear to differ by region, but total enlistments are quite evenly distributed.
- *Income class.* Are most recruits from lower-income groups? Surprisingly, available data suggest this is not the case.
- *The participation of women.* Are there opportunities that would expand the role of women in the military? This would appear likely, as women are now serving in military positions previously closed to them.

BLACKS IN THE ENLISTED FORCES

The vast majority of analyses, media reports, and congressional queries concerning representation have focused on the growing disproportionate representation of black youth in the enlisted ranks of the Army in particular and the Armed Forces in general.

The trend toward the increasing black content commenced during the draft era. This can be attributed in part to the dramatic increase in the proportion of blacks eligible for military services—specifically, the increasing number of black high school graduates and the larger percentage of blacks placing in levels on the mental aptitude tests required for service entry. There is also the combined push of the disproportionately high unemployment rate among black youth and the pull of the military services, which may have gone further than other institutions in offering equal opportunities for minorities.

Figure 7 shows the trends since FY 1964 in black accessions. In FY 1964 blacks made up about 10 percent of the NPS active-duty accessions. By FY 1979 under the AVF the number had risen to 26 percent. In the Army, blacks represent almost 37 percent of total active-duty NPS accessions. To put these figures in perspective, blacks represent about 13 percent of the total youth population and about 9 percent of the youth qualified for military service.

Figure 8 shows the number of black enlisted personnel by service. The increase in the black content since 1972 is a product of both the increasing accession rates for blacks and the higher-than-average reenlistment rates among black enlisted personnel. Under the AVF, the number of black enlisted personnel has returned to the levels of the Vietnam peak. However, because force sizes are down, this has resulted in major increases in the percentage of blacks in the enlisted force. In FY 1979, 20 per cent of the enlisted force was black, as compared with 10 percent in FY 1964. The Army has historically had the highest black content and the Navy the lowest. The pre-AVF trends have generally continued under the AVF, as shown in Figure. 9.

OTHER MANPOWER FACTORS

Three other manpower factors are important measures of the AVF: (1) discipline, (2) retention, and (3) first-term attrition.

Discipline

The state of military discipline in the active force as measured by the number of disciplinary infractions resulting in courts-martial or nonjudicial punishments has improved under the AVF. There are problems with this measure, because the rules and procedures governing such disciplinary actions have changed over the period. Under the AVF it is possible to release poorly motivated personnel without fear of encouraging counter-productive behavior.

In spite of these problems, the data are still interesting. In a conscripted force many people were incarcerated who today are simply released. The DOD-wide court-martial rate, defined as the number of courts-martial per 1,000 enlisted personnel per year, declined from a high of 36 in FY 1969 to about 11 in FY 1979. The steady increase in the nonjudicial punishment rate (defined as the number of punishments per 1,000 enlisted personnel per year under Article 15 of the Uniform Code of Military Justice) that occurred during the latter years of the draft was brought under control in the early AVF years. The rate peaked at 211 per 1,000 enlistees in FY 1974 and was down to about 160 in FY 1979.* The total disciplinary actions (courts-martial plus nonjudicial punishments) per 1,000 enlisted personnel per year has likewise decreased steadily since FY 1974. As another indicator of performance, desertions (absence without leave in excess of 30 days) have also shown a favorable trend under the AVF. The desertion rate declined steadily from an FY 1971 high of nearly 40 desertions per 1,000 enlisted personnel to about 17 in FY 1979.

---

* Complete data for FY 1979 are not yet available. During the first six months there were 5.5 courts-martial per 1,000 enlisted personnel for an annual rate of 11, and 77.8 Article 15 punishments per 1,000 enlisted for an annual rate of 156.

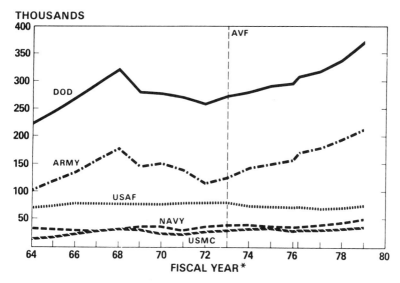

FIGURE 8
BLACK ENLISTED ACTIVE-DUTY END STRENGTHS

* Includes transition quarter between FY 1976 and 1977.

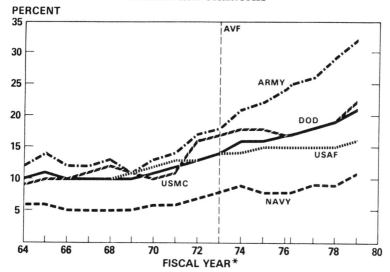

FIGURE 9
BLACKS AS A PERCENTAGE OF ACTIVE-DUTY
ENLISTED END STRENGTHS

* Includes transition quarter between FY 1976 and 1977.

In spite of many lamentations about the good old days, the evidence indicates that discipline is better in the AVF than it would be with a draft.

Retention

Retention refers to both first-term and career reenlistments. Table 4 presents the data since 1973. (Bear in mind that there are some data problems in determining who was eligible to reenlist, who was on extension, and so on.)

Table 4 shows a first-term reenlistment rate increasing from 24 percent in 1973 to 37 percent in 1979. Career reenlistments (second and subsequent reenlistments) declined from 82 percent in 1973 to 68 percent in 1979. Reduced pay increases, large and uncompensated increases in travel and moving costs, high costs in overseas assignments, and other factors have undoubtedly had a major effect on reenlistments.

TABLE 4

REENLISTMENT RATES (in Percentage)

	1973	1974	1975	1976	1977	1978	1979
First Term							
Army	38	33	39	21	33	36	43
Navy	23	33	40	35	37	40	38
Marine Corps	13	17	20	26	29	29	20
Air Force	20	31	40	37	39	41	38
DOD	24	30	37	30	35	37	37
Career							
Army	63	74	75	71	70	69	66
Navy	92	80	80	75	68	64	62
Marine Corps	82	80	73	78	72	69	52
Air Force	93	90	90	82	86	82	82
DOD	83	81	82	76	75	72	68
Total							
Army	50	51	53	43	52	54	56
Navy	46	54	58	50	49	50	47
Marine Corps	26	29	34	41	43	42	34
Air Force	53	58	68	62	66	66	60
DOD	47	52	57	50	54	55	53

But perhaps the largest factor contributing to increased first-term and decreased career reenlistments is the Selective Reenlistment Bonus (SRB). It would explain both the increase in first-term retention and the decline in career retention.

Many of those induced to serve an extra four to six years by an SRB are not career-committed but stay for the bonus and then leave. These extra years of return on the training investment, though very cost-effective, result in increased first-term reenlistment rates and reduced career reenlistment rates. Since the increased first-term retention is applied to such a larger base, it overshadows the lower career-reenlistment rates. Except for the Air Force, from which a large number of very senior people are retiring, every service has the largest career force in its history.

First-Term Attrition

First-term attrition is defined as the number of persons who are lost to the military before completing their initial enlistments. A major disappointment with the AVF has been the increase in attrition rates of first-term enlistees. As shown in Table 5, attrition rates grew markedly from FY 1971 through 1977. In the Army, for example, the three-year attrition rate for people who enlisted in FY 1971 was 26 percent, whereas in FY 1974 it was 38 percent. Apparently with the advent of the AVF, marginal performers and those with motivational problems tended to be released instead of counseled or punished. In short, the force was not only *volunteer-in,* but it was also *volunteer-out.*

Actions have been taken to reduce this costly waste of manpower. These are discussed in detail in the second part of this paper.

TABLE 5

ATTRITION PERCENTAGE OF ACTIVE-DUTY NPS MALE ENLISTEES
(fiscal years)

	Actual				Estimated			Projected	
Service	1971	1972	1973	1974	1975	1976	1977	1978	1979
Army	26	28	31	38	32	35	30	30	31
Navy	28	32	34	38	32	35	38	31	28
Marine Corps	31	24	32	37	40	37	34	31	30
Air Force	21	26	20	31	31	30	28	27	25
DOD	26	28	32	37	35	36	35	30	28

NOTE: The percentages refer to those who enlisted for three or more years in the fiscal year shown but left the service before completing three years of service.

Reserves

A determination of whether the AVF has worked or not should not be made on the basis of only the active force. The Department of Defense depends on several sources of manpower to meet its wartime requirements. These include the active forces, selected reserve components, pretrained individuals, and untrained individuals. Since the active forces provide our first line of defense in all contingencies, keeping them well manned and ready has been a primary concern of the Department of Defense under the AVF. They continue to have a high priority, but increasing attention now is being devoted to the other manpower categories. Personnel in these categories constitute the mobilization manpower of the DOD and must be considered before final judgment of the success of the AVF can be made.

THE SELECTED RESERVE

The selected reserve components provide manpower in organized units to be called to active duty as necessary to augment the active force units during mobilization.* Some reserve and national guard units also assist active-duty units during peacetime by providing services used by the active forces while the reserve units are training. For example, many of the strategic bombers are fueled on their peacetime missions by reserve tanker aircraft manned by aircrews in a drill status. These reserve components provide not only current services to back up our active force in case of a long-term conventional war, but also the rapid reinforcement capability needed early in a large-scale conventional conflict of short warning. The major manpower problem for the selected reserve component is a shortage of enlisted personnel, particularly in the Army Reserve and National Guard.

Strength Trend

The selected reserve strength decreased from 919,000 in 1973 (the year the AVF began), to 799,800 in FY 1979, a drop of almost 13 percent. As shown in Figure 10, almost all the decrease occurred in the enlisted forces. Figure 10 also compares total selected reserve strengths with the congressional authorizations during the AVF. Unlike those for the active force, congressional authorizations for reserves have, in fact, been adjusted downward, owing mainly to the reserve component's inability to attain higher strength levels.

Enlisted Strength Trends

The decline in enlisted strengths, as shown in Figure 11, is dominated by the reduction in the Army components. The most severe drop in enlisted

---

* The DOD selected reserve components are: Army National Guard (ARNG), Army Reserve (USAR), Naval Reserve (USNR), Marine Corps Reserve (USMCR), Air National Guard (ANG), and Air Force Reserve (USAFR).

FIGURE 10

DOD Selected Reserve Strength Trends
(paid drill end strengths)

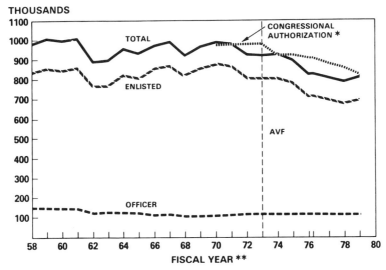

* Congressionally authorized floors began in FY 1970 and are based on average yearly strength totals.
** Includes transition quarter between FY 1976 and 1977.

FIGURE 11
Selected Reserve Enlisted End Strengths

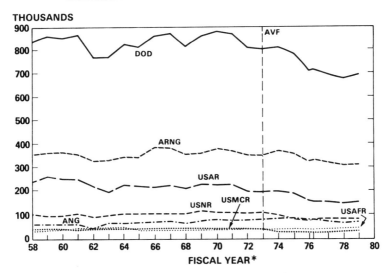

* Includes transition quarter between FY 1976 and 1977.

strength has occurred in the Army Reserve, which decreased by almost 22 percent (from 195,000 to 152,000) between FY 1973 and FY 1979.

Under the AVF we have enlisted fewer people in the selected reserve than during the draft, and a greater proportion of our reserve accessions have had prior service before enlisting. However, Figure 12 shows that both the total number of accessions and the mix of NPS and prior-service accessions for the DOD as a whole have remained relatively constant under the AVF. Experienced prior-service personnel are, of course, more productive than untrained recruits; they are also older, trained, and more expensive. However, prior-service accessions who enlist for one year at a time add turbulence and uncertainty for reserve force managers.

The trend for blacks in the reserve is much like those for blacks in the active forces, and the same trends are true for women (Figures 13 and 14).

Quality of Enlisted Accessions

As with accessions for the active forces, the tools for measuring accessions into the selected reserve are mental group ratings and educational levels.

Differences between the reserve and active components require that trends in quality of NPS reserve accessions be viewed somewhat differently from the treatment of the active force. First, reserve recruit "quality" during the Vietnam War was swollen by college-trained "recruits" seeking to avoid the draft. Second, prior-service enlistments provide an important—

FIGURE 12

DOD Selected Reserve Enlistments

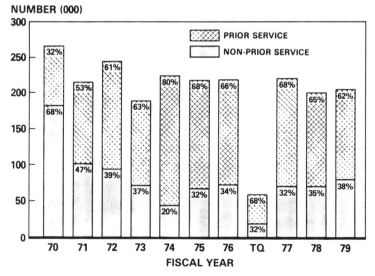

FIGURE 13

Black Strength as Percentage of Total
(by reserve component)

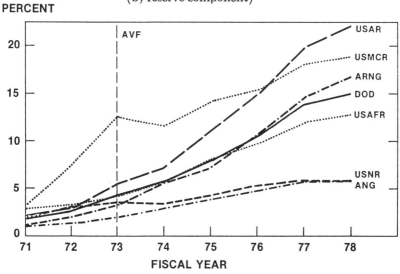

FIGURE 14

Total Number of Women in the Selected Reserves

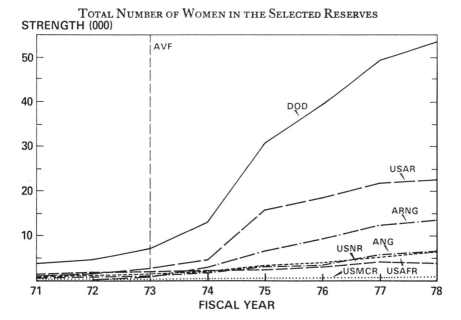

TABLE 6

QUALITY OF SELECTED RESERVE ENLISTED ACCESSIONS IN FY 1979
(in percentages)

	Non-prior Service	Prior Service	Total
Education			
High School Graduates*	49	81	67
Non-high school graduates†	51	19	37
Mental Categories			
I and II	24	41	34
III	64	52	57
IV	12	7	9

* May contain an indeterminate fraction of accessions with high school certificates rather than diplomas.

† A significant proportion of the non-high school NPS accessions are persons who join the reserves during senior years of high school and become graduates before their initial active-duty training.

TABLE 7

QUALITY OF ARMY NATIONAL GUARD
ENLISTED ACCESSIONS IN FY 1979
(in percentages as of July 1979)

	Non-prior Service	Prior Service	Total
Education			
High school graduates	52	86	69
Non-high school graduates	48	19	31
Mental Categories			
I and II	21	40	31
III	69	53	61
IV	10	7	8

TABLE 8

QUALITY OF ARMY RESERVE
ENLISTED ACCESSIONS IN FY 1979
(in percentages as of July 1979)

	Non-prior Service	Prior Service	Total
Education			
High school graduates	39	70	53
Non-high school graduates	61	30	47
Mental Categories			
I and II	23	36	29
III	60	55	58
IV	17	9	13

TABLE 9

QUALITY OF NAVAL RESERVE
ENLISTED ACCESSIONS IN FY 1979
(in percentages as of July 1979)

	Non-prior Service	Prior Service	Total
Education			
High school graduates	57	76	74
Non-high school graduates	43	24	26
Mental Categories			
I and II	41	38	38
III	49	53	53
IV	10	9	9

TABLE 10

QUALITY OF MARINE CORPS RESERVE
ENLISTED ACCESSIONS IN FY 1979
(in percentages as of July 1979)

	Non-prior Service	Prior Service	Total
Education			
High school graduates	43	47	45
Non-high school graduates	57	53	55
Mental Categories			
I and II	32	35	33
III	56	54	58
IV	12	11	9

perhaps the most important—source of manpower for the reserve forces. And, with prior-service recruits, experience and skill level are more significant than the less direct measures of quality applied to NPS personnel. Table 8 compares, by education and mental category, NPS and prior-service selected reserve accessions in FY 1979. Prior-service accessions are of higher quality than the NPS accessions and, because they account for two-thirds of the accessions, are sustaining the overall quality of selected reserve-accessions.

Although the overall DOD record in selected reserve recruiting (Figure 12) can be judged satisfactory for FY 1979, a closer examination shows major disparities between the six selected reserve components. As Tables 7 to 12 illustrate, the Air Force National Guard and Air Force Reserve compiled significantly better recruiting records than the other components. Conversely, the Army Reserve and the Marine Corps Reserve compiled

TABLE 11

QUALITY OF AIR NATIONAL GUARD
ENLISTED ACCESSIONS IN FY 1979
(in percentages as of July 1979)

	Non-prior Service	Prior Service	Total
Education			
High school graduates	88	88	88
Non-high school graduates	12	12	12
Mental Categories			
I and II	42	63	57
III	58	35	42
IV	—	2	1

TABLE 12

QUALITY OF AIR FORCE RESERVE
ENLISTED ACCESSIONS IN FY 1979
(in percentages as of July 1979)

	Non-prior Service	Prior Service	Total
Education			
High school graduates	82	90	89
Non-high school graduates	18	10	11
Mental Categories			
I and II	36	49	46
III	64	50	53
IV	—	1	1

FIGURE 15

EDUCATIONAL ATTAINMENT OF SELECTED RESERVE NPS ACCESSIONS

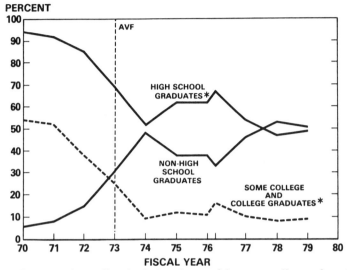

* High school graduate line includes those with some college education and college graduates.

FIGURE 16

SELECTED RESERVE NPS ACCESSIONS BY MENTAL CATEGORY

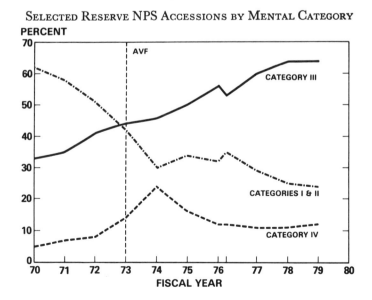

records significantly below the DOD averages.

Data on the education level and mental category of NPS accessions during the last decade is shown in Figures 15 and 16. (Similar information on prior-service accessions is not available.) Adding high school and college together shows that 94 percent of the reserve NPS accessions had high school diplomas in 1970. In FY 1979 this percentage had fallen to 49 percent. There has also been an obvious decline in the proportion of reserve forces enlistees with college training. For instance, over 50 percent of the FY 1970 accessions had some college training but only about 6 percent had been to college in FY 1979.

The decline in college youth in the reserves is attributable to the AVF. During the draft years, the reserve forces were "havens" for college-trained youth who desired to avoid active service. In each of these years, almost 100,000 men with some college training enlisted. However, many of these draft-motivated, college trained accessions were overqualified or otherwise unsuited for the positions to which they were assigned. And, as a result, retention rates beyond initial enlistment were very low. Following the end of the draft, the number of college-trained enlistees dropped dramatically. This decline in educational level is correlated with a decline in mental group I and II enlisted reservists. Figure 16 shows the change in the mental category distributions of NPS accessions.

Under the AVF, mental categories I and II of the NPS accessions have declined while categories III and IV have increased. Category IV enlistments hit a peak of 24 percent of the NPS accessions in FY 1974 and declined to about 12 percent in FY 1979. Although the percentage of mental categories I and II is now half of what it was in FY 1970, the reserve force tends to be much more "average" today under the AVF than it was under the draft or the early years of the AVF.

The decline in the quality of NPS accessions since the beginning of the AVF is partially balanced by the lower percentage of accessions they represent. The increase in high-quality, experienced prior-service accessions has tended in large measure to offset the decline in the number and quality of NPS accessions.

One can also argue that these more experienced and motivated reserve forces would be more likely to meet challenges of mobilization than would a force composed of persons who joined to avoid active-duty services.

Selected Reserve Turnover

The preceding sections have shown that while enlisted accession levels have remained relatively constant under the AVF, enlisted strengths of the selected reserve components have declined. Table 13 shows the severity of the problem.

TABLE 13

SELECTED RESERVE STRENGTH, ENLISTED LOSSES,
AND TURNOVER RATES

(strengths and losses in 000s; rates in percentages)

	FY 1977		
	Strength	*Losses*	*Rate*
Army National Guard	390	113	29
Army Reserve	212	56	26
Naval Reserve	97	28	29
Marine Corps Reserve	34	13	38
Air National Guard	93	15	16
Air Force Reserve	52	11	21
Totals	878	236	27

	FY 1978		
	Strength	*Losses*	*Rate*
Army National Guard	382	104	27
Army Reserve	211	57	27
Naval Reserve	87	23	26
Marine Corps Reserve	32	11	26
Air National Guard	93	15	16
Air Force Reserve	52	9	17
Totals	857	219	26

	FY 1979		
	Strength	*Losses*	*Rate*
Army National Guard	362	84	23
Army Reserve	196	44	22
Naval Reserve	87	19	22
Marine Corps Reserve	33	10	30
Air National Guard	92	13	14
Air Force Reserve	53	7	13
Totals	823	177	22

NOTE: This table uses the Congressional Selected Reserve strength levels that do not differentiate between officers and enlisted as the base against which to compare losses in enlisted personnel only. If an enlisted-only strength had been used, the turnover would be somewhat higher.

As noted in Table 13, the Marine Corps Reserve has by far the greatest turnover problem, while both the Air National Guard and the Air Force Reserve have had consistently low rates. Though very high, the rates for both the Army National Guard and the Army Reserve appear to be declining.

These simple statistics suggest that the reserve manning problem is not so much that of inability to recruit people as that of an inability to retain them—or, simply, the turnover problem. One reason for the increasing turnover is the greater dependence or prior-service accessions who may enlist for only one year at a time.

Initiatives

The DOD has undertaken several steps to alleviate the reserve manning problem. These initiatives include the selected reserve initiative package, reserve attrition initiatives, and more varied initial training options for reserve recruits.

Selected Reserve Initiative Package. The services—primarily the Army—have initiated major programs to improve reserve readiness and manning. These initiatives include additional full-time manning to aid in training and some increases in funds for recruiting and advertising. The Army has limited eligibility for these incentives to persons joining, or extending their time in, units scheduled for early deployment. The Navy is limiting their incentives to reenlistment bonuses only. The cost of the programs during FY 1980 will be about $30 million.

In addition, the Army Reserve components are offering new enlistment options that allow recruits to spend three years with a selected reserve unit, then the remaining three years of the six-year Military Service Obligation (MSO) in the Individual Ready Reserve (IRR). Similar programs are being considered by the other three services.

Reserve Attrition Initiatives. As noted earlier, enlisted attrition is a key contributor to the Army reserve manning problem. Yet, the reserve components currently are not equipped to manage the problem. For instance, the reserve component information systems are not structured toward tracking and monitoring attrition losses, and there appear to be few, if any, tools designed specifically for decreasing attrition. Simply stated, to date not enough attention has been paid to reserve attrition. The DOD is now taking steps to improve this situation. These include establishing a reserve attrition data base and tracking system and sponsoring research to determine how and why people are leaving the reserves in such great numbers.. Once the data base is established and the results of the research known, the DOD will increase its efforts to reduce attrition.

Initial Training Options. The selected reserve would like to attract people in the 20–25 age group. However, each NPS accession must receive about 12 or more weeks of basic and initial skill training. If taken at one time, this can present an unnecessary hardship on potential recruits, especially for those who have jobs and are settled. To alleviate this problem, the DOD is now providing a split-training option whereby an individual can take basic and initial skill training in two separate periods rather than all at once. In addition, the Army is testing two programs: in one, persons with certain skills can conduct and accomplish their initial skill training in the community; and in the other, a recruit receives initial vocational teachnical training during his senior year of high school while he is attending drills.

PRETRAINED INDIVIDUALS

Pretrained individuals are needed upon mobilization to augment units that are not at full combat strength and during a conflict to provide replacement personnel in the early phases of the conflict before untrained individuals can be called to active duty and properly trained and equipped for combat. Under the AVF and since the end of the Vietnam War, the number of pretrained individuals in the IRR and the Standby Reserve (SBR) has declined dramatically, until today there is serious concern that the numbers of pretrained individuals are inadequate to meet military requirements.* The change in scenario calling for a high-intensity war with short warning has also increased the need for pretrained individuals. Again, the major problems are centered on meeting the requirements for the Army.

IRR Strength Trends Through FY 1979

The Individual Ready Reserve consists of trained officer and enlisted personnel who have left the active or the selected reserve forces but are available in case of a major war. Most of the enlisted people in the IRR have time remaining on their initial six-year military obligation, while the officer complement is made up of both obligated officers (that is, those who have time remaining on their MSO) and non-obligated officers, many of whom are awaiting retirement. Until recently, the number of persons in the IRR far exceeded expected wartime mobilization requirements.

---

* The IRR is composed primarily of persons who have completed some active-duty service but have part of their six-year military obligation remaining. The SBR contains members of the IRR who request SBR status during the last last year of their military obligation. Currently the SBR can be called up only following a determination of availability by the Selective Service System, while the IRR can be recalled directly by the DOD upon mobilization.

FIGURE 17 .

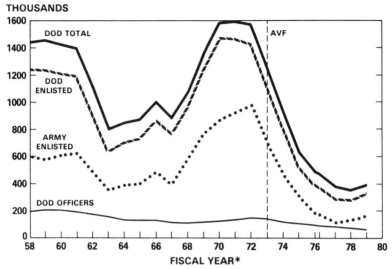

STRENGTH TRENDS IN THE INDIVIDUAL READY RESERVE

* Includes transition quarter between FY 1976 and 1977.

FIGURE 18

PROJECTIONS OF 17- TO 21-YEAR-OLD MALE POPULATION

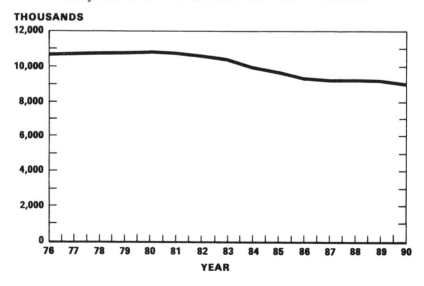

As shown in Figure 17, the size of the IRR has declined dramatically since the beginning of the AVF, making IRR strength levels a major concern for the first time since the early 1960s. The figure shows that, as in the selected reserve, the major IRR problem is the Army's enlisted force. In fact, while the total size of the enlisted IRR decreased from about 1.5 million in FY 1971 to about 310,000 in FY 1979, the Army enlisted IRR dropped from about 921,000 in 1971 to about 159,000 in FY 1979.

Past management actions to preserve the strength in the active and selected reserve forces have seriously reduced the amount of time personnel spend in the IRR and have depleted the sources of trained manpower available for the IRR. These actions included: (1) increasing most active-duty enlistments from two to three or more years, (2) enlisting people in the delayed entry pool for up to one year prior to commencement of active duty, and (3) increasing the number of prior-service accessions admitted to the selected reserve. In addition, the high attrition rates under the AVF, together with the policy of releasing from their military obligation those who fail to make the grade in the active and selected reserve forces, have decreased the size of the IRR.

Still another factor in paring down the IRR was the active force decreases that occurred after the Vietnam War. Reductions in the size of the active force decrease the number of people separating and available for the IRR.

Army Enlisted IRR Strength Initiatives

In light of the decrease in the size of the IRR and policy decisions to plan for an intense conventional conflict with a shorter warning period, the Army has taken several initiatives that will double its enlisted IRR force by 1984. These initiatives include terminating the automatic transfer from the IRR to the Standby Reserve after completion of the first five years of service obligation, screening active and selected reserve losses for entry into the IRR, and reenlisting or continuing people in the IRR after their initial obligation has been satisfied.

Even with these IRR initiatives, the DOD could still be faced with shortages of pretrained people under current wartime planning scenarios. Thus, additional initiatives are needed to increase the size of the pool of pretrained people under some conditions. Several of the alternatives are being considered within DOD. Two of these are: (1) additional initiatives to increase the size of the IRR, such as changing the military service obligation and recruiting people directly into the IRR; and (2) using other sources of pretrained manpower, such as recent retirees and, in an extreme World War II type of conflict, veterans who have satisfied their military obligation. These initiatives, together with those already taken, should provide the DOD with the management flexibility needed to institute an adequate supply of pretrained people.

Untrained Manpower

The final category of mobilization manpower resources is the untrained manpower—those persons who have no military training on mobilization day, but who are subsequently trained to meet a military requirement.

Since minimum training has been set at 12 weeks, the time between mobilization announcement and commencement of training is the primary variable in determining how long it takes these new personnel to begin reaching the theater. Some of them could be in theater in as little as three months, if they could be put in training on mobilization day. This subject is currently under review by a presidential study group in response to a request by Congress.

Summary

The status of military manpower at the end of FY 1979 can be summarized as follows:

- The active force is meeting its manpower objectives, both quantitatively and qualitatively, although recruiting in FY 1979 was very difficult. On balance, at the end of FY 1979, we conclude that the AVF has worked. Of course, the crucial question that remains is: Will it continue to work?

- Although Navy, Marine Corps, and Air Force reserve components have been able to meet congressionally authorized strengths, both the Army National Guard and the Army Reserve have sagged. A number of programs are being tested or have been adopted to increase both the strength and readiness of Army Reserve components.

- The pool of trained individuals who have a military obligation and are able to meet mobilization manpower needs has shrunk since the end of the Vietnam War. Current levels of the IRR and other pools, such as military retirees, are probably not sufficient to meet all requirements for individual replacements in a major war. A variety of programs are being implemented that will increase the level of resources in this important area.

Will it Work?

The successes of the AVF in the 1970s do not necessarily mean further successes in the decade ahead. Three major problems threaten the AVF in the 1980s.

First, our trends in population portend a decline in the pool of prime enlistment age youth from a peak at the beginning of the 1980s to a trough in the early 1990s. Population growth favorable to the AVF can no longer be used to sustain it.

Second, recruiting for the AVF—measured by enlistments of male high school diploma graduates—has declined significantly in the past four years. This decline casts a shadow over the prospects for the AVF, even in the early years of the next decade.

Third, the statistics of success for the DOD as a whole hide more troubling differences in the quality of recruits among the services. These differences may not be in line with legitimate differences in the manpower demands of the services.

We will address each of these problems in turn.

Population and Labor Market Trends

The effects of population trends on military recruiting depend not only on the number of youth of military age but also on other developments in the youth labor market that might either dampen or reinforce the effects of the decline in the number of youths of prime military age.

The prime recruiting pool for the active military consists of males 17 to 21 years old. Figure 18 shows the latest estimates for this population through 1990. After a peak of 10.8 million in 1978, the number of 17- to 21-year-old males will begin to decline and continue to decline through 1990. The drop is modest from 1979 to 1982—less than 1 percent per year. However, in the period 1983–1987 it increases to 2.5 per year. Thus, from the peak levels of 1978, the number of these males will decline 15 percent by 1987, 17 percent by 1990, and possibly more than 20 percent by 1992.

With a smaller population, we expect that the number of males completing high school each year will also decline. This will result in more intense competition for high school graduates among colleges, vocational schools, private employers, and the military. If educational institutions are able to prevent a fall in enrollments and private employers continue to hire young workers in similar numbers as today, the decrease in the supply of enlistees to the military could be proportionately greater than the decline in population. This set of assumptions would provide a very pessimistic view for the future of the AVF. The effects of this decline in the number of youth, however, tend to be both offset and reinforced by the other factors at work in the labor market.

COMPETITION FROM OLDER WORKERS AND WOMEN

During the period 1978–1990, the labor force as a whole will increase by about 20 percent, but the composition will change as follows:

- The 17- to 21-year-old population will decrease by 17 percent.
- The 21- to 55-year-old population will increase by 20 percent.
- The participation rate of women in the labor force will increase 17 percent.

The overall growth caused by the increases in the number of women and older persons of the labor force will be somewhat of a handicap for youth. Young people will always be at a relative disadvantage in competition with the more experienced and more highly trained segments of the labor force. Increases in the size and participation rates of competing groups will reduce the civilian economic opportunities for youth, the amount depending on the relative substitutability of these groups with youth. Military enlistment becomes a more attractive opportunity for all segments of the youth population. This effect could reduce—and perhaps offset—the effects of the population decline—and lead to an optimistic forecast.

Thus, high-quality enlistments may not be directly proportional to the change in the youth population. But because the direction of the bias from proportionality is unclear, we shall assume proportionality of recruits with population. Accordingly, we project a decline in recruits of 12 percent by 1985 and 16 percent by 1990.* In the Air Force, and perhaps in the Navy and Marine Corps as well, the decline would be less. The Army appears to be less competitive for recruits with the Air Force and the other services.

Two obvious strategies have been suggested to deal with the population-linked decline in recruiting: (1) find policies that would lead to fewer recruits being needed from the marketplace, or (2) find policies that would expand the supply eligible for military service.†

---

* The numbers do not track exactly with population declines because other variables were included in the projections, including unemployment and relative pay. (See Fernandez, in References.)

† A third strategy is to increase the supply of recruits by increasing the rewards and incentives for enlistment in the military. Only recently has this appeared to be a possibility, and we defer this subject until our discussion of recent trends in recruiting.

Policies of the first kind include those that would produce reduced turnover of military personnel and hence smaller recruit goals. This result can be produced either by increasing reenlistments or by reducing losses prior to reenlistment of first-term personnel. (First-term attrition had increased sharply with the end of the draft.) Policies of the second kind (supply expansion) might include relaxed physical, mental, or educational requirements either by reducing standards or by more closely matching skills with jobs. Another method of enhancing the supply base would be to use more female recruits. In FY 1971 only 1.3 percent of active-duty enlisted personnel were female. That number had increased to 8 percent by 1979.

In combating the future decline of recruits due to population changes, the DOD chose to emphasize (1) a reversal of the trend toward higher attrition for first-term personnel and (2) a significant reliance on the use of women for noncombat military positions.

First-Term Attrition

As shown in Table 5 (see page 249) the first-term attrition rate for enlisted men has grown markedly since FY 1971. High attrition is costly and requires more recruits than would otherwise be necessary to sustain a given force size. The impact of different attrition levels on trained man-years and accession levels is illustrated in Figure 19. In this figure, the expected trained man-years for accession over three years of service is computed for the Army under the 1971 and 1974 attrition behavior.* As shown, the 1971 cohort attrition implied that about 1.92 trained man-years were obtained per accession over a three-year period. This number dropped to 1.65 for the 1974 accessions and attrition experience. Thus, 17 percent more NPS accessions were needed in 1974 over 1971 to obtain a constant trained strength for the first three years of service.

Figure 20 plots attrition by month of service from FY 1971. The greatest attrition increase has occurred in the 0–6 months of service period owing to introduction of the trainee and "expeditious-discharge" programs. These programs were begun to facilitate the release of individuals who did not adapt to military life. Although it is important to be able to release malcontents and people who do not adapt to military life, the services went too far and were releasing many persons who could have had productive careers in the military.

---

* In this discussion, a person is considered trained after completion of six months of service. Additionally, for the purposes of demonstrating the impact of attrition, this discussion assumes that all NPS male accessions had a three-year commitment in FY 1971 and FY 1974, even though 63 percent and 23 percent, respectively, had a two-year obligation.

FIGURE 19

TRAINED MAN-YEARS PER MALE NPS ACTIVE-DUTY ENLISTED ACCESSION FOR THE FIRST THREE YEARS OF SERVICE
FY 1971 ATTRITION EXPERIENCE

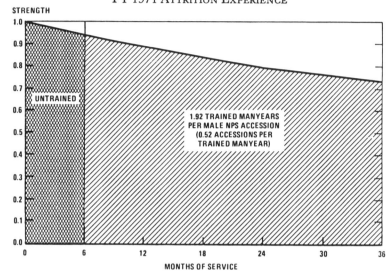

TRAINED MAN-YEARS PER MALE NPS ACTIVE-DUTY ENLISTED ACCESSION FOR THE FIRST THREE YEARS OF SERVICE
FY 1974 ATTRITION EXPERIENCE

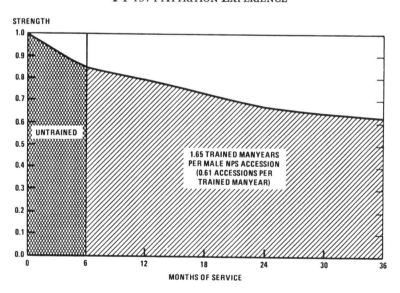

Another important factor to consider when discussing first-term attrition is high school attainment. Recruits who enter any of the services with a high school diploma have one-half the attrition rate of those who do not (Figure 21).

The DOD has adopted as interim goals figures that would represent a reduction in first-term attrition of approximately one-fourth. Although still higher than draft-era attrition, where the prevailing spirit understandably was to keep persons on active duty against their will, the new goals are 23 percent attrition for high school diploma graduates and 44 percent for nongraduates. These numbers reflect prevailing differences in attrition rates between the two groups.

WOMEN IN THE MILITARY

Figure 22 shows the supply and demand for women in the military from 1964 through 1994. Women represent a major underutilized manpower resource. This is especially true in the enlisted force, where the recruiting market for high-quality young men is very competitive.

Before FY 1973, women provided less than 2 percent of the total enlisted strength, but, under the AVF, the percentage rapidly grew. All services about doubled their percentage of female content between 1977 and 1979. In 1979 it was 8 percent and it is programmed to reach 12 percent by

FIGURE 20

ACTIVE-DUTY NPS MALE ATTRITION PERCENTAGES, TOTAL DOD

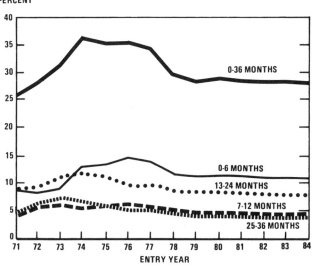

FY 1984. Figure 23 shows this growth by service. All services project major increases in the enlistment of women during the next five years. The Air Force projects the highest growth and the Marine Corps the lowest.

As Table 14 shows, the DOD plans to increase the number of enlisted women to 208,000 by FY 1984. The Army and the Air Force each should then have 80,000 enlisted women.

Women are now serving in military occupations previously closed to them. Figure 24 shows by occupation the percentage of enlisted positions filled with women. Since the total force was 5.8 percent female, any percentage above that level indicates higher than average concentration of women, and any percentage below it indicates underrepresentation. The greatest density of women is in traditional skills—the medical/dental and administrative/clerical occupations.

Current analysis indicates a potential to increase the number of women in the military even further—in part because more women want to enlist than are now accepted. But too rapid a rate of growth can result in an imbalance of women in the junior ranks, because it takes years for recruits to be trained and promoted into positions as qualified supervisors. Moreover, the DOD cannot be certain how many women will be attracted to traditionally male occupations, nor if they will reenlist in those occupations

FIGURE 21

ACTIVE-DUTY NPS MALE ATTRITION PERCENTAGES,
TOTAL DOD, BY EDUCATIONAL ATTAINMENT

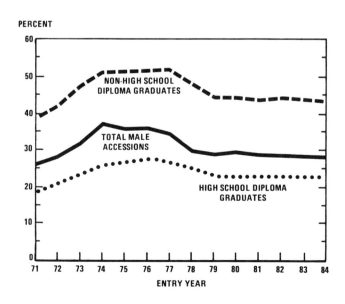

FIGURE 22

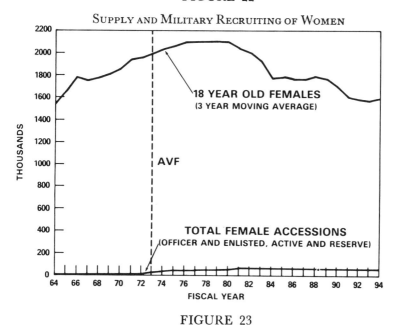

Supply and Military Recruiting of Women

18 YEAR OLD FEMALES
(3 YEAR MOVING AVERAGE)

AVF

TOTAL FEMALE ACCESSIONS
(OFFICER AND ENLISTED, ACTIVE AND RESERVE)

FIGURE 23

Enlisted Women as a Percentage of the Total
Active-Duty Enlisted Strength

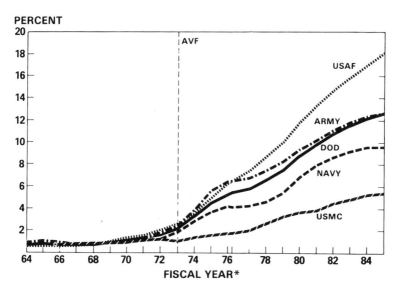

* Includes transition quarter between FY 1976 and 1977.

in sufficient numbers to meet career force requirements. Retention by the DOD occupation code for men and women is shown in Figure 25. Enlisted women had much higher retention in traditional skills than men, but much lower in nontraditional skills.

While Figure 25 shows comparative retention of men and women who enlisted in FY 1973 by occupation, Figure 26 compares the average retention of six cohort groups. Women, on average, are retained as well as men. Taking Figures 25 and 26 together, one concludes that women are retained at higher rates than men in skills more traditionally identified with women and at lower rates in the nontraditional skills, such as electrical equipment repair, technical work, mechanical repair, and crafts. One reason often cited for poorer retention of women in nontraditional occupations is the absence of women to provide support and to serve as role models for the female soldier. In recent years, the services have been striving to increase the number of women in nontraditional occupations, as shown in Figure 27.

Effects of Attrition and Women in the Military

To offset the decrease in quality male accessions due to demographic factors, the DOD will slow turnover through reduced first-term attrition and will increase the use of women in the military. Taken together, these moves will permit the DOD both to increase the number of quality accessions entering the force and to obtain more use out of the people recruited.

TABLE 14

Active-Duty Enlisted Women
(in thousands by fiscal years)

	1964	1968	1971	1973	1976	1977	1978	1979	1984
Army	8	11	12	17	44	46	50	57	80
Navy	5	6	6	9	19	19	21	22	40
Marine Corps	1	3	2	2	3	4	5	5	8
Air Force	5	6	10	15	29	35	41	48	80
Total DOD	19	25	30	43	95	104	117	132	208
% of total enlisted	0.8	0.8	1.3	2.2	5.3	5.8	6.6	7.5	11.6

FIGURE 24

Distribution of Enlisted Women by DOD Occupation Group
(as of end FY 1978)

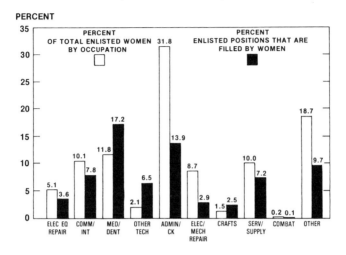

FIGURE 25

Retention of Men and Women by DOD Occupation Code
(in percentages)

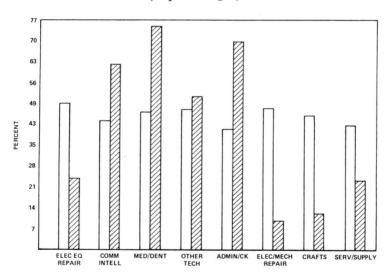

NOTE: The percentages refer to those entering a skill in FY 1973 who were still in the skill at the end of FY 1976, DOD average.

FIGURE 26

PERCENT OF FY 1971–1976 MALE AND FEMALE ACCESSIONS ON ACTIVE DUTY AS OF END FY 1977

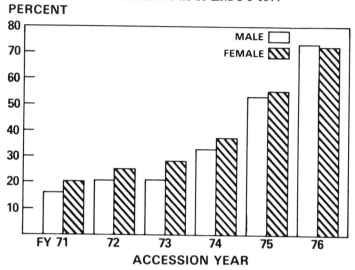

FIGURE 27

ACTIVE DUTY WOMEN

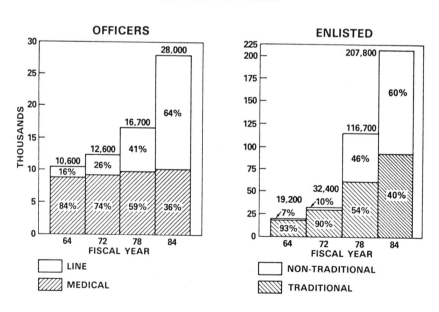

Table 15 shows the estimated effect these initiatives will have on Army accessions in the 1980s. Because of its size and its history of recruiting difficulties, the Army is a bellwether precinct in the tally on the success of the volunteer force. Projections of the Army's recruiting capability under the new policies use fiscal year 1977 as a base and indicate a decline in male high school graduate recruits of 14 percent by FY 1985 and 19 percent by FY 1990.

Without action, the percentage of Army NPS accessions with high school diplomas would have dropped from 59 percent in FY 1977 to 52 percent in FY 1984 and 47 percent in FY 1990. The projections assume an un-limited supply of non-high school graduates. But with the reduction in first-term attrition and the increased use of women, we now expect 66 percent high school graduates in FY 1984 and 61 percent in FY 1990. These projections, which also include pay and employment projections, assume the mid-range economic forecasts prevail in the 1980s (see *America's Volunteers*, Chapter 3).

In the past ten years, Army accessions have ranged between 61 and 77

TABLE 15

EFFECT OF FEMALES AND ATTRITION INITIATIVES ON ARMY NPS
ACCESSIONS OF HIGH SCHOOL DIPLOMA GRADUATES
(in thousands)

	1977	1980	1982	1984	1986	1988	1990
Without Initiatives							
Male HSDG	86	86	83	78	74	73	71
Female HSDG	14	13	12	12	12	12	12
Total HSDG	100	99	95	90	86	85	83
HSDG % of NPS accessions	59	55	55	52	49	48	47
With Initiatives							
Male HSDG	86	86	83	78	74	73	71
Female HSDG	14	20	23	23	23	23	23
Total HSDG	100	106	106	101	97	96	94
HSDG % of NPS accessions	59	67	68	66	63	62	61
Total Enlistees							
Without initiatives	169	180	173	173	176	177	177
With initiaties	169	158	156	153	154	155	154
Difference	0	−22	−17	−20	−22	−22	−23

percent high school diploma graduates (HSDG). The projected high school graduate percentage of over 60 percent compares favorably with the percentages in the first few years of the AVF. Thus, moderate controls on first-term attrition and the use of women in no more than 12 percent of enlisted jobs would appear to offset the decline in population. Further use of these policies, as well as other ones—most notably, higher reenlistments—would improve the quality of recruits and enhance the prospects for sustaining the AVF.

The Dip in Recruiting, 1975 to 1979

If the only problem faced by the AVF were the declining youth population, prospects for success in the 1980s would be bright indeed. But since 1975 the number of male high school graduates has declined from 243,000 to 191,000 or 21.4 percent. If we take into account that the population of 18-year-olds actually grew by 4 percent between 1975 and 1979, the decline was larger—24.3 percent. Thus, for reasons we have yet to explain, the rate of enlistments of high school graduates shrank by a quarter in the past five years.

We shall examine six hypotheses to which we can respectively attribute recruiting declines:

1. A reduction in youth unemployment rates in the past five years.
2. A decline in military pay for recruits relative to civilian alternatives.
3. The elimination of the GI Bill in 1977 as a recruitment incentive.
4. Restricted funds for recruiting and advertising.
5. Reduced requirements for military recruits.
6. Other reasons, such as a bad press on the volunteer force, low public opinion of military service, and a trend by youth away from military service and perhaps other manual occupations as well.

The first four factors are essentially economic arguments, and here we can present some evidence and guess at the magnitude of these effects.

1. *Unemployment.* In 1975, the United States hit the bottom of the deepest recession since the 1930s. Unemployment for the labor force as a whole exceeded 9 percent for the first time since before World War II. Youth unemployment for males aged 16 to 19 years averaged 20.1 percent for the year. Although 1979 would not appear to qualify as a boom period, the overall unemployment rate of 5.5 percent represents a major change from 1975. Unemployment among 16- to 19-year-old males averaged 15.7 percent, an improvement of 24 percent over the earlier period.*

---

* Calculated as $(10.157 - 0.20) \div \frac{1}{2} (0.175 + 0.200) = -0.240$.

Substantial empirical evidence links recruiting to youth unemployment rates (see Addendum B). Low-range estimates of the effect of unemployment indicate an elasticity of 0.20 in that a 10 percent increase in youth unemployment produces a 2 percent increase in enlistment supply. The high-range elasticity estimate is 0.5, suggesting that a 10 percent increase produces a 5 percent increase in enlistment supply.

America's Volunteers expresses the concern that current labor market statistics do not reflect the true tightness of the labor market, and more women and youth and others frequently considered marginal workers have entered the labor force. The greater participation of marginal workers, with greater probabilities of unemployment, produces a higher unemployment rate for each level of economic activity. This fact suggests one reason unemployment has not declined below 5.5 percent at the peak of the recent business cycle. Therefore, today's unemployment rates are not truly comparable with those of earlier periods, and the decline in unemployment since 1975 understates the changes in the labor market. This would "explain" an even greater decline in recruits due to labor market conditions. We have chosen not to account for this factor, both because of uncertainty as to the strength of its effects and because our empirical estimates (based on 1970s data)—may already account for this effect.

2. *Military vs. Civilian Pay.* Trends in military pay in the 1970s were generally unfavorable to first-term military pay. There are two reasons for the sluggish growth in military pay. First, military pay is linked to the overall average increase for general schedule employees—federal white-collar workers. Their pay is in turn related to that of private sector white-collar workers through the PATC Survey.* Pay rates have grown less rapidly for white-collar workers than for blue-collar workers in recent years. Second, in the past five years a change in the survey definition and two consecutive pay caps have retarded both military and federal white-collar pay increases by about 6 percent.†

Empirical researchers have never found a fully satisfactory measure of civilian wage rates available to prospective military recruits. Hence, to measure the decline in military pay relative to civilian wages, we have listed five separate indices: (1) average weekly earnings in the private sector, (2) the annual PATC Survey, (3) average weekly earnings in manufacturing; (4) the aggregate of blue-collar surveys used to set rates in the federal wage system, and (5) the minimum wage. Table 16 gives

---

* Professional, Administrative, Technical and Clerical Survey.

† Omitted from this calculation (and others) is a reallocation of base-pay increases into quarters allowances. Since first-term personnel typically live on post or base (or ship), this results in a reduction of take-home pay.

the value of the index in 1979 (1975 = 100) and the percent change in regular military compensation relative to these indices.* (The fifth index—minimum wage—is discussed separately below.)

Empirical results based on AVF-era data show a supply elasticity with respect to pay of around 1.0. This value means that a 10 percent increase in military pay produces a 10 percent increase in the enlistment rate. The Gates Commission used an elasticity of 1.25, which was itself near the conservative range of estimates produced by its own studies. (See Gilman, 1970, for a discussion.) More recent estimates of supply elasticity indicate a decline in recruits since 1975 due to a pay decrease of at least 9 percent, based on average private-sector earnings. If blue-collar workers are relatively more important, the decrease would be 12 percent or more.

A pay relationship that deserves note (and certainly deserves further research) is between the minimum wage and military enlistment. From 1975, when the minimum wage was $2.10, to 1979, when it reached $2.90, the minimum wage grew 18 percent. Today, military basic pay—calculated on a 40-hour week—is below the minimum wage and regular military compensation in cash is less than the minimum wage if the longer work week of military personnel is considered.

There are a number of ways to compare enlisted pay and minimum

---

* Regular military compensation in cash is defined as basic pay plus the cash value of quarters and subsistence allowances.

TABLE 16

COMPARISON OF CIVILIAN AND MILITARY PAY

	Index for 1979 (1975 = 100)	Percent Change in Military Pay Relative to Index
Average weekly private sector earnings	136	−9
PATC Survey (white collar)	133	−7
Average weekly earnings in manufacturing	144	−16
Aggregate of federal wage rate surveys (blue collar)	142	−14
Regular military compensation	124	−

wage. These include using basic pay or total regular military compensation in cash and comparing it with pay either for a 40-hour work week or for a more realistic (longer) work week with overtime. Our market research indicates that to the extent prospective recruits are aware of these items, they tend to compare basic pay with the minimum wage at 40 hours per week. Table 17 compares E-2 pay with the minimum wage over the past decade, with projections for FY 1980 and 1981.

Standard economic analysis of the effects of the minimum wage points to the increased youth unemployment a higher minimum wage is supposed to generate. At the same time, the military is attempting to attract the healthiest, the most highly educated, and the most intelligent part of non-college-bound youth. These youths would not be expected to have unemployment problems and would be likely to benefit from higher minimum wages. In the past five years, these rates have outstripped military pay increases by around 12 percent. While tending to increase unemployment rates among youths as a whole, higher minimum wages may have increased pay rates for high-quality youth without seriously affecting employment

TABLE 17

Comparison of Basic Pay with Federal Minimum Wage

FY	Basic Pay	Hourly wage*	Minimum wage	Percentage
1970	$127.80	$0.74	$1.60	46
1971	149.10	0.86	1.60	54
1972	320.70	1.85	1.60	116
1973	342.30	1.97	1.60	123
1974	383.30	2.10	2.00	105
1975	383.40	2.21	2.20	105
1976	402.60	2.32	2.30	101
1977	417.30	2.41	2.30	105
1978	443.30	2.56	2.65	96
1979	467.40	2.70	2.90	93
1980	500.10	2.89	3.10	93
1981	537.00†	3.10	3.35	92

* Hourly wage is calculated as 12 months' basic pay divided by 52 weeks at 40 hours per week.

† Assumes a FY 1981 pay raise of 7.4 percent.

rates. This has the effect of causing wage rates for youth to increase faster than other pay rates, and would increase the competition for military-age youth.

3. *The Elimination of the GI Bill.* At the end of 1976, new enlistees were offered a reduced and contributory educational benefit in place of the GI Bill. The GI Bill provided tuition payments and cash stipends for up to 45 months at a total value of $14,000 for single veterans ($16,500 for married).

The GI Bill was discontinued because of concerns over its lack of efficiency. High discount rates for new recruits would give a deferred benefit less recruiting effectiveness than a much smaller cash payment. It also carried high economic rent in that for many people it was not a strong drawing factor at time of enlistment. Yet many took advantage of the benefit. Thus, it was not a cost-effective recruiting incentive. Moreover, it often was not cost-effective in the broader societal context. Because it was of benefit only to those who took formal training and education, persons who derived only a marginal benefit from this training would still make use of this generous benefit.* None of these arguments state that the GI Bill had no recruiting punch but rather that the punch was weak relative to the high cost. The annual cost of the GI Bill in a steady-state AVF was $1.5 billion per year.

The new Veterans Educational Assistance Program (VEAP), begun for those signing enlistment contracts after 1 January 1977, is a benefit whereby the government matches the recruit's educational savings at a

---

* The best-known examples of marginal-value courses are pilot-training courses, supposedly for those who would become commercial pilots, and electronics courses that result at completion in construction of a color television.

TABLE 18

GI BILL vs VEAP

Discount Rate (Percent)	Present-Value Comparison	
	GI Bill	VEAP (No Kicker)
0%	$14,000	$5,400
10	8,000	2,800
20	4,800	1,400
30	3,100	600

two-for-one rate. The maximum government matching contribution under this formula is $5,400. In addition, the Secretary of Defense is authorized to make additional contributions (VEAP kicker) as may be necessary for accession and retention incentives.

The VEAP (without a kicker) has attracted about 25 percent of Army and Navy recruits and substantially fewer in the Air Force and Marine Corps. These numbers are far below GI Bill participation rates. A comparison of the present values at enlistment of the maximum GI Bill versus the maximum VEAP for single veterans reemphasizes the superior value of the former benefit (Table 18). (In 1980, the Army will begin to test a VEAP kicker of up to $6,000 for four-year combat-arms enlistment and for certain other MOSs.)

The needed research on the valuation of educational benefits for recruits has not been done. However, for the sake of argument assume a 20 percent real discount rate, and assume further that educational benefits are worth only 75 cents on the dollar for the average high school graduate recruit* and that only one-fourth of the total dollars are used.† Then the effect of the reduced educational benefits on initial enlistments is equal to
% change in enlistments = pay elasticity x average value of benefit x fraction of dollars used

$$\frac{x \ (\text{VEAP value} - \text{GI Bill value}) \times 100}{\text{First-term pay value}}$$

or

$$4.3\% = 1.0 \times 0.75 \times 0.25 \times \frac{(1,400 - 4,800) \times 100}{14,700}$$

Thus, the change in educational benefits may affect recruiting of high school graduates by approximately 5 percent. For the effect to be as large as 10 percent, the discount rate would have to be lower—around 10 percent —and the percentage of dollars used would have to be higher—50 percent. Our personal view is that this is not an unreasonable magnitude for the effects of eliminating the GI Bill.

---

* As an upper bound, educational benefits would be worth full value for those military personnel planning to obtain higher education on their own. The lower bound per dollar would be greater than zero because training would involve substantial investments of veteran's time. The 75-cent figure is the mean of a uniform distribution between 50 cents and one dollar.
† The limited available data suggest a GI Bill participation rate of 65 percent and an average utilization of $5,200, or 37 percent of the maximum benefit. This yields a utilization of 24 percent. High school graduates would be expected to be optimally situated to use the maximum benefit. Hence, this is a very conservative assumption.

4. *Reduction in Recruiting Resources.* A further economic factor, resources devoted to recruiting and advertising, relates not to the incentives to enlist but to the effort devoted to spreading information on military enlistment opportunities.

Recruiting offices functioned at a relatively low level during the draft era and, indeed, served a very different purpose. With the elimination of the draft, recruiting activities expanded rapidly (Table 19). But, after FY 1975, because of the success in 1975 (owing to a depressed labor market, reduced numbers of accessions needed, and other competing defense priorities), recruiting resources were reduced. Between 1975 and 1979, funds for recruiting and advertising were reduced about 15 percent in real terms, or about $80 million in FY 1977 dollars.

Estimates of the marginal cost per male high school graduate recruit have tended to vary between $3,000 (DOD estimate) and $6,000 (Congressional Budget Office estimate) in FY 1977 dollars. Such reductions might "explain" a decline of from 6 to 10 percent but such estimates tend to be extremely tricky. Both recruiting and advertising dollars face sharply diminishing marginal productivities once a market is saturated; moreover, the effectiveness of such programs depends to a degree on how attractive an option military enlistment is for America's youth. Since we have seen how

TABLE 19

RECRUITING, ADVERTISING, AND BONUS COSTS (in millions of dollars)

Fiscal Year	Advertising Actual $	Advertising 1977 $	Recruiting Actual $	Recruiting 1977 $	Bonuses Actual $	Bonuses 1977 $
1970	6.5	10.2	119.5	212.2	—	—
1971	22.7	35.5	139.7	231.3	—	—
1972	40.6	60.9	191.4	281.5	1.5	2.2
1973	68.3	98.0	256.0	342.6	40.9	54.7
1974	96.1	126.2	299.1	372.0	43.0	53.5
1975	89.1	102.6	346.8	397.9	58.8	67.5
1979	67.8	72.8	311.2	337.6	68.5	74.3
1977	64.4	64.4	327.6	327.6	30.3	30.3
1978	73.9	69.0	379.2	354.1	56.7	53.0
1976	74.1	65.2	380.2	355.1	60.9	56.9

the economic initiatives to enlist have declined in recent years, it may also be that additional dollars spent on recruiting resources are less productive.

5. *Fewer Military Recruits Needed.* Because of higher retention rates and reduced turnover and because of reductions in the number of military personnel, the number of recruits sought has been below average for the past two years. It has been thought that with lower recruiting objectives, the recruiters have tried less hard to get all the high school graduates available as long as the percentage of graduates remained high. In 1978, this appeared to be a definite possibility, but in 1979 the services ended up with fewer high school graduates and with fewer total recruits than planned.

A more sophisticated version of this effect, however, does appear to have some relevance. Military service represents a range of jobs and working conditions. Some are more attractive than others, and although bonus awards and other techniques are used to make less desirable jobs more attractive, they remain harder to fill. The implication of this is that, when fewer jobs are available, fewer good jobs are available, and it may be harder to attract high school graduate recruits. Between FY 1975 and FY 1979, NPS male recruits declined from 382,000 to 274,000—28 percent. The percentage of high school graduates among new male recruits actually rose from 64 percent to 70 percent. Thus, the argument goes, if more positions were available, more high school graduates would be recruited.

Although this hypothesis helps explain the 1978 recruiting experience, it will be of little help in explaining what happened in 1979. When requirements returned to more normal levels, the number of high-quality recruits remained low. The *net* effect of higher recruiting totals is to make the recruiting problem harder, not easier.

6. *Other Reasons.* A number of other reasons are heard for why recruiting may have suffered in recent years:

- A bad press on the problems of the AVF
- A low public opinion of military service, buttressed by continued anti-Vietnam sentiment
- Trends by youth away from blue-collar jobs and military enlisted service and toward college and white-collar jobs
- Large-scale CETA programs offering jobs to many youths who otherwise would enlist in the military
- Growing federally-sponsored scholarship programs that make it possible for low- and moderate-income youth to attend college without a military service commitment (a GI Bill without the GI).

Such reasons are not entirely without merit and indeed further research may shed light on some of these effects. There is no way, however, to gauge the magnitude of any of these effects over the past four years.

SUMMARIZING THE CAUSES OF THE RECRUITING DIP

In summarizing the possible reasons for the sharp decline in male high school graduate enlistment rates, we return to the economics of the military youth labor market. Over a five-year period (1975–1979), youth unemployment declined significantly. Moreover, pay for the military recruit fell relative to any civilian pay index measured and—during the same period—a valuable educational benefit was replaced by another far less valuable. If we look at these three measurable effects simultaneously, the strong effect on the market for military recruits is apparent.

Table 20 summarizes the cumulative effects of these changes. The more conservative estimates of these economic effects indicate a decline in recruits of 17 percent between 1975 and 1979. The less conservative estimates suggest a reduction in high school graduate enlistments of 10 percent. The reduction in enlistment rates for male high school graduates was 25 percent. Thus, a decline of at least 60 percent, and perhaps 100 percent, was due to improved employment opportunities, combined with reduced financial incentives for military enlistment.

The population decline of the 1980s and the recruiting dip of the 1970s are ominous portents for the AVF. Although reduced turnover and increased reliance on female personnel will, as in the past, help offset these effects, it is clear that the United States must improve the economic incentives for military personnel. In that sense a useful target would be to reverse the trends that have occurred in recent years. A 15 percent increase in the calculated present value of military pay and other benefits would increase the number of high school graduate enlistments by a similar number.

TABLE 20

EFFECTS OF ECONOMIC FACTORS ON MILITARY RECRUITING
BETWEEN 1975 AND 1979 (in percentages)

	More Conservative Estimates	Less Conservative Estimates
Reduced youth unemployment	−5	−12
Reduced military pay	−9	−12
Elimination of the GI Bill	−4	−10
Cumulative effect	−17	−30

Increases of this magnitude are *fair* in that such an increase would help recoup ground lost since 1979, and are *needed* to sustain the volunteer force through the 1980s.

The cost of such increases depends on how they are accomplished. If military pay were increased across the board, the annual cost would be around $4 billion. If raises were tailored to junior personnel, the annual cost would be about $1 billion. If increased financial incentives were given in the form of enlistment bonuses to high school graduate recruits, the costs would be less than $1 billion per year.

The DOD has already begun to recognize the seriousness of the recruiting situation. It is too early to state whether higher pay increases will be requested in the 1981 budget, but the DOD has greatly extended the VEAP kicker for Army enlistments in the combat arms and selected other skills.

Recruiting Differences by Service

Throughout the AVF era the Army has had the most difficult recruiting problems. It is not necessarily the case that the Army is the least attractive service; in fact, the Army attracts its share of recruits of all ability levels. The Army, however, has by far the highest accession requirement, and this more than anything else makes its recruiting problems unusually difficult.

Figure 5 (see page 239) underlines the average quality difference among recruits by service. And, although all services have remained at or near full strength, the Army's relative difficulty in attracting recruits is shown in the differences in test scores of recruits among the services.

The solution to this problem is not difficult or imaginative or expensive. The preceding section called for a significant increase in pay, benefits, and bonuses or other incentives for first-term military personnel. To correct the Army's problems and to equate more nearly supply and demand for personnel by service, such increases should be tilted in favor of the Army and perhaps the Marine Corps as well. This is most easily done with such discretionary items as bonuses and VEAP kickers rather than with separate basic-pay increases by service. A package targeted by service would be less expensive than a package that gives the same benefits across the board.

Summary

It is the authors' view that the knowledge and tools are available to continue the AVF through the 1980s.

- The population decline just ahead calls for efforts both to reduce personnel turnover and hence requirements for new recruits and to expand the supply base through the greater use of women and other measures. The policies already being pursued by the DOD should offset the effects of the population decline over most of the next decade.

- From an economic standpoint, the military is losing its competitive position for new recruits. A more vigorous economy, retarded military pay raises, and the abolition of the GI Bill have caused male high school graduate enlistments to decline between 15 and 25 percent in the past five years. To restore its competitive position, the DOD must reverse this trend by increasing the economic incentives for recruits to enter military service.

- Different supply-and-demand conditions by service need to be recognized by favoring the Army and perhaps the Marine Corps in enhancing the economic incentives to enlist.

- Finally, even a rich array of incentives to improve recruiting and permit the AVF to continue its successes of the 1970s would cost less than 5 percent of an annual defense budget of $150 billion.

Figure 28 summarizes graphically what this paper has addressed. Regarding supply, it shows the growth in the population of 18-year-old men that occurred over the past two decades and the decline that will occur over the next 15 years. The eligible line reflects the decrement in supply that may be expected as a result of mental, physical, and moral disqualification.

Demand is also shown at two levels. The first is total male accessions, that is, all men—active and reserve, officer and enlisted—that are brought on active duty each year. The second demand line is for active-force enlisted personnel. Both demand lines show the Vietnam buildup and the post-Vietnam decline.

The ratio of the eligible supply line on Figure 28 to the total demand line (that is, minimum supply to maximum demand) is shown in Figure 20. The figure reveals why a draft was necessary in the 1950s, when one out of every 1.2 eligible young man was needed. As the population increased and the post-Vietnam drawdown occurred in the early 1970s, the ratio rapidly dropped until only one out of every three young men was needed in 1973 when the AVF became a reality. Today less than one of every four eligible young men is needed. Although the trend will reverse in the coming years, the ratio will remain more favorable than the 1 : 3 ratio.

˙ Of course, these data do not prove the AVF will work, but they do indicate that there will be a sufficient supply of young men to meet the demand, if the American people are willing to support an all-volunteer force. The AVF is not without problems, but it is working and it can continue to work.

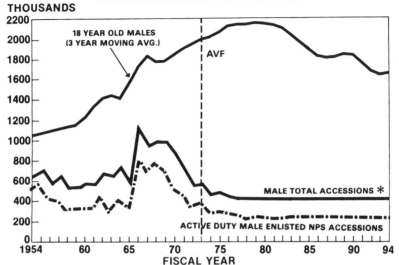

FIGURE 28

Sᴜᴘᴘʟʏ ᴀɴᴅ Dᴇᴍᴀɴᴅ ꜰᴏʀ Yᴏᴜɴɢ Mᴇɴ

THOUSANDS

18 YEAR OLD MALES
(3 YEAR MOVING AVG.)

AVF

MALE TOTAL ACCESSIONS *

ACTIVE DUTY MALE ENLISTED NPS ACCESSIONS

FISCAL YEAR

* Officer and enlisted, active and reserve

FIGURE 29

Rᴀᴛɪᴏ ᴏꜰ 18-Yᴇᴀʀ-Oʟᴅ Mɪʟɪᴛᴀʀʏ Eʟɪɢɪʙʟᴇ
Mᴀʟᴇs ᴛᴏ Tᴏᴛᴀʟ Mᴀʟᴇ Aᴄᴄᴇssɪᴏɴs *

RATIO**

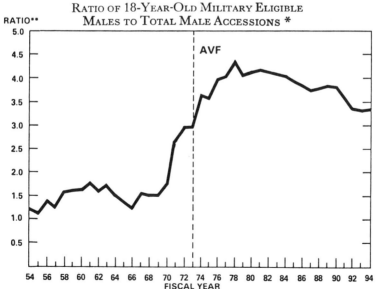

AVF

FISCAL YEAR

* Total male accessions are active and reserve officer and enlisted.
** Ratio = number of military eligibles per male accessions.

Addendum A

This addendum examines four representational issues:

- Are black military personnel concentrated in high-risk combat jobs and low-skill noncombat jobs?
- Are military enlistments geographically representative?
- What is the socioeconomic representation among military recruits?
- Are there opportunities to increase the role of women in the AVF?

Distribution of Blacks by Occupation

As the proportion of blacks in the services has increased, there have been corresponding increases in the proportion of blacks within service occupational groups. As Table A-1 indicates, however, the distribution of blacks

TABLE A-1

DISTRIBUTION OF BLACK ENLISTED PERSONNEL AMONG OCCUPATIONAL
GROUPS, ACTIVE-DUTY PERSONNEL, ALL SERVICES, FY 1978
(in percentages)

Occupational Groupings	Proportion of all Enlisted	Proportion of Black Enlisted
Infantry, gun crews and seamanship	15	19
Electronic equipment repair	9	4
Communications and intelligence	8	8
Medical and dental	5	4
Other technical	2	1
Functional support and administration	15	20
Electrical/mechanical equipment repair	20	14
Crafts	4	3
Service and supply	9	11
Other		
Totals	100% (1,774,000)	19% (342,000)

among the occupational fields is generally equal to the distribution pattern for all enlisted personnel.

As the greatest number of blacks are enlisting in the Army, their distribution among the Army's occupational groups also merits documentation. Yet, as Table A-2 illustrates, the proportion of Army enlisted blacks in each of the skill areas is about the same as that of all enlisted personnel.

Racial balance is not an easy issue. The blacks are qualified and are enlisting voluntarily. Is it right to deny a black a job he or she wants and is qualified to fill and to force a white to serve who does not want to serve? Do we want quotas by race? Do we want different pay and incentives by race? Clearly the answer to these questions is no. On the other hand, since casualties are usually proportional to exposure, the current trend will result in black casualty rates in excess of black representation in the society. Yet that is a clear risk of military service.

TABLE A-2

DISTRIBUTION OF BLACK ENLISTED PERSONNEL AMONG OCCUPATIONAL
GROUPS. ACTIVE-DUTY PERSONNEL, ARMY, FY 1978
(in percentages)

Occupational Groupings	Proportion of all Enlisted	Proportion of Black Enlisted
Infantry, gun crews and seamanship	25	25
Electronic equipment repair	4	3
Communications and intelligence	10	9
Medical and dental	5	5
Other technical	2	1
Functional support and administration	15	19
Electrical/mechanical equipment repair	14	12
Crafts	2	2
Service and supply	11	11
Other		
Totals	100% (669,000)	29% (195,000)

TABLE A-3

COMPARISON OF FY 1974, FY 1977, AND FY 1978 NPS ACCESSIONS BY REGION AND SERVICE

	Youth Population 1977	Army			Navy			Marine Corps			Air Force		
		1974	1977	1978	1974	1977	1978	1974	1977	1978	1974	1977	1978
Number (thousands)		182.2	168.4	124.1	90.4	101.6	80.3	47.5	45.0	39.6	73.8	72.5	68.0
Percent	100.0	100.0	100.0	100.0	100.0	100.0	100.0	100.0	100.0	100.0	100.0	100.0	100.0
Region (percent)													
New England	5.3	3.7	5.2	4.8	5.5	6.0	5.8	3.6	6.2	6.7	5.9	7.2	7.0
Middle Atlantic	16.3	10.7	15.3	13.3	14.9	16.8	17.6	14.8	17.6	18.5	14.0	16.6	17.0
East North Central	19.0	15.3	18.5	16.7	19.9	18.8	17.9	23.0	21.7	22.5	17.0	18.3	16.2
West North Central	7.6	7.1	7.0	6.3	9.2	7.3	7.5	8.3	8.9	7.9	8.1	8.1	7.7
South Atlantic	16.1	20.8	19.4	23.9	13.0	14.9	16.6	15.6	13.8	14.5	16.7	15.0	16.8
East South Central	6.6	8.9	7.5	8.2	6.2	5.6	6.0	6.0	5.1	4.9	6.8	5.4	8.0
West South Central	9.9	12.1	8.9	9.0	11.1	9.4	9.3	12.0	9.0	8.9	11.7	10.5	10.4
Mountain	5.0	5.2	4.3	4.1	5.9	5.5	5.4	4.4	4.8	5.0	4.6	5.6	5.6
Pacific	12.6	14.4	12.2	10.8	14.0	15.2	13.2	12.0	12.6	10.6	15.0	13.1	13.0
Other*	1.5	1.8	1.7	2.9	0.2	0.5	0.7	0.1	0.3	0.5	0.1	0.2	0.3

* Includes Puerto Rico, American Samoa, Guam, Canal Zone, and the Virgin Islands.

Geographic Representation

From a geographical perspective, the conscription system during the draft years generally provided a balanced pattern of accessions into the armed forces. Each state had its "quota" for Selective Service inductees that was related to that state's proportion of the draft-eligible population. However, differences in regional education systems, volunteer rates, health conditions, and so on created some qualitative differences among areas of the country. These conditions have persisted.

For example, though the ten most populous states with 52 percent of the 17- to 21-year-old population supplied 54 percent of male enlisted accessions to the DOD in FY 1978, a closer examination of data reveals both disparities between regions of the country and disparities within these regions for service preferences. The South Atlantic states were almost 50 percent overrepresented in the Army in FY 1978, while the same region was some 10 percent underrepresented in the Marine Corps. Many other such differences have taken place. Table A-3 summarizes the data for FY 1974, FY 1977, and FY 1976 by region, and Table A-4 summarizes the data for all states by order of youth population.

Since the AVF has brought about only minimal changes in the geographical representation of the draft years, the issue does not warrant corrective actions.

Economic Representation

The most elusive and hard-to-define socioeconomic characteristic of enlisted personnel in the armed forces is economic class; that is, the economic class of the member's family. In this area, to a far greater degree than the others, there are difficulties in obtaining adequate and accurate data. Compounding the problem are difficulties in data interpretation and definitions. Nevertheless various attempts have been made by the services and non-DOD researchers to better define the economic classes of the recruit groups. Unfortunately, such efforts can support only some general conclusions rather than definite answers. With these limitations in mind, therefore, the following comments are offered:

- It is clear that youths who attend a college or university are underrepresented. Only about 5 percent of enlisted accessions have some college prior to enlisting in the military. As a result, one can conclude, as Charles Moskos does, that upper-class America is underrepresented in the enlisted ranks of the Army. Yet many who enlist in the military continue on to college after service or attend college while on active duty.
- During the draft years, this same type of men used the Selective

TABLE A-4

STATES RANKED BY YOUTH POPULATION AND FISCAL YEAR 1978
NPS ENLISTMENTS (State Total as Percent of U.S. Total)

State	Youth Population* (Percent)	Enlistments (Percent)	Youth* Population (Cumulative) (Percent)	Enlistments (Cumulative) (Percent)
California	9.3	8.6		
New York	7.7	7.6	17.0	16.2
Texas	5.8	5.7	22.8	21.9
Pennsylvania	5.3	5.4	28.1	27.3
Ohio	5.0	5.6	33.1	32.9
Illinois	4.9	4.0	38.0	36.9
Michigan	4.4	3.9	42.4	40.8
Florida	4.1	5.5	46.5	46.3
New Jersey	3.3	2.8	49.8	49.1
Massachusetts	2.5	2.5	52.3	51.6
Indiana	2.5	3.1	54.8	57.0
North Carolina	2.5	3.1	57.3	57.0
Georgia	2.4	3.0	59.7	60.0
Virginia	2.3	2.5	62.0	62.5
Wisconsin	2.2	1.8	64.2	64.3
Missouri	2.1	2.3	66.3	66.6
Tennessee	2.0	2.1	68.3	68.7
Louisiana	1.9	1.5	70.2	70.2
Minnesota	1.9	1.7	72.1	71.9
Maryland	1.9	2.1	74.0	74.0
Alabama	1.8	2.0	75.8	76.0
Washington	1.6	1.5	77.4	77.5
Kentucky	1.6	1.5	79.0	79.0
Puerto Rico	1.5	1.1	80.5	80.1
South Carolina	1.4	1.7	81.9	81.8
Connecticut	1.3	1.3	83.1	83.1
Iowa	1.3	1.1	84.5	84.2
Colorado	1.3	1.4	85.8	85.6
Mississippi	1.2	1.2	87.0	86.8
Oklahoma	1.2	1.0	88.2	87.8

TABLE A-4—*Continued*

State	Youth Population* (Percent)	Enlistments (Percent)	Youth* Population (Cumulative) (Percent)	Enlistments (Cumulative) (Percent)
Arizona	1.2	1.4	89.4	89.2
Oregon	1.1	1.1	90.5	90.3
Kansas	1.0	0.8	91.5	91.1
Arkansas	1.0	1.1	92.5	92.2
West Virginia	0.9	0.8	93.4	93.0
Nebraska	0.7	0.7	94.1	93.7
Utah	0.6	0.3	94.7	94.0
New Mexico	0.6	0.8	95.3	94.8
Maine	0.5	0.7	95.8	95.5
Rhode Island	0.4	0.4	96.2	95.9
Idaho	0.4	0.3	96.6	96.2
Montana	0.4	0.4	97.0	96.6
Hawaii	0.4	0.5	97.4	97.1
New Hampshire	0.4	0.5	97.8	97.6
South Dakota	0.3	0.3	98.1	97.9
North Dakota	0.3	0.3	98.4	98.2
Delaware	0.3	0.3	99.7	98.5
District of Columbia	0.3	0.4	99.0	98.9
Nevada	0.3	0.3	99.3	99.2
Vermont	0.2	0.3	99.5	99.5
Wyoming	0.2	0.1	99.7	99.6
Alaska	0.2	0.1	99.9	99.7
Guam, Virgin Islands, Canal Zone, and American Samoa	0.1	0.3	100.0	100.0

* 1970 Census projected to 1977, youth ages 17 to 21.

Service deferment and exemption options to avoid military duty. As a result, there was a smaller proportion of recruits from this segment of society than from the so-called middle class.

- Officers, who bear a proportionate share of casualties in wartime, are all college graduates.
- At the lower end of the economic spectrum, the substandard education and health care of many poor families have precluded proportion-

ate numbers from qualifying for enlistment or induction. For example, during the draft years, up to 65 percent of the examinees from lower socioeconomic backgrounds were rejected, and the higher enlistment standards of the AVF have continued this trend.

- No group is unrepresented; rather, the question concerns the degree of under- or overrepresentation. Though opinions differ as to the significance of the levels of under- or over-representation, several survey efforts have documented the relatively small deviations from a truly proportionally representative force. This work admittedly is based on uncertain knowledge of recruits concerning their parents' earnings. Table A-5 summarizes the outcome of the yearly DOD effort to survey the economic status of the entering recruits by level of parents' earnings. Other analyses as shown in Table A-6 have attempted to document economic status by relating Zip Codes of recruits' home areas to Census earning patterns.

While admittedly imprecise both approaches tend to show underrepresentation of youth in enlisted occupations both from families with very low incomes and from those with very high incomes. Lower middle-income families are overrepresented in the AVF just as they were during the draft. Today, however, the overrepresentation is at least the result of the choice of the individual given the economic options open in the labor market.

Charles Moskos has combined the economic and race issues and concluded that, for the enlisted force of the Army at least, the black accessions are more representative of the black economic community than the white accessions are of the white economic community.

There is evidence that much of the lower half of the black economic community may be ineligible to serve. Thus, it appears that the enlisted force may well be underrepresentative of white middle and upper classes and black lower classes.

The question remains: Does this overrepresentation of those who want to serve present a problem? Its adverse effects in combat are somewhat mitigated by the plan, indeed the need, to reactivate the draft in the early stages of any mobilization and by the presence of middle-class youth—both black and white—in the officer corps.

Women

Women, of course, are the most underrepresented subset of those who are qualified to serve in the armed forces. Yet, major increases in the numbers and proportion of women serving in the military have been made during the AVF years. The move is toward increased representation, but even when the current strength goal for women in the armed forces is achieved, they will not be proportionally represented. By 1985, women may represent twelve percent of personnel in the armed forces. To achieve proportional representation some 51 percent of the ranks would have to be women. The DOD does not propose such a goal. Nonetheless, increasing numbers of women are volunteering and serving well. The AVF of 1979 was far more representative of the sexes than the draft-era force. The increased use of women is one potential solution to current and future recruiting requirements (see pages 269-276).

Addendum B

In regard to evidence linking recruiting with youth unemployment, the most comprehensive studies based on AVF-era experience for total DOD enlistments are by Cooper (1977) and by Grissmer (1979). They produced the following point elasticities for unemployment:

TABLE A-5

ACTIVE-DUTY NPS ENLISTEES BY PARENTS' EARNINGS (in percentages)

Income	CY (Calendar Year) 1969 U.S. Family Income Distribution	Distribution of CY 1969 Median Income of DOD Enlistees' Residences (fiscal years)					
		1974	1975	1976	TQ*	1977	1978
Under $6,000	26	7	6	5	6	6	6
$ 6,000 to $ 7,999	14	25	24	22	22	23	24
$ 8,000 to $ 9,999	14	32	32	33	32	32	32
$10,000 to $11,999	13	24	25	26	26	26	25
$12,000 to $14,999	14	10	11	12	12	11	11
$15,000 to $24,999	15	2	2	2	2	2	2
Over $25,000	4	†	†	†	†	†	†
Total	100	100	100	100	100	100	100

* Transition quarter
† Less than 0.5 percent

TABLE A-6

Distribution of Male Enlisted Accessions by SMSA Zip Codes Ranked According to Average Family Income (in Percentage)

Percentile[a]	Income Range[b] ($000s)	Enlisted Accessions[c] Draft	AVF	16–21 Male Population[d] All	N.S.
99	$24.5	0.38	0.34	1.06	0.43
95–99	$17.0–$24.5	2.84	2.67	5.13	2.59
90–95	$14.7–$17.0	5.08	4.93	7.36	4.61
75–90	$12.2–$14.7	19.33	18.95	20.83	16.65
50–75	$10.3–$12.2	29.88	29.70	28.56	28.01
25–50	$8.4–$10.3	25.17	25.23	22.63	27.70
10–25	$6.3–$ 8.4	13.21	13.99	12.13	16.70
5–10	$1.3–$ 6.3	2.88	3.02	2.10	2.91
5	$ 1.3	1.24	1.19	0.18	0.42

Source: U.S. Census and Manpower Research and Data Analysis Center, OASU (M&RA), provided the data tapes.

Note: This table reports the percentage distributions for total DOD enlisted accessions (inductions and enlistments) by percentile rankings of five-digit Zip Codes located in Standard Metropolitan Statistical Areas (SMSAs). SMSA five-digit Zip Codes were ranked according to average family income within the Zip Code, and then grouped into percentile groupings. Accessions were then matched with these percentile groupings by using the home address Zip Code for each enlistee or inductee.

[a] Percentile rankings, based on within Zip Code average family income, for five-digit SMSA Zip Codes. Based on 10,708 five-digit Zip Codes out of 11,972 Zip Codes located in SMSAs (data on either population or income were not available for the remaining 1,264 Zip Codes).

[b] The range of within Zip Code average family incomes for each percentile grouping. Based on 1969 incomes reported in the 1970 census.

[c] Percentage distributions for DOD enlisted accessions (see Note above). Time periods: draft, 1/71 through 12/72; AVF, 1/73 through 6/75.

[d] Percentage distributions for all 16- to 21-year-old males residing in these Zip Codes (All) and those not enrolled in school. (N.S.)

Cooper: Male high school graduates, mental categories I-III 0.19
Grissmer: Male high school graduates, mental categories I-II 0.485
                                        mental categories III 0.223

The range here (0.2–0.5) is taken as representative. More recent work by Fernandez (1979) has produced generally higher elasticities, although his results for male high school graduates, mental categories I-II, in the Army are consistent with those cited here.

There are other somewhat compelling reasons for the range of unemployment elasticities. Take the simple constant-elasticity supply model that relates enlistment rates (e) to military pay (m), civilian wages (c), and the employment rate (l-u), where u is the unemployment rate:

$$e = aM^{b_1} (c[1-u])^{b_2} (1-u)^{b_3}$$

where the expression in parentheses measures the expected civilian wage.
    The elasticity of supply with respect to unemployment is

$$- (b_2 + b_3) u / l\text{-}u$$

A reasonable lower bound on the elasticity assumes $b_3 = 0$. That is, there is no separate effect on enlistments beyond the effect on expected earnings. At the two data points observed for 1975 and 1979 (0.157 and 0.20, respectively), the unemployment elasticities are 0.19 and 0.25 if we further assume that the civilian pay elasticity (b_2) and the military pay elasticity (b^1) are 1.0.
    The upper bound of 0.5 is consistent with the separate effect of unemployment (b_3), being just as strong as the effect through the pay variable. Thus, the following unemployment elasticities are produced:

u	$b_2 = 1.0, b_3 = 0$	$b_2 = 1.0, b_3 = 1.0$
0.157 (1975)	0.19	0.38
0.20 (1979)	0.25	0.50

The range of estimates suggests that improvements in unemployment rates contributed to a 5 percent to 12 percent decline in male high school graduate enlistments between 1975 and 1979.

References

America's Volunteers: *A Report on the All-Volunteer Armed Forces.* Washington, D.C.: Department of Defense, 31 December 1978.

Cooper, Richard V. L. *Military Manpower and the All-Volunteer Force.* R-1458-ARPA, Santa Monica, Calif.: Rand Corporation, September 1977.

Fernandez, Richard L. "Forecasting Enlisted Supply: Projections for 1979–1990." N-1297-MRAL. Santa Monica, Calif.: Rand Corporation, September 1979.

Gilman, Harry J. Supply of Volunteers to Military Service.
In *Studies Prepared for the President's Committee on an All-Volunteer Armed Force,* Volume 1. Washington, D.C.: Government Printing Office, November 1970.

Grissmer, David W. "Supply of Enlisted Volunteers in the Post-Draft Environment." 1977. In *Defense Manpower Policy Presentations from the 1976 Rand Conference on Manpower,* ed. Richard V. L. Cooper, Santa Monica, Calif.: Rand Corporation, 1979.

Nelson, Gary R., Robert F. Hale, and Andrew Hamilton. "Defense Manpower Issues for 1977." Congressional Budget Office Budget Issue Paper, January 1977.

XXIII

NATIONAL SERVICE: UNWISE OR UNCONSTITUTIONAL?

Philip Bobbitt

National Service, like the draft, would employ conscription and various inducements to enlist vast numbers of our citizens but, unlike the military draft, would do so with the aim of directing this manpower toward civilian tasks. Owing to this difference in aim, it is not always easy to appreciate the origin of the idea of national service in the older idea of the draft.

The term "national service" occurs first in the context not of social action but as the name for a twentieth-century version of the draft. With our century's gift for euphemism, "national service" was the phrase applied in debate in 1917 when Congress reinstated conscription.[1]

And the seminal essay in 1910 by William James, which is usually thought of as suggesting the national service idea, also originated not in ambitious schemes for social reclamation but in war. This essay, which bears a title somewhat embarrassing for us today (a proof that not only are there relatively few new ideas, there are not even very many catchy phrases), was called "the Moral Equivalent of War."[2] In that essay, James surveyed the sanguine history of mankind and, doubtless anticipating the possibilities for blood letting on a truly apocalyptic scale that the new century presented, concluded that since war held a compelling fascination for man, it must be sublimated by more abstract and benign conquests. This, he suggested, might be accomplished by conscripting young men into a sort of war on poverty, augmented by attacks on unmined coal, unharvested grain, unbuilt

---

dams, and so forth. One cannot read this passionate program without being constantly aware that war —not the agenda of social action—is the primary target. James, who was a pacifist, was of course fated for disappointment, it is therefore tempting to say that he was ahead of his time. His essay reveals to us the birthmark of the idea of national service. From our perspective we can see that idea arising from the modern manpower problems of the warfare-welfare state. James's scheme was not merely *coincidental* with the twentieth-century draft.

Of course, in our day, we are aware of the binding of national service to the draft: the former is often suggested—and more often supported, I suspect, than suggested—as an ameliorative adjunct to the draft. If it's unfair to draft only a few young men into the military since our requirements don't dictate wholesale conscription, this can be alleviated by drafting everyone and augmenting the military tasks with civilian ones. The tasks mentioned usually share with defense needs a resistance to private solution, perhaps owing to technical barriers like transaction costs or perhaps because the aggregation of private values of caring for the elderly, cleaning up the environment, and staffing day-care centers adds up to something less than the value we publicly put on these objectives.

These tasks suggest the other basis on which national service is propounded: that it will solve a number of social problems by employing unemployables to accomplish what otherwise would be left undone.[3]

The two ideas are usually separated. "Youth and the Needs of the Nation," the Report of the Committee for the Study of National Service,[4] has little to say on the role of the draft, except to repeat the puzzling prediction that enlistments would rise if national service were instituted. At the same time, Robert McNamara's endorsement of national service seems clearly a by-product of the controversies precipitated by conscription for the Vietnam War.[5]

Actually these two ideas are descendants of a common reality, the inequality arising from the modern necessity of mass manpower, highly differentiated. In this paper I will show the implications of this origin for national service schemes: that, insofar as they are proposed as ameliorative adjuncts to the draft, they will eventually exacerbate the very difficulties such schemes are devised to solve; and that, insofar as national service is a means of accomplishing other than draft-related ends, it is unconstitutional.

II

To see how national service arises from the draft, and how it will prove unwise as a draft ameliorative, it is necessary to understand the ineluctable tensions that are responsible both for the suggestion in the first place and for its ultimate unsatisfactoriness.

There are three paradigms for the ways in which a statutory allocation of "goods" and "bads" can be made. These paradigms are: the pure market, the political agency, and the lottery. Each of these approaches has its peculiar advantages and shortcomings in the context of the draft.[6]

Market mechanisms—of which our current All-Volunteer Force is an example—confer several benefits. The principal benefit, which the perhaps misleading term "volunteer" seeks to exploit, is the lack of overt coercion. Particularly when the certainties of death and injury are being allocated, the apparent absence of coercion acts to absolve society from committing a particular person to a horrible fate. At the same time, market decisions are highly decentralized: because individuals are doing the choosing, the society as a whole is not expressing preferences for one group over another, or putting the burden on any particular class.

Of course, market decisions cannot be wholly allowed to govern in the draft situation. The total need for military manpower, as well as specific needs for doctors and engineers and so forth, must be determined by political judgments. Thus, much of the advantage of market procedures is lost to us, because we cannot use them to determine the social cost of each extra soldier by simply letting the market aggregate costs.

Once particular category levels are determined, however, we face the fact that markets make certain statements about relative value that, in the circumstances of risking life and well-being, we may find intolerable. It may be perfectly all right to *say* that a doctor is more valuable to society than a mechanic (although, in my experience, the similarity in their work doesn't seem to have escaped the attention of either party). But when we are forced to pay several times as much to induce the doctor to risk his life as we are to bring about the induction of the mechanic, we may discover the comparisons are a bit too vivid. By what justification, after all, do we accept the market's valuing of utility when it is life we are apportioning?

Yet the greatest shortcoming of the market as a draft mechanism is its dependence on the existing distribution of wealth. This dependence is accentuated when the market is used only to determine which persons shall fill the slots and not to decide the ultimate force levels. In such a situation it is unconvincing to maintain that by using the market we have merely given a resource to those who are willing to give up what it takes to produce it. Instead, since we are using the market solely to test relative desire—the amount of product to be allocated already having been determined—we must face, without excuse, the fact that the measure of desire has a different significance depending on the wealth of the choosers. A $10,000 salary isn't much of an inducement to a very wealthy man; forgoing it is a measure of his relative desire, *vis-à-vis* a poor man's, only in a very relative way. Indeed, insofar as the current voluntary system is financed by an accurately gauged inclining income tax system—as one fears it is not—we have a system much like that of the Civil War, in which the rich are hiring substitutes to serve for them. Such a system, from the perspective of each participant, is often said to make those who choose to participate in it better off while not worsening the lot of anyone else. If the poorer person chooses to enlist while the wealthier man does not, this simply means that the poorer person thinks he is better off in the Army than out of it. One reply to such a view is that since it assumes a market system, it does not help us to tell whether or not the participants are in fact better off under a market system than under some other arrangement. Indeed it is impossible to do so. For one thing, the choice to join the Army is a choice of a different kind when made in the market setting than when made in a society that regards such service as a citizen's duty. For another, we can never fully calculate the benefits a participant might have been able to reap in negotiating the changeover from one system to another, a loss he suffers if one system, rather than another, is assumed in place. And since such changeovers are not themselves the product of some meta-market choice, we have no way even of knowing if they are changes for the betterment of some and the detriment of none. In any event, the reply I have chosen to make has nothing to do with protecting the poor per se, but rather with protecting society's interest in not conceding and exploiting the fact that some of its members can be made better off, even at the risk of their lives, by the inducement of a relatively slight wage.

Finally, the market presumes that relative desire—even as warped by the existing distribution of wealth—is the sole criterion for deciding who shall serve in the military. But this is quite risky where civic duties are concerned, and the more so the more perilous the duty becomes, for the true volunteers—who would enlist for money alone when there is real danger—will often be those persons the society wishes to preserve rather than sacrifice. In other words, the market, when it is allocating incommensurables like death and great suffering, doesn't discriminate between persons whose social utility to society is not reflected in their relative desire to avoid harm. Cowards may die a thousand times but they have the comfort of expecting frequent restorations.

Political approaches remedy each of these shortcomings. When draft deferments or exemptions operate to exclude farmers, geniuses, Congressmen, or engineers, it is because these are felt to have a greater social utility at home. And, although the system of college deferments may have operated to the benefit of the middle class, a political approach can, in principle, avoid dependence on the prevailing wealth distribution. Furthermore, since conscription does not have to bid for the service of the numbers it needs, the explicit valuing of each additional life is avoided. Thus the superiority of using political agencies in the draft is a result of their ability to reflect nonwealth comparisons and to enforce general social standards that the pure market does not incorporate. We can decide to use criteria such as health and age as standards by which to allocate wartime service at the same time that we decide that wealth or race or class or alienage should not be used as an allocative principle. We can defer the conscientious objector even though he can't buy his way out; we can exempt the great research chemist or violinist; we can draft the heart surgeon when no monetary inducement would succeed.

But this flexibility and insensitivity to wealth distribution account also for the shortcomings of the political approach to the draft. By abandoning the market we give up an efficient mechanism of measuring individual desire. We are apt to draft the pacifist and leave the militarist at home. At the same time, the standards meant to reflect individual social utility impose a demand for information quite unnecessary in the axiomatic determination of utility that the market provides.

As a result, political agencies have an insatiable need for information gathering. This is reflected in the current action by Congress, which, rejecting a new conscription system based on politically determined allocations, passed measures designed to set up registration mechanisms. The insatiable need for information accounts for many of the shortcomings of using the political process here: its high cost and bureaucratization; its manipulability by lawyers; its personal intrusiveness; its susceptibility to corruption and bias.

Apart from the information gathering necessary to effectuate the politically determined standards, there are problems arising from the standards themselves. In addition to the costs of determining such standards, we must bear the cost imposed by having to name which persons society considers more valuable than others. Even if we were to agree that graduate students are less expendable than, say, gardeners—a dubious proposition perhaps—it is extremely costly for a society to say so, much more costly than the vague, partially chance-governed preferences that wealth positions reflect. Also, because the standards to be applied originate in the society, they are likely to reinforce whatever social discrimination currently exists. Since the meting out of infantry assignments is more painful than not getting an invitation to a coming-out party, this reiteration of preferences must be counted as a potential shortcoming of the political approach in this area.

These shortcomings are avoided by the third paradigm of social choice, the lottery. Because lot systems represent choices not to choose, they require neither elaborate information nor definable, neutral principles. In a lottery either all have an equal chance at the good (or bad as the case may be) or payoffs are distributed in an equal amount to all group members.

Lotteries, of course, have a limited usefulness in the context of manpower for war. Naturally, they cannot be used to set force levels. And they must depend on crucial political decisions to determine the perimeters of the pools within which they operate. Few would suggest, for example, that the blind and disabled be included in a draft pool. These obvious limitations suggest further shortcomings of this approach.

Even when initial force-level determinations of the total manpower needed are made, lot systems display defects at the allocative level that resemble those associated both with markets and with political approaches. In the market it was difficult to reflect those differences among individuals that were not expressed in their choices. In the political process, individual desires were difficult to give weight to. Lotteries, whose virtue is their blindness, are insensitive to both individual and collective preferences. It's not just that the "dove" is drafted while the "hawk" stays home: it's a near-sighted research scientist approaching a breakthrough who happens to be the dove; and a crack-shot with a particular taste for the endangered heron who happens to be the hawk.

In addition to the high cost of randomness, lot systems exert pressure to lower force levels because they highly dramatize the initial, "first-order" determination.

Each of the "pure" approaches, then, has pluses and minuses in its application to the problem of the draft. What is not always appreciated, however, is that each embodies a particular vision of egalitarianism. Whether this is the case because they reflect underlying human values of a structural kind (that is, a relatively few variations in attitude that are dictated by human cooperation and competition in the world), or whether these different rules of egalitarianism arise from those societies whose economic arrangements demand them, I cannot say. In any event, each of the three paradigms I have presented may be paired with a rule of equality, derived from different conceptions of egalitarianism.

Simple or *naive* egalitarianism treats everyone alike and admits of no discrimination on the basis of interpersonal comparisons. Such a conception is embodied, for example, in first-come-first-served distributions. It is the ideology of the lottery. *Formal* or *laissez-faire* egalitarianism requires the equal opportunity to move within categories that may properly be the basis for discrimination. Equals must be treated equally; that everyone is not in every relevant aspect equal is not only an assumption, it is a necessity, because it allows discriminating criteria to be identified and to function. *This* conception of egalitarianism is compatible with a reliance on markets. *Corrected* or *qualified* egalitarianism accepts the premise of formal egalitarianism that discrimination is proper so long as likes are treated alike, but it "corrects" the operation of this rule, rejecting it as an absolute and refusing to apply it whenever its results correlate a permissible discriminating criterion—in the draft context, say, health—with an impermissible one, such as wealth or race. Every culture's concept of equality is an amalgam of such paradigms; yet concepts of equality differ greatly from society to society in regard to which of these conceptions is dominant. Thus, to stay with examples drawn from the allocation of military service, until Gladstone's first ministry it was the accepted practice for an English officer to purchase his commission in a regiment; in America promotion is earned on the basis of educational tests and peer review with the additional factor of affirmative action when testing and recommendation fail to produce the "appropriate" number of officers from minority backgrounds; in China, in some recent periods, officerships were rotated among the soldiers.

Of course no society accepts one of these conceptions of egalitarianism to the complete abandonment of the others. The tension caused by their coexistence may result in a society's adherence to one dominant rule with respect to the distribution of one sort of good while employing another conception with respect to other goods. Even in the allocation of a single good, we may observe the use of different rules at different points in the process of allocation, resulting in a seriatim mixture.

At the same time, societies will employ such mixtures of the various "pure" allocation approaches in an effort to compensate for the shortcomings of the dominant approach. It is scarcely conceivable, for example, that the United States would employ a lot system to draft into military service without appending some political agency to circumscribe the eligible pool (by excluding, say, the handicapped). Two features, then, of allocation devices—their mutual compensation when used in combination, and the competition of values that underlie them—account for the use of mixtures of approaches in any nontrivial allocation.

Beyond such mixtures or combinations of mixtures, there is a more subtle type that one finds with respect to particularly precious allocations of life— and the draft is, of course, among these. This is the mixture or alteration of mixtures. It is an intricate strategy of successive changes demanded by the irreducible shortcomings that even the richest static mixture displays. When the cost to social cohesion and to society's values of choosing a single, though mixed, approach becomes sufficiently high, this strategy becomes worthwhile.

Many of you have been to other conferences on the draft before this one. Why, you may ask yourself, do approaches to such allocations change? Why wasn't the last change enough? It was not mindlessly made. It was the outcome of rational responses to pertinent criticism preceded by lucid debate—or at least as rational, pertinent, and lucid as discussions of policy usually are. Conferences were held. The critics of the then-existing system described in generally accurate detail the fundamental flaws; these critics invoked the values the system degraded. Of course the defenders of that system were no less rational. They were quite penetrating in their recognition of the flaws inherent in the proposed reform. Indeed, when the reform had become the system, it was eventually conceded to have the very shortcomings *its* critics had predicted and to degrade those values they had sought to protect. Does this mean that the adoption of the reform was a *mistake*? If it was not, why do we move restlessly from one system to another? If it was, why is each system in turn proved inadequate?

The answer, as Guido Calabresi and I have described it, is that a society may limit the destructive impact of tragic choices, allocations like the draft, by choosing to mix strategies over time. By this alternation, endangered values are reaffirmed while the cost to other values is initially postponed. Change brings two dividends. First, a reconceptualization of the problem arouses hope that its price can somehow be avoided. The certainties of the discarded method are replaced. Second, the society is acting, and action itself has a palliative benefit since it too implies that necessity can somehow be evaded if only we run faster, stretch our arms farther, work harder, plan better than those we supersede. Third, and most important because not an illusion, is our deep knowledge that change will come again. This is the birth of hope: values currently degraded will not be abandoned.

This phenomenon may be observed in an account of the draft in this country. For while the first-order determination of the number of soldiers needed has remained stable, virtually all of the classical approaches to allocation have, in various arrangements, been used as devices for resolving the issue of forcing some men to fight while others are left safe at home. Yet none of these mixed approaches has long survived.[7]

The Militia Act of 1862 was the first national draft statute in the United States. Reaction to it was immediate and unfavorable. It was said that the draft was insulting to citizens who would otherwise have volunteered; that it would impede that year's harvest; that it was unnecessary. But the most violent objection centered on the market component of the allocation mixture, a provision that enabled a drafted citizen to hire a substitute in his place. As any neoclassical economist could have told Congress, the immediate effect of this provision was to stop all voluntary enlistment. This in turn increased the need for draftees and therefore also increased the cost of hiring substitutes. Although this development was somewhat remedied by a draft reform act in 1863 that set a flat fee of $300 for exemption from induction, the proceeds of which were to be used as bounties to induce enlistment, the public outrage at such overt pricing was ended only by the end of the war. Although 292,444 names were drawn during this period, only 9,881 persons were impressed into service. For various reasons, including disability, 164,345 men were exempted; 26,002 furnished substitutes; 52,288 paid the commutation fee.

In 1866 a study was commissioned to review Civil War conscription. Its recommendations were the basis of the next statute, passed in May 1917, which reinstated the draft. Utterly rejecting the market reliance on volunteers, bounties, and hired substitutes, this act provided that conscription was to be the sole means of recruiting and maintaining a national army. Bounties and substitutes were forbidden. Ministers and divinity students, some public officials, and men in certain occupations were exempted. This system also was the subject of widespread criticism, though the criticism was not so violent as that aroused by the statutes of the Civil War, when draft officials were murdered in Indiana and Illinois, federal infantry were fired upon by draft resisters in Ohio, and the great draft riots in New York killed more than a thousand. Nevertheless, during World War I there were riots and there was widespread resistance. By August 1918, 16,000 men were being held in New York City for failure to register or appear when drafted. The system was incorporated, with some modifications, in a statute that would have established a permanent system of universal military training. The predictable arguments were made; the act failed to pass the Senate. At the end of the war, the draft lapsed.

The Selective Training and Service Act of 1940 authorized the reinstitution of a national draft. Liability to the draft, however, was limited to 900,000 men whose *order* of induction—which determined who was actually called up—was to be determined by a lottery. By 1942, various modifications were introduced. The lottery was discarded and registrants were called by order of date of birth. All males between 18 and 65 were registered. Voluntary enlistments were severely restricted, thus reducing the market component of the mixed approach. This act of 1940 continued until March 31, 1947. Its successor, the Selective Service Act of 1948, requested by President Truman, remained the basic method of conscription until its repeal during the Vietnam War. During this period vigorous criticisms were made of the criteria required by the chosen political approach to allocation. Under the 1948 act, all 18-year-old males were registered with a local agency. The agency used a classification scheme to determine the order of induction. Force-level requirements by the Department of Defense were prorated among the local boards with deductions for volunteers. All sorts of appeals were available to the registrant seeking to overturn his classification. Furthermore, a complicated system of deferments operated to reorder college students, graduate students, those physically or mentally unsuitable for service, fathers, farmers, Peace Corps and VISTA volunteers, medical students, and others.

This system of broad liability and broad, though vague, deferments operated with various modifications during the period when draft calls went from a little more than 100,000 in 1964 to almost 300,000 in 1966. It employed a decentralizing component (the local draft board) grafted onto a political allocation scheme (the classification and deferment system). As a result it attracted the two sorts of criticisms occasioned by such a modification, namely, criticisms both of the criteria and of their not being applied. When a decentralized agency acts according to discriminating rules, two things can happen: the agency will apply the rule, and the offense to formal egalitarianism, as well as the rules' highly debatable justifications for discrimination, will become apparent; or, sometimes, the agency will *not* apply the rule, and this is just as bad because it suggests corruption. On campuses during this era (I was an undergraduate then) there prevailed a sullen and restless irritability that stemmed partly from anxiety at the prospect of being called and partly from one's guilt in the knowledge that one's contemporaries, without the benefit of an academic refuge, were being sent to war.

Therefore, in November 1969, the Administration introduced a conscription scheme making draft selection wholly dependent on a lottery. First deferment for graduate students and then occupational and paternity deferments were phased out. In September 1971, an extension of the act provided for the elimination of college deferments and a uniform national call. Fortunately, at about the same time force levels began to decrease significantly, obscuring some of the difficulties imposed by a national lottery. Yet these were doubtless well enough appreciated. in 1973 the statute was allowed to lapse. An all-volunteer combat force, with a small draft for physicians and added reliance on civilians for some support tasks replaced the former system. The key element, the Secretary of Defense wrote, was a substantial increase in pay. By this we were brought full circle to the system of bounties and substitutes, though one considerably more concealed than that which operated during the Civil War. I take this conference as evidence that we are possibly in store for yet another rearrangement of approaches.

It is because the ineluctable underlying conflicts are, at some irreducible minimum, not amenable even to enriched mixtures that we have witnessed such cycles. I imagine it is obvious what point I shall assert in making use of this background: it is that national service is merely a scheme that uses a political mechanism as an added component to enrich the current arrangement of approaches that make up the draft. It is thought that, by greatly expanding inclusiveness so that everyone is drafted, the inegalitarianism exposed by the wartime draft can be ameliorated. No privileged undergraduates, no crafty lawyers, no victims. This, I submit, was what many had in mind when the national service idea enjoyed a vogue in the mid-1960s. And a similar idea can be detected in President Carter's statement, on March 5, 1977, that universal national service with nonmilitary options should be considered if a military draft becomes necessary.

This sort of mixture enrichment—that is, adding a component to the process, much as the lottery was piggybacked onto a market mechanism in the 1970s or onto a political agency during World War I—will create benefits for a time. Since the added component is chosen to compensate for a perceived weakness in the status quo, typically by marrying variations of pure approaches, the new mixture achieves, for a time, an amelioration through complexity. But because the underlying conflicts are not ultimately ameliorable, this initial benefit will not last. And this is so with the national service modification of the military draft.

Initially the conflicts are muted. But one mechanism must be established to determine who is channeled into the Army option and who into, say, the Peace Corps. The Report of the Committee for National Service suggests that this might be done through "random selection," which means a lottery. This reflects, I believe, the deep appeal of national service as an ameliorative to the draft. And yet, to imagine the results, we have only to imagine the skilled agriculturist who is fluent in Swahili being sent to Iowa to watch oscilloscopes. Moreover, a *truly* random system could hardly be universal; there may be many social welfare tasks that the handicapped and the frail can perform, but we would, I think, be daunted by the prospect of including them in a pool from which combat soldiers are to be randomly picked. Of course, absurd results confer certain benefits; it is reassuring, perhaps even inspiring, to see Schwarzschild the astrophysicist and Roosevelt the polo player in the trenches together. But is it equally reassuring to have a Conservation Corps from which forestry students are virtually excluded owing to the small probability that a lot system would put them there; or a home medical extension service that, for the same reason, excludes persons who had nursing training?

The lottery approach seems an unlikely one to use in dividing up the military and nonmilitary composition of national service. It is attractive to us because we are under the erroneous impression that there are millions of daily tasks that uneducated, unskilled, poorly paid, and largely unsupervised 16-year-olds can and will perform. The fact that the national economy finds it more efficient to pay these persons *not* to work, that is, does not find it worthwhile to set up a market in their services, suggests that there are a good many flaws in the image of 4½ million industrious youth picking up litter, planting pines, and administering day-care centers. It is difficult to believe that this awesome logistical and training task will be rendered more tractable by our refusing to pay any attention to the abilities, training, and interests of those employed.

Far likelier, at least *initially*, is the use of accountable political agencies to direct persons into the various options. Yet it should be obvious that the very use of discriminating criteria to make these judgments will provoke the sorts of conflicts that national service was designed to alleviate. This is not happenstance; indeed, because national service simply replicates the draft dilemma, one can predict the ontogeny of its programmatic development.

First a proto-national service system will employ market mechanisms. This will be the nonmandatory "volunteer" superagency. The current VISTA and Peace Corps programs are models. The use of the market in this context will arouse considerable criticism once the numbers involved rise above the present small amount used. Yet I doubt we will have much time for this reaction to develop, because, if I am correct in thinking that national service is a creature of the draft, there will be a collateral, irresistible pressure to replace the market apparatus of national service once the military draft is reinstituted. It's not every family, after all, that can afford to have a child languishing at substandard VISTA wages while waiting for the military to fill its calls. So we will then see a political approach used to compel service and to distribute the so-called volunteers. After a time, the shortcomings so evident with the political approach during the mid-sixties will become apparent. I am inclined to think that, after the initial benefit, a national service component to the draft will actually enhance those conflicts of values that the draft dilemma lays bare. Thus we may perhaps see use of lottery mechanisms, at least to vary the mixture within the overall system. This will have the various disadvantages mentioned above but it will confer—at a high price—the simple egalitarianism that is the refuge of a society that does not wish to make interlife comparisons when life itself is at stake. When we later become aware that we have thereby perfected a system for the indiscriminate imposition of inequalities, we will have completed the cycle. If this projection of a history we have yet to live is correct, then I am justified in concluding that national service, as an ameliorative to the conflicts in values generated by military service, is unwise because it is ultimately ineffective.

III

Yet it is often maintained that the draft is rather a minor aspect of the national service idea. This is perhaps implied by those who view national service as a "policy option for attacking disturbing social trends," like youth unemployment, as a means of enhancing social and psychological development of youth, or as a shrewd exploitation of an untapped resource, or as some combination of these three perspectives. Persons with these aims for national service may find what I have just argued in Part II unconvincing or at least irrelevant since, for them, national service never had much to do with the draft. It is my conclusion that, if national service is justified from *this* perspective, it may indeed be a wiser course of policy, but it is unconstitutional.

The constitutional argument that leads me to this conclusion is a very straightforward one. If Congress is to provide for a compulsory national service, it must do so pursuant to some constitutional authority to regulate behavior. The broad delegation of power to Congress to tax and spend for the general welfare will not apply in the context of coerced behavior, as it would if the plan were purely voluntary, that is, if the national service scheme simply placed the government in the marketplace to compete with other employers. Since the spending authority provided by Article I, Section 6, is not sufficient with respect to a compulsary national service plan, what other constitutional authority, express or implied, can we find to support such an exercise of authority? I will consider several, in turn, in a moment. It is my judgment that there is no such authority. If I am correct in this, then this power—to draft a civilian work force—is one not delegated to the United States by the Constitution. Indeed, I think it can be shown that it is not even an implicit means permissible to the national government; if this is so, then it is a power that is also denied the states. It is therefore one reserved to the people and may not, absent constitutional action by them, serve as a basis for governmental action.

Let me now present this argument in more detail. I assume a compulsory national service scheme. At first blush, this may seem an unreasonable assumption; many of the proposed plans are voluntary. I may even be suspected of indulging this assumption to make the constitutional problem more interesting. Yet I think a closer review of the national service idea will justify my assumption.

In the first place, many of the voluntary plans, despite their disclaimers, are in fact coercive. The Report of the Committee for the Study of National Service makes the curious observation that though some of its members "favor the adoption of mandatory National Service . . . no member of the Committee favors sending anyone to jail who refuses to serve." A "novel" sanction is then proposed: "denying a driver's license to anyone who declines National Service."[8] What, one wonders, does the committee think will happen to the young person who "declines" the offer of national service but who drives anyway? Perhaps the committee thinks he will only be fined. But what if he won't pay the fine? Then he is going to jail.

A second reason to assume compulsory service is that a great many plans are based on this assumption. This is, I suspect, what the President meant when he called for consideration of a "universal" national service.[9] Universality is a characteristic that minimum wage incentives alone are unlikely to confer. Even plans that currently have a veneer of the voluntary about them are often frankly acknowledged by their designers to be little more than stalking horses for more ambitious, compulsory plans that are to come later, once the public becomes accustomed to the idea of national service.[10] I hope the discussion in Part II suggests how the shortcomings of such a voluntary plan will, in chain reaction, arouse pressures to make service universal and hence compulsory .

Moreover, other sorts of shortcomings that voluntary systems impose might be avoided by a compulsory plan. Thus the Congressional Budget Office study of national service concluded that a large-scale, voluntary national service with diverse nonmilitary options would siphon off youth currently entering the military.[11] This would increase the costs of military recruiting and worsen the alarming shortcomings in military personnel already predicted for the 1980s. I need hardly add that for reasons similar to those outlined in Part II, this eventuality would also increase the pressure to make national service mandatory when the draft has to be reinstituted to cope with these shortfalls.

Finally a voluntary system—which amounts to setting up a market in youth employment—is least defensible simply because the marketplace has already established that it is less efficient to employ these youth than to have them idle. If it is objected that the minimum wage threshold distorts the market in this regard, it need only be replied that employment at less than minimum wage is hardly likely to draw enough recruits to "enable Black youth to break the chains of poverty and discrimination that imprison so many millions of minority Americans,"[12] in a way that will "enhance social integration in American Society and improve the quality of civic spirit"[13] while providing "valuable learning experiences,"[14] to take but three of the predictions made for national service by its advocates.

If we assume, then, that national service is to have some element of coercion—whether to achieve universal induction, or to prevent on-the-job defections, or, in time, to reform a failing voluntary system—we must face the constitutional question of what authorization Congress has for such coercion. We begin by observing that there is no explicit authority empowering Congress to coerce large-scale labor, in contrast to the explicit authority for Congress to provide for the punishment of counterfeiters or to suppress insurrections or to establish post offices. This inquiry, however, does not end the matter. Congress is not given explicit authority to regulate labor unions or polluters or drug manufacturers either. We must look further[15] to see if there is implicit authority for compulsory national service, that is, whether the imposition of a national service scheme might be implied in one of the broader grants of Article I (or some other provision, such as Section 5 of the Fourteenth Amendment).

There are, I think, two candidates. First, it might be proposed that national service is merely an adjunct to the military draft, and therefore is a proper exercise of the congressional power to raise and support armies. Apart from the tail-wagging dog aspect of drafting 4½ million persons, only a fraction of whom are to serve in either the military or military support positions, there may nevertheless be a sound constitutional basis here. Certainly the courts are likely to defer to the judgment of Congress as to whether the various shortcomings of the draft I outlined in Part II do in fact necessitate a corrective, even a vast one; if Congress determines this is the case, the corrective measure is one following from an explicit grant of responsibility.

Yet this is precisely the situation that my analysis does not deal with in this section. In Part II, I argued that if national service were a draft palliative, it would be unwise; it would not be necessarily unconstitutional. The situation I address in the present section is not one truly arising from the draft dilemma, but rather a scheme aimed at curing social ills, a scheme that its architects merely wish to justify, constitutionally, as flowing from the power to raise armies. In other words, given the purpose I have posited in this section for national service, the argument that it is a necessary and proper means of raising an army is a sham. It would amount to Congress passing a statute for an impermissible purpose but deceptively packaging it so that it might be allowed to stand in light of some other, permissible purpose. I cannot assure you that the Supreme Court would strike such a statute down. It may be that the controversial case of *United States* v. *O'Brien*[16] presented us with just such a situation. There an anti-draft-card burning provision was upheld as an exercise of the management function implied by the grant of power to raise armies, despite the fact that at least some legislative history suggested that Congress's true motive was to punish political dissent, a plainly impermissible purpose. But whether or not the Court would presume to attribute an unconstitutional motive to a plausibly ambiguous act will not make the statute constitutional. It simply means that Congress has been given the decision; and Congress may decide wrongly. I hope that we shall not be treated to speeches by Congressmen proposing such a sham; and that if we are, the Court will look behind it. But in any event, to the extent that national service is not a true adjunct of the military draft, to that extent it cannot rely on the power of Congress to raise and support armies.*

---

* The same analysis would apply to reliance on the Fourteenth Amendment should it be determined that the inegalitarian features of the draft render it unconstitutionally underinclusive. Such reliance, however, is perhaps more fundamentally flawed: Section 5, from which congressional powers arise, applies only to the guarantee of equal protection by states. The due process clause of the Fifth Amendment, from which we may infer a guarantee of equal protection by the national government, does not similarly authorize enforcement legislation.

There is one other likely constitutional candidate to support a national system of drafted labor; that is the commerce clause. The provision in Article I, Section 8, that Congress shall have the power to regulate commerce among the several states has been held to be the justification for statutes as various as open housing and civil rights laws, agricultural production quotas, criminal narcotics, and antikidnapping acts. By the symbiotic device of holding that Congress may regulate not only noncommerce that affects commerce but also commerce, albeit local, that affects commerce among the states, the Court has gone a long way toward establishing an "omnicompetent" federal government.[17]

I think it can be shown, however, that Congress is not omnipotent, that is, that Congress may not legislate as to any purpose or deal with any subject. If Congress were omnicompetent, it would mean that, apart from structural considerations,[18] the only restraints on government action would lie in the specific prohibitions, such as those of the Bill of Rights, the Fourteenth Amendment, Article IV, and so forth. That something of an omnicompetent view has reigned since the early 1940s may indeed be inferred from the extremely broad, even fantastic, constructions given to clauses like equal protection and due process, as these have had to bear the burden of limiting government, unaided by any doctrines restricting the scope of affirmative power. Yet even very broad constructions of the specific prohibitions against government cannot, by themselves, serve sufficiently the rules of government the Constitution provides us.

We can observe this first in one of the most important of the specific prohibitions, the Ninth Amendment, which states simply that there are unspecified prohibitions. If the specific prohibitions—even amplified and broadly interpreted—were sufficient, there would be no reason to have the Ninth Amendment. Assuming, then, that there are unspecified prohibitions, how do we derive them? The answer to the problem also casts doubt on the idea of an omnicompetent Congress. For it can be shown that the nonspecific rights and prohibitions—an infinite list of them, which is why, I suppose, they are not specified—*can* be derived from the limitation on government imposed by the notion of enumerated powers. That is, we can, in a given circumstance, derive an unspecified right by asking whether the challenged governmental action employs a means not necessary and proper to carry out its affirmative grants.

This view finds support in the language of the Tenth Amendment, which says plainly that there are certain powers that are *not* the subject of the specific prohibitions applied to the states (and this is, today, most of the specific prohibitions that apply to the federal government) and that, in the words of the amendment, are "powers not delegated to the United States by the Constitution"—in other words, reserved to the states or to the people.

Of course we could not give meaning or force to this provision if we could not give content to the phrase "powers not delegated to the United States"; and we could not do this if we believed that the United States was all powerful and was restrained only by affirmative declarations of rights. Indeed this would confound the concept of "right"—the term used in the Ninth Amendment—with that of "power"—the word used in the Tenth Amendment, while at the same time denying us the ability to determine such rights by using the interrelationship between the amendments as a generative formula.

I conclude, therefore, that the idea of an omnicompetent Congress, which is to say the erasure of the notion of affirmative grants of power to Congress, is an erroneous view. I have gone through this argument—and, what is worse, made you go through it—because only if Congress is *not* omnicompetent can we sensibly answer (or for that matter, ask) the question whether or not a statute instituting compulsory national service is a law passed pursuant to Congress's power to regulate commerce among the states. Indeed once we put the question plainly, it would seem to be a simple one. Its answer is "No." I doubt that many persons would think of such a law as the regulation of commerce; and if they did, I submit that everything and anything is a regulation of commerce and then we are back to an omnicompetent Congress—which the Constitution says we do not have.

I am not predicting that such a statute would be struck down by the Court. In related areas[19] the Court has been willing to make Congress the final constitutional arbiter. But I am saying that if Congress passed a national service statute, claiming it to be a regulation of commerce, it would be an unconstitutional decision, whether or not the Supreme Court recognized it as such. After all, it is the phenomenon of our system that we are quite accustomed to the Court making such mistakes, even though, at least until the Court acknowledges them, these mistakes have legal effect.

There is another analysis, undertaken by one of the nation's most distinguished constitutional lawyers, Professor Charles Black, that also leads to the conclusion that compulsory national service is unconstitutional.[20] It is Black's view, "'with the tentativeness which ought to qualify a just-begun constitutional discussion,'" that the Thirteenth Amendment rules out compulsory national service. That amendment prohibits involuntary servitude except as punishment for a crime. Black applies this provision in three classic modes. First, arguing textually, he resolves the phrase "involuntary service" into the term "involuntary servitude." There is little common language distinction made between the two phrases, after all; and in Article IV the word "service" is used to refer to servitude. Second, Black counters the historical argument that since the Thirteenth Amendment was intended to apply to black slavery, it should be correspondingly limited in application. This he does by using doctrinal arguments, drawn from case law, which have held that attempts to punish the nonperformance of labor contracts are a violation of the amendment,[21] though these contracts did not involve slaves or former slaves. In the *Pollock* case, for example, the Supreme Court stated the aim of the amendment to be "not merely to end slavery but to maintain a system of completely free and voluntary labor throughout the United States."[22] Finally, Black marshals ethical arguments, asserting that "large-scale coercion of labor is foreign to our tradition and to our Constitution."[23] To these conclusions Black admits one exception: the draft.* For the draft must be an *exception*—that is, not available for analogical and *a fortiori* arguments—or there are not any meaningful restraints on government conscription of our persons. Only "iron necessity," Black writes, has forced us to allow this exception and we should insulate it.

This is a very different approach from my own. I happen to think that it is the abandonment of ideas such as the limits imposed by enumerated powers that compels us, first, to look to an explicit prohibition and, next, to wrestle with the exceptions that constitutional life is bound to have ready for us when the explicit prohibition does not explicitly cover the application we are urging. But in any event, Black's forceful and eloquent essay stands as a rebuke to any who are free of constitutional doubts about national service.

In addition to the two global attacks on national service, there are other specific constitutional shortcomings of most of the plans I have seen. These shortcomings—three of which I will discuss—are not, however, insurmountable. Modifications in a national service scheme can be devised to overcome these sorts of "contingent" constitutional objections. But I think it will be seen that once such modifications are made, the overall attractiveness of the national service program is considerably diminished. Since these objections are of constitutional dimensions and must be accommodated, it is important that we appreciate them if we are to have a true appreciation of national service itself. When I say "must be accommodated," I mean to indicate a constitutional analysis that is a prediction of what in fact the courts would hold.

The first of such specific objections arises from the discrimination by sex that has been a main feature of our military conscription. Although at least one court has held that a statute limiting the military draft to male citizens violated the equal protection clause,[24] this holding was promptly and summarily reversed,[25] and I have only some little doubt that, given the current

---

* Jury duty and a few days' labor in the community are not really analogous to any sustained national service.

state of constitutional doctrine, all-male draft liability could be reinstated today.* But to understand the basis on which such reinstitution would be upheld is also to understand the problems in this regard with respect to a nonmilitary national service.

In the 1978–79 term, the Supreme Court decisively abandoned the two-tier analysis of equal protection when confronting classifications based on sex. The two-level method of analysis required that the challenged state statute bear some rational relationship to a permissible state objective and that, if a "fundamental interest" was implicated, or an allocation made on the basis of some classification conventionally regarded as "suspect," the state must additionally show a compelling motive for its particular scheme. As you might imagine, it was a rare statute that could not meet the first test; the charges of irrationality so frequently leveled at state legislatures are usually fired by persons with a narrow view of what ought to be the legislative objectives. And, as you might also imagine, it was a rare racial classification—the paradigm for a suspect criterion—that survived such scrutiny. Naturally, feminists rejoiced when, in *Frontiero* v. *Richardson*,[26] a plurality of the Court appeared to have decided that sex, like race, was to be treated as a "suspect" classification. This view has not been accepted by a majority.

Instead, the Court has fashioned a middle tier of review for sex-based discriminations. Such classifications, in the language of the opinion that announced the new test, must "serve important governmental objectives and must be substantially [not mere rationally] related to the achievement of those objectives."[27] Thus, for example, the Court has recently struck down a state law that provided that wives, but not husbands, could be granted alimony payments, even though the Court acknowledged that there were permissible objectives—compensation for women whose housework left them unprepared for the job market, for example—that the statutory classification served.[28] Since the classification scheme was accompanied by a hearing, the state could not argue that the scheme was necessary to promote these objectives; the hearing, after all, could determine whether the spouse really was needy, was ill-equipped for the job market, and so forth. Therefore the state statute did not substantially promote the permissible objective claimed for it.

By this standard sex discrimination in the draft is probably permissible. It is not hard to think of permissible governmental objectives that all-male conscription substantially furthers, and indeed this has been so held by the Ninth Circuit.[29] The combat safety and compatibility of draftees are surely

---

* My colleague Professor Barbara Aldave does doubt that such a system could be upheld today. It is only her surety—and not the case law—that moves me to confess "some little doubt" rather than deny doubt altogether.

permissible government objectives. That an all-male force suitable for combat promotes these objectives is buttressed by the fact that women currently in the armed services, into which induction is not sex-related, do not operate heavy equipment, scale obstacles, operate mine detonators, or prepare for combat. Absent some a priori concern over the classificatory scheme itself, it does not seem implausible that drafting only males substantially promotes the combat effectiveness of the armed forces. This analysis could be changed, I should think, by the adoption of the Equal Rights Amendment or by a return—if we were ever there—to the treatment of sex classification as "suspect." Then the state would have to make the formidable showing of a compelling interest, although that is scarcely unimaginable, given the sensitive context of national security.

By contrast, national service schemes have no such permissible combat objectives to which sex classifications are easily—if erroneously—related. In *Orr v. Orr*, the alimony case summarized above, the Court explicitly ruled out the permissibility of ensuring that males be allocated primary responsibility for the family.[30] I should think this view casts considerable doubt on whether certain arguments would even pass a rational basis test: arguments, for instance, that women should not be conscripted into national service because they must learn homemaking skills or assist their own families; or that only men need be drafted into national service because they bear some special responsibility to learn job skills, or protect the society, and so forth.

This objection to national service, however, though constitutional, is hardly fatal to the scheme. It simply means that the ultimate plan by which national service is brought off must be one that drafts both men and women. But this not unappealing modification brings with it its own difficulties, a main one being that a co-vocational national service of conscripts cannot, I think, long coexist with an all-male system of military conscription. The offenses against egalitarianism are brightly exposed by such a system. I should think the pressure then to universalize the draft, national service and military, would be very great. For some of its advocates, this may make national service itself less attractive. I am not sure that the effects of a universally drawn army will be as salutary as, say, those of coeducating Princeton. It is hardly all to the bad that military service is viewed with distaste by most people and that, as a culture, we have been less mesmerized than bored by military life.

The second constitutional shortcoming of national service, of this treatable variety, derives from the guarantee against a deprivation of one's liberty without due process. Here, as in the Court's treatment of equal protection, we encounter a two-tier analysis. And here as well, the constitutional difficulties become acute only if we are forced to go beyond the first level of analysis—asking for a rational basis for the statute—to another, more demanding standard. Then the absence of military necessity that distinguishes national service from the draft will prove the constitutional undoing of the former because, at this heightened level of scrutiny, government will be deprived of its most forceful "compelling interest," viz., national security.

Therefore, we must ask: Granting a rational basis for national service, does it infringe some "fundamental right" as that phrase has been given constitutional significance by the courts? Does the statute, in other words, deprive persons of those liberties that case law has established are to be diminished only on a showing of compelling governmental need? Several possible features of national service, in relation to corresponding lines of decisional law, are significant here.

In *Moore* v. *City of E. Cleveland* the Supreme Court struck down a zoning ordinance that would have had the likely unintended effect of preventing a grandmother from sharing a house with her son's son and nephew. "Our decisions establish," Justice Powell wrote, "that the Constitution protects the sanctity of the family," which, in *Moore,* meant the right of an extended family to live together.[31] Two years earlier, also relying on the due process clause, the Supreme Court, in a right-to-treatment case, *O'Connor* v. *Donaldson,* had held that "a State cannot constitutionally confine without more, a nondangerous individual who is capable of surviving safely in freedom by himself or with the help of . . . family members or friends."[32] Taken together, I should think that these cases establish that a person has a "fundamental right" to live with his family, which the state may override on some compelling basis, such as that he has been adjudged dangerous or a criminal. If this is correct, national service may not compel a young person to live in training centers or move to a city where the national service work is to be done or punish him if, once having begun to work in some assigned locale, he decides to throw it all over and go absent without leave.

The due process clause has also been the basis for holdings establishing that sexual and marital privacy are protected by constitutionally cognizable "fundamental rights." It was the controversial case of *Roe* v. *Wade* that established that government may not, absent a showing of a compelling interest, infringe the right of privacy, a right that case law has found reflected in the decisions on whom to marry, whether to have children, whether to prevent conception by contraception or to prevent birth by abortion, how to educate and rear one's children.[33] Against this doctrinal background, it would seem that ordering a young person no longer a minor even to undergo certain educational instruction is at least open to question. A national service program that compelled its young men and women to live apart would appear also to infringe on fundamental rights. Certainly such a program could not forbid marriage during the duration of service or penalize pregnancies, two provisions that have been suggested as necessary parts of a national service program.[34]

Of course, these constitutional difficulties are, as I have said, remediable. A national service plan that had its members live at home, for example, would satisfy many of the objections raised by the case law. But this would make manpower at the Conservation Camps somewhat sparse, I should think, to say nothing of what effect it would have on the grand plans to get youth out of the urban ghetto. Similarly, a national service plan that permitted its members to marry and transfer so that they might live together, that made provision for its members to have children and care for them while serving, would remove features of national service plans that otherwise implicate fundamental rights. But the program that emerges with these modifications may well not be the vast Boy Scout Jamboree that some advocates of national service have imagined.

A third line of constitutional doubt, contingent like the other two on less-than-fundamental features of national service, concerns the elusive application of the "takings" clause of the Fifth Amendment. That clause prohibits the federal government from taking private property for public use without paying just compensation. Deciding, therefore, whether conscription of civilian labor constitutes a taking of "property" must be the initial constitutional question. It is by no means a simple question.

I do not think it is appropriate, for example, to rely on judicial constructions of the term "property" in straightforward due process contexts.[35] The welcome development of the modern notion of entitlements that has so remade our concept of property has not been as similarly clarifying with respect to the analysis of the "takings" clause. Indeed the very contexts of the use of the word "property" in the Fifth and Fourteenth Amendments suggest that a single definition is unworkable. The Fifth Amendment (as well as the Fourteenth, which tracks this language) admonishes us that no person shall be deprived of property without due process of law. This suggests, although it does not entail, that one may be deprived of one's property *with* due process of law. At the same time the succeeding clause in the Fifth Amendment enjoins government from taking private property for public use without just compensation. If the term "property" is to mean the same in both clauses, we confront a requirement that whenever one is deprived of property even with due process of law, one must be compensated if the property is put to public use. We know, for example, that a welfare recipient has a property interest in the continued receipt of welfare benefits and that he may not be deprived of it without due process of law.[36] Does this mean that once the hearing is over, and the recipient is thereby rightly "deprived" of his property, he must receive compensation nevertheless? If you are tempted to say that the hearing extinguished the property interest by establishing that the recipient no longer had a valid property interest, and hence need not be compensated for its loss, you may note that whenever the loss occurred—even if the hearing only ratified it—it must have occurred through the operation of law. That means that government —though perhaps not government acting alone—removed the property interest from its possessor. In the case of welfare benefits, the redistribution of the funds is surely a distribution for public use. It may be that the entitlement to a job conferred with tenure, or to social security benefits and the like, are not *private* property, in the sense perhaps that government creates them, but this implies a view of the rest of property—that it somehow exists apart from government recognition—that is scarcely free of its own difficulties. Better then, I conclude, to leave aside the recent case law determining what is "property" for due process purposes.

At the same time I think we should avoid concentration on the construction of the term "taking." We can thereby avoid the difficult question of whether a specific deprivation of property is a *regulation* or a *taking*. Mark Sagoff illustrates the kind of problem I have in mind.

> Suppose you buy a wetland knowing that filling it will make it commercially valuable; suppose the State then passes an environmental regulation which prohibits any dredging or filling of wetlands. Your property, once valuable, becomes worthless. Suppose the government, in order to achieve environmental objectives, requires every owner of two cars to garage one of them permanently. Your second car, which now cannot be driven, becomes merely a burden to you. You could go to court to find out. The State will argue that the wetland and the car have not been taken from you. All the government has done is to prevent you from using these things in ways that might hurt the environment. This is just a matter of regulation under the police power of the State; it is not an exercise of eminent domain. You argue that, on the contrary, your property has been dedicated to a public purpose, much as if your land were made into a park or your car were requisitioned as a bus. You could use a park or a bus, indeed, but you cannot use your property as things stand.[37]

This sort of question is not very much like the one we face in the national service context. If one's labor is one's private property, then drafting a person to conscript his labor full-time for one or two years is, I should think, clearly a "taking." It is not a marginal imposition or the collateral, incidental diminution in value worked by some regulatory scheme. It is precisely because the labor is valuable in itself and is private that it is being conscripted in the first place. Therefore we must forego, here as above, a large body of doctrine developed in the courts that is not really very useful to us. I have in mind those opinions that consider the constitutionality of minimum wage and maximum hour laws, the restriction of child and female labor, and the like.[38] Our case is not like these.

There is, however, some precedent treating the question of whether conscripted labor is a taking of property when it is concededly not merely a regulation. As you may have anticipated, much of this case law occurs in the context of the draft, a fact that will be of significance not only as a limitation of the analysis but as an indicator of what a like opinion on national service, stripped of military objectives, would be.

First I should note, however, that the case of *Butler* v. *Perry* does not decide this question in the national service context.[39] *Butler* involved a challenge to a Florida statute that required every able-bodied male between the ages of 21 and 45 to provide six days' labor on the county roads or provide a substitute or pay three dollars to the county. Superficially, it is an interesting amalgam of the allocation features I discussed earlier for nonmilitary purposes not unlike those envisaged for national service. Moreover, in the following passage Justice McReynolds might be taken to have decided the very issue with which we are presently concerned. For a unanimous Court, he wrote,

> There is no merit in the claim that a man's labor is property, the taking of which without compensation by the state for building and maintenance of public roads violates the due process clause of the 14th Amendment.[40]

The importance of this passage, however, is not that it validates a national service scheme. A reasonably close reading of the opinion will confirm that McReynolds did not decide whether or not the coercion of labor constituted a "taking" of property—a question raised by the Fifth Amendment—but decided instead that a taking of this property, if such it be, would not violate the Fourteenth Amendment, which forbids deprivations of property without due process. Thus in the line following the one I have quoted above, McReynolds writes,

> That Amendment [that is, the Fourteenth] was intended to preserve and protect the fundamental rights long recognized under the common law system. Conceding for some purposes labor must be considered as property it is evident from what has already been said [viz., that the duty to work on public roads was recognized at common law] that to require work on the public roads has never been regarded as a deprivation of either liberty or property."[41]*

---

* Of course, to the extent that Fourteenth Amendment case law determining what is a deprivation of property *is* relevant to the taking question, modern precedents (see, for example, *Mathews* v. *Eldridge*, 424 U.S. 319 [1976]) suggest that the extent of the loss is significant. There is little comparison between three dollars or six days and the sort of commitment national service schemes involve.

Apart from *Butler* v. *Perry,* there is a line of precedent that needs to be examined. Although these cases, like *Butler,* do not explicitly decide the "takings" question, they do provide us with some basis for answering that question because they appear to answer it themselves in route to the constitutional questions that are decided.

The two cases I have in mind are from the First and Ninth Circuits, decided in 1944 and 1949, respectively. They are styled *Weightman* v. *United States*[42] and *Atherton* v. *United States.*[43] Both involved challenges to the Selective Training and Services Act by conscientious objectors who were assigned to Civilian Public Service Camps where they were housed, fed, and paid a nominal wage. In Weightman's case the work was largely forest conservation. In both cases, no Supreme Court opinion was written, certiorari was denied, and we have, therefore, no authoritative statement as to the extent to which Congress is authorized to conscript civilian labor. We have, instead, two very similar opinions that structure the answer in the following way: If Congress has acted pursuant to its war and army powers, then an activity so related to war as to substantially affect its conduct and progress does not deprive civilians of their constitutional rights. These holdings are important for our inquiry* because both opinions appear to concede that a taking of property has occurred that the scope of the war power simply overrides. Thus the First Circuit wrote that "in view of the breadth of the war power" it had "no doubt that the [work camp] does not deprive [the plaintiffs] of any of their constitutional rights even though, in practical effect, it . . . requires them to work at a rate of compensation far below what could be earned in civilian life."[44] Similarly the Ninth Circuit, citing Weightman and having paraphrased the passage I have just quoted, wrote: "Men eligible for miliary service can be conscripted for duty without compensation and it follows that men conscripted for work of national importance can be likewise conscripted"[45] (that is, without compensation) since " 'Work of National Importance' means not all work but work which will assist in the preservation of the nation by winning the war."[46]

These opinions assume—though of course they do not hold—that a person's private property is taken when he is conscripted, and that, so long as this is pursuant to a war measure, compensation need not be paid. For our purposes, therefore, these cases suggest that a national service scheme

---

* They also stand as a roadblock against those who would try to find sufficient limitation to bar compulsory national service in the due process clause alone. Apart from the textual difficulties of such a position, and the problem of giving content to such a doctrine once the specific prohibition has been used up, it is hard to reconcile with holdings such as *Weightman* and *Atherton*. The doctrine of limitation based on a lack of affirmative power, however, does not encounter such problems. See pages 314–316.

that coerces labor and, by definition of coercion, pays it less than the market would to induce such labor, and that is not a mere adjunct to the power to raise armies and successfully wage war, violates the Fifth Amendment.

Of course, others will draw a different lesson from these cases. It will be suggested that Congress can somehow manage a sham of some sort by which to bring national service, though directed at social policy, under the broad power to raise armies, or even, given the twilight state of foreign affairs, the power to wage war. It has already been held by courts that, in exercising the power to raise and support an army, "Congress may legitimately require alternate service to alleviate the unfairness which results if [some] continue to enjoy . . . civilian life while their fellows are conscripted for onerous and sometimes hazardous duty,[47] or to bolster morale in the armed forces, doubtless affected by the perception of such unfairness.[48] Surely someone will suggest that national service can be advertised or at least dressed up as a war measure to evade the problems encountered by a straightforward system. This is the sort of subterfuge that, as Charles Black has said, "we ought to reject simply on hearing the issue stated."[49] If it is unconstitutional for the federal government to conscript labor without just compensation, it is no less so when the question is never straightforwardly presented.

Moreover, the objections as to just compensation are, as I have noted, merely contingent in the sense that they can easily be overcome by simply paying the inductees more. This would resolve the constitutional doubt, but, as with the first two such "contingent" objections, may make the program far less attractive to its sponsors, and to the rest of us.

There may be other constitutional difficulties that a national service plan, depending on how it is designed, will precipitate. For example, consider this advice of Willard Wirtz, former Secretary of Labor:

> There is a point at which the community's good sense has to be asserted— as it is now in the case of education up to age sixteen—with respect to someone who has clearly established his lack of any sense, or any sense of responsibility, at all. And that point is not necessarily, or even wisely, after he has committed a serious offense. The compulsory education concept could very sensibly be extended to cover types of training and discipline better suited to the "hard cases"—not as part of the penal system but as part of the educational system, and yet operated on the community's terms, not the boy's."[50]

It may be that a system of punishment that anticipates a boy's transgressions—if this is what Secretary Wirtz has in mind—violates elementary due process. I should think this would be true of a national service system that, for example, singled out for "education" those juveniles who showed promise of being delinquent but who hadn't yet committed a crime. Such arguments need not await the design of a national service that might accommodate the substantial, though contingent, constitutional objections I have mentioned, but I will not explore them further here.

Why should you be careful of constitutional arguments anyway? Not for any pragmatic reason, it would seem, since it is likely that courts would defer to Congress on the crucial determinations that will ultimately decide the lawsuits brought to overturn rather than merely modify such a system.

This is why: The Constitution makes certain, fundamental commitments as to the forms of constitutional arguments that are available (for example, Professor Black's textual argument about the Thirteenth Amendment), as to entitlements (the presumptions of perspective, for example, implied by the takings clause), and as to certain cultural arrangements. In regard to this last, we are not first a *state,* a nation. The Ninth and Tenth Amendments affirm as much. The Constitution is not, therefore, simply a process document. So the comparisons to China and Cuba so often drawn by advocates of a universal, compulsory national service are not apt. It is typical of those who ignore constitutional argument and who don't appreciate the cultural kinesthesis of it, that they talk as if we could "take the best part" of the Chinese or Cuban experience with national service plans. My own hunch is that if we could somehow graft such a scheme onto the constitutional body politic—perhaps through the subterfuges to which I have alluded—it would be the body that would be changed by the experience, not just the graft.

This should be borne in mind by those who would conclude that my dichotomized analysis of national service ignores a plain solution. I imagine it has occurred to someone that national service need not be either universal or unconstitutional, depending on which purpose it is to serve, but could be safely constitutional—that is, survive court challenge and reasonable precedent, by serving both purposes.[51] Even if it is unwise to expect such a program to overtreat the perception of inequality brought about by the draft, we cannot be certain of this; perhaps it might, to some extent, ease this difficulty. And there is no reason why national service might not be designed to accomplish more social good collateral to the draft problem, as an additional benefit. I have conceded that a draft-aimed national service plan would likely be constitutional; taken with a youth employment component, that is, taken as a whole, I have not shown that it would be unwise.

Yet I do think it would be unwise precisely because constitutional and programmatic goals are not brought into line with one another. The Constitution is an ongoing expression of the people we wish to be. I am deeply reluctant to depart from its vision of us. Moreover, to the extent that such a combination can be severed into separate goals, it might well be held to be unconstitutional because some far less intrusive means could be employed to ease as much the draft problem. This would mean the composite plan was both unwise *and* unconstitutional.

Conclusion

An optimist is one who retains the image of attractiveness cast by unmodified hope when most of its original hopeful features are gone. We are a nation of optimists; indeed, the sociobiologists tell us that human beings are a species of optimists. I fear that even those who share my programmatic and constitutional reservations about national service may not have a clear picture of what a national service plan would look like when all the disquieting objections are accommodated.

Such a plan would not make the draft more equitable or even seem to do so. It would not provide a structure within which all races, classes, and backgrounds would mingle. It would not be able to draw persons at both ends of the social scale, even though planners may most want to enlist them. It would draw some persons away from the volunteer army, even if we wished to exclude them. It will not be cheap; indeed, it will cost us more than we have already determined the labor of unskilled youth is worth. Finally, like the educational system, to which it can be properly analogized, it will require highly skilled personnel, some general agreement about its aims, and some social willingness to endure its discipline and boredom.

This does not mean that a truly voluntary program of public service would not be useful. On the contrary, if national service were arranged so as to perform as decentralized agencies to various distributive bureaucracies, much good might be accomplished. The two principal shortcomings of distributive bureaucracies—of which we shall see more as government becomes more and more a producer rather than merely a regulator—are a lack of individuation and the inability to avoid making general statements of value with which some portion of the community is likely to disagree. These two shortcomings are neatly paired with two features of volunteers— their representativeness and their responsibility. As such, volunteers are well suited as adjuncts to distributive bureaucracies and may well improve a situation currently characterized by an absence of creativity and realism.

Of course, this view suggests that current trends in the volunteer field to make volunteers more responsible (for example, by imposing tort liability) and more expert (by rigorous selection and extensive training) are moves in precisely the wrong direction. But these directions may change, and, if the alluring mantle of national service were draped, incongruously, on such modest schemes, perhaps even the advocates of national service might be the ones to bring about such a change. As it is, it is disheartening that the director of ACTION—whose apparatus in VISTA is well suited to the sort of bureaucratic adjunct activity I have in mind—should be a vigorous proponent of a universal, compulsory national service. I am inclined to think that neither he, nor John Connally, nor the President, nor any other of our leaders from all political points on the horizon who profess to detest bureaucracies, would be much satisfied with the little plan I have sketched.

I should like to conclude by actually concluding something, rather than just summing up. My paper has had two main parts: a discussion of the socioethical processes of various allocative devices that national service might employ in a role as supplement to the military draft; and a canvass of constitutional objections that a national service plan might encounter if its purposes were not largely military. From each of these parts I should like to draw a lesson. A great many absurd and fatuous claims are made for national service; I shall rely on your skepticism to puncture them. My conclusions, my cautionary lessons, are merely two, corresponding roughly to the analyses and descriptions of Parts II and III.

1. Don't create a revolutionary army of young persons who are embittered by having been forced to waste their youth in useless pursuits and whose frustration is compounded by the guilty knowledge that others, those who are not made to sit out their lives, are forced to risk and sometimes lose them.

2. Don't allow a benignly packaged national service plan to be a Trojan horse for a coercive plan. The dynamics discussed in Part II would, in such a circumstance, be peculiarly situated to exploit the subterfuges and constitutional deceptions alluded to in Part III. By such irresistible and yet moderate evolution, we as a people would be much changed and, I think, much for the worse.

Notes

1. See, for example, U.S., Congress, Senate, S. Rept. no. 22, 65th Cong., 1st sess., April 21, 1917, *Congressional Record* 55: 911, 912.

2. William James, "The Moral Equivalent of War," *International Conciliation*, no. 27 (February 1910).

3. See Donald J. Eberly, ed., *National Service: A Report of a Conference* (New York: Russell Sage Foundation, 1968).

4. Committee for the Study of National Service, *Youth and the Needs of the Nation: A Report ...* (Washington, D.C.: Potomac Institute, 1979), p. 10; see also Eberly, *National Service.*

5. "It seems to me that we could move toward remedying [the draft] inequity by asking every young person in the United States to give two years of service to the country—whether in one of the military services, in the Peace Corps, or in some other volunteer developmental work at home or abroad. . . . It would make meaningful the central concept of security: a world of decency and development—where every man can feel that his personal horizon is rimmed with hope" (*New York Times,* May 19, 1966, p. 11, excerpt from speech to the American Society of Newspaper Editors, Montreal, Canada, May 18, 1966). See also National Advisory Commission on Selective Service, *In Pursuit of Equity: Who Serves When Not All Serve? Report ...* (Washington, D.C., 1967).

6. A fuller treatment can be found in Guido Calabresi and Philip Bobbitt, *Tragic Choices* (New York: W. W. Norton & Co., 1978).

7. Ibid., pp. 158–167. This account is taken from *Tragic Choices* and sources cited therein at notes 12–47, Chapter 6.

8. Committee for the Study of National Service, *Youth and the Needs of the Nation,* p. 11.

9. CBS Radio interview, March 5, 1977; a similar statement was made in December 1978, in Memphis; see Committee for the Study of National Service, *Youth and the Needs of the Nation,* p. 17.

10. See, for instance, Terrence Cullinan, "National Service and the American Educational System," in *The Draft: A Handbook of Facts and Alternatives,* ed. Sol Tax (Chicago: University of Chicago Press, 1967), pp. 91–98.

11. See U.S., Congressional Budget Office, *National Service Programs and Their Effects on Military Manpower and Civilian Youth Problems* (Washington, D.C., 1978).

12. Vernon Jordan, "Black Youth: The Endangered Generation," *Ebony,* August 1928, p. 86+.

13. Harris Wofford, "Toward a Draft without Guns," *Saturday Review,* October 15, 1966, p. 19+.

14. See Carnegie Commission on Higher Education, *Toward a Learning Society: Alternative Channels to Life, Work, and Service* (New York: McGraw-Hill, 1973).

15. A particularly egregious example of constitutional analysis of this question may be found in Cullinan, "National Service," p. 97. The author, *inter alia,* derives constitutional authority for congressional action from the Preamble; confuses state and federal allocations of authority; and erroneously declares a "trend in Supreme Court decisions" that "makes it clear that public education is related to the 'general welfare of the United States' as a whole," apparently without appreciating that the phrase quoted has application in

the taxing and spending grant of Article I.

16. 391 U.S. 367 (1968).

17. The characterization "omnipotent" is from Charles L. Black, "Foreword: the Myth and Reality of Federalism," *University of Toledo Law Review* 9 (1978) :615.

18. Cf. *National League of Cities* v. *Usery*, 426 U.S. 833 (1976).

19. See, for example, *Prudential Insurance Co.* v. *Benjamin*, 328 U.S. 408 (1946).

20. Charles L. Black, "Constitutional Problems in Compulsory 'National Service,' " *Yale Law Report* 13 (1967) :19.

21. See *Pollock* v. *Williams*, 312 U.S. 4 (1949).

22. Ibid., at 17.

23. Black, "Constitutional Problems," p. 21.

24. *United States* v. *Reiser*, 194 F. Supp. 1090 (1975).

25. *United States* v. *Reiser*, 532 F. 2d 673 (1976), cert. den., 429 U.S. 838 (1976).

26. *Frontiero* v. *Richardson*, 411 U.S. 677 (1973).

27. *Craig* v. *Boren*, 429 U.S. (1976).

28. *Orr* v. *Orr*, 440 U.S. 268 (1979) ; see also *Califano* v. *Westcott*, 99 S. Ct. 2655 (1979).

29. *Campbell* v. *Beaugher*, 519 F. 2d 1307, 1309 (9 Cir. 1975). But see also footnote, p. 317, above.

30. *Orr* v. *Orr*, note 28 above, at 279–280.

31. 431 U.S. 494 (1977).

32. 422 U.S. 563 (1975).

33. 410 U.S. 113 (1973) ; referring to the right of privacy, the court wrote : "[Our decisions] also make it clear that the right has some extension to activities relating to marriage, *Loving* v. *Virginia*, 388 U.S. 1, 12 (1967) ; procreation, *Skinner* v. *Oklahoma*, 316 U.S. 535, 541–542 (1942); contraception, *Eisenstadt* v. *Baird*, 405 U.S., at 453–454; *id.*, at 460, 463–465 (White, J., concurring in result) ; family relationships, *Prince* v. *Massachusetts*, 321 U.S. 158, 166 (1944); and child rearing and education, *Pierce* v. *Society of Sisters*, 268 U.S. 510 535 (1925), *Meyer* v. *Nebraska*, supra [262 U.S. 90, 399 (1923)]."

34. See, for instance, Margaret Mead, "A National Service System as a Solution to a Variety of National Problems," in *The Draft*, pp. 99–109. Mead points out that "pregnancy could be treated as a severe breach of contract, comparable to going AWOL in males. Part of the institution of universal national service would be the postponement of marriage until the service was completed, if universal national service takes the form of a nationwide call-up at 18, or the possibility of the entry into national service as a working couple if proposals for extending the service period into the late 20's were to be

adopted. Universal national service would replace for girls, even more than for boys, marriage as the route away from the parental home, and provide a period of responsible and directed reappraisal before marriage and parenthood were assumed" (ibid., p. 108).

35. Cf. Roland Adickes, "The Constitutional Invalidity of the Draft," *Southern California Law Review* 46 (1973) : 385.

36. *Goldberg* v. *Kelly*, 397 U.S. 254 (1970).

37. Mark Sagoff, "Review," *Environmental Ethics* 1 (1979) : 89.

38. See, for example, *West Coast Hotel Co.* v. *Parrish*, 300 U.S. 379 (1937).

39. 240 U.S. 328 (1915).

40. Ibid., at 333.

41. Ibid.

42. 142 F.2d 188 (1 Cir. 1941).

43. 176 F.2d 835 (9 Cir. 1919).

44. *Weightman*, note 42 above, at 191.

45. *Atherton*, note 43 above, at 841, 843.

46. The following statement was made by the court: " 'The war power of the national government,' the Supreme Court recently said, quoting Charles Evans Hughes, War Power Under the Constitution, 42 A.B.A. Rep. 232, 238 'is "the power to wage war successfully." It extends to every matter and activity so related to war as substantially to affect its conduct and progress' " (*Kyoshi Harabayashi* v. *United States*, 320 U.S. 81, 93, 63, S. Ct. 1375, 87 L. Ed. 1774, cited in *Weightman*, note 42 above, at 191).

47. *United States* v. *Boardman*, 419 F. 2d 110, 112 (1 Cir. 1969), citing by contrast *Braunfield* v. *Brown*, 366 U.S. 599, 608 (1961).

48. See *Howze* v. *United States*, 272 F. 2d 146, 148 (9 Cir. 1959) ; see also *Brooks* v. *United States*, 147 F. 2d 134, 135 (2 Cir. 1945).

49. Black, "Constitutional Problems," p. 21.

50. Quoted in ibid., p. 20; see also Willard Wirtz, *The Boundless Resource: A Prospectus for an Education-Work Policy* (Washington, D.C.: New Republic Books, 1975).

51. "The 32 million Americans who are poor were not born without intellectual potential. They were not brain-poor at birth; but only privilege-poor, advantage-poor, opportunity-poor. To the extent that this nation loses the performance potential of these millions of human beings, to that extent this nation's ultimate security is diminished" (excerpt from speech by Secretary of Defense Robert McNamara to the Veterans of Foreign Wars Convention, *New York Times*, August 24, 1966, p. 18).

XXIV

CIVIL LIBERTIES, NATIONAL SECURITY, AND THE DRAFT

David Landau

> Safety from external danger is the most powerful
> director of national conduct. Even the ardent
> love of liberty will, after a time, give way to its
> dictates. The violent destruction of life and prop-
> erty incident to war, the continual effort and
> alarm attendant on a state of continual danger,
> will compel nations the most attached to liberty
> to resort for repose and security to institutions
> which have a tendency to destroy their civil and
> political rights. To be more safe, they at length
> become willing to run the risk of being less free.
>
> Alexander Hamilton
> *The Federalist No. 8*

On September 12, 1979, the House of Representatives overwhelmingly
rejected the resumption of draft registration.* Despite a well-organized
campaign by congressional supporters of the draft, most members of Congress had little choice in the matter. In the few months since the draft
had resurfaced as an issue, a nationwide antidraft movement had sprung
up.[1] The vote was thus a reaffirmation of what was up until the post-World

---

* The vote was 252 to 153.

War II period an historical fact: Americans find wartime institutions, including the military draft, unacceptable in peacetime.

For this nation, war has usually been a last resort when our security is significantly threatened. It demands special sacrifices from the citizenry. Those who are drafted into the military must have their individual rights curtailed to maintain discipline and order, and, of course, they must face the ever-present peril of serious injury (physical and mental), permanent disability, and loss of life. For civilians, national security institutions, such as the intelligence network and the military establishment, take precedence over all else. Inevitably the individual rights of the general population are impaired. Those are the inherent evils of war. Americans have demonstrated a willingness to accept this way of life when there is a declared war or when there is a consensus that the nation is faced with an imminent threat. Americans have also recognized, however, that because national security institutions and the military establishment are intrinsically anti-democratic, they ought to be tightly controlled in peacetime.

Alexander Hamilton followed this general theme in *The Federalist No. 8*. Later, on the floor of the House of Representatives in 1814, Representative Daniel Webster condemned the military draft in somewhat stronger terms: "The question is nothing less than whether the most essential rights of personal liberty shall be surrendered and despotism embraced in its worst form." "The people," he proclaimed, "have not purchased at a vast expense of their own treasure and their own blood a Magna Carta to be slaves." The draft is "incompatible with any notion of personal liberty."

Not until after World War II was the draft authorized in peacetime. Early in the postwar period, there was still a consensus that the nation was faced with an imminent threat to its security. But as the years progressed, the wartime national security state became a habit of mind for this country. At the same time, the theoretical foundation of this way of life, that is, the consensus of a direct threat to the nation, eroded.

The Vietnam War was the breaking point. Because the military establishment was in place and operating, the government did not have to obtain the consent of the American people to fight a war. The American people began to rebel when they discovered a war was being fought when their security was not directly threatened. The system responded as if in a declared war and attempted to silence opposition and maintain order and discipline. Intelligence operations expanded; law enforcement agencies disrupted political activity. In the end, the distinctions between war and peace, which in large measure are marked by the size of the national security establishment, became blurred.

By 1972, the national security establishment was being dismantled; the draft ended. This year, however, Congress debated whether to take the first step toward reinstituting the military system—draft registration. Others have called for stepped-up intelligence operations, both at home and abroad. Although proponents of the draft have attempted to prove that the United States is threatened, they have been unable to convince the American people that the threat is sufficient to justify the inevitable curtailment of individual rights and liberties that results from the draft.

The American people, in the end, apply a test similar to the one the courts employ in judging governmental abridgment of civil rights: there must be compelling proof that such measures are necessary. In the case of national security, the burden is particularly heavy, because, as this paper will discuss, the erosion of democratic principles is so great.

Individual Rights and the Military

Second Lieutenant Henry Howe, Jr., was stationed at Fort Bliss, Texas, in 1968. He had read in the newspaper that a group of professors and students at the local university were going to hold a demonstration against American policy in Vietnam in the main plaza of El Paso. He made a sign reading, "Let's Have More than a Choice between Petty Ignorant Facist [sic] in 1968." On the other side he wrote, "End Johnson's Facist [sic] Aggression in Vietnam." On the day of the demonstration, while off duty and dressed in civilian clothes, he drove to the plaza and joined a line of about 12 demonstrators who were carrying similar signs protesting the war. In the crowd of spectators surrounding the demonstrators were several military policemen who recognized Lieutenant Howe. He was tried and convicted by a general court-martial of making contemptuous remarks against the President and of conduct unbecoming an officer and a gentleman. Lieutenant Howe was sentenced to dismissal from the Army, forfeiture of all pay allowances, and confinement at hard labor for two years.[2]

Captain Howard Levy, an Army physician stationed at Fort Jackson, South Carolina, was a deeply committed individual. During off-duty hours he became very active in the local civil rights movement. His civil rights activities led him to speak out against the war in Vietnam, particularly because of its adverse impact on minorities. Captain Levy was dismissed from the service and sentenced to three years at hard labor. His crime was making public statements against the war to enlisted personnel. The Army found these statements to be "conduct unbecoming an officer and a gentleman"—that is, intemperate, defamatory, provoking, disloyal, contemptuous, and disrespectful. The Supreme Court upheld Levy's conviction for uttering such statements.[3] .

Roger Priest was stationed at the Pentagon as a seaman apprentice in the Navy. In spring 1969, on his own time and with his own funds, he published a newsletter that he distributed to active-duty military personnel in the Pentagon. The newsletter contained strong protests against the Vietnam War, such as "And to Those Who Hold Illegitimate Power over Our Lives We Say to You That We Will Not Accept the Continuation of This War. We Will Continue to Resist, and Encourage Others to Do the Same. SILENCE IS COMPLICITY." Roger Priest was convicted of "disorders and neglects" to the "prejudice of good order and discipline in the Armed Forces." The U.S. Court of Appeals for the District of Columbia Circuit affirmed the conviction.[4]

There are many similar cases. For example, Bill Harvey and George Daniels were given dishonorable discharges and ten and six years' hard labor, respectively, for stating that the Vietnam War was a white man's war; Dan Amik and Ken Stote, dishonorable discharges and four years for passing out leaflets. Young C. Gray, a dishonorable discharge and two years for leaving antiwar messages on his ship. Mark Avrech, one month for *attempting* to utter a disloyal statement.[5]

All these men were punished for expressing their personal political beliefs. They were not saboteurs or espionage agents engaged in covert activities. Many others in the country shared their views. Had they been civilians, they clearly could not have been punished for such verbal activity. The Supreme Court has repeatedly held that speech, including disrespectful and contemptuous speech, even advocacy of violent change, cannot be prohibited unless it is both directed to inciting imminently lawless action and likely to produce such action.[6]

Since the *Levy* case, this standard has no longer applied to the military. Although the Supreme Court and the Court of Military Appeals have given verbal support to the free speech rights of military personnel, cases such as *Levy* leave it entirely within the discretion of the military to permit or punish political speech. Moreover, a variety of speech-related activities, including political association, can be prohibited by the military. The Navy recently banned personnel from associating with the Ku Klux Klan during off-duty hours. Symbolic speech such as buttons or patches is made impossible by the dress regulations of the military. Political campaigning may be banned.[7] Military personnel can even be sanctioned for the speech activity of their civilian friends.

David Cortright was a member of the Fort Hamilton Army Band. During a Fourth of July parade on Staten Island, his fiancée and the wives of four other band members attempted to march with the band while the women carried antiwar placards. Because of this incident, Cortright was summarily transferred to Texas.[8]

In addition to free speech and association there are various other constitutionally protected activities that are substantially abridged by the military. The citizen who enters the military cannot select his or her employment free from government interference.[9] Although the military does make an attempt to provide job skills to enlistees, there is no contractual obligation. For example, a radio operator enlists because the Army has promised to teach him computer skills. The enlistee receives the training and is a computer operator for six months. Suddenly, the Army transfers him to a radio listening post at the outer rim of Turkey. There is little recourse.

Cases such as this are further aggravated when the person is fraudulently inducted into the military and receives no training. Army recruitment advertisements are big on promises. In far too many cases, the Army finds an excuse to renege.[10] Besides the lack of a right to contract, military personnel are forbidden by statute from collective bargaining.[11] Working conditions can be negotiated only on an individual basis. Grievances, however, are handled through procedures established by management, and the fear of reprisals is always imminent. In contrast, the right of civilians to band together to improve conditions and bargain on an equal footing with employers is unassailable.[12]

Beyond the employment aspect of the military, controls extend to every phase of private life from appearance and dress to personal relationships. In fact, the military still regulates marriages. The "right to marry" has long been recognized as one of the most fundamental rights of individuals. It is protected by the Constitution.[13] Yet, courts have upheld the power of commanding officers to disapprove marriages of military personnel stationed overseas.[14] Moreover, the overseas serviceman or servicewoman who wishes to marry must confront a variety of bureaucratic barriers. Forms galore must be filled out, including statements of assets and liabilities. Applicants must undergo counseling by clergy and attorneys on the moral and legal obligations of marriage. A commanding officer may even request character references of the prospective spouse.[15] The service person cannot marry if the application is disapproved. This is hardly the same right to enter marriage enjoyed by other American citizens living abroad. But the interference in privacy is not limited to marriage. There are also military regulations governing dating. And women, especially those stationed overseas, who choose to have an abortion are in many cases denied the free exercise of this right because the military is prohibited from funding abortions for service personnel.[16]

The military's domination of all aspects of personal life is typified by the Army's drug abuse program. This program authorizes warrantless drug inspections without probable cause. Everything from personal possessions to the body itself may be searched without suspicion of drug abuse. A U.S.

Court of Appeals upheld this search policy as "reasonable."[17] Search and seizure in the military are now virtually uncontrolled. As long as a particular search is under the guise of the drug rehabilitation program, it cannot be challenged.

Even more serious is the "rehabilitation program" for drug abusers. As part of the program, the military may withdraw the drug abuser's privilege of wearing civilian clothing and require the removal of civilian clothing from the barracks area; suspend his or her driver's license; require the abuser, whether married or single, to move into the barracks; segregate abusers in one part of the barracks; and require the soldier to keep his or her room unbolted when the room is occupied. There is no hearing before any of these measures are imposed. Whether or not these measures are part of a "rehabilitative program," they are clearly not medical remedies. Rather, they are sanctions imposed on drug addicts. The Supreme Court has held that a citizen cannot be criminally punished for mere drug addiction, as it is in essence an illness.[18] Yet, the military not only punishes drug illness, it does so without any due process.

The Army's drug abuse program is symptomatic of the entire military judicial system. Because of the vast restrictions upon every aspect of a service member's life, the military out of necessity has established an intricate system of enforcement that, other than the court-martial proceeding, mostly operates outside the framework of the Constitution. In civilian life, state and local courts punish by fine and/or imprisonment relatively limited types of behavior deemed by society to threaten other individual life or property. The military, on the other hand, has an entire hierarchy of procedures replete with varying punishments for violations of the Uniform Code of Military Justice (U.C.M.J.).

The best-known of these military proceedings is the court-martial. The court-martial can impose the severest penalties available in the military: a dishonorable discharge, confinement at hard labor, and even the death penalty in certain cases. Although service members facing court-martial enjoy many procedural rights guaranteed by the Constitution, such as the right to counsel and the right against self-incrimination, the most basic right guaranteed to criminal defendants in civilian courts is denied them— the right to a trial by a jury composed of one's peers. The general court-martial is an ad hoc court composed of at least five officers. One third of the court-martial members may be replaced by enlisted men, but this is hardly comparable to a civilian jury representing a cross section of the community.

The court-martial is the fairest of the proceedings that may be commenced against violators of the U.C.M.J. A special court-martial may only impose a maximum of six months' imprisonment, forfeiture of two-thirds pay per month for six months, reduction to the lowest enlisted grade, and a bad-conduct discharge in some cases. But this court usually consists of only three officers. The service member may opt for enlisted members to compose one-third of the court, and he or she is entitled in most cases to military counsel free of charge.

There is also a summary court-martial, consisting of only one officer. Although the possible penalties are somewhat lower, there are also less due process protections. There is no absolute entitlement to free counsel. The summary court-martial officer is prosecutor, jury, judge, defense counsel, and court reporter. A service member may elect a special court-martial instead, but this runs the risk of a more severe sentence. Summary court-martials are imposed for the most minute violations of the U.C.M.J. For example, a service member may be brought before a summary court-martial for trivial offenses such as missing a dental appointment arranged by a superior officer or carrying an umbrella.

The most common punishment meted out in the military, however, is the nonjudicial punishment, or Article 15 (Captain's Mast in the Navy). Officers in the service member's chain of command may impose an Article 15 for any violation of the U.C.M.J. and offer virtually no procedural protections. Service members are thus faced with a Hobson's choice: accept the Article 15 punishment because of its significantly lower penalty or opt for the court-martial with more due process protections, but with harsher penalties.

Although the actual sanctions imposed by nonjudicial punishment and summary court-martials are the least severe, the effect of these proceedings has subtle implications. Too many Article 15s or summary court-martials may result in a less than honorable discharge.

Dishonorable and bad-conduct discharges can be imposed only by sentence of a special or a general court-martial, both of which have at least some due process. The two other kinds of less than honorable discharges, general and undesirable, are imposed administratively without benefit of a full-blown adversary hearing. Yet, they too inflict a lifelong disability upon the veteran.

All holders of less than honorable discharges are routinely discriminated against by employers. One well-known study by Army Major Bradley Jones revealed that 69 percent of employers discriminate against holders of undesirable discharges, and 51 percent against holders of general discharges.[19] The courts routinely recognize the severe stigma attached to a less than fully honorable discharge. For example, the United States Court of Appeals for the District of Columbia Circuit has stated that "anything less than an honorable discharge is viewed as derogatory and inevitably stigmatizes the recipient."[20] In addition, holders of other than honorable discharges, such as undesirable, bad-conduct, and dishonorable discharges, are precluded in almost every case from receiving federal veterans' benefits.

Other than specific disciplinary violations, general discharges and undesirable discharges have been given for a variety of behaviors. For example, the Army used to characterize the service of individuals discharged for character and behavioral disorders as general. General discharges could be issued for, among other things, "unsanitary habits, financial irresponsibility, apathy, defective attitudes and inability to expend effort constructively." Until recently, undesirable discharges were given to homosexuals, as well as to drug users and alcoholics. They could also be issued for, among other things, "an established pattern of shirking" or "an established pattern of showing dishonorable failure to pay debts."

The military, then, has not only a well-developed system of punishing criminal behavior, but also an intricate system of punishing any aberrant behavior it deems injurious to military discipline. Most of the behavior resulting in other than honorable discharges could not be punished in civilian life. Yet, when the service member returns to civilian life with such a discharge, he or she suffers severe disabilities.

This discussion is not intended to challenge the appropriateness or necessity of current military regulations. Rather, it demonstrates the fundamentally antidemocratic nature of the military. The controls may be necessary and acceptable for the military. But we have never tolerated this type of control on the civilian population. Indeed, only during World War II was the total abrogation of the constitutional rights of American citizens ever sanctioned by the Supreme Court. In that case a divided Court upheld the forced internment of American citizens of Japanese ancestry.[21] But even during the war these cases were few; the Court continued to invalidate other government action that abridged the rights of American citizens. In *Duncan v. Kahanamako*, for example, the Court struck down martial laws in Hawaii that required civilians to be tried by military tribunals.[22] In the famous steel-mill seizure case, *Youngstown Sheet and Tube Co. v. Sawyer*, the Court overruled President Truman's seizure of steel mills during a labor dispute that he deemed would cripple the Korean War effort.[23]

In peacetime, the Supreme Court has taken an extremely narrow view of the circumstances in which constitutional rights may be summarily restricted by the Executive Branch, and has steadfastly refused to expand this view. When, for domestic security, Richard Nixon engaged in a program of electronic surveillance of American dissidents, the Supreme Court invalidated it;[24] other federal courts have frequently invalidated other aspects of the Nixon national security program.[25] The principle that emerges from these cases is that, except when the nation is faced with an imminent threat to its very survival, such as World War II, individual rights are to be given the widest possible leeway. The nation's defense will always be given great consideration, but, as the Supreme Court has said, "It would indeed be ironic if, in the name of national defense, we sanction the subversion of [one of] those liberties ... which makes the defense of the nation worthwhile."[26]

Just as the courts have been vigilant in refusing to sanction infringements of civil liberties based on claims of national security, the American people historically have also resisted the infringement of their rights by the government. The imposition of the military draft in peacetime would subvert the individual liberties of the draftee in the name of national defense. As the recent debate on the draft demonstrates, the claim of national defense is not a sufficient justification for the imposition of the military system on the citizen without consent.

The Military Draft and National Security

The impact of a draft on the citizen who is conscripted is alone sufficient to bar its imposition absent a compelling justification. But since it is an integral part of a national security state, the draft also has a broad adverse impact on society. Unless the nation is imminently threatened, an institution that undermines fundamental democratic principles will create hostility in the general population. It breeds contempt of the government for abridging the rights of its citizens and engenders militant opposition that is not afraid to take direct action against the system. The government, in turn, cannot permit this disruption. It therefore not only must enforce the system against those who resist it but also must take costly steps to prevent disruption and, even, in some cases, to silence its critics.

In 1967, Dr. Benjamin Spock, Reverend William Sloane Coffin, and two other protesters issued "A Call to Resist Illegitimate Authority." Eventually signed by hundreds of others, the document called on inductees to stay home and registrants to go on strike against the draft. Both Spock and Coffin were tried and convicted of conspiring to counsel, aid and abet Selective Service registrants to disobey the Military Selective Service Act.[27] Before this, on the morning of March 31, 1966, David Paul O'Brien had burned his Selective Service registration certificate on the steps of the Boston Courthouse. O'Brien was indicted, tried, and convicted.[28] Later during the Vietnam War, opponents to the draft took more violent action.

Daniel and Philip Berrigan led a raid on a suburban Baltimore County draft board office and destroyed 378 draft files. Hundreds of similar raids by others resulted in damage or destruction to thousands of draft files.[29] The Chicago Fifteen succeeded in destroying the records of 12 local boards.

The government reaction was predictably severe. Ten of the Chicago Fifteen were sentenced to ten-year prison terms.[30]

The Selective Service System itself was also used to silence criticism. Punitive reclassification for dissenters was encouraged by General Hershey. In December 1965, 35 University of Michigan students staged a sit-in at an Ann Arbor draft board. Within a month, several had lost their student deferments.[31]

As antidraft activity intensified, it became one of the excuses for widespread political surveillance and disruption programs. The CIA investigated to determine if these groups were being run by foreign governments. The FBI had to investigate criminal violations of the draft laws. The Army looked into the potential of the groups for disrupting the war effort. Some of the surveillance was legal; much of it was not. The prosecution of Benjamin Spock was necessary because his political opposition to the draft and the war threatened the entire system. Because the draft in the absence of an imminent threat to the nation fomented widespread hostility, particularly when draftees were used to wage an unpopular war, law enforcement and intelligence agencies were drawn into the political arena. Powers that were intended to weed out saboteurs, espionage agents, and criminals were directed at antidraft and antiwar activities. If these powers are unchecked, as they have been for the last 30 years, law enforcement and intelligence systems tend to operate outside the Constitution, stifling dissent.

The illegalities and abuses of the past from the FBI's COINTELPRO (Counterintelligence Program) operation to the prosecution of Benjamin Spock were not isolated incidents. An entire bureaucracy was established, involving hundreds of officials and aimed at thousands of people.[32] It is one thing for this type of national security state to exist during a national crisis, such as World War II. It is an entirely different thing when it operates during peacetime or is used to wage an unpopular war. One of the lessons of the Vietnam War is that the American people will not tolerate the latter.

The imposition of the draft at this time would begin in the resurrection of wartime national security measures in the absence of a compelling justification that has been recognized in society. As during the Vietnam War, hostility toward this system would grow rapidly and old enforcement mechanisms would be thrown into gear. Even though we would not be fighting a war, individual liberties would begin to erode in the name of national security just as they would during a war.

The Founding Fathers constructed a system of government in which the federal government would be under the control of the people. The Bill of Rights is a series of restrictions on the government's ability to abridge the rights of the citizenry. As Daniel Webster long ago recognized, the military has profound ramifications for the society, as it is "contrary to any notion of personal liberty" on which this nation was founded. To impose it as less than a last resort to preserve the existence of our nation would subvert the very principles on which our nation was founded. Indeed, the security of the nation, which in the end lies in our adherence to those principles, would be undermined. A peacetime military draft should therefore be rejected.

Notes

1. *Washington Star*, September 12, 1979, p. A10.

2. *Howe* v. *United States*, 17 U.S.C.M.A. 509,16 C.MR. 13 (1959).

3. *United States* v. *Levy*, 417 U.S. 733 (1974).

4. *Priest* v. *Secretary of the Navy*, 570 F. 2d 1013 (D.C. Cir. 1977).

5. David Addlestone, "Amnesty: Where It Stands," *Bill of Rights Journal*, December 1978. See, generally, Edward Sherman, "The Military Courts and the Servicemen's First Amendment Rights," *Hastings Law Journal*, 22 (January 1971) : 325

6. *Brandenburg* v. *Ohio*, 395 U.S. 444 (1969).

7. *Greer* v. *Spock*, 424 U.S. 828 (1976).

8. *Cortright* v. *Resor*, 447 F.2d 245 (D.C. Cir. 1971).

9. *Greene* v. *McElroy*, 360 U.S. 474 (1959). The right to hold specific private employment and follow a chosen profession free from unreasonable government interference is within the liberty and property clauses of the Fourteenth Amendment.

10. George Wilson, "Recruit Casualties High in Today's Military Class Struggle," *Washington Post*, November 17, 1979, p. A5.

11. P.L. 95-610, 92 Stat. 3085.

12. *NLRB* v. *Jones and Laughlin Steel Corp.*, 301 U.S. 1 (1937).

13. *Loving* v. *Virginia*, 388 U.S. 1 (1968).

14. *United States* v. *Wheeler*, 12 U.S.C.M.A. 387 (1961). See generally, Richard B. Johns, "The Right to Marry: Infringement by the Armed Forces," *Family Law Quarterly* 10 (Winter 1977) : 351.

15. Army Regulation 600-290.

16. Public Law 95-527.

17. *Committee For G.I. Rights* v. *Calloway*, 518 F. 2d 466 (D.C. Cir. 1975).

18. *Robinson* v. *California*, 370 U.S. 660 (1962).

19. Bradley Jones, "The Gravity of Administrative Discharges: A Legal and Empirical Evaluation," *Military Law Review* 59 (1973) : 25.

20. *Bland* v. *Connally*, 293 F. 2d 813, 853 (D.C. Cir. 1961).

21. *Korematsu* v. *United States*, 373 U.S. 214 (1944).

22. *Duncan* v. *Kahanamako*, 327 U.S. 304 (1946).

23. *Youngstown Sheet and Tube* v. *Sawyer*, 343 U.S. 579 (1952).

24. *United States* v. *United States District Court*, 407 U.S. 297 (1972).

25. *Halperin* v. *Kissinger*, 929 F. Supp. 838 (D-D.C. 1976). *Berlin Democratic Club* v. *Rumsfeld*, 410 F. Supp. 144 (D-D.C. 1976).

26. *United States* v. *Robel*, 389 U.S. 258, 264 (1967).

27. The conviction was later reversed. *United States* v. *Spock*, 416 F. 2d 165 (1st Cir. 1969).

28. *United States* v. *O'Brien*, 391 U.S. 364 (1968).

29. Lawrence M. Baskir and William A. Strauss, *Chance and Circumstance: The Draft, The War, and the Vietnam Generation* (New York: Alfred A. Knopf, 1978).

30. Ibid.

31. Ibid., p. 25.

32. Morton H. Halperin et al. *The Lawless State: The Crimes of the U.S. Intelligence Agencies* (New York: Penguin Books, 1976); p. 9.

XXV

MILITARY MANPOWER PROCUREMENT: EQUITY, EFFICIENCY, AND NATIONAL SECURITY

Richard V. L. Cooper

I. Introduction

Once again the possibility of conscripting young men (and women) into the nation's armed forces is emerging as a major public policy issue. This renewed interest in the All-Volunteer Force (AVF) and alternatives to it, including more broadly defined national service programs, can be seen in the media, the military, and Congress. Indeed, legislation to reinstitute peacetime registration was recently introduced in Congress. Though ultimately defeated, this effort is seen by some as but the first formal step in an attempt to reinstate the draft. The debate itself is likely to become lower keyed during the next year or so, as the 1980 elections near, but most signs point toward active, intense considerations of conscription beginning in 1981. The realities of a declining youth population and of a (presumably) improved economy will begin to be felt. Clearly, then, this is the time to make a careful assessment of where we have been and what the options for the future are.

Historically, the decision to implement conscription has been driven largely by military "necessity," not only in the United States but in the other English-speaking nations as well: in the United States during the War of 1812 (when the attempt to institute conscription failed), the Civil War, World War I, World War II, and the postwar draft, and in Great Britain, Canada, and Australia in both world wars. When the "necessity" was evident, conscription was used, though sometimes only after lengthy and hotly contested debates.

The problems of the last quarter of this century are, however, more subtle. They involve a different kind of military "necessity," not one of an ongoing or imminent war, but rather one of preparedness. The concern for national security is thus still very real and very important. But so are the concerns about the other effects of military manpower procurement, especially its fairness and its efficiency.

It is the purpose of this paper to examine military manpower procurement policy in the context of these concerns—equity, efficiency, and national security—as these are the factors that will in a large part shape the public policy choices that are made during the remainder of this century. The discussion here is intended to be broad and informal. A more rigorous treatment of the issues is given in some of my previous work,[1] and unless otherwise referenced, this previous work is the source of the various estimates presented here.

Section II describes in a general way the major military manpower alternatives. Which of these actually represent feasible alternatives for the United States today, and why, is discussed in Section III. Section IV presents an analysis of the equity issues, and the efficiency issues are explored in Section V. Conclusions are presented in Section VI.

II. Military Manpower Procurement Systems

What are the various kinds of systems that can be used to procure manpower for the military? Although there are theoretically many different policy alternatives, many of these are not practicable for the United States today. A brief review of the potential policy alternatives—and their limitations—serves to focus the succeeding analysis on the most relevant policy options.

Military Manpower Procurement Alternatives

There are essentially three classes of military manpower procurement systems: volunteer, selective service, and universal service. Volunteer systems are self-descriptive. Selective service and universal service, on the other hand, are both forms of conscription, differing basically with respect to who is required to serve. Whereas all (or nearly all) of the eligible population is required to serve under a policy of universal service, this is not the case under selective service. Rather, when the eligible population exceeds the military's requirements for conscripts, only some will be required to serve—hence, *selective* service.

There are, of course, many variations of these three basic types of systems. For example, three types of universal service immediately come to mind: universal military training (UMT), universal military service (UMS), and universal national service (UNS). Under UMT, all qualified individuals in the eligible population (usually male youth) are required to receive military training, except, of course, conscientious objectors, who generally are assigned to alternative service. UMT can range from just basic military training, to basic training plus individual skill training, to both of these plus some unit training. Upon completion of such training those persons who do not remain in the military would be assigned to the reserve forces (in the case of the United States, the Selected Reserves and/or the Individual Ready Reserve). The period of active service (that is, training) under UMT could thus range anywhere from eight or ten weeks to six or nine months; the period of reserve service could range from only one year to perhaps many years.

UMS goes one step beyond UMT in that all qualified eligibles not only must undergo military training but also must serve in a substantive capacity in the active military. For productive use of these conscripts, the active duty tour for UMS (including training) probably cannot be less than a a year, with two years representing a more reasonable minimum tour length. After this period of active service, UMS conscripts will generally be assigned to some form of reserve service that can last anywhere from one to several years.

UNS is like UMT and UMS in that all qualified eligibles must serve, but differs from these two in one important respect: whereas UMT and UMS conscript individuals to serve in the military, UNS conscripts individuals to perform other public service as well. Individuals can satisfy their obligation by performing either military service or some other public service that is designated as being in the "national interest." The tour length for UNS is typically envisioned as one to two years.

These three systems—UMT, UMS, and UNS—thus represent the main variants of universal service. There are, of course, further variations on each of them. For example, we can think of two different types of UMT models: UMT-draft and UMT-volunteer. Under the UMT-draft model, not only would individuals be conscripted to receive their training, but some of these would then be conscripted to serve in the active military (and also, possibly, the Selected Reserve). As such, this system is not too different from the selective service system described later. Under the UMT-volunteer model, by way of contrast, the military would rely only on volunteers to staff the active forces and the Selected Reserves, drawn from the pool of UMT (conscripted) trainees. That is, while all youth would be required (that is, conscripted) to receive military training, service beyond the initial period of training would be on a voluntary basis only. Those not volunteering for either the active forces or the Selected Reserves would be assigned to the Individual Ready Reserve for some period of time (say, a year or two). They would thus be free of further military obligation unless a national emergency was declared by the President, in which case they could be called into active service.

As noted above, selective service, the other main form of conscription besides universal service, differs from the latter in that not all eligibles are required to serve. It is thus the form of conscription used when the size of the qualified and eligible population base exceeds the military's requirements for manpower. In other words, when this situation prevails, the military or its agent (the Selective Service System in the case of the United States) must *select* only a portion from among the qualified eligibles to serve in the military.

As with universal service, there are many possible variations of the basic selective service concept. These variations involve (1) the purpose for which persons are to be conscripted and (2) the method of selection used. With respect to the former, conscription can be used to fill (or help fill, as with America's postwar mixed draft volunteer system) the active forces, the reserve forces, or both. (In fact, there have been proposals to use selective service to conscript both for the military and for public service jobs.)

There are likewise different kinds of selection methods. A random process, such as the lottery instituted by the United States in 1969, can be used; or, alternatively, deferments and exemptions can be used to channel out those who will ultimately serve. This in fact was implicitly the case in the United States before the 1969 lottery: a person could, for example, affect his probability of serving by going to school, getting married, becoming a father, or entering a sheltered occupation.

Despite the many possible variations, all selective service systems have one thing in common: they conscript only a portion of the qualified eligibles. Specific versions of selective service, then, differ according to both where conscripts are to serve and what type of selection process is used.

Finally, volunteer systems are what the name implies: they rely on individuals to join the military voluntarily, and not because of the threat of punishment if they do not serve. Volunteer systems do not use coercion but rather depend on such motives as monetary incentives, patriotism, job training and experience, the chance to "travel and see the world."

To sum up, there are three basic classes of military manpower procurement systems: universal service, selective service, and volunteer service. These alternatives, and their variations, provide the basis for the remaining discussion.

The Policy Environment

The choice of a military manpower procurement policy cannot be made in the abstract, but must instead be made in the context of the specific environment in which it must operate. That is, it can be argued that there is no absolutely "right" system. what may be "right" under one set of circumstances may be entirely inappropriate under another. Clearly, then, we need to understand the policy environment of the United States today (and, to the extent possible, over the next decade) in order to determine the appropriateness of the various alternative military manpower procurement systems described above.

Certain objectives—for example, economy, efficiency, and consistency with other social objectives—are important in making any public policy decision, and thus need not be detailed here. There are, however, certain unique environmental factors that need to be taken into account in the choice of a military manpower procurement policy. Two in particular stand out: defense requirements and the youth population base.

Defense requirements. The analysis presented here is based on the assumption that the military will require about 2.1 million individuals for the active forces, about 900,000 for the Selected Reserves, and several hundred thousand for the Individual Ready Reserve (IRR). There are, of course, ball-park figures. The point is not whether the manpower requirements for the active forces will be 2.1 million, or 2.5 million, or 1.5 million, but rather that the requirements will be much less than 4 or 5 million and considerably more than several hundred thousand. This means that the military will have to obtain some 400,000 to 500,000 recruits (or inductees) each year (active and reserve, officers and enlisted) in order to meet military manpower requirements.

Equally as important as these numbers is the kind of defense effort that is envisioned. In short, the U.S. Armed Forces, with their highly sophisticated technology, are structured primarily as expeditionary forces. The United States does not seek a home guard or militia to provide territorial defense of the U.S. mainland, but rather a large standing army capable of fighting both on a quick response basis and for an extended period of time abroad.

Given this statement of defense requirements, it will become clear in the next section how appropriate—or inappropriate—various military manpower procurement system are. Suffice it to say here that if future defense requirements vary markedly from these assumptions, evaluation of the alternative procurement strategies must of course change accordingly.

Population. The ratio of the military's manpower requirements to the population base is an important determinant of the attractiveness of the various military manpower procurement options. For instance, when manpower requirements are large relative to the population base, countries are drawn closer to some form of universal service. Conversely, universal service becomes impractical when manpower requirements are very small relative to the population base.

The "relevant" population base is typically thought of as all able-bodied males (though some countries, such as Israel, also include able-bodied females), whose ages range from 18 to 24, to 35, or even to 45. Using this as a population base, for example, the United States was able to mobilize from less than 500,000 individuals in uniform in 1940 to more than 12 million in 1945.

The military can draw from a large population base of the sort mentioned above on a one-time basis. But the military operates as an up-through-the-ranks personnel system and therefore is generally restricted to a narrower age window when the issue is one of *sustaining* a military force. As a practical matter, it is useful to compare the military's annual accession requirements with the numbers of 18- or 19-year-old males each year.

In the United States, the numbers of 18-year-old males increased from about 1.1 million in the mid-1950s to more than 2.1 million today. Because of the late "baby bust" in the late 1960s and the 1970s, this number will decline to about 1.8 million in the mid-1980s and 1.6 million or so by the early 1990s. By the latter 1990s, however, the number of 18-year-olds will once again increase, to somewhere between 1.6 and 2 million. In short, the population base potentially available will range between 1.6 and 2.1 million for the next two decades. Assuming that about 75 percent of these individuals could qualify for the military, the military will thus have a male youth population of some 1.2 to 1.7 million to draw on over the remainder of this century.

III.   The Policy Options

Owing to the policy environment just described, a number of the systems for procuring military manpower are not practical for the United States today or, for that matter, for the remainder of this century. This section examines the feasibility of these various systems, and concludes by outlining those that might be practical.

UMT and UMS

In many ways, there is something intuitively appealing about the concept of universal military service (or training). It would appear to go hand in hand with the notion of the "citizen soldier," which has long been a hall-mark of the American system. George Washington's view is perhaps most representative of this: "It may be laid down as a primary position, and the basis of our system, that every Citizen who enjoys the protection of a free Government owes not only a proportion of his property, but even of his personal services to the defense of it." This perspective has served as the basis for conscription in the past, and is a good part of the rationale that underlies both UMT and UMS today.

Nevertheless, UMS and, to a lesser extent, UMT are highly impractical for the United States today. The issue in both cases is one of need: there simply does not appear to be a need for the numbers of military personnel that would be generated by either UMT or UMS. This is most obvious for UMS, but is probably true for UMT as well.

In the case of UMS, two years is probably the minimum active-duty tour length that would be acceptable from a military standpoint. If about 70 percent of male youth qualify for military service, there would be between 1.2 million and 1.7 million males entering the military each year. With the two-year tour, this would mean between 2.4 million and 3.4 million service members with less than two years of service, exclusive of *any* female participation in the armed forces. Assuming that another 1.3 to 1.5 million servicemen with more than two years of service would be needed, UMS would thus lead to an armed force of some 3.5 to 5 million members, if women were not allowed to join. But women would probably be allowed, if not required, to join, so UMS would probably mean a force of 4 to 6 million members.

The above numbers are obviously only approximate, but the basic point is clear. What would the United States do with a military force of 4 to 6 million individuals? Moreover, such a force would be expensive: another $10 billion to $20 billion per year for manpower alone, not counting the additional expenditures for equipment to use and support this manpower effectively. Given the questionable need for an armed force this size, UMS would thus appear to be highly wasteful of the nation's resources.

Like UMS, UMT does not appear to be practical for the United States for the foreseeable future. Under UMT, all able-bodied males (and females?) would receive some military training and then be routed to the active forces, some to the Selected Reserves, and the remainder to the Individual Ready Reserve (IRR). To be effective, such training would at a minimum probably have to include both basic military training and some individual specialty training, which would mean 12 to 16 weeks of training for each UMT conscript. Assuming that the active forces would take about 400,000 new recruits each year, and the Selected Reserves about 100,000, UMT would thus put 600,000 to 1 million newly trained UMT conscripts into the IRR each year (given that about 75 percent of the male age cohort would be mentally and medically qualified for military service). Further, if each year every UMT conscript had a one-year obligation in the IRR, and 300,000 or so active-duty separatees entered the IRR (for one or two years), the IRR would have between 1 and 1.5 million members at any one time, again exclusive of any female participation.

How useful would an IRR this size be? Even under the most demanding scenarios considered by the Department of Defense (DOD), an IRR this large does not seem justifiable. Moreover, unlike many European countries, where territorial defense is paramount, the United States envisions largely an overseas war. Yet, it is precisely for this type of expeditionary force that UMT conscripts (serving in the IRR or its equivalent) are of the least use. Thus, because the greatest value of UMT conscripts lies in territorial defense, UMT does not provide the kind of manpower needed by the U.S. military.

In general, UMT would not appear to be strictly "needed" according to military requirements, but it should be recognized that UMT would help to shore up two areas in which the present volunteer force has had some difficulties: the Selected Reserves and the IRR. In other words, although an IRR of the size generated by UMT might not be needed, DOD plans suggest that an IRR larger than the present one probably would be useful. Therefore, even though there are other means for enhancing the size of the present IRR, UMT probably cannot be rejected out of hand as a policy option.

Some see UMT as having desirable social consequences in that it might promote better integration of military and civil life. This view is not, of course, unanimous, but it must be considered.

Finally, although not as expensive as UMS, UMT would be costly. Training costs alone would probably add another $3 to $6 billion to the defense budget, not counting the additional capital expenditures that would be required to develop the military installations and facilities for training this volume of new recruits.

In sum, the U.S. military probably does not "need" UMT, although it can be argued that UMT would serve some military and social objectives. In the end, the not entirely convincing advantages of UMT must be weighed against its very real shortcomings. Should UMT be adopted, then the choice centers on the two different models described earlier: UMT-draft and UMT-volunteer. The UMT-draft model is essentially a variant of selective service, and thus carries with it all the advantages and shortcomings of selective service. The UMT-volunteer approach, on the other hand, is more like the current AVF.

Universal National Service

As envisioned by its supporters, a national service draft would serve two principal purposes: It would help supply the manpower required to staff the nation's armed forces; and it would provide a means for utilizing the remainder of young men (and possibly young women) in nonmilitary functions designed to benefit the "national purpose." Because of the enormous impact that a compulsory national service policy would thus have on defense in particular and on society in general, the discussion below briefly addresses some of the benefits and problems that might result if such a policy were implemented.

Support for a compulsory national service program is both philosophical and practical in nature. On the philosophical side, national service is seen by some as a vehicle for encouraging a new "sense of commitment" to the country—a hoped-for result of the direct labor contribution that each young participant would make. In other words, some view compulsory national service as a vehicle for combating the erosion of "national purpose" that has supposedly taken place during the past 10 to 15 years. Participants would perform a number of tasks and duties that would presumably benefit society as a whole. Youth would be more effectively brought into the mainstream of American society; and society in general would become better acquainted with the aspirations, needs, and ideas of youth. National service is also seen as a means for encouraging a certain "socialization" process among the nation's youth—specifically, a mixing of individuals from different backgrounds and with different interests—that might not otherwise take place under a strictly market economy.

Of course, proponents of national service do not expect these things to happen overnight or see national service as the sole means for achieving these objectives. Rather, national service is seen as the beginning of a long evolution toward a more effective interaction between the individual and society.

In addition to the philosophical base of the argument, there is a more practical side to the case for national service. Specifically, one has only to consider the very high youth unemployment rates—approaching 30 percent or more for certain minority groups—to see the economic rationale for compulsory national service. Not only would a national service draft reduce youth unemployment rates directly, but a possible side benefit would be decreased future unemployment rates for national service participants thanks to the skills and maturity presumably gained during their period of service. Thus, compulsory national service is seen as a tool for making youth more employable.

Although the above objectives are clearly laudable, it is important to recognize that they are a *possible* outcome of compulsory national service, *not a certainty*. Indeed, a national service draft could do far worse than the current system in trying to achieve these objectives. For example, resentment among those subject to a national service draft might lessen rather than heighten the "sense of commitment" to the country. Alternatively, a national service program might have little or no effect in lowering unemployment rates.

Not only are its supposed benefits uncertain, but compulsory national service raises some possibly severe problems as well. First, there is the equity question. How would national service workers be distributed among the various national service jobs—especially between military and nonmilitary assignments—given that the distribution of individual preferences would be unlikely to match the distribution of jobs? For example, it is hard to argue that cutting down a tree in Wyoming as part of the forestry service is equivalent to cutting down a tree on the border between North and South Korea in the military. In general, then, an excess supply of applicants for nonmilitary assignments would be expected.

This problem could be solved by a random selection process, though history tells us that the better qualified would stand a better chance of getting their preferences. Alternatively, a pay or period-of-service differential could be introduced. Military pay might be set at a level higher than for other national service jobs, or other jobs might have a three-year commitment as opposed to two years of military duty.*

Second, a national service draft would be enormously expensive. Total program cost would depend on a number of factors, including the number of young Americans serving in the program (which in turn would depend on disqualification rates and the extent to which young women would participate), the length of the service commitment, the pay for national service, the costs of accession and training, and the costs of administering the program.

Although it is difficult to pinpoint the exact costs of a national service draft, Table 1 illustrates some of the potential magnitudes. For example, assume that there are about 2 million 18-year-old males (and about the same number of females), that about 90 percent of males would qualify for military service or national service,† that about 75 percent of females would qualify, and that the military would require about 400,000 new

---

* President John F. Kennedy, for example, proposed that a three-year period of service in the Peace Corps might serve as an exemption from the two-year minimum military service. Although this proposal was never implemented, it is illustrative of how a period-of-service differential might be applied.

† It is unlikely that the disqualification rate or a national service program would be above those rates experienced during the selective service draft, since the same rationale (force readiness, and so on) could not be used to exclude the large numbers of persons who were in fact disqualified for physical or mental reasons during the draft. Moreover, viewed as a social policy, national service might have its greatest positive impact on those who would have been disqualified under a selective service draft.

recruits each year. Assuming a one-year tour for nonmilitary national service, there would be about 1.4 million national service members under a male-only program, and about 2.9 million if both males and females were required to serve. Assuming further that the pay for national service would be around $3.00 per hour,* the total salary cost would be about $8.7 billion for a men-only program and about $18.1 billion for a program including women.

The second cost element, accession and separation, would probably run about $1,500 per national service member, thus generating a total program cost of $2 to $4.5 billion. This would include the costs for travel, examination, processing, counseling, and so on. Depending on how much training would be provided, total training costs, exclusive of the national service members' own salaries, would probably amount to between $3 and $6

---

* It is interesting to note that even if the 1971 first-term pay increase had not been implemented, existing federal law would have resulted in regular military compensation of about $6,290 per year for the first two years of military service in fiscal 1980— about $3.00 an hour. To expect that pay could be reduced much below this level, which was viewed as a poverty wage during the 1971 AVF debate, is at best unrealistic.

TABLE 1

Cost of Universal National Service: Nonmilitary Portion

	Men only			Men and Women		
	Number (000s)	Av. cost ($/year)	Total cost ($billion)	Number (000s)	Av. cost ($/year)	Total cost ($billion)
Salary*	1,400	$6,240	$ 8.7	2,900	$6,240	$18.1
Accession/ separation	1,400	1,500	2.1	2,900	1,500	4.4
Training	1,400	2,000	2.8	2,900	2,000	5.8
Administration†	70	15,000	1.1	145	15,000	2.2
TOTAL			$14.7			$30.5

* Annual salary based on minimum wage of $3.00 per hour. Number based on one year of national service obligation, 2-million-member age/sex cohort; 90 percent qualification rate for males; 75 percent qualification rate for females; and 400,000 military inductions per year.
† Based on one administrator (clerical, etc.) per 20 national service members.

billion per year.* Finally, the costs of administration could easily amount to $1 to $2 billion per year.

The total cost of the nonmilitary portion of a men-only program would therefore appear to be about $15 billion, assuming that nonmilitary members of the program were required to serve only one year. Requiring a longer commitment, or allowing (or requiring) women to participate, would drive the cost up further. For instance, a compulsory program for both men and women, assuming only a one-year tour, would probably cost more than $30 billion in fiscal 1980.

Third, a national service draft would probably displace some currently employed workers. Moreover, because national service workers would tend to be less educated, less trained, and less experienced, the persons most likely to be displaced from their current employment would be the black, the poor, and the undereducated—those with the most difficulty in finding alternative employment offers. Thus, a national service program might reduce unemployment among the nation's youth, but it might increase unemployment among other hard-to-employ segments of society.

Fourth, the removal of 1.5 to 3 million young men and women from the workforce and/or student rolls for one or more years each could cause possibly severe economic dislocations. For example, since about half of all high school graduates go on to college each year, compulsory national service would create difficult transition problems for the nation's colleges, universities, and trade schools. In addition, the high youth unemployment rates during the 1970s are clearly cause for concern, but the fact that 80 percent or more of those in the youth work force do find employment means that a national service draft would deprive the economy of many productive workers.

Fifth, finding and managing the 1.5 to 3 million jobs needed to support universal national service would be an administrative nightmare. Many, if not most, of these jobs would likely be "make work," because the fact that government and industry do not presently support these kinds of jobs suggests that the value to society of the tasks that would be performed by national service members is less than their cost.

Finally, there is considerable doubt about how well a program of compulsory national service would work, because many of those subject to this type of conscription are unlikely to see the "need" for it. The Vietnam War

---

* Training costs could obviously be held to less than this amount, as some have suggested. But, this would reduce the national service benefit of making youth more employable. If national service is to be more than menial labor, it is necessary to provide a reasonable amount of training. Past experience in the DOD suggests that $2,000 would provide a "bare bones" minimum.

amply demonstrated the effects of an unpopular conscription and the lack of a national commitment on the ability to maintain conscription successfully. Whereas the importance of defense may be well recognized by the American population, thus providing a certain credibility for a *military* draft when needed, drafting for "nonessential" purposes might seriously dilute support for a nonmilitary draft. In other words, the same arguments used to support a military draft—that is, a youthful fighting force and the necessity of defense—cannot be used to justify conscripting young men and women for nonmilitary purposes.

The use of compulsory national service also raises a number of philosophical and legal problems, including those resulting from the use of coercion to allocate labor resources in a free society. In this regard, a Senate speech by Robert Taft of Ohio just before World War II is particularly relevant:

> The principle of a compulsory draft is basically wrong. If we must use compulsion to get an Army, why not use compulsion to get men for other essential tasks? Why not draft labor for [essential] occupations at wages lower than the standard? ... In short, the logic of the bill [for a draft] requires a complete regimentation of most labor and the assignment of jobs to every man. This is actually done in the communist and fascist states which we are now apparently seeking to emulate.[2]

The imposition of compulsory national service would seem to directly contradict the long-held principle of individual freedom. Indeed, for this reason, it is not clear whether a nonmilitary draft is even constitutional. In short, universal national service does not appear practical, feasible, or desirable for the United States.

Selective Service Volunteerism

As a practical matter, then, the choice really boils down to one between selective service and a volunteer military. Neither UMS nor UNS appears feasible or desirable for the United States. UMT is probably not needed, but does not pose as severe problems as does either UMS or UNS. Moreover, if UMT were adopted, the two versions—UMT-draft and UMT-volunteer—are really more akin to selective service and the volunteer force, respectively. In other words, selective service and the AVF would seem to represent the viable policy options. The remainder of this paper accordingly focuses on these two alternatives.

IV. Equity

Equity and the elimination of inequities have long been important social objectives of this country. Equity is therefore one of two key concerns that we must consider when examining the choice between selective service and volunteerism, the other concern of course being efficiency.

Historically, the inequity of conscripting young men (and, on occasion, young women) for military service has been a controversial issue nearly every time the draft has been imposed. However, as the result of some demographic trends (for instance, the number of young men eligible for military service more than doubled between 1955 and 1975), the equity issue became critically important beginning in the late 1950s, and will continue to be so for at least the remainder of the century.

The burden of conscription was limited to a relatively small segment of American society—young men of military age—but the growing number of such eligible men, combined with relatively stable military force sizes, meant that increasing numbers would not be called upon to serve. This situation made the postwar draft more inequitable over time.

Equity was thus a paramount issue in the move to end the draft in the 1960s, and will continue to be a focus whenever a return to selective service is considered in the future. There are two parts to this equity issue: the burden of conscription and the selective way that burden is applied.

The Burden of Conscription

Draftees are forced to bear a burden that other members of society are able to avoid. The specific aspects of this burden are many, and include the risk to life and limb, personal hardship, arduous working conditions, low pay, and the disruption in the lives of the conscripts. It is not that many civilian occupations do not have some of these attributes, but rather that those serving in such civilian occupations are there *voluntarily*, not because the government has forced them.

Selectivity

The imposition of a burden does not in itself constitute inequity, for society must frequently impose "burdens" on its citizens. These burdens are usually in the form of taxes, although there are certain kinds of nontax burdens, such as the right of eminent domain and the prohibition of illegal acts.

The issue of inequity does arise, however, when these burdens are applied selectively, with the result that only some citizens must pay the price. This does not mean that a burden must be shared equally to be equitable, but rather that there must be some design to distribute the burden "equitably" among society's members.

FIGURE 1

MILITARY MANPOWER PROCUREMENT AND THE POPULATION BASE

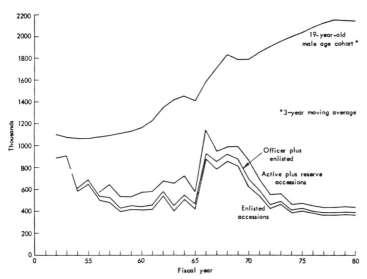

In the case of conscription, there are several kinds of selectivity. To begin with, the burden of conscription is generally limited to young men. Those beyond the age of eligibility thus benefit at the expense of those in the vulnerable age group. This in itself need not, however, constitute inequity, because if universal service is maintained, everyone will eventually serve. Therefore this could be an acceptable means for distributing the burden "equitably."

When only some in the age cohort are forced to serve, however, the inequity of conscription does become a serious issue. It was in this regard that some simple population dynamics brought the equity issue to the forefront of public policy beginning in the late 1950s and early 1960s. Except for the Vietnam War period, the number of annual accessions into the military has remained roughly constant over the years. In fact, as Figure 1 shows, it has actually declined somewhat since the 1950s. However, beginning in 1954, the number of young men turning 19 years old increased every year, and dramatically so starting about 1961.

In fact, by 1957 only about one in every five young men was required to serve in the military. This clearly indicates the selectivity of military service, and the inequity of this selectivity. Indeed, no matter how fair the selection process is before the fact, after the fact selective service will be inequitable.

This does not necessarily rule selective service out as a viable policy option, for we can envision circumstances (such as existed in the mid-1950s) in which, from a public policy perspective, these inequities are worth incurring. What it does mean is that we need to gauge the magnitude of these inequities and their consequences and compare them with other elements that must be factored into the public policy decision process.

The remainder of this section is devoted to a more specific examination of these inequities and their consequences.

The Conscription Tax

Conscription is essentially a vehicle for reducing the budget cost of military manpower. That is, it provides a method for bypassing standard market allocating mechanisms.

One of the consequences of the draft, then, is the implicit tax that conscription imposes on young men of military age—the so-called conscription tax. Although this "tax" never appears on an IRS Form 1040 or in the accounts of any government agency, it is nonetheless very real to those forced to pay it.

Explicit consideration of this tax is central to the question of military manpower procurement policy, because whether or not by design, the conscription tax is itself an important element of public policy in general and tax policy in particular. It reduces the amount of direct taxes that must be levied on the general public; it redistributes income within society; and it requires its own bureaucracy for administering and enforcing collection. In short, the conscription tax has many of the attributes of other, more conventional methods of taxation, and thus needs to be examined in this context.

We can consider the conscription tax from two different angles, the first being the financial burden that conscription imposes on young men forced to enter the military. To the extent that military pay is less than the pay that one could earn from civilian employment, the individual forced to serve in the military bears a financial burden. Figure 2 indicates that this burden was substantial during the postwar draft. For example, military pay was about $2,100 less than the average earnings for all 18- to 24-year-old civilian workers in 1964, and $3,200 less in 1970. Using this measure as a rough estimate of the financial burden borne by the typical individual, we can estimate the collective financial burden imposed on those forced to serve in the military as about $2.1 billion in 1964, and about $4.0 billion in 1970.* To put these figures in some perspective, it should be noted that

---

* This was determined as follows: for 1964, 496,000 accessions times $2,100 times two (because the minimum period of service was two years); and for 1970, 631 accessions times $3,200 times two.

FIGURE 2

ANNUAL MILITARY AND CIVILIAN WAGES

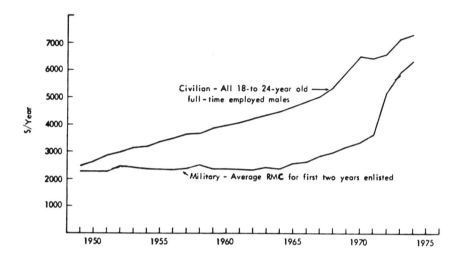

total military personnel budget costs amounted to about $12 billion in 1964 and $23 billion in 1970. Clearly, then, the postwar draft put an enormous financial burden on those forced to serve.

But the financial burden is only part of the picture, as it does not deal with the nonpecuniary aspects of military service. In this regard it is perhaps more appropriate to think of the conscription tax in terms of the wage that would just induce the individual to join the military—that is, his reservation wage, or supply price. The rationale for this measure rests in the fact that the individual who is coerced into the military forgoes not only his alternative civilian earning potential but also (the monetized value of) the nonpecuniary aspects of civilian employment, relative to the military. Since these nonpecuniary aspects of military service may be positive or negative, this measure of the conscription tax can theoretically be less than, equal to, or greater than the financial burden.

This measure, which we can refer to as the narrow definition of the conscription tax, makes the implicit, but important, assumption that the confiscation of economic rent by the government does not constitute taxation. That is, in the absence of a draft the government would have to pay a competitive wage in order to attract the requisite numbers of personnel, so that even those with supply prices less than this competitive wage would still earn the competitive wage. For these individuals, this difference is rent, but rent of this sort earned by other individuals (postal clerks, employees covered by collectively bargained contracts, and the like) is not normally confiscated by the governmnt. Sjaastad and Hansen argue that forgone economic rent is as much a part of the conscription tax as is the difference between the individual's supply price and his actual military wage.[3] The conscription tax, under this broad definition, is thus measured as the larger of (1) the difference between the competitive wage and the draft wage and (2) the difference between the individual's supply price and the draft wage.

The importance of this distinction is not so much that the two measures, the narrow definition and the broad definition, differ in magnitude, but rather that they have very different meanings with respect to the larger public policy questions concerning the income redistribution caused by the draft. The narrow definition views only those with high reservation wages as having to pay the tax, whereas the broad definition explicitly recognizes that the draft extracts a tax from all those serving in the military, including the less affluent. Therefore, the narrow definition, which does not recognize the tax paid by the less affluent, hides some of the most undesirable economic and social consequences of the selective service conscription tax.

Measurement of the conscription tax must thus at best be imprecise because it depends on knowing the supply price of each person serving in the military. However, we can make a few rough estimates based on some assumptions about the supply of labor to the military. In particular, based on the Gates Commission assumption that about 60 percent of enlistments in 1964 were "true volunteers" and that the supply of labor to the military is given as a constant elasticity function with an elasticity equal to 1.25, the conscription tax under the narrow definition can be estimated as about $2.1 billion in 1964. For the broad definition, these assumptions yield an estimate of about $3.2 billion for 1964.

Thus, whether one views conscription as a financial burden imposed on those forced to serve or in terms of either the narrow or the broad definition of the conscription tax, it is clear that the postwar draft imposed a significant penalty on those forced to serve.

"Who Serves When Not All Serve?"

What made the postwar draft so onerous was not just that conscription extracted a tax from young men of military age, though greater efforts should have been made to minimize the amount of this tax, but that this tax was extracted from only a small proportion of these men. This, then, raises the natural question: "Who serves when not all serve?"

The folklore is replete with story after story about the extremes to which some young men went to avoid induction.[4] There were cases of men purposely maiming themselves, spending thousands of dollars on lawyers or unnecessary medical care, and fleeing the country or going to jail. Although most did not go to such extremes, it is probably fair to say that the vast majority of those subject to the draft engaged in at least some draft-avoidance activities.

Part of the reason for this is that the Selective Service System institutionalized many methods for avoiding the draft. The Selective Service was faced with the problem described earlier—namely, an increasing population of young men and constant (or decreasing) force sizes—and had to find ways for picking the young men who would actually have to serve. Deferments and exemptions were thus used to pare down the choices, for they helped reduce the size of the classification I-A population. Initially, there were deferments for hardship and for college students. Later came additional deferments: deferments for postgraduate study; more liberal hardship deferments; deferments for fatherhood. and, finally, deferments for marriage.

Draft avoidance (in the guise of these many deferments and exemptions) became as much a part of official U.S. policy as was the draft itself. Although initially envisioned as a means of "channeling" American youth into activities that served the national purpose, the underlying purpose for

TABLE 2

Blacks as a Percentage of the Mental Categories I-III
Youth Population and Enlisted Accessions

Years	Blacks as a Percentage of Categories I–III Population	Blacks as a Percentage of Categories I–III Accessions
1953–57	2.2	4.7
1958–63	2.9	5.4
1964–68	3.6	6.0
1969–70	4.5	6.5
1971–72	5.0	10.5
1973–75	6.8	16.5

SOURCE: Richard V. L. Cooper, *Military Manpower and the All-Volunteer Force.* R-1458-ARPA (Santa Monica, Calif., Rand Corporation, September 1977), p. 215.

many (if not most) of these deferments and exemptions was to provide the Selective Service with a way to select which young men would actually have to serve.

Not surprisingly, those who served when not all served turned out to be largely the poor, the black, and the undereducated—hence the inequity. Although youth from all stations of life did serve in the military, it was these less advantaged citizens who bore the disproportionate share of the burden.

For example, Table 2 shows that, consistently throughout the postwar era, mental categories I–III blacks served in numbers roughly twice as large as their share of the categories I–III youth population.* The reserves, a last resort for those able to get in, were disproportionately populated by college graduates. Blacks made up less than 2 percent of all reservists in 1970, but college students and graduates made up more than 50 percent of all new reserve enlistments that same year.

In general, then, those with the most to gain from not serving in fact

---

* When a person is tested for military service, he is classified into one of five so-called mental categories. Categories I–III represent the upper 70 percent of the population, and are thus the military's prime recruiting pool.

TABLE 3

Distribution of Male Enlisted Accessions during the Lottery by SMSA Codes Ranked According to Average Family Income
(Percent)

Zip Codes with Average Family Income in Percentile	Enlistments	Inductions	All	16- to 21-Year-Old Male Population
> 95	3.1	3.4	3.2	6.2
90–95	4.7	5.4	4.9	7.4
75–90	18.8	19.5	19.0	20.8
50–75	29.7	29.9	29.7	28.6
25–50	25.4	24.9	25.2	22.6
10–25	14.8	12.2	14.0	12.1
< 10	4.0	4.7	4.2	2.3

faced the least chance of having to serve. This, of course, should not be viewed with surprise, because with enough resources, ingenuity, and knowledge of the law, one could almost be certain of (legally) avoiding the draft, and the more affluent were likely to have these resources and this knowledge.

Much of the above inequity can be attributed to the specifics of the postwar, prelottery draft. Although the deferments and exemptions of that draft were not as blatant as the World War I draft—in which individuals were classified, and inducted, according to their "value to society," with those of "least value" drafted first—they nevertheless worked primarily to benefit white middle- and upper-class youth. A variety of draft reforms emerged in the late 1960s, culminating with the introduction of the lottery draft in 1969. Marriage deferments were ended, student deferments were reduced, and the order of induction was changd from an oldest-first policy to a youngest-first. These, and the lottery itself, helped reduce the inequities and lessen the burden.

Despite these draft reforms, the less affluent continued to serve in numbers greater than their proportion of the population. In this regard, Table 3 shows the distribution of 16- to 21-year-old males and of enlisted accessions (that is, enlistees and inductees) *during the lottery* according to the average family income in their home address Zip Code.* These figures reveal that those young men living in the highest income areas stood only half the chance of having to serve as those young men living in middle-income areas, and only one-quarter the chance of young men living in low-income areas. For example, about 6 percent of all 16- to 21-year-old males resided in Zip Codes that ranked in the upper 5 percent of all Zip Codes in terms of average family income, but only 3 percent of enlisted accessions came from these areas during the lottery draft. Conversely, only about 2 percent of 16- to 21-year-old males resided in the bottom 10 percent of Zip Codes, but these same Zip Codes accounted for 4 percent of all enlisted accessions.

Interestingly, these patterns held for both enlistees *and inductees* during the lottery draft. In other words, despite the closing of many draft loopholes, those from lower-income families continued to be forced to serve in numbers larger than their "fair share."

---

* That is, all Zip Codes in Standard Metropolitan Statistical Areas (SMSAs) were ranked according to average family income. These Zip Codes were then grouped into categories: the top 5 percent, the next 5 percent (that is, the 90th to 95th percentiles), and so forth. Table 3 shows the distributions of 16- to 21-year-old males and of enlisted accessions during the lottery (1970–72) according to these categories. For example, the table shows that 6.2 percent of all 16- to 21-year-old males live in Zip Codes that fall in the upper 5 percent of all Zip Codes ranked by average family income; 3.2 percent of all enlisted accessions between 1970 and 1972 came from these same Zip Codes, and so on.

Again, the above should not be viewed with surprise, because it is impossible to eliminate all draft loopholes. The Selective Service System, through its policies and procedures, can reduce the degree of inequity (for instance through a lottery), but it cannot eliminate it altogether. So long as some have an incentive to avoid induction (as the above discussion on the conscription tax has indicated, this will *always* be the case), some will find a way out. And those who do will tend to be the more affluent and better educated.

Redistribution of Income under the Conscription Tax

Because conscription is essentially a mechanism for collecting tax revenue, it should be examined within the broader context of U.S. tax policy in general. In this regard, two issues, which are corollaries of each other, warrant particular consideration: the burden of paying the conscription tax, and the redistribution of income that accompanies the imposition of

TABLE 4

THE ABILITY TO PAY: CONSCRIPTION TAX AS A PERCENTAGE OF LIFETIME EARNINGS

| Race | Education | Tax Burden: Percentages of Life Cycle Earnings | |
		Narrow Definition	Broad Definition
		(1)	(2)
White	Some high school	0.7%	2.2%
	High school graduate	2.0	1.8
	Some college	3.0	1.6
	College graduate	4.1	1.3
	Postgraduate	5.4	1.1
Black	Some high school	0.0	3.4
	High school graduate	0.4	2.6
	Some college	2.8	1.9
	College graduate	3.4	1.5
	Postgraduate	5.2	1.2

SOURCE: Cooper, *Military Manpower and the All-Volunteer Force*, p. 90.

that burden. By examining this income redistribution, we can evaluate the efficacy of conscription as a means for collecting tax revenue.

From the earlier discussion, we know that conscription causes two kinds of income redistribution: intergenerational and intragenerational. Intergenerational income redistribution occurs because it is generally young men who are subjected to the conscription tax. As noted earlier, this need not be inequitable, but neither does it imply that the younger generations should have to bear both the financial and other burdens imposed by conscription.

Intragenerational income redistribution, on the other hand, occurs because only some young men have to pay the tax while others escape. The discussion below, which summarizes some of my previous work, focuses on this aspect of income redistribution.

The intragenerational redistribution of income is a result of the magnitude of the tax and who pays it. Column 1 of Table 4, based on the narrow definition of the tax, shows the magnitude of the tax expressed relative to a taxpayer's lifetime earnings. This perspective, which would seem to imply that the conscription tax is very progressive, is inappropriate for two reasons. First, the narrow definition fails to account for the fact that those with low supply prices also paid a tax under the draft, in an amount equal to the difference between the low draft wage and the competitive wage. Second, it does not take into account that those with higher reservation wages in fact stood a smaller chance of serving. Although individuals with a high supply price who were actually forced to serve ended up paying a substantial tax, as a group these people paid a smaller percentage of their lifetime earnings in the form of the conscription tax, as shown in column 2.

To illustrate, column 2 of Table 4 indicates that blacks with only some high school education paid a tax roughly three times as large as that paid by whites with postgraduate training. The reason for this, of course, is again that those with opportunities for higher earnings and with greater resources faced a lower probability of having to serve.

Therefore, the conscription tax, which on the surface appears to have been quite progressive, was in reality just the opposite. It redistributed income away from the poor to the more affluent and thus ran contrary to most of the stated goals of U.S. social policy. The practical implication, then, is that conscription enabled the general public to pay less for military manpower—at the expense of those least able to afford the burden.

The Inequity of Selective Service

Life is not always fair, and cannot always be made to be. But should the U.S. government deliberately pursue policies that lead to greater inequities?

Most would argue not. Yet this is precisely what the government did throughout most of the postwar draft era.

Selective service will, by its very nature, always be at least somewhat inequitable. But there are ways for reducing the worst of these inequities, even when selective service is the only feasible alternative. A step in this direction was taken with the introduction of the lottery system in 1969. Other steps would have to be taken if selective service is ever to be resumed. Perhaps the most important of these is that inductees should be paid a "fair" wage, so that they do not have to pay a large financial burden in addition to the other burdens of involuntary service.

In sum, there were and always will be inequities associated with selective service. These by themselves may not necessarily rule out selective service under all circumstances, but greater efforts should be made to reduce the magnitude of these inequities.

V.   Efficiency

In addition to the equity issue, military manpower procurement policy raises important efficiency concerns. By efficiency, we mean the amounts of society's resources that are required to sustain a given level of defense effort. This section examines the efficiency of conscription vis-à-vis a volunteer military.

Economic Cost of Military Manpower

When the government can by fiat conscript persons into the military at whatever wage it sets, the budget cost of military manpower is less a measure of the "value" of the labor resources used by the military than it is an indicator of government policy toward conscripts. Yet it should be recognized that society forgoes something by employing these persons in the military. It forgoes the amount of productive output that would have been realized had these persons instead been employed in the civilian sector. The value of this productive output is what we refer to as the economic cost of military manpower.

The economic cost of military manpower is at a minimum when the allocation of labor resources takes place in a free market. In this instance, labor resources are sorted into their most productive uses via the market mechanism—that is, wage rates. This, of course, is what happens with a volunteer military when the military wage is set to clear the market.

How badly does conscription vary from this minimum?* The answer depends on the selection process used to conscript young men into the military. For example, suppose that the draft is structured so as to conscript individuals according to their value to society, with those of the "least value" drafted first. As mentioned earlier, this was essentially the selection process used during World War I. The result of this "lowest-value-drafted-first" (LVDF) draft policy is as the name implies. It minimizes the economic cost of those serving in the military, much as a volunteer military does by using the market mechanism. Indeed, this minimization of the economic cost was the primary reason that the LVDF draft policy was used.

The LVDF conscription policy was repudiated by the United States following World War I as being socially repressive, and efforts were made to structure a more random selection process when peacetime conscription was introduced after World War II. The effect of introducing more randomness into the selection process, however, is to raise the economic cost associated with those serving in the military. As a result, this economic cost under the prelottery draft was less than that when the lottery was used. The reason, of course, is that the wide variety of deferments and exemptions available during most of the postwar draft allowed persons to self-select themselves out of the military. The ones most likely to self-select themselves out were the ones with the most to gain—that is, those with the highest valued civilian alternatives. When these deferments and exemptions were reduced or eliminated with the draft reforms of the late 1960s, the inequity was reduced, but the economic cost associated with those actually serving increased on account of the increased randomness of the selection process.

Thus, achieving a representative selection of individuals is not costless. According to some of my previous estimates, the excess economic cost of the prelottery draft appears to have been about $850 million in 1964. Had the more random lottery draft been used then, the excess economic cost of the draft would probably have been about $1,350 million. These are rough estimates at best, but they help make an important point: When the number of eligibles exceeds the military's requirements for personnel, there is no conscription policy that minimizes both economic cost and inequity. In other words, when conscription is used, the policymaker has the unenviable task of choosing between inequity and inefficiency.

---

* It can be argued that a volunteer military might in practice also deviate from this minimum, because if the voluntary wage is set higher than the competitive wage, the military has an excess of applicants to choose from. In this instance, the military is likely to set screening standards higher than necessary, thereby selecting the most capable out of the group, who on average would also be expected to be those with the highest valued civilian alternatives. This would thus lead to an economic cost greater than the theoretical minimum. As a practical matter, the excess economic costs resulting from this are not likely to be severe.

Labor Utilization

Conscripting individuals into the military at less than the market wage does more than hide the "true" cost of military manpower; it also distorts the incentives faced by the DOD, and thus encourages an inefficient allocation of resources. Paying junior military personnel less than the market wage means that the budget cost for them is less than the economic cost. This encourages the DOD to use too many junior personnel relative to more experienced military personnel,* too much military manpower in general relative to other types of labor, and too much labor relative to other kinds of resources. Moreover, it encourages the Administration and Congress to allocate too much money for defense relative to other uses of society's resources.

In short, to the extent that the DOD, the Administration, and Congress respond to budget incentives—and the evidence suggests that they do—the conscription of individuals into the military at less than the market wage results in a misallocation of society's resources. This misallocation means that there are resources diverted to the military that have higher valued uses elsewhere in society, the result being that society "pays" more than necessary to maintain a defense effort.

The effects of this overemployment of first-term military personnel, combined with the excess economic costs of any other than the LVDF selection process described earlier, can be visualized as shown in Figure 3.† Assume that the demand for first-term labor is given as a downward sloping function of its cost, as shown by the curve DD′ in Figure 3, and that the supply of first-term labor is given as an upward sloping function of wages, as shown by the curve SS′. Assume further that the draft wage is w*, which is less than the market clearing wage of w′. Then the military will hire OB first termers, as opposed to the socially optimum amount OA. If other than a LVDF selection process is used—that is, if there is at least some randomness to the selection process determining who is actually drafted—then the curve SS″ represents the locus of supply prices for those first termers who actually serve in the military. Assuming that supply price is equal to the

---

* There is also a more subtle argument as to why the military hired too much first-term labor during the draft. Specifically, the draft not only depressed the first-term wage rate but also guaranteed an almost infinite supply at that wage, so that the marginal costs of first termers equaled the average cost. In marked contrast, the supply of careerists was clearly upward sloping during the draft (as it is today), which means that the marginal cost for careerists was more than the average cost. Thus, whereas the average cost for careerists was roughly twice as much as that for first termers during the draft, the marginal cost was about 3½ times as much.

† "First termers" are those in their first tour of duty. Empirically, we can think of first termers as those personnel with less than four years of service.

FIGURE 3

OVEREMPLOYMENT OF LABOR WITH THE DRAFT

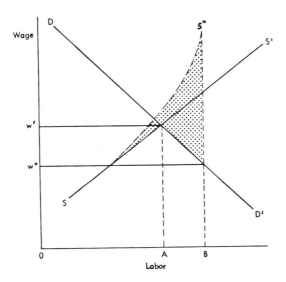

individual's alternative civilian earnings opportunity,* the shaded area lying above the SS′ curve then represents the excess economic cost associated with introducing some randomness into the selection process. The shaded area lying below the SS′ curve, on the other hand, represents the excess economic cost resulting from the military employing too many first-term personnel. The shaded area as a whole, then, represents the excess economic cost associated with those first termers actually serving in the military.

We can make some rough estimates as to the magnitude of this social welfare loss by assuming that the supply curve has a constant elasticity equal to 1.25, that the elasticity of demand for first-term personnel equals 1.5, and that first termers were paid a draft wage equal to 75 percent of the market clearing wage. Together, these assumptions imply that the military will demand about 55 percent more first-term personnel than is socially optimal, with the result that the shaded area lying below the SS′ curve in Figure 3 equals about 16.5 percent of the entire compensation paid to first termers. Given that first-term compensation was about $4.2 billion in 1969, the social welfare loss associated with this overemployment of first termers was on the order of $700 million in that year. When this loss was combined with the approximately $850 million in excess economic

---

* Relaxation of this assumption does not materially affect the results.

cost due to the prelottery selection process, the total social welfare loss associated with this overemployment of first termers was on the order of $700 million in that year. When this loss was combined with the approximately $850 million in excess economic cost due to the prelottery selection process, the total social welfare loss associated with those first termers was around $1.5 billion in 1964, more than one-third the total compensation paid to them.

These are obviously only rough estimates of the magnitude of the additional costs resulting from the draft. The more general—and more important—point is that the presence of the draft encouraged the military to misuse society's resources by introducing the wrong budget incentives.

A volunteer military, on the other hand, may generate social welfare losses by using too few labor resources, a point first raised by Borcherding.[5] As the military faces an upward sloping supply of first termers in the absence of a draft, the marginal cost of first termers is more than the average cost. Assuming again that the military responds to budget incentives, we find that the military will demand labor up to the point where that labor's cost equals its military value, which is less than the social optimum. But there are at least two factors that serve to mitigate the actual amount of social welfare loss generated by this underemployment of labor; the first is that the military does not face a strictly upward sloping supply curve because of the current "comparability" pay principle; and the second is that the military can act partially as a discriminating monopsonist. The result is that the social welfare losses generated by the underemployment of labor under the AVF probably amounts to less than $75 million today.[6]

The above provides a theoretical discussion of the misallocation of labor resources under the draft, and thus implicitly points to the improvements that would be expected under a volunteer military. But what has been the actual experience with the AVF? Although I have been critical of the DOD in the past for failing to move quickly enough, the evidence nevertheless indicates that there have been improvements (and in some cases substantial ones) in the military's allocation of resources since the end of the draft.

With respect to the experience mix of the enlisted force, progress has perhaps been the slowest of all. About 59 prcent of all enlisted personnel in 1974 were first termers, the same percentage as in 1964. But by 1978, this had fallen to 58 percent, and the services' goals call for the first-term percentage eventually to be about 57 percent. This is still more than the longer-term 50 percent objective that I feel may be more appropriate, but it does represent progress.

In the area of substituting civilians for military personnel, the military has made considerable progress. For example, Figure 4 shows that the mix of military personnel and direct-hire civilians (that is, those civilians

FIGURE 4

MILITARY AND DIRECT-HIRE CIVILIAN PERSONNEL
UTILIZATION AND COSTS

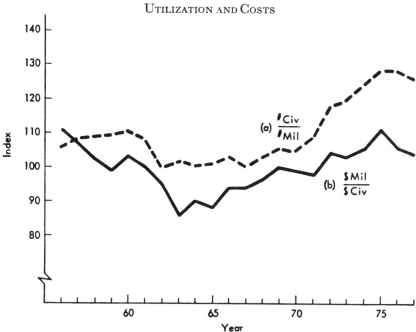

^a Ratio of numbers of civilians not in training to numbers of military personnel not engaged in training (index, 1964: 100).
^b Ratio of average cost of military personnel to average cost of civilians (index, equal average cost: 100).

directly on the DOD payroll) has been very responsive to changes in the costs of these two types of labor. Thus, by making the budget costs of military personnel more nearly equal to their economic cost, the AVF has led to greater efficiency in the mix of military and civilian personnel.

This substitution has not been limited to direct hires for military, for Table 5 indicates that the DOD has increased its use of contract hires substantially over the past ten years. Contract hires are persons employed by private companies under contract to provide services to the DOD. They perform a number of functions formerly carried out by uniformed personnel and direct-hire civilians. For example, maintenance functions and base operations at Vance Air Force Base are now performed almost entirely under contract. Indeed, Table 5 shows how misleading it is to focus solely on uniformed strengths as the measure of DOD labor input, for many functions in the military can be and are performed by civilians either directly employed by the DOD or employed by private firms under contract to the DOD.

In sum, by underpricing military manpower, the draft encouraged the military to allocate its resources inefficiently. These inefficiencies wasted society's resources.

Other Resource Costs

Besides the costs of individuals actually serving in the military there are other costs associated with the process of maintaining a military labor force. In the case of a volunteer military, for example, the main examples of these costs are the incremental expenditures required for recruiting and advertising and the additional costs resulting from enlisted attrition, which has been higher than experienced under the draft. Together, it is estimated that these costs were about $300 million in 1976.

A conscripted force, on the other hand, requires a selective service system to administer the induction process, expenditures for expanded training activity to train the larger numbers of new recruits, and an alternative service program for conscientious objectors. The costs of the first two alone would have amounted to about $270 million in 1976 had the draft then been in place.

In addition to these costs that can be directly related to the draft, it can be argued that the GI Bill was implemented in part to help compensate those who were drafted. The cost of the GI Bill was more than $5 billion in 1976. Although this program is said to have helped further certain social goals, it also appears to have involved considerable wastage.

An interesting sidelight is that although most of the additional resource costs associated with the volunteer force are carried in the DOD budget, most of such costs associated with the draft were not. Indeed, one of the principles underlying the implementation of the volunteer force was that

TABLE 5

THE MIX OF DEFENSE PERSONNEL
(000s)

Year	Military	Direct Hire	Contract Hire	Total
1964	2,687	1,030	219	3,936
1972	2,323	1,083	394	3,800
1976	2,087	994	455	3,536

manpower costs be made visible, rather than being hidden in the form of the conscription tax or put in the budget of some other government agency.

The Costs of Collecting the Conscription Tax

One of the most important resource costs associated with maintaining a military labor force under conscription, and one that is not captured by the standard budget measures, is the cost of collecting the conscription tax. Whenever a government imposes a tax on some or all of its citizenry, there are certain costs associated with the collection of that tax, a fact well recognized in the public finance literature. These collection costs include, among other items, the costs for tax collectors, the costs of enforcing payment of the tax, and, particularly important in the case of conscription, the costs incurred by those attempting to avoid payment of the tax.

We would expect the amount of costs incurred by those trying to avoid payment of the tax to be a function of (1) the magnitude of the tax and (2) the difficulty of escaping payment of the tax. In the first case, the relationship is clear: The larger the tax, the more will be spent in attempts to avoid payment. In the second case, the relationship is a bit more subtle. When the authorities make it more difficult to escape payment, fewer persons will engage in draft avoidance activities, but those who do are likely to spend more in their efforts. In other words, it makes sense to incur tax-avoidance costs only if those expenditures can be expected to have a reasonable chance of success. And to be successful, more must almost invariably be spent.

As noted earlier, many persons took advantage of the numerous legal and illegal means of avoiding induction. For example, Baskir and Strauss estimate that there were about 570,000 draft offenders during the Vietnam era out of what they define as the 27 million Vietnam generation males.[7] Though this was a sizeable number, perhaps more important were the 15 million young men who were deferred, exempted, or disqualified throughout this period. When marriage deferments were introduced, the marriage rates jumped roughly 10 percent almost immediately. It is estimated that 6 to 7 percent more males attended college than would have done so had the draft not existed. And so forth.

Clearly, then, so long as there was an incentive to avoid the draft—and for most there was—individuals would try. Not only did this result in larger numbers of the less affluent serving, as described previously, but it also entailed substantial amounts of resources being spent on draft avoidance.

It is probably impossible to catalogue completely the costs of draft-avoidance activities, but the work of Sjaastad and Hansen offers some interesting insights into the potential magnitudes of these costs. Sjaastad and Hansen's model was developed under the assumption that individuals attempt to maximize their expected incomes, and that their probability of serving (and, hence, their expected income) can be reduced by expending resources in the pursuit of draft avoidance.[8]

The results of this procedure, as estimated in some earlier work of mine, suggest that the costs of collecting the conscription tax amounted to between *$2.6 and $3.6 billion* in 1964, a sum as large as or larger than the conscription tax itself. Had the lottery draft, with its reduced draft loopholes, been used instead, the costs of collecting the tax would have been less, by about a half to two-thirds, but still would have been substantial.

Thus, not only does conscription impose a significant burden on those forced to serve, but it is an extremely inefficient method for collecting tax revenue.

Selective Service versus Volunteerism

Although a selective service draft appears to be less expensive than a volunteer military, because its budget costs are lower, it is in reality just the opposite. A selective service draft actually leads to higher costs than a volunteer force. Selective service only hides many of these real costs from society.

VI. Conclusions

Much of the recent AVF debate appears to be a case of "the tail wagging the dog." At the broadest level, legitimate concerns have been expressed about problems such as high youth unemployment rates. Yet, is a military draft or compulsory national service the answer? It seems not. A military draft is a mechanism for procuring military manpower, and not much more. Although a military draft, if needed, should be made as consistent as possible with the nation's broader social goals, conscription itself is a very poor tool for directly achievinging these goals.

Compulsory national service poses even greater problems. Not only would such a program be enormously expensive, but conscripting young men and women for nonessential tasks at what would amount to the whim of the government raises important questions about the legitimacy of such an effort. Indeed, these problems are likely to undermine whatever social gains such a system might promise. Compulsory national service would thus seem to be an inefficient and ineffective way to solve the nation's ills.

This takes us back to the basic problem at hand: how to best provide the manpower needed for our armed forces. As a practical matter, the choice is one between a selective service draft and volunteerism. Although a selective service draft is frequently sold on the basis that it reduces the cost of military manpower and distributes the burden of providing the nation's defense more equitably, in reality it does neither. In real resources expended, a selective service draft is far more costly than a volunteer military. All a selective service draft does is to hide these costs from public view.

In regard to equity, the problems are perhaps even more severe. No matter what process for selecting young men for service has been used in the past, or can be envisioned for the future, the burden of providing the nation's defense has always fallen disproportionately on the less affluent. So long as there is an incentive to avoid conscription—and there always will be under a draft—individuals will try. And the ones who succeed are likely to be the ones with the most to gain—that is, the most affluent. The main difference between a volunteer force and a conscripted one, then, is not in who serves, for there will be little difference in this regard. Rather, the difference between them is that the AVF, in paying a "fair" wage, does not discriminate against the poor the way that the draft did.

In short, a volunteer military is not only more efficient than a selective service draft, it is also more equitable. Further, it removes the worry about designing an alternative service program for conscientious objectors, about finding and prosecuting draft offenders, about resolving the arbitrariness of deferments and exemptions. If half the effort that had gone into these concerns during the postwar draft had gone into making the volunteer force itself work better today, perhaps the present debate would not be taking place.

For all this, it is possible to envision circumstances in which a peacetime selective service draft would be needed. Should such a need arise in the future, the mistakes of the past should be avoided. At a minimum, those actually forced to serve should be paid a "fair" wage, and the draft reforms put in place in the late 1960s should be continued.

There seem, then, to be three options: make the volunteer force work, let it and our military capability erode over time, or enact a selective service draft. Making the AVF work better is the only one of these options that satisfies the three objectives outlined in the introduction: equity, efficiency, and national security.

Notes

1. See Richard V. L. Cooper, *Military Manpower and the All-Volunteer Force*, R-1458-ARPA (Santa Monica, Calif.: Rand Corp., September 1979).

2. For the full text of Taft's speech (delivered in September 1940 to oppose the Burke-Wadsworth bill, which, for the first time in U.S. history, proposed

peacetime conscription), see Robert A. Taft, "The Anti-Militarist Tradition," *New Individualist Review* 4 (Spring 1967): 43–47.

3. Larry A. Sjaastad and Ronald N. Hansen, "The Conscription Tax: An Empirical Analysis," in *Studies Prepared for the President's Commission on an All-Volunteer Armed Force* (Washington, D.C.: Government Printing Office, 1970).

4. For a fascinating account of some of these stories, see Lawrence M. Baskir and William A. Strauss, *Chance and Circumstance: The Draft, the War, and the Vietnam Generation* (New York: Alfred A. Knopf, 1978).

5. See Thomas E. Borcherding, "A Neglected Social Cost of a Volunteer Force," *American Economic Review* 61 (March 1971).

6. See Richard V. L. Cooper, *The Social Cost of Maintaining a Military Labor Force* (Santa Monica, Calif.: Rand Corp., 1975).

7. Baskir and Strauss, *Chance and Circumstance*, p. 5.

8. Sjaastad and Hansen, "The Conscription Tax," passim.

XXVI

SERVING IN THE RANKS: CITIZENSHIP AND THE ALL-VOLUNTEER FORCE

Charles C. Moskos, Jr.

Since January 1973, the United States has sought to accomplish what it has never attempted before: to maintain 2 million persons on active duty on a completely voluntary basis. Now into its seventh year, the All-Volunteer Force has been analyzed in a seemingly endless series of studies and reports. The commentators tend to divide into two groups. On the one side, there are those who convey their belief that the All-Volunuteer Force has been generally successful. On the other, there are those who see little prospect of a viable defense force short of returning to a form of compulsory military service or registration. I place myself in neither group.

The problems of the All-Volunteer Force are not found in the end of conscription, or in the declining youth cohort of the 1980s, or in the efforts of service recruiters (who have accomplished a task of immense proportions). The grievous flaw has been a redefinition of military service in terms of the economic marketplace and the cash-work nexus. The redefining process was given powerful expression by the 1970 President's Commission on the All-Volunteer Force—the Gates Commission.[1] It is a theme that recurs in officially sponsored assessments of the All-Volunteer Force.[2] This has contributed to moving the American military away from an institutional format to one more and more resembling that of an occupation. It has corroded the standard that military participation ought be a citizen duty.

This paper focuses on that component of the All-Volunteer Force that relied most directly on the draft—the enlisted ranks of the Army. The draft was also the major impetus for recruitment into reserve and guard units. It is important to stress, moreover, that all services were beneficiaries of the Selective Service System. It is estimated that about 40 percent of all voluntary accessions into the military in the peacetime years between the wars in Korea and Vietnam were draft-motivated. Nevertheless, it is the enlisted ranks of the Army, the largest of the services, where the outcomes of all-volunteer recruitment have become most evident.

Let me state at the outset that it is a great exaggeration to characterize the all-volunteer Army as being in a state of crisis. The Army of the late 1970s, by many indicators, whether unit effectiveness, disciplinary rates, or race relations, is noticeably improved over the Army of the early 1970s. To place the all-volunteer experience in a more balanced light, however, it would be better to use the immediate pre-Vietnam period as a benchmark rather than 1970–73, the worst years in modern Army history. Furthermore, as the information to be presented will show, enlistment of an Army primarily based on marketplace competition most likely cannot ensure a sufficient number of qualified entrants and may well have a corrosive effect on service integrity. To raise questions as to the future viability of the all-volunteer force, however, is not to advocate restoration of conscription. The choices before us are not limited to tinkering with the all-volunteer status quo, on the one hand, or bringing back the draft, on the other.

The plan of this study is straightforward. First, data from the end of the draft through 1979 are given on the social background of the Army enlisted ranks. Whenever possible, comparable data are presented from the early 1960s in order to assess demographic trends over two peacetime periods. Second, there is a discussion of the issue of "representativeness" and how this relates to soldierly performance. Third and finally, in an effort to counterbalance prevailing econometric analyses of the All-Volunteer Force, military service in the ranks is linked to broader questions of citizen participation and national service.

Manning the Force, and Social Composition

The most obvious effect of the shift to the All-Volunteer Force has been the marked decline in active-duty strength, from over 2.6 million in the peacetime period of the early 1960s to slightly over a million in 1979. Even at the declining force levels since the end of the draft, the armed services have been hard pressed to recruit every year some 350,000 to 400,000 enlisted persons.

The Army has been recruiting between 150,000 and 200,000 enlisted persons annually since 1973, of whom over 80 percent have been non-prior-service (NPS) males. From 1974 through 1978, Army recruitment achievements met or were close to recruitment goals. (The overall size of the Army, however, has been reduced from an active-duty strength of over 900,000 in the early 1960s to 759,000 at the end of 1979.) But in 1979 the Army fell short of its enlistment objectives by more than 16,000 recruits. This was also the year in which all services, for the first time, experienced recruitment shortfalls.

Since the advent of the All-Volunteer Force there has been a precipitous drop in Army reserve components and the Individual Ready Reserve, or IRR (soldiers with prior military training who are available for replacement requirements during the early days of a war). Depending upon how the data are presented, the IRR in 1979 was between 200,000 and 500,000 below required levels. Thus debate on the All-Volunteer Force has come to include questions of the quantity of soldiers joining the active-duty and reserve forces as well as the more controversial issue of the "quality" of entering soldiers.

Although recruitment objectives in the active-duty Army have generally been achieved, excepting 1979, inescapable demographic constraints appear on the immediate horizon. In 1980 some 2.13 million males will reach age 18. This figure will drop to 1.8 million by 1985 and 1.7 million by 1990. Inasmuch as the recruitment pool consists overwhelmingly of NPS males, this is the group with which most of the ensuing discussion will deal. The increasing role of women in the all-volunteer Army will also draw our attention.

Educational Levels

Examination of trends in educational background show major differences between the services. The Air Force has the highest proportion of high school graduates, the Army the lowest, with the Navy and Marine Corps in between. These gross data do not, however, fully describe effective trends. During the all-volunteer period, the data include the increased number of females, virtually all of whom are high school graduates, who are, for practical purposes, excluded from combat. (Starting in late 1979, the Army began to recruit females who do not possess a high school diploma.) One must also be cognizant of the tremendous pressures on service recruiters to meet goals and the probability that at least a few have falsified educational credentials of recruits. Thus, if anything, the officially reported educational levels of recruits may overstate the actual number of high school graduates. There are, moreover, studies showing that among high school graduates who do enter the military, the tendency is to come from the lower levels of their graduating class, especially for those entering the Army.[3]

By reanalysis of available data, it is possible to highlight the realities of Army recruitment. The educational levels of male enlistees in the all-Volunteer Army are markedly lower than either the equivalent civilian population or the Army entrants of 1964, the last peacetime year before the war in Vietnam. (Because of higher draft calls, educational levels of

TABLE 1

EDUCATIONAL LEVELS OF ARMY MALE ENTRANTS
(Non-prior-service)

Educational Level	1964 Draftees	1964 Enlistees	FY 1975	FY 1976
Some college	17.2%	13.9%	5.7%	4.1%
High school graduate	54.1	46.2	48.6	51.5
Non-high school graduate*	28.7	39.9	45.7	44.4
Total	100.0%	100.0%	100.0%	100.0%
Number	151,194	108,303	165,610	164,291

	FY 1977	FY 1978	FY 1979	18- to 19-Year-Old Males (1978)
Some college	5.1%	4.5%	3.2%	40.1%
High school graduate	51.1	65.5	55.4	39.9
Non-high school Graduate*	43.8	30.0	41.4	20.0
Total	100.0%	100.0%	100.0%	100.0%
Number	153,434	106,512	112,088	3,464,000†

SOURCE: Accession data from Department of the Army statistics. Civilian data from U.S. Bureau of the Census, *Current Population Reports*, P-20, No. 335.

* Includes General Equivalency Diploma (GED).
† 511,000 enrolled in high school not included.

Army accessions increased during the Vietnam War period.) As reported in Table 1, 41.4 percent of NPS males in fiscal year 1979 did not possess a high school diploma, in comparison with 20 percent of 18- to 19-year-old males in the general population, and 28.7 percent of draftees and 39.9 percent of enlistees in 1964. The contract between the educational levels of the all-volunteer Army and the peacetime draft Army is more noteworthy when placed in the context of the overall increase for male high school graduates, aged 18 to 24 years, in the United States: from 66 percent in 1964 to 83 percent in 1978.[4] Thus while national trends have been toward a higher percentage of high school graduates, Army accessions have been moving in the opposite direction.

The data in Table 1 also reveal an even sharper decline in the proportion of Army entrants with some college between the pre- and post-Vietnam periods. Whereas 17.2 percent of the draftees and 13.9 percent of the enlistees in 1964 had some college, the corresponding figure in the all-volunteer Army has been around 4 percent. This contrasts with 40 percent of 18- to 19-year-old males who matriculated at the college level in 1978.

Racial Composition

The rising proportion of black entrants has generated more heat than any other topic in the debate on the All-Volunteer Force. This topic has been particularly sensitive with regard to the Army enlisted ranks. In the early 1960s, blacks accounted for about 12 percent of Army enlisted entrants, a figure corresponding with the black share of the 18 to 24 age group in the total population. During most of the war years in Vietnam, blacks made up about 15 percent of Army accessions. Since the advent of the all-volunteer Army, the proportion of black entrants has tripled over pre-Vietnam levels. As shown in Table 2, black accessions reached 36 percent of NPS males in 1979 (42 percent for females). Although the number of other minorities is not as reliably tabulated, an increasing number of Hispanics has also been entering the all-volunteer Army. That well over 40 percent of those now entering the Army's enlisted ranks are from minority groups would be a reasonable estimate.

Within the enlisted ranks racial content varies by branch and career management field. The following figures are drawn from 1979 Army statistical data. Black membership in the infantry is 30.6 percent. Thus, it cannot be stated that blacks are overrepresented in the combat arms in terms of total enlisted blacks. Of course, blacks are overly proportionate in the combat arms in relation to their numbers in American society, but this is because whites are underrepresented in the all-volunteer Army. Within the Army, however, it is in support units where racial imbalance is most clearly evident. Blacks tend to be concentrated in low-skill fields: 57.1 percent in petroleum handling, 46.8 percent in supply, and 45.1 percent in wire maintenance. Whites, on the other hand, are disproportionately found in such high-skill fields as intercept equipment, signal intelligence, aviation, and electronics.

The changing racial composition of the Army is shown in Table 3. Blacks made up 11.8 percent of enlisted personnel in 1964, 17.5 percent in 1972, and 31.3 percent in 1979. Even at senior noncom levels (E7–E9), blacks are considerably better represented in 1979 than at any earlier time. The proportion of black noncoms can be expected to increase further owing to the black reenlistment rate being 1.6 times greater than that of whites. Blacks can be expected to play an increasingly positive role in the NCO corps. Blacks continue to be underrepresented in the officer corps at all levels, although the direction of change is toward greater black participation. Army projections are for black officer entrants to reach 20 percent by the end of 1980. Whether this goal will be achieved remains to be seen, but there certainly has been a sharp rise in newly commissioned black officers since the start of the all-volunteer Army.

It is important to stress that the trend toward increasing black content in the Army predates the All-Volunteer Force. The rising percentage of blacks operates somewhat independently of the end of conscription and can be attributed in part to the dramatic increase in the proportion of

TABLE 2

PERCENTAGE OF BLACKS AMONG ARMY ENLISTEES, MALE AND FEMALE
(Non-prior-service)

Fiscal Year	Male	Female
1973	20.9	18.9
1974	27.9	19.1
1975	23.3	19.3
1976	24.9	18.2
1977	30.1	21.5
1978	34.9	30.3
1979*	36.1	42.2

SOURCE: Department of the Army statistics.
*First three quarters.

TABLE 3

PERCENTAGE OF BLACKS IN THE ARMY BY GRADE

	1964	1972	1979
Officers:			
O-7 and above	—	1.8	4.6
O-6	0.2	1.5	4.4
O-5	1.1	5.3	5.2
O-4	3.5	5.0	4.6
O-3	5.1	3.9	6.9
O-2	3.6	3.4	9.5
O-1	2.6	2.2	10.0
Warrant	2.8	4.5	5.9
Total officers	3.3	3.9	7.0
Enlisted:			
E-9	3.3	8.6	18.2
E-8	5.8	14.4	23.0
E-7	7.9	19.9	25.2
E-6	12.2	23.9	22.2
E-5	14.8	16.9	27.9
E-4	12.5	14.1	32.5
E-3	11.9	16.7	36.3
E-2	11.6	18.5	38.3
E-1	6.4	18.4	36.3
Total Enlisted	11.8	17.4	31.3

SOURCE: Department of the Army statistics.

blacks eligible for military service, specifically, the increasing number of black high school graduates and the larger percentage of blacks placing in the upper levels of the mental aptitude tests required for service entry.[5] There is also the combined push of the astoundingly high unemployment rate among black youth and the pull of an institution that has gone further than any other to attack racism.

Race and Education

It is a well-recognized fact that the educational levels of blacks in America have trailed far behind that of whites. The trend, however, has been toward a narrowing of the gap. Among males 18–19 years of age in 1967, for example, 30.7 percent of blacks, as compared with 15.4 percent of whites, had not completed high school. By 1977, the high school dropout rate for blacks had declined to 23.8 percent while the rate for whites *increased* to 17.0 percent.[6] Still, even for the more recent period, black educational attainment falls below that of whites.

Contrary to national patterns, however, the intersect of race and education is quite different among male entrants in the all-volunteer Army. Since the end of the draft, the proportion of black high school graduates entering the Army has exceeded that of whites, and this is a trend that is becoming more pronounced. In 1979, as shown in Table 4, high school graduates accounted for 65 percent of entering blacks, as compared with 54 percent of entering whites. In fact, today's Army enlisted ranks is the only major arena in American society where black educational levels surpass those of whites, and by quite a significant margin!

What may be happening in the all-voluntary Army, I suggest, is something like the following. Whereas the black soldier is fairly representative of the black community in education and social background, white entrants of recent years are coming from the least educated sectors of the white community. My stays with Army line units also leave the distinct impression that many of our young enlisted white soldiers are coming from nonmetropolitan areas. I am even more impressed by what I do not often find in line units: urban and suburban white soldiers of middle-class background. In other words, the all-volunteer Army is attracting not only a disproportionate number of minorities, but also an unrepresentative segment of white youth, who, if anything, are even more uncharacteristic of the broader social mix than are our minority soldiers.

Women

Perhaps no change in the makeup of the all-volunteer force has received as much media attention as the growing numbers and role of woman soldiers. An argument could be made that it has been the sharp rise in female entrants (virtually all of whom through mid-1979 were high school graduates) that has been the margin of success in the all-volunteer Army. As given in Table 5, the proportion of women in the enlisted ranks climbed from 0.9 percent in 1964 to 7.6 percent in 1979. Table 6 shows that females accounted for about one in seven of all enlisted accessions in 1978 and 1979. Thus the Army seems well on its way toward the goal of a 10 percent female enlisted force by the early 1980s.

The increasing utilization of women in the all-volunteer Army is an indisputable fact. Starting in the early 1970s virtually every occupational specialty except those in the combat arms has been opened up to women. There has also been a steady elimination of discriminatory practices: in 1971, the Army lifted its ban on the enlistment of married women; in 1973, a Supreme Court decision required that married women in the military get the same family allowances that married men have long received; in 1975, the Army dropped its policy of discharging women soldiers who became mothers; in 1976, the minimum 18-year-old enlistment age for women was lowered to 17, the same as that for men; and in 1979, the Army announced it would accept female high school dropouts, again the same as for men.

The crux of the issue remains the prohibition of women in the combat arms. Congressional statute presently bans women from duty on combat aircraft and ships, a principle that has been codified into Army regulations pertaining to exclusion of females from the ground combat arms. A

TABLE 4

PERCENTAGE OF HIGH SCHOOL GRADUATES AMONG ARMY ENLISTEES BY RACE
(non-prior-service males)

Fiscal Year	Black	White
1975	59	53
1976	63	53
1977	65	53
1978	76	65
1979	65	54

SOURCE: Department of the Army statistics.

removal of the ban cannot be viewed as a solution to all-volunteer recruitment. There are already indications that the available pool of highly qualified women is being tapped close to its maximum. More important, it is highly unlikely, to say the least, that women will show any greater

TABLE 5

PERCENTAGE OF FEMALES IN THE ARMY BY GRADE

Fiscal Year	Officers	Enlisted
1964	3.4	0.9
1973	3.7	2.4
1975	4.9	6.1
1977	5.7	6.7
1979	6.4	7.6

SOURCE: Department of the Army statistics.

TABLE 6

FEMALE PROPORTION OF ARMY ENLISTEES

Year	Percentage Female
1973	4.5
1974	7.7
1975	9.1
1976	8.0
1977	8.2
1978	14.0
1979	13.2

SOURCE: Department of the Army statistics.

eagerness than men to join the combat arms.

Yet, for sure, there is a certain fraction of Army enlisted women who are capable and willing to be assigned to combat units. But to allow women the choice of whether or not to volunteer for the combat arms would lead men to ask for the same prerogatives—including the option not to serve in the combat area. If regulations were changed so that women could be compelled to serve in the combat arms, as is presently the case for men, the result would almost certainly be a sharp drop in the number of women who would volunteer to join the Army in the first instance. It is this conundrum, as well as considerable normative and organizational obstacles, that preclude the utilization of women in the combat arms.

Given the pressures of recruitment in the all-volunteer era, it is understandable that the Department of Defense has moved to greater reliance on female personnel. But, in all likelihood, further utilization of enlisted females in "nontraditional" tasks even outside the combat arms will be increasingly difficult in the years ahead. Already attrition rates for females, as shown in Table 7, greatly exceed those of males of like educational level. It is estimated that 1 in 9 enlisted women is pregnant in any time period, and 1 in 11 heads a single-parent family (compared with 1 in 50 among male soldiers). Such considerations can only plague realistic plans for military mobilization and deployment. Moreover, the 1979 decision to accept female recruits who do not possess a high school diploma can only aggravate the ongoing difficulties of incorporation of women into the military.[7]

TABLE 7

ATTRITION RATES OF MALE AND FEMALE SOLDIERS
(Fiscal year 1976 entrants)

| | Percent Attriting before 30 Months of Service | |
	Male	Female
All enlisted personnel	36.8	40.7
High school graduates only	27.1	39.1

SOURCE: Department of the Army statistics.

Marital Status

Though usually uncommented upon by students of all-volunteer trends, there has been a significant change in the marital composition of the junior enlisted force in the Army. From 1964 to 1978, the proportion of enlisted marrieds at the pay grade E-4, the modal junior enlisted pay grade, increased from 25.3 percent to 41.4 percent, an increase dating only since the end of the draft in 1973. Today just about every major military base in the United States is ringed by trailer camps or shoddy apartment complexes where many of the young enlisted marrieds live an existence close to the poverty line, a condition that exacerbates what are often already unstable family lives. In Germany, young Army couples living "on the economy" face cultural isolation as well as financial distress. The new phenomenon of intraservice marriages in the enlisted ranks has hardly been acknowledged, much less assessed for its effect on organizational readiness.

The change in the marital composition of the enlisted ranks runs directly counter to national trends. Table 8 summarizes some of the relevant data. From 1967 to 1977, the median age of white males at first marriage increased by one year, and the number of never-married men in the age bracket 20–24 years rose from 53.0 to 62.3 percent. An anomaly is evident, however. The number of never-marrieds between ages 17 and 19 actually decreased slightly in recent years.

The anomaly revealed by the census data on marriage rates—generally later marriages coexisting with an increase in marriages among 17- to 19-year-olds—is striking because it parallels the previously described census data that indicate generally rising educational levels accompanied by an increase in the high school drop out rate for 18- to 19-year-old white males. These anomalies in the census data suggest, in effect, that we now have

TABLE 8

MARITAL STATUS OF WHITE AMERICAN MALES

Year	Median Age at First Marriage	Percent Never Married Ages 17–19	Percent Never Married Ages 20–24
1967	23.0	97.4	53.0
1977	24.1	97.1	62.3

SOURCE: U.S. Bureau of the Census, *Current Population Reports*, P-20, Nos. 170 and 323.

two quite different youth groups within the white population. One group, the numerical majority with middle-class origins or aspirations, is characterized by increasing educational attainment and later marriage. The other group, with declining educational levels and propensity to enter early marriages, seems headed toward a marginal position in regard to both class and culture. It is from this latter white group, along with racial minorities, that the all-volunteer Army has been overrecruiting.

Service Differences

The Army, of course, is not the only service competing for qualified people in the all-volunteer era. It suffers, moreover, by being identified, according to youth surveys, as the least attractive service by those high school males who are most qualified for military service. The Army then starts out as the most handicapped service in the recruitment effort. This state of affairs is reflected in a comparison of the average proportion of high school graduates among NPS male entrants since 1973; about 90 percent for the Air Force, 70 percent for the Navy, 65 percent for the Marine Corps, and less than 60 percent for the Army.

All the services, with the partial exception of the Air Force, have encountered recruitment difficulties since the end of the draft. More telling, each of the services has experienced shockingly high attrition rates. Between 30 and 40 percent of service members do not complete their initial enlistments and, instead, are discharged for disciplinary problems, personality disorders, or job ineptitude. The majority of these losses occur six months after service entry. In some ways it may be the all-volunteer Navy that is confronting the most severe problem. Recruiters publicly bemoan that many high school graduates seeking to join the Navy simply cannot read at acceptable levels. Moreover, the Navy's desertion rate in the late 1970s was higher than in any previous time in its modern history, including the Vietnam War period. The Marine Corps has adopted a deliberate policy of accepting recruitment shortfalls and reductions in authorized strength in order to maintain the quality of its recruits. The Air Force continues to remain the best situated of the services in enlisted recruitment, perhaps because its enlisted force is essentially precluded from direct combat roles. Yet in 1979, even the Air Force saw the proportion of high school graduates among NPS males drop below 80 percent for the first time.

Whatever the all-volunteer parallels between the Army and the other services may be, it is the Army's social composition that most contrasts with its pre-Vietnam form. Certainly the lower ranks of the peacetime Army between the wars in Korea and Vietnam were never a mirror image of America's class system. It is undeniable, however, that the all-volunteer

Army is much less representative of the American middle class than was the pre-Vietnam Army. Whether or not this speaks to the success or failure of the all-volunteer Army is a separate issue. But there can be no question that since 1973 the Army has undergone a metamorphosis in its enlisted membership. The real question is how high-powered commissions and well-financed DOD studies come up with the opposite conclusion.[8]

Is a Representative Enlisted Force Desirable?

It is incontrovertible that the enlisted ranks of the all-volunteer Army are much less representative of middle-class youth than the peacetime draft Army. It is, however, another kind of question whether this is good, bad, or irrelevant.

The clearest and strongest evidence bearing upon the effects of social background or soldierly performance deals with enlisted attrition.[9] One of the main presumptions of the Gates Commission was that, with longer-term enlistments and professionally committed soldiers, there would be less personnel turnover than in a military system that was heavily dependent upon draftees and draft-motivated volunteers. This has turned out not to be the case. Personnel turnover has increased at such a pace that the All-Volunteer Force is becoming something of a revolving door for many of its entrants. Seven years after the end of conscription, the Army, along with the other armed services, is confronting an unacceptably high rate of enlistees who do not complete their first term of service

The striking finding in all available data is that high school graduates are twice more likely than high school dropouts to complete their enlistments. More revealing, this finding is virtually unchanged when mental aptitude is held constant. High school graduates from the lower aptitude levels are actually much more likely to finish their tours than high school dropouts in the higher aptitude levels. Supplementary data that make black-white breakdowns indicate that overall attrition rates between the races are comparable, with the exception that blacks in the lower aptitude levels do better than their white counterparts.[10]

Other measures of soldierly performance, such as enlisted productivity and low disciplinary actions, show precisely the same correlates as found for attrition rates.[11] High school graduates significantly outperform high school dropouts. Possession of a high schol diploma, it seems, reflects the acquisition of social traits (work habits, punctuality, self-discipline) that make for a more successful military experience. The conclusion is inescapable. The all-volunteer Army would be better served by attracting more high school graduates or, even better, college-bound youth, to gain a more representative cross section of American young men.

Despite the overwhelming evidence that the higher the quality, the better is soldierly performance in the aggregate, it is too frequently argued that there are many manual tasks for which bright soldiers are less suited than the not-so-bright. One Congressman has seriously proposed that the services recruit more heavily from the less intelligent precisely in order to fill menial jobs.[12] This assertion has the apparent attraction of making a virtue out of a perceived necessity. But it is patently contradicted by the facts. The evidence is unambiguous that on measures of enlisted productivity, higher educated soldiers do better in low-skill jobs as well as in high-skill jobs.[13]

Most of the discussion about representativeness has centered on the racial content of the all-volunteer Army. As noted earlier, the rise in black content reflects both the large increase in the proportion of blacks eligible for military service and the unprecedentedly high unemployment rates among black youth in the 1970s. Nevertheless, to look at the racial composition of the Army solely in terms of social forces impinging on and internal to the black community ought not to foreclose attention on the participation—or, really, the lack of it—of the larger white middle-class population. To what degree the changing racial composition of the Army also reflects white reluctance to join a truly integrated system is unknown. I am unpersuaded that any significant number of middle-class whites—or middle-class any race, for that matter—would be more likely to join the Army, under present recruitment incentives, even if the Army were not disproportionately black. Yet it would be a setback of historic proportions if the Army were to back away from racial integration under the guise of equal opportunity.

The military has always recruited large numbers of youth, white and black, who had no real alternative job prospects. The recently advanced view that the armed forces ought to be an outlet for otherwise unemployed youth, while seemingly persuasive in the short term, is deceptive on several grounds. It fails to take into account the preponderance of disadvantaged youth in low-skill enlisted jobs that have marginal, if any, transferability to civilian employment. Moreover, with such a large proportion of volunteers—white and black—failing to complete their enlistments, the All-Volunteer Force is producing large numbers of what are, in effect, two-time losers. Each soldier who drops out or is forced out of the military is a personal matter. But if the attrition rate begins to overtake the success rate, we have to wonder not about what has gone wrong with a specific soldier but about what is happening to the military institution.

Rather than regarding the military as part of the marketplace with its attendant social tracking in the economy, it would be better to redistribute less advantaged soldiers into positions requiring extended literacy and skill training along with a correspondingly longer commitment, and, at the same time, to draw middle-class youth into low-skill occupations where short enlistments are most practical. The military, however, will continue to draw disproportionately from young blacks as long as they are victims of certain structural defects in the national economy—specifically, the steady flow of manufacturing jobs away from cities where so many poor blacks are trapped.

The rising minority content in the Army actually masks a more pervasive shift in the social class bases of the lower enlisted ranks. From the 1940s through the mid-1960s, the military served as a bridging environment between entering low-status youth and eventual middle-class employment.[14] Whatever successes the military had as a remedial organization for deprived youth were largely due to the armed forces being legitimated on other than overt welfare grounds, such as national defense, citizenship obligation, even manly honor.[15] In other words, those very conditions peculiar to the armed forces that serve to resocialize poverty youth toward productive ends depend directly upon the military not being defined as a welfare agency or an employer of last resort. Present trends toward labeling the Army as a recourse for America's underclasses are self-defeating for the youth involved precisely because they directly counter the premise that military participation is one of broadly based national service.

By no means does being middle class necessarily make one braver or more able. There are many outstanding soldiers in the all-volunteer Army who have modest educational attainments. But our concern must also be with the chemistry of unit cohesion, which requires an optimum blend of talents and backgrounds. The distinctive quality of the enlisted experience starting with World War II was the mixing of the social classes and, starting with the Korean War, the integration of the races. This gave poor youth an opportunity to test themselves, often successfully, against more privileged youth. Such enforced leveling of persons from different social backgrounds had no parallel in any other existing institution in American society. This was the elemental social fact underlying enlisted service. This state of affairs began to diminish during the Vietnam War when the college-educated avoided service; it has all but disappeared in the all-volunteer Army.

One of the crucial aspects of combat groups is the effect of social composition on combat performance. A summary of years of research stated that level of schooling was the strongest predictor of effective combat performance.[16] Studies for the Army during the Korean War also show that educational background is positively correlated with combat effectiveness.[17] All such evidence serves to confirm the observations of commanders and noncoms from the draft period of the importance of college-educated members in enriching the skill level and commitment of military units, in peace as well as in war. These observations are to be placed in the context of recent studies that show all-volunteer soldiers displaying levels of alienation far exceeding those of the contemporary youth population or of World War II soldiers.[18]

From a historical standpoint, the evidence is also clear that military participation and combat risks in World War II were more equally shared by American men than in either the Korean or the Vietnam War.[19] The draft per se is thus no guarantee that military participation will ensure class equity. In fact, soldiers in World War II reflected a higher socioeconomic background than that of the general population. On the other hand, a careful study of Vietnam War casualties documents that low social class (not race!) was the factor most responsible for the higher casualties suffered by segments of American society in that war.[20] It is informative that both supporters and critics of the American military concur that at least some of the deterioration of American troop behavior in the Vietnam War was due to the accurate perceptions of lower-ranking enlisted men that the sacrifices of war were not being equally shared.

In the post-Vietnam context, if U.S. forces are to fulfill their function of military deterrence, representational concerns are still germane This is not to argue that the makeup of the enlisted ranks be perfectly calibrated to the social composition of the larger society, but it is to ask what kind of society excuses its privileged from serving in the ranks of its Army. It is a social reality that the combat arms will never draw disproportionately from middle- and upper-class youth. But to foster policies that accentuate the tracking of lower-class youth into such assignments is perverse. If participation of persons coming from minority or blue-collar background in military leadership positions is used as a measure of democratic character, it is even more important that participation of more advantaged groups in the Army's rank and file also be a measure of representational democracy.

Serving in the Ranks of the All-Volunteer Army

The time is ready to reassess our stock of knowledge concerning the all-volunteer Army. Such a reassessment must be based on clear analysis of seven years of experience and future probabilities. It ought not be constrained by policy alternatives—the economic model versus a return to conscription—that dominate the debate on the All-Volunteer Force. What considerations must be raised in determining who should serve and what kind of an enlisted force is desirable? What are the relations between citizen participation and national security? Econometrically based analyses tend not to ask these kinds of questions, but we must.

Let us summarize the discussion up to this point. The all-volunteer Army has its difficulties but it is working. In comparison with the peacetime draft, however, today's Army is much less representative—and becoming increasingly so—of American youth. Accompanying major demographic changes, there has been a shift away from organizational factors conducive to an institutional framework toward one more resembling that of an occupation. A more representative force will have beneficial consequences for the Army in terms of military effectiveness, enlisted life in the ranks, and civic definition.

Present and anticipated difficulties of recruiting an all-volunteer Army have led to renewed talk of restoring conscription. This possibility is viewed as remote. A return to the draft would pose anew the question of who serves when most do not serve. Under present manpower requirements, less than one in four males would be drafted or otherwise serve in the military. (If women were to be drafted, the proportion of youth serving would, of course, be only one in eight.) One of the key factors that operated favorably for the peacetime draft during the 1950s was that, because of the small youth cohort (the maturing "Depression babies"), over three-quarters of eligible men served in the military. This fostered a legitimization of the peacetime draft. In actuality, a higher proportion of men were drafted in the 1950s than during the Vietnam War.[21]

To have a workable conscription also requires a national consensus of its need, especially within the relevant youth population. Such a consensus does not presently exist (see Tables 9 and 10). A 1979 Gallup poll reported that the draft was opposed by a three to one margin among those aged 18 to 24 years.[22] Induction would likely lead to turbulence on many college campuses. It might well result in troop discipline problems exceeding what the Army could accommodate. If compulsion is used, moreover, many will attempt to avoid military service, which will lead to further problems. Practical as well as political considerations foreclose the draft as a real alternative in the foreseeable future.

Another option, and it is one that will be increasingly mentioned in the near future, is to reduce considerably the size of the force.[23] Such an alternative, however, would only further reduce an already severely reduced force. Unless accompanied by a major retrenchment of America's defense commitments, such a resolution of all-volunteer problems would only compound the already "hyper" atmosphere of military units in which too few people are charged with too many tasks. A major reduction in force levels accompanied by a redefinition of America's military purpose deserves consideration. At the present time, however, it runs counter to the growing sentiment for an increase in military capabilities. In any event, whether the military force is large or small, it must answer the test question: Is this the best we can have?

Granting conscription is not feasible and a major reduction in the force is not in the offing, what about management steps that could be taken to improve manpower utilization within the all-volunteer framework? Here we run into the difficulty that most proposals in this vein—a kind of sub-optimal approach—do not address the core issue: getting young qualified men into the combat arms.[24] Neither lowering physical or mental standards for men, nor increasing the number of women, nor greater reliance on civilian personnel, nor more utilization of older military members suits the imperatives of the combat arms. It is highly questionable that increasing the proportion of women, civilian, or less physically qualified men in support units would result in releasing more soldiers for assignment into the combat arms. What would probably happen is that the all-volunteer Army would experience even greater problems among its male soldiers than presently exist.

Underlying many of the difficulties in the all-volunteer Army is a source of enlisted discontent that had no counterpart in the peacetime draft era. This is what I term postentry disillusionment. In all-volunteer recruitment, a consistent theme—out of necessity, to be sure—has been the self-serving aspects of military life, notably, what the service can do for the recruit in the way of training in skills transferable to civilian jobs. The irreconcilable dilemma is that many military assignments (by no means exclusively in the combat arms) do not and cannot have transferability to civilian occupations. And it is precisely in such military assignments that recruitment shortfalls, attrition, and desertion are most likely to occur.

Large raises in military pay for lower enlisted personnel, a central Gates Commission recommendation, have been cited as the principal rationale to induce persons to join the All-Volunteer Force. But this has turned out to be a double-edged sword. Youth surveys show that pay motivates less-qualified youth (for example, high school dropouts, those with poor grades) to join the armed services while having a negligible effect on college-bound youth (see Tables 9 and 10).[25] To use salary incentives as the primary motivating force to join and remain in the military can also lead to grave morale problems. If future military pay raises were to lag behind civilian scales, as now seems likely, the present grumbling that throughout the career force is now limited to perceived erosion of benefits would then become a rumbling chorus of complaint. An occupational model of the armed forces turns service members into "employees," with the recent talk of military unionization as a natural by-product.

The central issue remains: Is there a way without direct compulsion or

TABLE 9

COLLEGE STUDENT ATTITUDES TOWARD MILITARY SERVICE, PAY, AND EDUCATIONAL BENEFITS: MALES (in Percent)

	Strongly Favor	Somewhat Favor	Undecided	Somewhat Oppose	Strongly Oppose	Total (N = 146)
Return to the draft	2.1	12.3	8.9	24.0	52.7	100.0%
Draft registration	13.0	44.6	12.3	17.8	12.3	100.0%
If draft includes women	23.3	32.9	12.3	16.4	15.1	100.0%
USA more military power than any other nation	21.2	41.8	14.4	15.8	6.8	100.0%
Require 2 years of national service	11.0	28.1	8.9	20.5	31.5	100.0%

	Very Likely	Somewhat Likely	Undecided	Somewhat Unlikely	Very Unlikely	Total (N = 146)
Will join Army	—	—	—	7.5	92.5	100.0%
Will join Army, $1,000 monthly	—	1.4	0.7	13.0	84.9	100.0%
Will join Army, $2,500 monthly	1.4	10.3	6.8	28.1	53.4	100.0%
Will join Army, $5,000 monthly	12.3	28.8	8.2	20.5	30.2	100.0%
Will join Army, 2 years tuition + $500 monthly	2.1	19.2	13.0	24.7	41.0	100.0%
Will join Army, 4 years tuition + $500 monthly	12.3	22.6	20.5	15.8	28.8	100.0%

Data collected at Northwestern University, Evanston, Illinois, December 3, 1979, by Charles C. Moskos, Jr.

TABLE 10

COLLEGE STUDENT ATTITUDES TOWARD MILITARY SERVICE, PAY, AND EDUCATIONAL BENEFITS: FEMALES (in Percent)

	Strongly Favor	Somewhat Favor	Undecided	Somewhat Oppose	Strongly Oppose	Total (N = 151)
Return to the draft	1.3	15.2	7.3	34.5	41.7	100.0%
Draft registration	15.2	45.7	11.3	18.5	9.3	100.0%
If draft includes women	13.2	32.5	9.9	11.9	32.5	100.0%
USA more military power than any other nation	15.2	45.7	14.6	20.5	4.0	100.0%
Require 2 years of national service	7.3	34.4	7.9	25.2	25.2	100.0%

	Very Likely	Somewhat Likely	Undecided	Somewhat Unlikely	Very Unlikely	Total (N = 151)
Will join Army	—	—	2.0	7.3	90.7	100.0%
Will join Army, $1,000 monthly	2.0	2.0	3.3	14.6	78.1	100.0%
Will join Army, $2,500 monthly	4.0	13.9	7.3	25.1	49.7	100.0%
Will join Army, $5,000 monthly	15.2	27.2	8.6	19.9	29.1	100.0%
Will join Army, 2 years tuition + $500 monthly	5.3	31.1	11.9	19.2	32.5	100.0%
Will join Army, 4 years tuition + $500 monthly	20.5	30.5	11.3	11.9	25.8	100.0%

Data collected at Northwestern University, Evanston, Illinois, December 3, 1979, by Charles C. Moskos, Jr.

excessive reliance on cash inducements by which a cross section of young men can be attracted into the combat arms and related tasks? Or, to put it differently, is there a way we can obtain the analogue of the peacetime draftee in the all-volunteer era? I believe there is.

One step would be a two-year enlistment option (the term of the draftee) to be restricted to the combat arms, low-skill shipboard duty, aircraft security guards, and labor-intensive jobs. The quid pro quo for such assignment would be generous postservice educational benefits along the lines of the GI Bill of World War II. This formula—a college education or vocational training in exchange for two years in the combat arms—would be a means to attract highly qualified soldiers who could learn quickly, serve effectively for a full tour, and then be replaced by similarly qualified recruits.[26] Because there would be no presumption of acquiring civilian skills in the military, the terms of such short service would be honest and unambiguous, thus alleviating a major source of postentry discontent in the All-Volunteer Force. The added costs of postservice educational benefits would, at least in part, be balanced by lower attrition, reduced recruitment outlays, the end of combat arms bonuses, and most likely, fewer marrieds among junior enlisted personnel.

To go a step further, the military could set up a two-track personnel system recognizing a distinction between a "citizen soldier" and a "career soldier." ("Soldiers" as used here refer also to sailors, marines, and airmen.) The career soldier would be assigned and compensated in the manner of the prevailing system. The citizen soldier, however, would serve a two-year term in the combat arms or labor-intensive positions with low active-duty pay, few, if any, entitlements, but with deferred compensation in the form of generous postservice educational or vocational training benefits. Such benefits ought to be linked with reserve obligations following active duty. Without extensive reliance on prior-service personnel, there seems to be no way to salvage Army reserve components in the all-volunteer context.

The immediate goal is to break the mind-set that sees the All-Volunteer Force in terms of econometric models. Experience to date has shown that the market system is not the way to recruit an all-volunteer Army. To regard the military as an occupation also raises nagging issues on the future of the armed services in American society. The All-Volunteer Force as presently constituted has come to exclude enlisted participation by those who will be America's future leaders, whether in government, business, or the intellectual and academic communities. Will enlisted service become viewed as a place for those with no other options? Will the career military acquire an increasingly distorted view of American youth and civilian society? Rotating participation of middle-class youth would leaven the enlisted ranks and help reinvigorate the notion of military service as a widely shared citizen's duty. It would prevent labeling the Army as a recourse for dead end youth, a characterization hard to escape, even if unfair, unless enlisted membership reflects a cross section of American youth.

A more broad proposal assumes that the definition of military service needs overhauling as badly as the machinery of selection. Now is the time to consider a voluntary national service program—in which military duty is one of several alternatives—that would be coupled with postservice educational benefits. For purposes of discussion, a two-year national service program aimed at youth—male and female—is proposed.[27] Such service would be expected to take place between school and job, or between school and college, or between college and professional training. Voluntary servers would receive compensation comparable to that given draftees in the pre-Vietnam era: subsistence plus a little spending money. They would be directed toward diverse tasks that are intrinsically unamenable to sheer monetary incentives; caring for the aged falls in this category as well as serving in the combat arms. These are the very kinds of tasks that are probably best performed when not regarded as a long-term commitment. It would certainly be to the advantage of society to have such service performed by lowly paid but motivated youth. In fact, for many in their late teens and early twenties a diversion from the world of school or work would be tolerable and perhaps even welcome.

Congress must attend to governmental policies that undercut the All-Volunteer Force and the notion of citizen service. I refer to the several billion dollars a year spent on assistance given college students in the form of federal grants or loans. It is surprising that, given the current debate on providing governmental relief for middle-class families with children in college, no public figure has thought to tie such student aid to any service obligation on the part of the youths who benefit. It would be philosophically defensible as well as downright practical to hold that any able-bodied young person who did not perform national service, whether civilian or military, would be ineligible for federal student aid.

The overriding strategy is to make governmental subsidies of youth programs consistent with the ideal that citizen obligation ought to become an essential part of growing up in America. The cupboard of those who view military manpower as an exercise in labor economics is bare. It may also be that we must come to a realization that many of the things we need as a nation we can never afford to buy. Such a realization would also clarify the military's role by emphasizing the larger calling of national service.

Notes

1. *The Report of the President's Commission on the All-Volunteer Force*

(Washington, D.C.: Government Printing Office, 1970).

2. Most influential in this regard has been Richard V. L. Cooper, *Military Manpower and the All-Volunteer Force* R-1450-ARPA (Santa Monica, Calif.: Rand Corp., 1977). See also, *America's Volunteers: A Report on the All-Volunteer Armed Forces* (Washington, D.C.: Office of the Assistant Secretary of Defense, 1978).

3. Ralph R. Canter, "Organization Management and the Volunteer Force," paper presented at the Security Issues Symposium, U.S. Army War College, April 17–19, 1978; and John H. Faris, "Adaptation of the All-Volunteer Force," paper presented at a conference sponsored by the Center for Peace, War, and Defense, University of North Carolina, January 22–23, 1976.

4. U.S. Bureau of the Census, *Current Population Reports*, P-20, no. 333.

5. Cooper, *Military Manpower*, pp. 209–216.

6. U.S. Bureau of the Census, *Current Population Reports*, P-20, no. 333.

7. Lest we forget. In January 1943, during World War II, entry standards for women soldiers were lowered to increase enlistments. The resultant problems were so unmanageable that the earlier standards were restored within the year. Mattie E. Treadwell, *The Women's Army Corps*, Special Studies, United States Army in World War II (Washington, D.C.: Office of the Chief of Military History, 1954), pp. 168–190. For a balanced discussion of enlisted women in the All-Volunteer Force, see Cecile S. Landrum, "Role of Women in Today's Military," in *The All-Volunteer Force and American Society*, ed. John B. Keeley (Charlottesville: University of Virginia Press, 1978), pp. 150–165.

8. For example: "There is no evidence to suggest that armed forces are now or are in danger of becoming a 'poor man's Army' " (Defense Manpower Commission, *Defense Manpower: The Keystone of National Security* [Washington, D.C.: Government Printing Office, 1976], p. 167). "The evidence presented here thus shows that the American military has not been nor is it becoming any Army of the poor or the black" (Cooper, *Military Manpower*, p. 231).

9. A good overview of the attrition phenomenon is found in H. Wallace Sinaiko, ed., "First Term Enlisted Attrition," proceedings of a conference held at Leesburg, Virginia, April 4–7, 1977. (Mimeographed)

10. A. J. Martin, "Trends in DOD First-Term Attrition," in ibid., pp. 20–21.

11. On the correlates of formal education and mental aptitude levels on enlisted productivity and disciplinary actions, see Cooper, *Military Manpower*, p. 131.

12. Les Aspin, *Sergeant York Isn't Welcome Anymore* (N.p., n.pub., 1979), p. 8. Another proposal to recruit from the lower mental categories to man purposively menial jobs is found in Robert G. Lockman, "First-Term Success

Predictions for Class A School and General Detail Recruits," Center for Naval Analyses, December 1978.

13. Cooper, *Military Manpower*, p. 139.

14. Harley L. S. Browning, Sally C. Lopreato, and Dudley L. Poston, Jr., "Income and Veteran Status," *American Sociological Review* 38 (1973): 74–85; Sally C. Lopreato and Dudley L. Poston, Jr., "Differences in Earnings and Earnings Ability between Black Veterans and Nonveterans in the United States," *Social Science Quarterly* 57 (1977): 750–66; Wayne J. Villemez and John D. Kasarda, "Veteran Status and Socioeconomic Attainment," *Armed Forces and Society* 4 (1976): 407–420; Melanie Martindale and Dudley L. Poston, Jr., "Variations in Veteran/Nonveteran Earnings Patterns among World War II, Korea, and Vietnam Cohorts," *Armed Forces and Society* 5 (1979): 219–243; and Roger D. Little and J. Eric Fredland, "Veteran Status, Earnings, and Race: Some Long Term Results," *Armed Forces and Society* 5 (1979): 244–260.

15. Bernard Beck, "The Military as a Welfare Institution," in *Public Opinion and the Military Establishment*, ed. Charles C. Moskos, Jr. (Beverly Hills, Calif.: Sage, 1971), pp. 137–148.

16. A. Holberg and N. H. Berry, "There's No Doubt about It, A Diploma Goes a Long Way for Combat Efficiency," *Marine Corps Gazette*, September 1977.

17. Roger L. Egbert et al., "An Analysis of Combat Fighters and Non-fighters," *HumRRO Technical Report* 44 (Washington, D.C.: Human Resources Research Organization, September 1957).

18. David R. Segal, Barbara Ann Lynch, and John D. Balir, "The Changing American Soldier: Work-Related Attitudes of U.S. Army Personnel in World War II and the 1970s," *American Journal of Sociology* 85 (1979): 95–108; and Stephen D. Wesbrook, "The Impact of Socio-political Alienation on Combat Readiness," *Armed Forces and Society* (in press).

19. John Willis, "Variations in State Casualty Rates in World War II and the Vietnam War," *Social Problems* 22 (1975): 358–568; Neil D. Fligstein, "Who Served in the Military, 1940–1973," *CDE Working Paper* 76-8 (Madison: Center for Demography and Ecology, University of Wisconsin, 1976).

20. Gilbert Badillo and G. David Curry, "The Social Incidence of Vietnam Casualties: Social Class or Race," *Armed Forces and Society* (1976): 397–406.

21. Richard W. Hunter, "Decision: To Draft or Not to Draft," paper presented at the Conference on the Citizen Soldier, St. Michael's College, October 4, 1979. Because of the larger youth cohort during the Vietnam War era, a larger absolute number of men were drafted than during the peacetime 1950s.

22. Gallup Opinion Index, "National Service Program," *Report No. 169* (Princeton, N.J., 1979).

23. Alan Ned Sabrosky, *Defense Manpower Policy: A Critical Reappraisal*

(Philadelphia: Foreign Policy Research Institute, 1978); William L. Hauser, "A Smaller Army? Adapting to the All-Volunteer Situation," *Parameters* 9 (September 1979): 2–7. The analyses of the All-Volunteer Force given by Sabrosky and Hauser closely parallel my own. We differ in that I hold that the All-Volunteer Force can be made to work at present or even larger force levels.

24. See, for example, Martin Binkin and Shirley J. Bach, *Women and the Military* (Washington, D.C.: Brookings Institution, 1977); Martin Binkin with Herschel Kanter and Rolf H. Clark, *Shaping the Defense Civilian Force* (Washington, D.C.: Brookings Institution, 1978); and Martin Binkin and Irene Kyriakopoulos, *Youth or Experience? Manning the Modern Military* (Washington, D.C.: Brookings Institution, 1979).

25. Market Facts, *Youth Attitude Tracking Study* (Chicago: Market Facts, 1977), pp. 123–127.

26. An insightful discussion on the value of postservice educational benefits in lieu of active-duty pay is found in Jerald G. Bachman, John D. Balir, and David R. Segal, *The All-Volunteer Force* (Ann Arbor: University of Michigan Press, 1977), pp. 145–148. The weaknesses of in-service college programs are documented in Stephen K. Bailey, *Academic Quality Control: The Case of College Programs on Military Bases* (Washington, D.C.: American Association for Higher Education, 1979).

27. For a study containing both factual information and original thinking on the relationship between military needs and national service, see William R. King, *Achieving America's Goals: The All-Volunteer Force or National Service?* Report prepared for the Committee on Armed Services, U.S. Senate, 95th Cong., 1st sess. (Washington, D.C.: Government Printing Office, 1977).

INDEX

ABOUT THE AUTHOR

MARTIN ANDERSON is Assistant to the President for Policy Development and a member of the Military Manpower Task Force established by President Reagan in 1981. He is also a Senior Fellow (on leave) at the Hoover Institution at Stanford University, and served as a member of the Defense Manpower Commission (1975–76) established by President Ford to study the short- and long-term manpower requirements of the Department of Defense.

While serving as Special Assistant and Special Consultant to President Nixon (1969–1971), Dr. Anderson was deeply involved in the formulation of military manpower policy. He served as the chairman of an interagency task force that evaluated the report of the President's Commission on an All-Volunteer Armed Force and developed the legislation that abolished the draft in 1971.

A summa cum laude graduate of Dartmouth, Anderson received a Ph.D. in Industrial Management from the Massachusetts Institute of Technology and taught economics and corporate finance at Columbia University's Graduate School of Business for six years before becoming involved in national politics. He is the author of *Conscription: A Select and Annotated Bibliography* (1976), *Welfare: The Political Economy of Welfare Reform in the United States* (1978), and *The Federal Bulldozer: A Critical Analysis of Urban Renewal, 1949-62* (1964).